THE 'HALLA

(Modern Tales of Old Valhalla)

Volume One

VALLEY OF THE DAMNED

DOUGLAS M. LAURENT

International Standard Book Number
ISBN-13: 9780692598917
ISBN-10: 069259891X

Library of Congress Control Number: 2015960682
laurentbooks

Scripture taken from the HOLY BIBLE, NEW INTERNATIONAL VERSION®. NIV®.
Copyright©1973, 1978, 1984 by International Bible Society. Used by permission of Zondervan.
All rights reserved.

Scripture citations marked (*kjv*, King James Version), are taken from *The Defender's Study Bible*, and
annotated by Dr. Henry M. Morris, (*www.icr.org*.). World Publishing, Inc. Iowa Falls, IA, 50126.
1995. *See* also the *New Defender's* 2006 version.

Printed in the United States of America

First Printing 2016

DEDICATION

To my beautiful good Mother, Agnes Battistelli-Laurent,
A brave Lady who endured many storms for me—and still does.

TABLE OF CONTENTS

THE 'HALLA

No force can oppose Love in Earth or Heaven above, No, not even the damned of Hell can stop relentless Love.

—Kari, *Chapter Sixteen*

Preface to the First Published Edition

I. INTRODUCTION: NOTES OF DRIPPING BLUES—COMPOSITIONS ON THE SYMPHONIC THRUST

When I was growing up, I remember spending many fascinating hours touring Hell with Dante Alighieri (1265-1321) in *Inferno (ca.* 1321). John Ciardi's wonderful translation both mesmerized and riveted me as I read the old poet's masterpiece in my father's creaky basement with its musty cobwebs, thin spiders and falling shadows—just right for firing the imagination of a young, aspiring writer. In time, I wanted to see if I could write like Dante, and well, *Valley of the Damned* and its cognate sister volumes, *Cold Steel Eternity* and *Garden of the Dragons* are the products of that fevered effort.

It has been many years now since I have personally visited the strange, unseen mental Underworld in the trilogy of poems known collectively as *The 'Halla*. At first the stories were meant to be a romanticized study of northern European literatures, but the eternal teenage Valkyrie Kari's fantastical, morbid, yet somehow appealing primordial swordslinging Underworld became much more expansive than that. In time the poems came to embrace ideals of eternal soul and spirit, of our own selves, the mirror of literature serving to help illuminate what we all have inside of us. Largely, the 'Halla series represent experiments in both literature and how our minds interface with literature, the poems ultimately being a study of our own personal nature and how this shapes our destiny.

As these poems however are the stuff of which dreams are made of, to continue the series almost requires the help of a computer. Because for these works, not only should the poems run in a 'horizontal' chronological or parenthetical normal reading fashion, but 'vertically' and 'diagonally' as well, as if their poetic structure were also a type of fluid 3-D visual art. Imagine for a moment artist Piet Mondrian's *Victory Boogie-Woogie* (ca. 1944) as being 3-D with all its wonderful colored cubes stacked at various lengths, widths and heights representing a connected symphony of images, sounds, words, rhythms, story parts, realizations, *etc.* Now imagine that this could be 'read' or painted in 3-D, becoming part of an overall moving geometric design that makes complexity out of simplicity as we might see in colorful blooming flowers or expanding frost patterns on a cold autumn morning windowpane.

This is in part what I had in mind when I wrote these poems. Subsequently, after I had finished the third poem, *Garden of the Dragons*, strictly in an *avant-garde* sense, I felt that I could progress no further at the time with the genre type and structure I had set out to create. I believed that the art form had hit repetitive snags on these and other levels, and therefore, as a experiment to compliment the fluent human mind with literature to parallel that fluidity, the work had somehow failed.

The failure was in my *intellectual* self of course as I tried to overcome the structural boundaries of formal story telling. I had much to learn about the art form. I had to realize that it did not matter *what* stories were being told, for stories of love and romance, tragedy, revenge and heroism, are as old as the hills and they have their established patterns and archetypes. No, what mattered was *how* these timeless elements were told, and so we have these poems *a priori* to that greater, albeit simple realization. Okay, perhaps for some the plots or structures are not so great, but the real worth of the poems lies in the concepts, ideas and *intuitional* fluidity behind them, and with a little luck, how these are conveyed *through our own minds.*

Surely, there could be many more stories to be told of Kari and other intriguing Underworld denizens, all based on rich characterizations and elaborate plot torsions, but basic storytelling using formal methods, as said, was not exactly the original goal of the art form itself. The original premise of this work was to follow the flow of the intuitional mind and not lose the story line within this state of mobile, fluid awareness. The *flow* or *fluent state of the mind* refers to intuitional 'knowing' or 'doing,' much as when we drive automobiles. Being so used to driving, we do not 'think' to turn left or put on the brakes; we just *know-flow* and *do.*

Ergo, built into the sub-stratum of the text and footnotes are three, barely-visible strands of perception goal-objectives to seize upon and track this line of thought in their "thousand cunning windings" as Sherlock Holmes says in *The Final Problem,* in which to heighten our state of personal awareness.

The *first* is once the basic block-mechanics of how the story is built and works are understood, is to switch out from the rational and use the central principle of *clarity* and *fluidity* of mind as *the basis of learning itself. Second* is learning to see realities independently without extraneous, superfluous influence or interfering self-bias, seeing situations before 'they happen,' *intercepting* them at the vanguard of the moment, making oneself invulnerable. *Third* is to sharpen our sensibilities to the fine web of subtle causal underlying tensile connections that are in all relationships by eliminating distracting mental preoccupations, fixations and attachments that overworked intellects, emotions and wills often produce.

These three principles are derived from studies of ancient Japanese swordsmanship and other *vea mārtiālis ars,* making for a most efficient warrior, strategists using these tools, particularly the *third,* in order to learn how oppositions will respond to the perceived possibilities of a given time so let us readers of such said material become 'reader-warriors' in our own lives. A hand leaning more toward simple intuitional flow then is what paradigm-model guided this writing, not full-throttled chunky stoic reasoning, which has a tendency in the West to divide itself against itself producing doubt, confusion, double-mindedness, circular reasoning, *paralysis through analysis, to wit*, the sum outcome equals spiritual impotency, a most decidedly negative, un-warrior-like virtue. In all, *Valley* incites readers to take part in the work using it as a tool for personal assessment, stanzas representing aspects of our psyches, and to a certain extent uses intuitive ambiguity to mirror our mindsets and personalities through our own interpretations of the text and our reactions to it.

As a matter of fact, if readers get lost in the shuffle of finding the work too stuffy and 'intellectual' causing them to stumble, they are encouraged to just cut through this *Gordian mind-knot* with their spiritual mind-sword and read the poetry as it is meant to be read. That is, it is meant to play with, not agonized over as if running a hundred yard dash with an anchor strapped to ones back. It is just that the more complex the mind, the more complex the play. This means returning full circle to the greater need for the cultivated simplicity of play–which we adults often forget–so get under the covers at midnight with a flashlight and read the work like the great big fat comic book that it is and have fun. The work is adjustable, so readers, as always, should bring it to their "*Aha!* Now I get it" level and enjoy. Do not make it hard.

Indeed, the very mechanics of how these stories work–the 'ever-shifting' lucid and *Twilight Zone* boundaries of our own minds–make the stories a never-ending workable flowing meditation. We are supposed to cook up story lines, characters and conclusions all on our own, the *very essence* of what these writings are about, not lock them down into a 'beginning—the end' limited format that conditions us to stop learning, enjoying–and living. As we are living, the stories are meant to live as well, growing with us, not stopping just because the story line must have boundaries for obvious spatial and layout reasons. It is just as wise old King Solomon said, "Be admonished: of making many books *there is* no end; and much study *is* a weariness to the flesh" (Ecclesiastes, 12.12). Consequently, with the structural form of the compositions toned down for readability and complementing the freedom of fluency, they taking place in the imaginative moving grounds of our minds, in this respect, the poems do all right. Even the poem's footnotes–a whole bunch of other off-tangent stories unto themselves–reveal this fluent shifting as well, as they give us choices, options for perusal.

VALLEY OF THE DAMNED

As is often the case, artistic works are the results of internal pressures artists have in attempting to balance their inner frame of mind, setting it in equilibrium with the external world. Communication between the artist's inner mind and the outside world is what is meant by balance. With this, another reason why I stopped writing 'Halla poetry was that these works were the products of disbalance—of having a bi-polar mental state, hallucinatory paranoia, a nearly non-working thyroid, severe asthma, major debilitating chronic depression, a touch of schizophrenia and autistic savantism to boot! (Hey, even batteries have terminal negatives to draw electrobutes 'electric-attributes' from, so positively, charge up.)

From these orange squeezings of the soul–pits and pulp included, sprang their rank children: lunatic ravings of a feverish midnight mind, which by nature made everything, look broodingly dark, slow and ponderous. Oh, how the poor-begotten, crawling, ground tongue-scraping, sledge-hammered psyche, making mistakes at every corner and creating horrible turns and twists in its own road, tries to claw its way up to greater life. Yea, so very few people understand the immense grip dissipating mental 'challenges' have upon a loved one—or the 'time' and compassion to deal with it.

Why, it is enough to make one feel as though they were a corporeal see-through ghost that 'never was'–there and yet not so there, the world passing them by. In the end, they become ghosts–worse, wanting to become ghosts and disappear, because that is what they are, being invisible to others and all, because that's all there's left—simply to fade away, as lost, failed dregs into time's dust bin. Their only worry is whether they will end up on Level 5ive of Dante's Inferno, where in the stygian evil, the wrathful and the gloomy irascible sullen hang out. The angry ones tear at each other whilst the glum, morose, bitter, ill-resentful sour ones lie beneath the brackish, stagnant muck, withdrawn, "into a black sulkiness which can find no joy in God or man or the universe" (Sayers, Canto Seven). Unquestionably, they are all alone; forgotten and forever unknown, eternally pouting and gurgling up bubbling sputumy lamentations no one cares about or hears. What a head trip–to find out that your whole life has been as a waning ebb, a pale, colorless, silhouette and has been nothing more than a sham and an illusion—but that is what the

Deadlands are 'in business' for—the likes and ilk's of so many of us. Beware of the *Ides of Death*.

Cumulatively speaking, these combined maladies and more made a simple task like taking out the garbage or getting the mail a major slug-paced, tooth-pulling, anchor-laden, cement-shoed, tunnel-visioned undertaking. I guess that is why story lines were so difficult to make up. With haranguing illnesses snapping at my rear and life screeching for more life, these life challenges acted as the pressurized, maniacal magma to fire these stories, they acting as metaphorical pressure release valves, converting much mental abuse, highly distilled angst, ghosts and demons (personal and otherwise) into symbolic tales—an iconic language I could communicate to the world through. Words and phrases were invented to convey my *torquetured-twistorted* soulish meanings because they did not exist in plain-Jane English. If truth were told, these were very bad days at *Black Rock* (*MGM*, 1957) indeed. As such, these stories act as symbolic, fragmentary records of very dark days, unhinged awry rusted gates, and to return to them forces open long corroded-shut doors that perhaps should best be left barred, bolted and eternally time-locked. The mental quicksand's within these works are very seductive and the meanings behind the images that cross the soul, my soul, are painfully black-neon electro-frying. Perhaps it is just as Dr. Abraham Van Helsing said to his associate, Jonathan Harker in the 1931 *Universal* film *Dracula*. "Mr. Harker. I have devoted my lifetime to the study of many strange things, little-known facts which the world is perhaps better off for not knowing." Then again, wisdom that never sees the light of day is such a waste and so the doors, like the tin man, must be oiled to creak and 'grown' open once again.

Within the three compositions, there is a definite progression of the art form. The first story, *Valley of the Damned*, reflects a tight analysis of northern European folklore and the Eastern martial arts *e.g.*, kung-fu and karate, made immensely popular in the last few decades with their vast commercialization through movies and TV shows. As an experiment, *Valley* was an attempt at understanding and putting the mechanics together for the machinery of the poem itself, much as a clumsy child playing with oversized blocks would try to do. It is with regret that some of the more fluid original lines are lost to time (but they *are* out there—snag 'em yourself), the poem having been set to a harder musical beat with the idea of making a movie or a heavy metal-blues opera out of the story. The second story, *Cold Steel Eternity*, succeeds in putting the machinery together for the Underworld genre and the third story, *Dragons*, finally rolls, at least in my mind, much like an act of Zen-calligraphy writing, where thoughts and realizations flow well, dispensing with rule-bound intellectual formalism. It is definitely a free-flowing tri-work all on its own. In fact, *Dragons* is the only one of the three stories that was not planned out or written chronologically, but rather written in a broken rhythm sort of fashion, when scenes popped into my mind. These scenes were later pieced together like a borderless jigsaw. Although I wished to try this more natural approach to study how my mind placed things in order, it took a far longer time to put the third poem together because of this method.

For this first *'Halla* edition, very little editing of what remains of the original works has been done. I have left the texts mostly in their original edited state from several years ago except with slight modifications to make the reading a bit more colorful and fluid. Footnotes however have been given a new going over in order to establish continuity to them as a trilogy-series, as they address various aspects of the *'Halla* universe as a whole body of literature. The notes stand pretty much on their own merit giving an indication of the development of my thinking concerning the structure of the three work's maturation at a particular time. The introductions too have been reworked, clarifying some points.

Perhaps someday, more stories will be written. Certainly, there are plenty of deliberately partialized *pseudographic* notes from the *confabulous* figmented ghost-authors (*see* Bibliog.). Their scribings offer tantalizing facts and clues, but no real cohesion to suggest definite outlines. Fragmentation and we putting things together personally for ourselves *is the art form*. Of much more importance, the study of humanity, the way we perceive reality and the telling of our own spiritual story are the poems inner more profound secrets, and so, their fascination and never-ending cycle. Undeniably, it is as the *Introduction* to *Valley of the Damned* rightly says, "we are the Valhallans."

II. *FLORA AND FAUNA OF THE DEADLANDS*

Having reviewed the poems in preparation for publication, I realized too that there were not enough descriptions of the plants and animals found in the Mortuuslands. Plants and animals, including birds, mirror our own species and then some. Since everything is dead in the Deadlands, nothing can become 'extinct.' Every plant and animal that ever came into being in this dimension and beyond is accounted for in the Chthonics. Nevertheless, they are different, so vastly different.

On Midgard, programmed *micro-evolutionistic* genetic heredity and environment forcefully dictate what types of plants and animals will live where and how. Polar bears would not do well in the tropics. A macaw would freeze at the poles. However, many claim that this present world is 'fallen,' in ill-repair. It is *less* than its original state. The point is that in the celestial realms, plants and animals are true, full, exact—and 'solid.' Can anyone imagine 'unfallen' peonies, not subject to the physical and genetic laws of this world? Our beautiful peonies, compared to those in the heavens, would be like lumps of sludge. Plants and animals in the great beyond are beyond radiance, crystalline-like, shimmering with thousands of colors, many that are unknown. On Earth, we get the inexact copies. Like the six-thousandth year copy of a single extremely splotchy, grainy scratched up black and white videotape of Adam as we all are, our plants and animals—our reality, are highly ripped, *distorsioned*, pressurized and morphed over to fit the harsh Earth environment. By logical Underworld extension, plants and animals in the wastes are greater and tougher aberrations of the fallen forms we find here. They are even stranger manifestations of things living here.

Take your basic nether-pinecone for example. About the size of a large watermelon, it is glossy, iridescently heavy-metaled, having the weight and appearance of blocks of oily lead or bronze. It is thick, with hooked spikes on the end of it for digging in. It can easily shred a spirit, much more a human. Another example might be the nether-thistle. It is exceedingly coarse, thick, dense, glimmering and heavy weighted. A field of them would be a bad dream for any mortal to try to cross. Carnivorous plants, as do many others, move about, feeding on whatever they want. Flowers of such delicacy, however, are found everywhere. Magnificent flowers *hum and coo* in the wind, they diamond with all the glistenings of light-minute plasma rainbows. They show the past and future. They too, though, are made of the same hyper-solid elements that make up the Nether. A bloom can be toxic or intoxicating. Petals are solid as hunks of tungsten and at times as sharp as razors. On the other hand, some spark something like electro-nethicity. Some are mere outlines, representing what a flower just might look like in the twinkling of our mind's eye as we catch a glimpse of it on a dusky, lavender sun low. Still, others are so exceptional, rare and exquisite they exist only *if we wish them to be*—within our very hearts.

Animals in the Nether, living, extinct and exotic, are unbelievable. In our world, we hear of werewolves, bears and tigers. Allegedly, these are pretty tough and violent critters, but compared to some legitimate animals in the wastes, these are mere pups, cubs and kittens to be sent to their corners when naughty. Even the likes of the extinct short-faced bear, much fiercer and larger than modern giant kodiak or grizzly bears, would seem like Yogi and Boo-Boo bear or Gentle Ben compared to bears down in the Wastes. Our descriptions of the slathering, snapping, salivating three-headed, dragon-tailed dog *Cerberus* the vicious guardian dog of Hades are too, poor indeed. Measured against the dog-like creatures of the Underscape, Cerberus would seem like Lassie out on an adventure with Timmy. The fact is whatever passes for bears dogs or other beasts in the Nether are beyond description. Metaphorical depictions can only dream of describing such *Animalia*. The talents of Picasso, Dali and Rembrandt, merged together, could not capture these beasts on canvas and *National Geographic* with their finest crews and cameras could never document them on film.

Then there are the beasts that belong to the Undernether proper. To say that great translucent beasts, showing every ripple of glowing acrylic cubism-like muscles in their moving is an understatement. They move about the 'scape as fragments, blocks, rectangles and geometric shapes in general. Like peering through binoculars, they have a decided, blocky, depth-perception dimensional look to them. Their individual sections undulate, conforming to the land, going up down over rocks in independent block motion. Many elongate in speed, becoming cohesive when they slow. They change their forms to hunt, sleep, and graze on ada*m*antines and so on. Like the toy *Transformers*—cars that switch out to become robots and back to vehicles again—beasts appear and disappear as rocks, plants, airs, waters and other indescribable otherworldly rudiments. There are some that are invisible and large, the size of houses, visible only to Underworld eyes. Some of them only exist during certain times, such as the waxing phases of the rare squared moons events falling into a spread-out looseness until their next phase. Others, like the mighty *Diagons*, only exist when they move in and out of living solidity when slanted shadows and light strike them. Markings such as these make some beasts have movements that look like stop-frame photography or choppy early *Claymation* under a strobe light disappearing and re-appearing, these beasts may live like this for millennia, going through the so-called 'yearly' cycle of the five-aught *tortuosymmetric* ('crookedness-balance') Deadlands seasons. Oddly, mighty creatures arise from this dimension that is a wilderness of nought-nothingnesses made up of balances having many uncanny twists, bents and turns. And we may as well ask right now, why the number five? Who knows, but in some eastern Midgard societies such as China, the number bodes very ill, so look *ye* to it. (For further visual insight on these creatures, check out *Claymation* master artist Ray Harryhausen's work, *The 7th Voyage of Sinbad*, 1958 and *Jason and the Argonauts*, 1963 *Columbia Pictures*.)

Great phantom creatures fill the skies and space. Many are not birds. Some are like fluorescent squids with glossy, peacock-like iridescent plumage, the feathers being the consistency of metallic bottlebrushes or combs. Their delicacies of transparent steel-like shapes are suited perfectly for their heavens. Some creatures are made of hot glowing metals, rock-like matter, or consist of beyond ultra-violet light material, they roosting in the great fiery cold pits. Compared to our mythology, some of these flying beasts would make our vision of the beautiful shimmering white Pegasus look ill. These beasts, with their '*bellow*ings,' smells, tastes, feelings, imaginings, dreamings and interphasings, are quite a remarkable lot. And as for bugs, cooties and other microscopic creatures, let us not even go there.

These are the healthy beasts. There are other, lesser beasts and plants however. They are malformed through the unnatural, unholy vomitings of nature. They are more depraved, predatory, and wispy, shadows of our minds that 'once were.' They show their lowliness in their level of decay, the gaunt splint'ryness of their nearly invisible haggard bones and rotted muscles.

As the citizens of the Deadwastes, all things there follow the decreed rule that the stronger and better are on top. This is why it is said that the landscape will consume the weak. Wildernesses of nether-metal, rock, water, plants and animals are eternally heavy, thick. Skies are solid and stifling. Moving through a sunny meadow on Earth with a horse is a very pleasant experience. In the Underworld even though the nether-horse is adaptive to its environment, it would have to push its way through swaying sharply dull nubby plants that may be as heavy as the core of a black hole.

Nature itself is weird in the Deadlands. Atoms with their orbiting electrons may be as big as basketballs. Some black shiny river shores are like red iron with rivets. The sun, in many instances, especially during necroclipses, is negative-negative black or some other too wonderful for words non-color. It is reported as a yellow sun sometimes, but its radiance is in our eyes. We must catch a meteorhorical glimpse of it in our minds as it whizzes by. Sour storms rip the face of the land off. Geysers belch steam and emotions. Vast dried ocean plains glow red. Grassy steppes have the consistency of yards-high metallic iridescent porcupine quills. Heated mud pools blop on their surface, telling of inexpressible things far, far below. Lone star's, those visible and invisible in black, white and unknown colored and energy-banned space, bend, torque, and hunt. Some suns are cool enough to walk upon, having delights of their own. Nearby galaxies, octopus-like, reach in and around and are made of those real surrealities we have as when we dream. Dimensions within dimensions exist, all with their own bizarre quirks. It's up to the reader to experience these things.

Naturally, everybody in the 'scape is used to such things, but, like an oiled up eel, it is still a very elusive, slippery, deceptive environment. Suffice to say, spirits need to know their way about. These dynamics advise us to the hardiness of those who abide there and what may become of us if we enter in.

DOUGLAS M. LAURENT

III. *SOME NOTES ON TRANSLATING CHTHONIC LITERATURE*

Originally, there were supposed to be five poems based upon the development of a new literary genre and analytical discipline, variously named *Deadlands*, *Chthonic*, *Underworld*, *Mortuus* or *Nether* Literature. For the *'Halla* texts, the term *chthonic* means several things. Classically speaking, this generic term pertains to spirits, deities and other remarkable citizens living 'under' the earth. Just because you can't *see *'em*, it doesn't mean they are not there (Rev. 9.1-11).

The term *chthonic et al.* henceforth, is both broad and diverse, but it is also used in several unique ways. On one level, *chthonic* means anything and all that pertains to the *Nether* or *Underworld* proper, but especially so, what we in our own minds *personally* conceive this foreboding place to be. Secondly, what we are attempting to capture with this term is *how and why* our minds stir up certain images, *etc.* within us that attempt to define and make sense of occurrences that gas up our personal positives, negatives or the neutrals of it all. Where does all this phenomenon come from, it all linking? Both the how and the why, from propagandistic and conditioned points of view, are important for understanding the under-texts, as may become apparent later on in the stories. On perhaps the deepest definition of the term, *chthonic* implies how these spirits taken as real actual living entities influence us Midgard mortals, particularly through historically recorded art, literature and science.

As to how our minds generate certain images, thoughts, feelings and conclusions, this is common enough as we do this all the time. When reading stanzas we naturally develop positive or negative thoughts, images or feelings about someone or something in them. But is this not in part the result of our education, of our own personal conditioning? Categorically, from the lowliest 0.981 candlepowered sewer brain to the most erudite quasar-illumined radiating mind, bias for or against a subject is something of an 'acquired taste.' For example, everybody's ideas of the juvenile Valkyrie Kari will be different. We will form opinions as to what she is or is not, what she should do or do not and so on. Our minds will lead us to imagine all sorts of things good or bad about her. We will love her, despise her, sympathize for her, be disgusted by her or cheer her on. Thus in our minds she will always be changing, yet constant, and like the shifting background of our own mentalscape from whence she springs, she will always be in flux. So, the only *real* poetry presented here is like an iceberg, much of it 'lying' beneath 'the smiling surface.' Consequently, the poetry being a partly visible, but mostly submerged intangibility of soul, solidly existing yet elusively not, is a nebulous interface and as miraging model, *demonstrates* how our souls 'work' these familiarities out. In this vein the understanding of how Chthonic Literature operates is found in our minds own pliant and conditioned quintessence. *'Halla* Literature is a warp-driven paradoxically complex Occam's *razor* yet cuts; a sharp stainless steel kitchen sink strainer, the remaining *ek* of an *ek'ō*, a box of shadows, rippling eclipses to our own souls—much like outgoing radiating wrinkles on a still-water pond that runs deep when a pebble is tossed into it.

To illustrate further, how Deadlands Literature performs we must know that in the nether-stories *naturalism*, more often than not, rules. In Western literatures, naturalism is the genre of how the relentless *forces of nature*—primarily heredity and environment—eventually pummels compulsive, instinct-ridden protagonists down to nothing in the end, disintegrating and dissipating them, in general wiping them out. A pawn to their unchecked bodily appetites, such as greed or sexual desire, along with crushing social and economic forces, pressurizes them, killing them off for a grand, dismal finale—an apropos parallel to both Western and Eastern 'despairing' martial writings. Stephen Crane's *The Red Badge of Courage* (1895) is a masterpiece example of a novel gone South towards naturalism. It displays nature and fate being a much larger force than what mortal man is. It not only pits bleak man against himself, but even bleaker determinism, survivalism and fatalism as well (*see* the 1951 *MGM* movie with Audie Murphy).

Because this is the norm in the floodpain of the Nethers, there is definitely a certain amount of despair as everybody there is already dead or never having been human to start with, and in all cases, everyone is stuck there. No one there is in a classical Christian Heaven or Nordic Valhalla proper, but is in a Heaven or a Hell, a *Valhalla* of his or her own making. All spirits there are on one plane of existence—*their own current mindsets* so to speak, they working out their life-equations for the good, bad, ugly or *nil* of it all. With this metaphorical thought, we are the 'soul' creators of our own nether-realms, our constantly shifting spirits, minds and emotions—our selfsame souls being the fertile naturalistic grounds on which these stories of light and shadow, good and evil, of love, life and death take place.

The structure of the Under Literature also helps us to see ourselves in these lights here. As we will find, lines and stanzas have been clipped tight and broken down into fragmented form. It is not a perfect, pretty poetry in any way, shape or form. Aside from humdrum human error, it is flawed and is intended to be that way. Editorially 'correct' punctuation is not exactly there. Commas and the like are missing or are misplaced. As the doomed, 'never was' nondescript, nameless forgotten Eleanor Lance (Julie Harris) said in *The Haunting* (*MGM*, 1963), an extremely brilliant evil haunted house movie (esp. with the lights out), "Add up all these wrong angles and you get one big distortion in the house as a whole." Enough said? This gone awry misshapen disfigurement adds to the works' overall crack'edness, its pent-up off beam mirthless momentum and its dis-jointing cumulative about-to-burst dam effect. If the jagged, pock-marked work (as in *Valley*) tries, tasks, heaps upon and challenges the reader then good, because that is what its desperate cornered rat nature is meant to do.

And there are four reasons for this. Art comes from the soul. One is *attention deficit*. I write 'em as I *seez* 'em. *Star Wars* Han Solo at this point might say, traveling through *hypergraphs* ain't like dusting crops, boy! My eyes always hurdle back and forth through outer graph-space like a maniacal, steroid-driven baboon playing hopscotch. Going to and fro like a plumb loco *pīngpāng* express ball it is very hard to grasp the initial slurpage of info as my eyes and mind skip madly about, and so are forced to go over the same data time and again until understanding is had. Definitely, this asymmetrical spurting mental patterning affects my attempted fluid-state on-the-spot writing style. Secondly, the sharded angular highly visual style allows us to read the poems words and serrated soul-cutting fragmentary images in our own broken reading rhythm ways as our eyes and concentration usually wander, trace and stray about anyway. Once we grasp the meaning to the smashed glass images and phrases, like sitting on a pincushion, the hacked imagery and slivered wording should nettle our souls long enough for us to stop fidgeting, stand up and go soulishly about. In keeping with the spirit of the Deadlands, Zen-like 'editing of no-editing' has allowed its poetry to remain derelict and splint'ry. Fractu'*red* rhythms are more important than 'proper' English–whatever that may be. Thirdly, this *zencrypticus* askewed style is good for mediation and musing upon the subject, as it 'forces' the reader, a decidedly Deadlands trait, to seek out deeper illuminations and matters of the heart.

But surely, the fracture-red images that zip through our minds concerning these stories are not groundless or incoherent. Though images, thoughts, memories, realizations, *wouldashouldacouldas* (the disembodied lands of the *wsc* are dangerous to enter alone, laced with rusted barbed-wired soul-snagging yearning regrets and remorse that lust) and conclusions concerning the stories may appear in broken jumbled forms in our minds days, weeks or even years after reading them, the images that are stirred within us are nonetheless connected. How our individual minds order and interpret them *are the stories*. They do have a personal continuity to them, a string of humanity–of spirit, of soul, of *us* running through them, ⇨ *as we our own selves are the stories themselves*. Jumbledness is just a reflection of how we (I) move things about in our minds, un-jumbling stacks of seemingly unconnected bits of jig-sawed data and placing them in an order that suits us.

This is the Zen flow-state intuitional mind performing on 'jigsaw-less jigsaw puzzles.' Like a scattered about, all over the coffee table picture-less, faceless, clueless jigsaw puzzle that would require a nearer-to-comatose meditational zen-crypto jigsaw puzzle master to restructure (and they *do* have them, *see* Ravensburger's *krypt silver* j-puz on line), this mental un-jumbling *is* the *élan vital*, the 'life vitality' required of how we are supposed to interact with the story lines. These stories are simply designed to this end. Perhaps it is just my chunked-apart self trying desperately to express itself the only way it knows how. Still, although for the sake of makeup the stories are built somewhat chronologically, '*Halla* texts are not supposed to be read in a linear 'story' fashion. They are not 'straight' histories *per se*. They are open-ended, designed for pondering and personal *meditation*. They are metaphorical parables designed to help us see ourselves in the light of what is all around us.

Overall, humanity is the thread we must seize upon to feel the soul-pulse of the poems and it is to humanity's end the poems seek to address and capture.

At the very least, an analysis of Hallan Literature finds itself concerned with the *why* of how it functions and tries to find the meaning behind our 'eyes of childhood,' we being conditioned to see painted devils as Lady Macbeth might say. As we know, children spook easily. With a fun-scary thrill in their hearts, they look for witches and goblins at dusk in the autumn Hallowe'en season and for the mysterious little leprechauns on St. Patrick's Day. The superficial tops to these kinds of commercialized pop-myths are not the important things here. What are important are the 'grains of truth' ingrained into such myths and the feelings, thoughts, realizations and consequent actions they generate. In terms of myths and legends, we understand that all such stories carry within them the seeds of truth that enable them to carry down through generations. The stories may be fantastical, full of romance, heroism or tragedy, but their core meanings, their universal truths communicate to us, touching us all deeply in some way. That is why stories such as these endure. Undoubtedly, literature, as all great storytelling is, is designed to evoke in us certain thoughts and moods, and so we identify with the persons, situations, mores and ways, their reflections, we pondering their—*and our lives.*

As for the feelings and thoughts stories like these create, Nether Literature seeks to explore those areas where the soul and things toward the darker side meet and mingle in terms of conditioning processes. Here we are speaking of things that go 'bump in the night,' and how these occurrences give us the 'willies,' the 'creeps,' the 'heebie-jeebies' thrill of the unknown, and the sincere humanity and desire *to know.* Yet, in order to have the willies and the creeps and to know, we must first go back to a simpler foundation and *relearn.* We must learn to see and believe as a child does in the impossible *as* the possible, the improbable *as* the probable, and to see ourselves as we truly are and can be, for these stories are broody, dark parodies of historical, literal realities—of ourselves. In *The Sign of the Four*, it is as the illustrious fictional detective Sherlock Holmes said to his pal Dr. Watson, "How often have I said to you that when you have eliminated the impossible, whatever remains, *however improbable*, must be the truth?" *Valley*, like her weird sister other poems, founds itself on the basis of the *however improbable*.

This returning to a simpler, clearer vision is the essence, or feeling or belief we need to have when we read Deadlands Literature, as childlike wonder and believability is where truer hearts lie and are the catalysts for these lucidly macabre, bent and disjointed *daystallion* (opposite of nightmare) poems. Parallel to this, this jet-black inky electro mind-poetry attempts to get behind those conditioning processes that cause us to get the creeps and willies. What is more, it undertakes to capture our feelings concerning the unknown through symbolic formats. These formats, the readable story forms with its many devices, serve as common grounds, starting points for investigations into our deeper soulish reality and the very fabric of *what is* itself.

Going beyond the *façade* of how and why our minds play conditioned tricks on us all—the tired results of educational methods that are designed to make us vacillating and *stultified*—a nearly invisible instructive process that is calculated to make one "systematically stupid," *'Halla* poems unpeel information that at first glance appears mind-boggling and illogical. Certain ideas within the texts will undoubtedly look archaic, perhaps absurd, but this is because modern education has lost its more formal, original spiritual mooring and has brilliantly failed to address certain bodies of knowledge, an acute "sharp-dull" *oxymoron*. By default, this makes for things outside its very narrow parameters *seem* mind-blowing, far-fetched and illogical.

Consequently, the Nether-texts take the bull by its horns. They are designed to analyze, in a literal and practical sense, what impact spirit beings, mythic, angelic and demonic, have historically made in our world. Certainly, *the gods of this world* know of their past, present, future and final reckonings, so why should not we be let in on their secrets in a vigilant, practical working sense as well? All alert intelligences in the universe know the *zeitgeist* 'spirit-times' they live in and can read the signs of the seasons and the handwriting on the wall. Here we must ask ourselves if our feelings and suspicions concerning their Nether-realm are indicators of their actual existence. Most likely, it is the *fallen ones* who make things go 'bump in the night,' conditioning children to be frightened and awestruck for later manipulation as adults.

This makes for an easily controllable, gullible population. Science itself has proven the mathematical possibility of at least nine dimensions of existence (we exist in four—length, width, height and time) and people of faith do not question the existence of such beings as angels, good or bad.

While we do not wish to indulge in flighty speculation, there are far too many sightings of spirits and whatnot to turn a deaf ear to. Indeed, it is terribly hard for modern 'rational' man with all his pompous sophistication and derisive verbosity, to invest himself in the belief of the spiritual realm although the darker aspect of this trend is growing. That is exactly what his civilization is for; it is designed for willing unbelief, to buffer him against greater realities he cannot possibly comprehend without first trying to prove it with a microscope. Being full of holes Swiss-cheese style, civilization is a very thin and poor *Band-Aid* indeed, used as a quick-fix replacement to those who desperately need brain-surgery.

Accordingly, it is even more trying for us mortals to grasp what exactly Mortuuslands Literature is trying to tell us. Beyond the normal pale and scope of ordinary incursions into basic literature, *'Halla* Literature is definitely most fantastical. It is quite beyond the ken of normal, pragmatic worldly educated reasoning. Midgard politically speaking—for even angels and demons are creatures of politics—as a pre-view, the unseen, unrealized 'coming-soon-to-a-world-near-you' realities behind the stories are the *real game.*

Nether Literature is based on shadows of mind, spirit and other unseen forces, where we have our sneaking suspicions as to things that *do* go bump in the night. Consequently, for our lame otherworldly translations then, I have combed the finest literary, artistic, scientific, mythological, religious and historical devices and references to find the best instructive parallels to track this elusive graspless dimension. These disciplines will help us glimpse-relate to the ideas presented at hand. Common and uncommon examples from history, literature, philosophy, music, science and art, such as *Disney's* animated *Night on Bald Mountain* (*Fantasia*, 1940) with its ghastly skeletal riders and foul dancing spirits, are the tools that will help capture the effervescent changing texts that our own souls are and the titanic hidden propensities of the world around us. These examples will serve as handrails to support us as we study our changing *life-stories* in the light of the texts. They will also help us maintain an overview of the stories themselves. As it stands, these dark looking-glass Nether-poems can only ever be crude translations of what is going on 'out there' and 'inside of us,' we using our own poor earthbound references, embellishments and sensibilities to try to capture fleeting, nearly transparent images of what the grandeur of this otherworldly, and soul-oriented Literature—*us, we*—is all about.

Douglas Laurent,
Round Lake, IL
March 28, 1993
Mitchell, NE
November 7, 2001
August 27, 2004
April 23, 2013
Scottsbluff, NE
February 19, 2016
Friday, 6:21 am

*Concerning *conceptual visuals* in the text, it needs be recalled much is hidden and it is up to readers to blast through to discovery. This invisible gig running through the volume is akin to the Japanese *kata*, the kill-oriented dance-like forms of self-defense. Kata has both 'surface' and 'interior' forms, *i.e.*, surface and content, or *omote* and *ura*. *Omote* is the visible, the obvious, the given, the reachable through nominal understanding, it is what's 'up front.' *Ura* is the reverse to this. It implies the hidden, the secret, invisible, the *conceptual*, what is 'not shown' readily. Both are linked. Again, it is all about the intuitive ability to perceive and realize. As a teaching device, the tools to help in illuminating perception and understanding are embedded in classical kata. On top, the public sees the glitzy *omote* surface techniques, while strategists see kata as hidden reefs with much of their formidable powers and meanings lying just below the surface. Many ships have been wrecked by the unseen. The idea is that the form studied may not contain a 'specific,' surface visible technique, but the 'thought' or 'perception' for the hidden underneath technique *is always there*. *E.g.*, straight kicks with an uplifted knee dominate old karate forms but modern-day hook-kicks *etc.* are absent. However, the uplifted knee 'allows' for the *concept* of a front hook-kick to be there. Just because a formal kata does not 'show' a technique on its *omote*-surface, it does not mean that the *ura*-hidden concept for the technique is not there. *E.g.*, shōrin karate's neutral looking knee up front kick position can kick three different 'hidden' ways, the front, hook and side-kick. It thus 'camouflages' any of the three kicks one might desire to execute at any given time. Although the katas do not show this, the concept is there nonetheless. It is the same in the world of the spirits. They are extremely well hidden, but sometimes we on the Midgard can catch glimpses of the more sloppy, careless or proud ones who like to 'strut their stuff.'

VALLEY OF THE DAMNED

The Valkyrie's heart was wrought of dazzling gold full of the most finest and firmest of loves, this being the secret of her many moods and akimbo inspirangular mercies.

—On Kari, *Chapter Fifteen*

I. *INTRODUCTION—POETICS & STRATEGIES: ABSTRACT PRISMATICS*

To quote a common life *cliché* that "life is a battlefield," may well turn out to be the most apt illustration for *Valley of the Damned*. *Valley*, both for its participants and us, is an immense life battlefield, the work being designed to engage our minds and souls.

As this piece is the study of souls in action, one group of readers, those whose interests lie in the broad field of *martial arts* such as Chinese kung-fu, Korean taekwon-dō and Japanese karate-dō, jūdō and kenjutsu (sword) will at once recognize that *Valley* is both a social commentary and philosophical treatise on the arts. In these and other aspects, the document functions as a classical military exercise, or what the Japanese call *kata*. *Katas* are pre-arranged sequences, forms or patterns of set physical offensive and defensive techniques that are practiced relentlessly. They are the architectural 'blueprints' found within an art. Akin to a literary classic, *katas* make up the *alpha-beta*, philosophies, principles, theories and actions—the detailed plans and outlines, that is an arts own unique 'storyboard,' giving that particular art its distinctive flavor, identity and place in history. This means that every martial art, every kata has a 'tale to tell,' things that are obvious, like fundamental movements, advanced technique, power and quickness, and things that are not so obvious, like their ancient roots, and an unknown, forgotten fighting master's individual prowess, success and ultimately personality that is 'genetically' imprinted and embedded within the kata form.

But kata is not just merely a physical self-defense construct; it is also an *idea* and a *concept*. Kata is a *lens*, a way of seeing, *of perception*, a 'method of analysis' that goes far beyond the boundaries of meager physical limitations. A lightning rod, kata is an inner reflection of the person, the physical and mental nature of which producing self-scrutiny as one sees their limitations through kata as a barrier that must be broken. A journey in self-discovery, kata can be anything in *thought*, *word* or *deed* as it is a close-knit triad, a three-fold construct-stimulus of *spiritual, mental and physical* endeavor of which man and so his creation kata is uniquely made up of.

There are many hidden *attributes* and essences in the *cosmos of kata* that can be mined from the *psyche of kata*. But what is a *martial cosmos*? From the Greek *kos'-mos,* we find that it is a 'highly designed, heavily ornate, orderly arrangement or decoration.' Extra pointedly, the martial cosmos is 'an adorned world or system with its tinsely and glitzy beautifications, including its literal, figurative and moral prettifications' with more than enough eye-candy to fool eye, body and soul. With his sprawling, steeled iron death-clutch gripping the world, such is the throbbing, pulsating, orbiting galaxy of Mars' martial arts global corporate conglomerate along with its katas and everything else that tags along after it, including the kitchen sink.

Mining kata, one can dig up a lot of *neat-o* things—intriguing, sparkling multi-colored diamonds, emeralds, sapphires, rubies—and sometimes the blackest lumps of Christmas stocking coals—of wisdom, understanding, moral command, council (power to originate and plan), might to carry out, fear (respect), knowledge, shrewdness, acumen, discernment, foresight and hindsight. All these and more can be discovered. The life-perceptions and strategies found within these classical exercises have existed for ages and are applicable to anything in life metaphorically or in the real; each 'kata experience' is personal going down to the roots of one's own being, as they embody the human condition and soul. One's attitude and actions displayed during kata training sessions and in daily life is the *soul* of kata itself.

The application of formal *kata* self-defense strategy, known in Japanese as *bunkai*, is one of the trademarks of *Valley*, offering interesting glimpses into the minds of ancient warriors. As a whole, this information pertains to the old military arts and their current pop-cultural modern state of affairs such as sports, business or a spiritual life-path known as the 'way' (*dō*, or *tào/dao*). *Bunkai* literally means "disassembly," "to break apart," or "draw out" and is the *formal interpretation* of a kata technique in its combative functional context. In order for a kata self-defense technique to have proper *bunkai*, that is, to be classified as a functional, official technique, a technique must work in a combative vein. If not, it is chucked. Bunkai then is the ever-expanding process for a more accurate 'vision' of personal art, of personal understanding, strategy and efficiency in word, deed and thought. If a kata can be considered to be a diamond with many hidden facets, the role of bunkai in the hands of the reader is to discover, explore and polish each particular *fascia*; kata holding many unseen wonders for us that in time we come to realize. And so it is with *Valley*. In view of this, the poem 'requires' from the reader at least three things: 1) the analytical bunkai ability to disassemble and break apart stanzas and lines. 2) The faculty to find, interpret or (Gk. *exegesis*) "lead out" their intrinsic meanings, values, significances, implications, worth and consequences and finally 3) the work calls for aptitude to adapt and apply their *functional* applications to one's person and everyday life experiences factually or in the abstract.

Hence, just as a *kata* is a spiritual, mental and physical *riddle* to be mused upon and solved, even the poem's footnotes are part of the larger cryptogram to be figured out. They may or may not appear to give satisfactory answers and in some cases, are left purposely misty. As a parallel, in Zen Buddhism there is something known as the *kōan*. A *kōan* is a metaphor; sort of like a 'Chinese puzzle' labýrimaze brain-teasing sphinx that cannot be solved through ordinary rational means. Like a square round trying to be jammed into a hole peg, this scalene triangle of thought, emotion and will, poses an intangible perplexing *perpugnax* (Lat., "very fond of fighting") stickler to students that can only be grasped intuitively. Grappling with it perhaps will bring them, upon the realization of it, into a greater awareness of life beyond their own narrow, furrow-minded garden variety prejudices and self-limiting mephitic *dis*-aromatic *oponions*. The question, "What is the sound of one hand clapping?" is *the* classic example of a Zen *kōan* puzzling monkey wrench. Rational thought cannot answer this strainer of brainers as reason runs out of room here; intuition is the key needed to grasp the essence of this and other extremely vital life mind-hurritwistnadoes (like this one, "what is the taste of one donut hole eating?").

Consequently, there are two reasons for the poem's *kōan*-like nature. One is that words simply cannot possibly capture or convey all that the poem is trying to move or say. Secondly, notes are sketchy so that we may interpret the story according to *our own* intuitional metaphoric inclinations, perhaps transcending our 'boxed-in' perceptions of rule-bound reason itself, seeing directly into the matter *with our hearts*, which is what *Valley* is about. It is not dictatorial telling us what to think. In this way, the *Valley* text again acts as the classical *kata* in which life-enthusiasts and strategists can exercise their wits and souls on spiritual, physical and mind-labyrinthine stratums, self-illumination being the very hinge-pin of the kata-poem itself. *Valley* affords us myriads of thoughts to explore and enigmas to consider, personal applications of the poem-form being just one of the many goals of the work. These life-thought applications take on many ways, shapes, sizes and outlines from the classical to the abstract. In dance lingo, these might be uplifting vertical lines of movement and thought, earthy, powerful, horizontal lines or soaring in the air spirit-freeing diagonals. Even curly-cued and squiggly lines to the highly elegant spiral and curvaceous lines of movement—of spirit, mind, body and soul, the poem fulfills many multi-dimensional purposes.

One purpose of application, for example, is to exercise our *suki-points*. *Suki* for Japanese swordsmen is a term that describes the "space that occurs between two objects." It is a mental gap, breach or *hole* for opportunity. When one swordsman's tension-filled mind begins to relax, he lets down his guard. At this point, a *suki-gap* occurs making a hole in his defenses. The swordsman's opponent instantly exploits this mental gap by attacking through this *suki-hole*. In fact, the sword masters became so good at reading suki, they were able to key in upon their opponent's psyche, it for instance 'resonating' fear or doubt coming up through their blades. And this is what the sword masters focused in on—not the technique of the opponent *per se*, but what the opposition's spirits were 'radiating.' Therefore, for us, a *suki-point* is any mental gap or lack in our concentration that allows an attack to penetrate, disrupt, enter in, destroy and kill—verbally spiritually, physically, emotionally or otherwise.

The *suki-point* describes an undisciplined mind with strategic and mental breaches that has a tendency to 'mosey about,' drifting away even in the face of danger. Further, suki-points, weaknesses in our psychological makeup, are the products of our own 'self-generated biases.' They are quite natural for meandering day-dreaming minds, for example, as when we are listening to friends speak but we are thinking about soccer scores. To further the example of the *suki*, as our minds may skip about while looking at the poem, our attention will undoubtedly waver and drift onto other topics, perhaps such as getting a snack. It is then that the book from the Deadlands, the concerned teacher that she is, will exploit our mind-gaps catching us flat-footed in our mental wanderings and laxness. Thus, the '*Halla* will 'claim' more victims. The metaphor is that in the Land of the Dead, drifting thoughts do one in, just as it was in the days of yore when one had to duel for one's life—just as we ourselves are now 'dueling' with the dark poem herself for our very souls. She reveals to us, whether we like it or not, what we are truly like on the inside. Indeed, the land of the Nether teaches that an undisciplined, unalert, inattentive straying mind is the one thing that gets a person killed. Thus, suki is 'mental drift,' especially at a crucial or dangerous time. Overall, the *suki* premise and more are designed to induce further inquiries into our gap-ridden selves and our living art, how we perceive and interact with the world around us. These gaps of mental wandering can be filled in if we are but aware of them.

For help in this area, *chthonic marsology*, a very obscure and little-known branch of the martial arts, seeks to investigate the martial realm of the Underworld. There, methods, techniques, and attitudes, although quite different, nevertheless parallel the ways of this world, and so grant us an enormous opportunity to look into the deepest workings of the arts, theirs and ours, those in the here and now, and should not simply be passed over.

From our mortal aspect, what is covered on the surface of this work is a survey of the pop-American martial art scene with its subsequent philosophies from the late 1960s to today. Events described, or more so parodied, are written facetiously, in a hyperbolic, exaggerated manner. This is because the poem is a vehicle that serves only to heighten those areas of critical interest and concern that act as sore spots and cover-ups to the greater truths found in the arts. These agitating, characterless 'less than true truths' hamper the greater appreciation of the arts, the principles of which can be applied to many areas of life.

This seeming antagonistic approach to the arts is not aimed at them directly, although the text could easily be accused of that. Rather, the attack on modern martial arts is a critique of the vaporous myths, base commonalities and silly notions to which many in the commercialized arts fall prey. The fact is many things in life are accompanied by deception and illusion. The arts are no different from this, although in this respect, the field of god Mars is filled with illusion even more so. Strategic deception is ultra-fundamental; part and parcel of the art of war.

What is meant by all this is that what were once necessary 'killing' arts, where true heroic endeavors of valor and self-discipline flourished, many of today's arts, are packaged to make them blandly commercial and generic. They are made to fit all too neatly in with the bulk public. True honor here cannot abound, and if it does squeak through, at the very most it can only be democratic and artificial, as the modern student's life is hardly at stake. With gore removed and marketed for the mass consumer, many arts today lack in vitality, individuality, or more to the point, a type of gallant zeal that existed long ago, calling for one's utmost, but is no more. Today's artists practice but the shadows, the trace fumes of 'what once was.' In many cases, the arts have been made into hobbies and social activities, just another time-consuming 'thing to do.' The modern era, it appears, has made the once noble arts into mere curiosities. Trendy, egg-head intellectualizations are the real culprits of the arts' greater perceptive loss. They enshroud the truer, more chivalric, meaning of the arts.

So, what shows up in this life-poem are the displaced ghosts from once worthier, or rather, real warrior eras. These ashen wan pallid shadows both reveal and denounce the glory and depths that the arts, as a magnifying glass to life, are capable. These *mesmirrorizing* relic ghosts point out what is good or worthless in the arts, everything from false, unworthy movements and cheap philosophies to the high ideal of great words and deeds, the true mother of all martial arts.

As will be seen, in the entire poem there are only two scenes, Chapter's 2 and 34 that take place in normal 'Earth-time.' They are the most visible and ordinary to the mortal eye, the only 'real' chapters in the story we can relate to. Shadows of the mind cannot touch the subjects here, for these images are to us as solid as our own lives. These scenes are packed with a familiar, but hidden and necessary legitimacy. Perhaps dull familiarity amid a fantastical Nether-realm is an unwelcome intrusion. Nonetheless, familiarity is a tool that focuses minutely and negatively on the despairing *naturalism*-oriented elements found within the arts, and through various connections, we discover the soul of the arts in anguish. Adherents of the arts, more often than not, do not address these despairing elements, either because they do not see them or do not 'wish' to see them, mega-vulnerable *suki* blind spots at best. Certainly, this is a case of admiring the rose, but paying little heed to her thorns, yet both make for the beautiful flower—if we are not pricked.

Undoubtedly, the souls found in Chapter 3 have grappled with the same elements many of us have had or may now be grappling with. The text, a chronicle of both ancient Valhalla and this turbulent Deadlands era, is a child of the times. Life in any Age is to be wrestled with and won over. Let the deepest secrets be wrested from life though, for like her mother, Nature, life does not yield up its secrets willingly.

Let not we in our wildest dreams ever want to end up in *Market of the Soul* (Ch. 3), or become crippled like many of these spirit-*phasma* remains are. They are there because they did not heed the wise teachings of their masters, of life, but succumbed to the coal-ish egocentric diseases found within the body of the arts and the art of the body and soul. They do not live anymore but merely exist and imbibe within their all-consuming appetite-ridden dull-minded selves, the unfortunate penalty of not understanding the essence of their arts, *which is ourselves*, the very self-same soul that abides within us all.

Classically speaking, *Valley of the Damned* is predicated on the finest aspects of the old European North Country, and is a metaphorical document of what was there in ancient times. This includes both Christian and Pagan elements. *Pagan* is a term that originally meant "country dweller." It was a phrase used by the early Church to describe the rustic, common working folk, so we should not exactly be thinking of wild people, witches and the like running amok here. Chiefly, the work is really neither Pagan nor Christian. No, what we are viewing here *is life*, and these tools of perception help us to see what is behind the scenes just past our every workaday reality.

Coupled with European influences, Eastern thought expounds much of the martial aspects of the text, providing missing links to the warrior mentality that appears to be so similar worldwide. Classical Eastern martial arts are used because they are for the most part still intact, the Western arts having long ago been superseded by the firearm. The real, non-commercial Eastern arts yet encapsulate much of the active and living warrior ideal, which as with the European knights, existed in the West long ago. Essentially, this odd mixture of perspectives found in the work is meant to be a microcosm of what we have in the world today, a unique blending of definitive cultures from all over the globe.

Classical Valhalla is a place where warriors do battle daily. Many die, and die continually, only to be resurrected at night. Then they are welcomed at the Great Hall to feast all evening. The general facts concerning these historical beliefs have been faithfully reproduced for this work, although these facts have been stretched a bit *via* poetic license to fit the story line, after all, it is a "*Modern Tale of Old Valhalla.*" This tactic is quite becoming for the type of Netherworld that is to be presented—a Valhalla that springs out and devours the unwary.

Based loosely on the patterns of Icelandic *Sagas* and other northern litera-tures, we must be reminded that this particular tale of the *Valley*, set in the vast wastes of the eternal Deadlands, is a minor occurrence, one of many, really, that occupy the daily lives of the deadlanders. On this note, we should not be too moved by the poem's trappings. If we are mesmerized by what is going on we are lost, for this story is but one daily nightmarish occurrence of grinding terminal-velocity reality that goes on and on and on and on forever in this Land of the Dead. For all intents, we should feel the gross, leaden dead weight of this deadly savage nether-ending place pressing in on us. Murky, horrible feelings of despairing entrapment and suffocating anxiety are the more appropriate colors that fly here. Unimaginable feelings are sickeningly suppressed and buried deep in its quicksands. In short, the text spells it out plainly—this is "*a forgotten tale that no one knows, except those who enter therein.*" It is not a game. Knowledge here is applicable to our lives. We should watch our step.

As for the poem itself, it should be considered more of a short story set to rhyme. Although the work is not meant to be an epic-style piece, it does follow certain epical guidelines. Of importance though, *Valley* was meant to be an experiment to recalibrate language structure, most notably visible in the action sequences, where thought and action at the same time of occurrence, become an '*a'one'ening.*'

Cinematically speaking, those who appreciate the films of Japanese and Italian directors Akira Kurosawa (1910-1998) and Sergio Leone (1929-1989) will find *exact similarities* to their film work, the poem heavily utilizing the genre of the *Spaghetti Western* and the *Chambara* (*Sword Theater*) of the samurai film. Stanzas and individual lines are to be literally taken as camera shots, compacted into poetic cuts, and modeled after these two film masters. Thus, the story is highly visual in style being impressed with a 'cinematic' mode of expression. Within this cinematic matrix, poetic descriptions and single words convey the function of the camera in terms of close-ups or long shots, *etc.* for full visual, audio and sensual impact, words being used to pull readers in and out of *poetic mental focus.* These shots are the media that brings things into sharp focus. Using words such as '*the, that, those, they, these* and *them,*' we are pulled in and out of the action, made to see what is vital and what is not. Most of these mental word-crispers, however, go un-*italicized*; readers must perceive and interpret their own living poetic mind-focals placing perceptive emphasis where they will.

But there is a deeper meaning to '*the*' specific words mentioned here as well. They tend to express the secret of the tale. It is as if the story itself were alive, demanding of us to be intimately acquainted with its materials, as we are to 'look over *there*,' and 'see *that* thing,' personal involvement and familiarity (with our lives) being keys to help us move through the poem. It is a tale most desperate to tell us of itself–that it is alive. It demands, nay, screeches to be heard, terrified that its shrieks of inner torment will never be heard and of being forever consigned to the lonely damning darkness that is the pit to be heard of no more. *Wow.*

This activity, of being manipulated in and out of focal range by such *poetic word-mind focuses* is linked to the term *maai* in Japanese martial arts. *Maai* is the "timing, space and distance that separate two opponents." *Maai* allows them to judge these three factors accordingly in order for them to execute proper technique. The greater the grasp of *maai* by one of the opponents allows his or her battle tactics to be successfully carried out. The poem's *maai* should be taken into account as a device for movement. The construct of the poem forces the study of its tactics as it presses and shoves and jerks us about in our minds, daily life and poetic-metaphorical focal life connections.

Like faded still-photos, there are also certain words and phrases that freeze specific actions, the words becoming memorials to the character's personages. These 'recordings' of their work, rather than their technical skills, gives the characters a far greater chance at immortality, (at least in our world) than any of their own actions. Their action-art of swordplay occurs in a fraction of time and long after their deeds are done and forgotten, the words set here will act for them as a far great legacy and learning experience for those who will come after.

As for the Hallan deadlanders themselves, they live not by the edge of the blade as we are likely to think, but on the hair's-breadth difference of speed that lies *between* the drawings of blades. They all take a dim view of living on this razor difference however, as they, like us, can be here one moment and gone the next. For them the quick-draw lightning act conveys numerous concepts—wit, bluff, body language, the masterly use of energy, time and distance, and most importantly, the idea of eternal preparedness. High-noon fast draws also take into account ideas concerning fate and destiny. To borrow from the old nursery rhyme, 'For want of the nail the kingdom was lost,' speaks of how their eternity is shaped by the net accumulation of the smallest, most trivial of movements, so nothing is ever taken for granted. For *them who is we*, like a high performance vehicle, directional life changes are often quick, occur in very small spaces and are dreadfully tight, major events turning on a dime.

Because of this, one might suggest that entering into this particular *Valley* is a journey we must prepare for, and to be sure, to come out in one piece in the sense of self-realization from the wilds, or rather the 'wiles' of the Underland is a superb accomplishment. This is a truism, for the passage through the Deadflats is the metaphorical journey of life, a crossing over that lasts forever. It is a pilgrimage into our own souls, with all the soul's puzzling little movements and what these may mean, according to Hamlet in his famous line, "The undiscovered country, from whose bourn no traveler returns—puzzles the will . . .?" (III. i.). In a final sense, all in the Nether must trod this path alone, choosing wisely, and for those who do so successfully; this is the greatest mark of their warriorship.

Thus, the excursion into the Land of the Dead calls for us to engage our spirits. To be found in this loathsomely powerful territory means that we must use all our wit to out-maneuver adversaries who at any moment may do us in. Adversaries in the Nether come in all sorts of disguises, sincere or diabolical, beautiful or ugly, and we cannot be too trusting of any of the characters found there, especially if there is a reward to be gained at our expense.

Another thing, just as an enemy in the Deadlands may deceive us with words, so the idea of an illusory Underworld carrying the dominant theme of deception is no poetic slip of the *sword of ink-pen* either. The wastes and their naturalistic writings are deceiving, except to those who have the spiritual eyes of a falcon to cut through the diminishing returns and blanket fogs of life's despondent illusions. In *The Japanese Art of War* (Cleary, pp. 53-54), Master samurai Suzuki Shōsan (1579-1655), a contemporary of the sword duelist Musashi writes:

Those who have mastered the Way use reason and justice as a forge to temper the mind daily, getting rid of impurities to turn it into a pure, clear, unopposed mind-sword, which cuts through the thought-root of selfish greed and conquers all thoughts, so that the Way-farers ride on top of everything, untroubled by anything, beginningless and endless. But ordinary people take deception for realities, creating attitudes biased by fixation on appearances, thus starting up thoughts of craving, anger, and misunderstanding. Having produced all sorts of psychological afflictions and lost the original mind, they find that their minds are distracted and unfocused, giving in to whatever thoughts arise. As a result of this, they suffer from handicapped mentalities that make them hurt. They have no psychological buoyancy; they are gloomy and depressed, living aimlessly and without self-understanding, fixating their attention on things. This is called the mentality of the common man.

The natural world of the underwastes, like our world, camouflages its insidiousness in order to survive. Beautiful, flowering cacti have coarse prickly thorns, bees that make the sweet honey sting unmercifully, and gorgeous tigers have no claws until they spring open. All these are wonderful and calm—until they reach out for us and strike.

For this reason, while the whole of this Nether-region's existence is based on the idea of truth and illusions, warriors and sojourners alike must have one single mind here. The disciplined mind to the warrior is the difference between sweeter life and further death. There are no falsehoods whatsoever in this dead land. What is meant by no falsehoods is that all things are done with an exacting purpose of mind, for a barely detected wrong thought or action here means instant death. This is *the* Valhallan concept to be reckoned with. For we who travel into these wastes, the discernment between truth and error means survival or oblivion.

This keen-edged mentality found in the Deadlands has an equivalent on Earth in the difference in what the Japanese call *jutsu* and *dō*, as related to their martial arts. *Jutsu* may be likened to the application of battlefield techniques used for the sole purposed of killing efficiently, while *dō* is more of a personal, spiritual path, using concepts derived from the art of war to improve oneself. That the characters found in the Netherzone use both these ideals at least implies to them that their arts have not gone stale. Their arts at such a honed level enable them to see through the minutest elusive illusion and so act accordingly.

VALLEY OF THE DAMNED

Unfortunately, just as people here on Earth use their arts for improvement's sake, sometimes they are used negatively, leading to the destruction of the doer. The same is found in *Valley*; only here, the pain is much more intense and longer lasting, the sullen, plutonian-dyed eternal blade cutting much deeper than temporal steel ones.

II. *MAIN CHARACTERS*

Concerning Mark Theman, one of the *5ive* main characters of the story, he is the only one we can relate to. Like us, he is human. The other creatures of the story—Kari, Storm and Angel, are insubstantial, graspless and are far more of an interrethereal-trapped mystery to us than basic Theman, the ruthless movie star.

Theman's character is the only one of the four whose essential identity has been obliterated. A piece of merchandise himself, Theman is a perpetrator and a trafficker of the sterile business wasteland that surrounds the once-noble martial arts, a waste industry much in vogue today that uses the ancient arts for commercial gain. His is a time when great words and deeds—the very essence of the old arts—are seen only as old-fashioned scraps and images in movie houses. Mark Theman, aka 'the man,' thus identified, is a product of his times, a shadow himself, subsisting on the smoldering embers of 'what once was.'

As a symbol, his sterility represents the faces of countless sincere students of the modern arts who are swallowed up yearly by the despairing falseness that many unscrupulous teachers and arts (political and money-making systems) advocate. His life at the end of the story is a mock tragedy. His character is not deep enough (and is deliberately made so) to elicit from us a touching response. On the other hand, as he is a selfish arrogant man, a cool 'tough-guy' in the movies, to see the virtues of the higher arts only to reject them in the end, is indeed a tragedy. As we travel through the story, we come to know the bittersweet fate that awaits him, and like the other characters of the drama, know him as fool.

As the story unwinds, we first find Theman hollow, not that 'bad' really. He is after all becoming 'The Mean.' Theman is tragically caught up in a system. He has an image he *must* keep up. This not only enlists him to *naturalism*, the false cause, but also in the end destroys him, as he, 'the big badass movie star,' will not let go of his vanity. Theman's self-enslavement to his self-made gooey egotistic, but ultimately vacuous image is what does him in, not the sobering reality of the Deadlands, which is only a mirror to his bleaker side.

As for the four main characters in general, it may be noted that they are not fully described and are left purposely hazy. Without hesitation, we can naturally describe Theman because he is like us, but he however being the devious human that he is can always make up excuses for himself so set him aside. As for the other three, they are as Lady Macbeth might possibly describe them, being murd'ring ministerial "sightless substances" that "wait on nature's mischief" (I. v.). These soul-pursuers ride on as killer-phantoms. They are *obliquitious* and thus obscurely traced, because if exposed their truer interior illuminosities and terrors would be too much for us to take, like being locked inside a sealed chest with an insane hopped-up supernova to keep watch over us. Their intensities are as such that like the poem as when one dyes, they reveal the darker *pigments of our imachinations*. And that is why they are kept under lock and key—always. They are *achromatic gloom*, 'without color,' vague, impalpable dreams that fleet in the night that one cannot quite recall, soundless deafening bells, claspless, discarnate—the nightmarish muffled screams and sobs of ours never heeded in the dead of night.

Macbeth (II. i.) would say they are mind-daggers, false creations knifing out of our heat-oppressed brains, illusions that do not exist—*or do they*? They are what we make them out to be. In studying the poem or characters, we should be aware that the characters, as wayfarers in the *Valley*, are never on solid ground as the *Prologue* imposes, and neither are we.

When the characters make their bold claims of truth or love or hate, we are the ones who have to decide who is telling the truth or not. The trick to understand is that the only way we have of knowing a character's worth is to observe their actions and what their actions produce. This is one of the most difficult realities found in the Netherscape, as a seeming bad action at the end may prove to be very fruitful (but to whom and why might be the safe and smart questions to ask). Apparently, it is the same in our world: a person is only as good as their word as to what they do.

All the characters too, are off-kilter. They have quirks to show that in the world of spirits and people, nobody is perfect. The result of this is that strange reality we call life, with all its small innuendoes and mysteries. This mixture, much like the lotus rising out of the mud, makes life abstractly beautiful. That depravity and genius have their own idiosyncrasies in this world and in the Deadlands should not surprise us, and whether we wish to admit it or not, like love and hate, genius and madness are twins.

Regardless, in the chthonic flatlands, genius succeeds where often time's madness fails. In the Nethers, the idea of genius, both light and dark, takes on a terrifying 'out of proportion-ness.' Genius runs at optimum levels for the most successful spirits found there. No one there is totally good or evil. They are all an odd bunch. One day we might find a Michelangelo-type sculpting a beautiful figure only to find him the next day hacking his way across an immense battlefield with all the coolness as if he were back at his studio sculpting.

This point can be most clearly seen in the three characters of St. Kari of the Blade, Dark Storm and the swordslinger Angel-Heart. It might be thought that with such a lofty title, Kari would be pure saint. But as a High Mass-battle artist, hers is a religious fervor based on motion, the 'now-doing' of actions, which to her vast and disturbed mind takes precedence above all things. Her looks are deceiving but she should not fool us. This 'saint' by any stretch of the imagination is full heartedly Valkyrie, and a happy one at that. She is a spirit that would no doubt cut off our heads if she had to, while singing a song about it.

Conversely, villainess Dark Storm is a ruthless killer consumed by revenge and ambition, but she is also a consummate artist of high ability. Having certain 'attitude' problems makes her 'artwork' all the more intense. As for Angel, he prefers the thrill of the hunt and personal duels while Mark Theman, in light of his run-ins with these spirits, becomes unglued as he seeks to find, then ultimately murder his own mediocre identity. Such (bi-)

polar exaggerations found in these four serve only to heighten the effect of what is found in the Deadscape and in our everyday waking universe.

The key to understanding these characters with all the mind shape-shifting Nether-currents swhirling about them is to be found in looking at the play as a *mirror*. In particular, we must look upon the composition as if it were a broken mirror with a sword's razor edge, having the ability to cut deeply if not carefully handled. As the work is but a mirror, it too is deceptive in the sense that it only reflects back a flat 'past' image of a real, living form, there being a certain amount of lag-time between the reflection and the reflectee. It is the true life form that is to be studied and not the mirror. The image reaps nothing, only the form, the real, upon reflection of itself, can harvest the grace of wisdom that is derived only from a deep contemplation of its innermost nature. It is like what Cassius and Brutus in Shakespeare's *Julius Caesar* (I. ii.) spoke of when Cassius was trying to convince Brutus into helping him do in Caesar (abridged):

> *Cassius*: Tell me, good Brutus, can you see your face?
> *Brutus*: No, Cassius; for the eye sees not itself, but by reflection, by some other things.
> *Cassius*: 'Tis just: and it is very much lamented, Brutus, that you have no such mirrors as will turn your hidden worthiness into your eye, that you might see your shadow.
> *Brutus*: Into what dangers would you lead me, Cassius, that you would have me seek into myself for that which is not in me?
> *Cassius*: Why, man, he doth bestride the narrow world like a Colossus, and we petty men walk under his huge legs and peep about to find ourselves dishonourable graves. Men at some time are masters of their fates: the fault, dear Brutus, is not in our stars, but in ourselves, that we are underlings.

As the mortality play rambles along, we find that Cassius wishes Brutus could see what everybody else does about him—namely that he is conscientious, gentle and thoughtful, a true Roman son of the Republic in every respect, a real genuine hero. Upon observing that no mirror could reveal

Brutus' worthiness to himself, coy, clever Cassius then butters Brutus' brain up. He plays the role of a 'humble human mirror' so that the nobleman may 'conveniently discover' himself and see his own person in new and positive lights, helping to sway Brutus into aiding Cassius and his cutthroat gang to 'bump off' the mobster-emporer Caesar and 'put him on ice.' This is what the *mirror-poem* postulates. She 'sways' and 'flatters' us so that we might see our hidden 'worthiness,' our 'shadows' in the eye of her brokenness. This is so that, upon being pompously inflated like a leaky tire, made to look and feel good about ourselves, we might in our own self-righteousness, 'assassinate' our own self-made Caesars, a double whammy leaving us either blind or dead with perhaps no one the wiser. Those forbidden, secret, hidden desires to waste our own alter-egos, our own ugly monstrous selves in lieu of her shàt'térèd'nes's are the very tattered soul-clothes the poem wants to rip off of us, she burning to point to, and expose in us our own personal *de-enlight*enment, a most grave and sobering view. What are her ends we may rightly ask? For what it is worth be wary of her interior-minded *skipta hömum* "shape-shifting" propensities. As a condensed thumbnail sketch of life, she *is* life, and takes many smoothly barbed and saw-toothed pliant forms in our everyday (mind) world.

A Deadlands spirit though knows a terrible secret, and perhaps we should be let in on it as well. It knows that it is both form and image. It is form in that the spirit exists internally as an individual and as an outer, external image. But like the mirror, this external image is a 'past' reflection of a spirit's being, in that it is 'no more,' even more appallingly so, in that it always is a 'once was' to begin with. What this awareness calls for on the part of a spirit is a reckoning. It calls for a doubly-deep contemplation of itself, *form and image*, and its responsibilities to itself and to other spirits, as many spirits see each other only through their outward 'once was' image, and not so much by their inner, truer, current form. In the wastes, as on Earth, many judge books by their covers and so pay the price for their spiritual sloth and superficiality.

In a final sense, the mirror is a critical icon in understanding one of the major themes of the Nether-play, which is the virtues or falsehoods found within the work. Even though the Deadlands are eternal and unchanging, people there are in a state of flux, each growing at their own pace. As the tale is a story of greed and manipulation, a dark mirror by which we may see many hidden undercurrents, the solution to the mystery of the *Valley* and its inhabitants is quite simple. All we need to do is look *through* ourselves in the (poem) mirror, and we will understand what the aware deadlanders see on any given day—the true character of a person behind their *façade* of face. Whether we like it or not, the most appalling, the most dreaded secret to Valhalla is that we are of the Land of the Dead—*we are the Valhallans.* In Earth dialect, this means that whatever forms the poem takes in your mind and soul, just remember—that you and you alone, *are the poem.* It is but a *spittin'* vanity mirror image to your well-hid essence, that *thing* behind your eyes that *must* not be named—let alone confronted. You do not read it; she thumbs you and this she does very well and *will eventually come* for you. "Magic mirror on the wall, who is the fairest of them all?"—"these were shadows of the things that have been," said the Ghost. "That they are what they are, do not blame me!" *All is vanity/Ku-soku-zeshiki* says the Preacher and *the* Japanese karate master—and that accursed viper does sink its illusory fangs in deep (Eccl. 1.2).

Again, in the Zen literature of Suzuki Shōsan, he quills of the alarming and pending Samarran-style date the "killer ghost of impermanence" has with us all, especially when it comes to sucking the souls (soulpirism) out of even the very strong. Cleary translates:

So people who stir up the courage of bloodlust with afflicted minds may at some point have the force to break through iron walls, but there is inevitably a time when bloodlust is exhausted and moods change. A sturdy heart, in contrast, is immovable and does not change. If warriors cultivate it, why wouldn't they develop such a sturdy heart? If they have afflicted minds, even people of tremendous martial valor will find that when they face the end of their lives and the killer ghost of impermanence comes after them, their usual forcefulness will run out, their courageous ferocity will be gone and they will be unable to muster any strength (p. 55).

In truth, the characters are all phantom killers, but they are in their own way working toward a 'form' of good, a state of equilibrium in their lives. Underneath their seeming nasty motions, Angel's, Kari's, and Storm's motives are essentially the same. There is no winning or losing, there is only survival. They train themselves to survive, and, as the pop adage goes, to 'survive, strive and thrive' in a blistering dimension where any foolish thought or action may be their last. Using life experiences as their training regime, they practice relentlessly so that they may have a mental edge on themselves as keen as their blades as befitting warriors in the Darklands of mind and soul. This point should be well taken, because it provides the atomic fuel rods for the Underscape and our own minds. The characters in a strong sense are representations of the fragmented, sharded human mind that seeks to define its place in the universe, and to balance itself in the common, everyday world.

St. Kari, while resting on a hill after a great battle, once turned to her companion, Hamlet's father, and said,

> Our memories will be dim shadows one day to the mortals,
>
> Let us make heritage of them therefore, lest they forget glory's toils.
>
> They shan't suffer us gladly, yet let us turn cheek and give sway,
>
> If lessons are not to be learned by our bloody hands, their memories too shall ebb away.
>
> Thus, I decree that as a man moves toward his own sunset his shadow shall lengthen in stride.
>
> A legacy of sorrows he shan't have, our shadows to remind him hence, shall ne'er leave his side.
>
> Let us then stir a worthy cause, for our motion's deep penitence,
>
> And mark it down forever by a shadow's recollection—
>
> That they may have an understanding of their own vaporous inheritance.

This statement is the *summatim* whole of our Deadlands *'Halla* experience, with all its ways and personages. Perhaps it was this conversation too, that, being buried deep in the mind of young Hamlet (once being spoken of between himself and his father—Shakespeare never did record *all* their conversations, you know), that prompted his words to Polonius (II. ii.) as actors entered Elsinore to entertain the King:

> Do you hear? Let them be well us'd; for they are the abstract and brief chronicles of the time. After your death you were better have a bad epitaph than their ill report while you live. . . . Use them after your own honour and dignity. The less they deserve, the more merit is in your bounty. Take them in.

What better advice for those who descend into the recesses of the *Valley of the Damned*?

Douglas Laurent,
Round Lake, IL
March 28, 1993
Mitchell, NE
November 7, 2001
August 27, 2004
April 23, 2013
Scottsbluff, NE
February 19, 2016
Friday, 6:21 am (hooray)

VOLUME ONE
VALLEY OF THE DAMNED

Finis Meus Principium Meum Est

—The Ourobóros

"My end is my beginning." The *Ouróboros*, the gluttonous snake (or dragon) wolfing down its own tail as if it were a Big Mac with cheese and fries, is the prototype of the *vicious circle*. What could be more diabolical than to sink your pearly white incisors deep into yourself with a view, presumably, of gorging upon yourself? But, this is impossible—for the snake anyway, maybe not so much for people. Perhaps for some, who are as proud as peacocks and as dumb as an ox, it is a case, after eating like a horse, pigging out and running around like a chicken with its head cut off, of making sure that they get their own "just desserts." The fangs cannot consume the fangs, nor can the belly digest itself. This act is the ultimate in dog-eat-dog masochism, *i.e.*, soul and body consumptive hunger. This labor, of *diening* from both ends at once, is hellishly painful, futile and unproductive, not to mention fashionably tasteless. At the final leg, it is impossible and stands tall as a solid definition for an ironic polar poetic paradox. Heraclitus of Ephesus once mentioned, "In the circle the beginning and the end are common." Our toothsome mouthy little *Ouróboros* is out to prove him right, the twistorted circle becoming in the end a symbol of infinity—a most apropos tortwisted icon for the belly of this beast from the *Valley*, and all therein this forgotten tale entails.

PROLOGUE

The Nether is a land that is ne'er on solid ground,
Its boundaries always shifting, illusions never found.
A land of distant adventure and of thoughtful care,
Existing only for the hearts of those who sojourn there.

Come, dear Muses and stay this night,   5
Instructing those who seek the light.
For those of us who have lost our way,
Grant the power to love, let come what may.

And to those of us who have lost our cunning,
We warriors of past and present becoming,   10
Teach us, we, who fumble for truth in the night,
To instruct our minds, to purpose for right.

Tell us of tales that are no more,
Of warrior lands and their forgotten lores.
Speak to us of tales beyond dim memories show,   15
That we may share with our children, as we grow old.

Educate us in the ways of gone faded shadows,
Those histories consigned, and their faintest echoes.
Of spirits that are vanished long into the past,
Vapors to the mortal mind that never once does last.   20

In thy kind teaching direct us please,
Of the way of poetry martial and how she frees.
This tale of the four and their mystery,
A tale to learn dark stragedies.

And Lady Art, with sword so fair,   25
Show us the riddle of those who repose there.
This wondrous mystery of word and thy blade,
Of actions b'speaked and actions displayed.

That thy riddle would inspire they with good hands,
To be gentle in spirit and strong in soul as ironed bands.   30
And for those of us whose minds be wit,
Let wisdom blaze forth with mercy's swift.

In the end reveal to us things not seen by mortal eye,
Of works unheard, and of motions lost to time.
Legends of warriors and their ways,   35
To evoke the parables of masters—
Those truths mislaid.

The way of motion and thought esteemed by the blade,
A study in dark honor—
To those who live it triumphant or to their great shame.   40
And now, dear Muses, for us who stay,
Help us to act on this small, illumined play.

VALLEY OF THE DAMNED

Prologue Valley Footnotes

The *Prologue* introduces us to the main tenets of our story. It is a tale of power, struggle, greed and wit, of revenge and redemption, of souls contending in and for their eternal state, a journey into mind and soul—just like any 'ordinary' day on Earth! The poem is an askewed mirror, a dark parody through which we are invited to see ourselves. Not apparently intended to be a poem solely in the epic sense, *Valley* is designed around the ideals of classic literature, that is, the poem is made to both 'entertain as well as to instruct.' An adventure, the tale is a study of souls in conflict, a most timeless tale—a tale of ancient times, a tale for today, a tale of the near and distant future.

5. *Come, dear Muses.* As accorded by ancient epic literature, it is fashionable to invoke a guiding spirit to instruct those who would understand and learn from a work. For this play, fortunately, three Muses have shown up to help us poor mortals out, Clio of History, Calliope of Epic Poetry and Melpomene of Tragedy. Poet Homer (*Hómēros ca.* 750 B.C.) says there were nine Muses in all and it is suggested by later writers that the Greeks took into their pantheon Egyptian goddesses with kindred attributes. According to this logic, Egyptian god Osiris always brought along with him the nine because he liked song, gaiety and dance. Osiris apparently was 'personality front' for the evil and tyrannical King Nimrod of *Genesis Ten* fame (Hislop, p. 328).

24. *To learn dark stragedies.* Strategy + tragedy. The *Valley* text is wonderful in that it not only affords analyses of strategy and conflict but drama as well, it being a tragedy in the end.

25. *And Lady Art, with sword so fair.* The text, citing traditions, has personified martial arts as an elegant female spirit, such as the Greek *Alce/Alkê*, a female spirit-personification of battle prowess, courage and strength, and a member of the *aigis* or "armed unit" who guarded Zeus. This underscores the ancient concept that the core internal dynamics of war are ultimately soft and feminine, or *yīn* in scope and not so *yáng* or hard, as many believe, which is a superficial, exterior culturally 'male dominant' view of the arts. Warfare is indeed destructive, but it is sort of a 'birth-pang,' it

'giving birth' to a new order, just as a phoenix, a universal symbol of resurrection and immortality—of death and rebirth by fire, arises anew out of its own spent ashes. Soldiers in the heat of battle are definitely known to call out to their mothers.

37. *Those truths mislaid.* These are great truths carelessly forgotten or lost upon us.

39. *A study in dark honor.* In translating this cryptic phrase, I have rendered it as close to the original Chthonic language as possible. It does not speak of a 'bad' or 'evil' honor, but a mystery, a puzzle, a *dark saying*, *i.e.*, a riddle that we need to figure out for our own benefit.

42. *Help us to act on this small, illumined play.* Literally, "Help us to act out this small play in our lives." *Illumined.* Linguist Jonathan Mycroft cites this term as 'ill-you-mind,' or more succinct, 'ill-mind,' implying that the tale is actually a study in what modern psychiatrists, such as Dr. Greta Hastings, would term *psychosis*, or the truly darker, aberrant aspects of the human soul.

ONE: DARK STORM RISING

Tempestuous plains tell the tale,
Windswept wastes do bewail,
Haunting Spirit of the land,
Seeks the living, seeks the damned.

Horizoned edge sheared with grass,   5
Dark Storm Rising in the pass,
Ageless Spirit seeks the path,
To torment souls to the last.

Brooding Spirit upon the plain,
Thunderhead gathers for the rain.   10
Light grows dim then bolts with pain,
On dry Earth her sin is stained.

Burning Prairie razed a red swollen eye,
Flames leap heavenward
Ahhh, with bowstring does she fly!   15

(Frightened creatures do stampede,
Into night, they do recede).

Ungodded hand on seasoned blade,
Reaps the harvest of the Age.
Burning spirit of ancient woe,   20
How many have you killed—
How many did you know.

Released from her eternal din,
Spirit of the Age rises again.
Seeking to plunder and consume, 25
Those who were proud, those who presumed.

Spirits rage while storm draws nigh,
Upon burning plain and emblazoned sky.
It is said giants grapple in the Earth so deep,
To contend for souls that they might keep. 30

The Storm spirit now searches the high and the low,
To seek her manchild victim in the fields below.
Leaves bad wasteland to claim but a fallen man,
Denying *it* Heaven, crowning *it*, 'Son of the Damned.'

Treacherous Spirit of the far lost night, 35
Tramples souls down denying them light.
Storm seethes with furious hiss,
Leads men on to bottomless pit.

This most ancient of foes has come from her den,
To seek the living, to make ready those dead. 40
A living sacrifice is her soul desire,
To snatch the soul for black funeral pyre.

A double-damned devil, that is she,
This one who lies, who claims to make free.
A lying spirit, that is her domain, 45
A storm-wracked Fury of self-proclaim.

Onward she seeks, this bleak Northern wind,
Searching for naught but for a soul akin.
Amidst the howling and the rage,
To murder again, *that* is her trade. 50

As she went forth, she was heard to say:
"Gather unto me my children on this lovely day,
For I have come to set your hearts free,
From *heh*, all yore wants and your miseries.
Come with me all you who hear,   55
Draw to me both far and near,
Cleave to me as I certainly shall cleave to you,
For I must show you what I speak is perfectly true."

As this spirit of graves left the plain,
She left a wake of dead in shrouded train.   60

Burning Prairie, she smiled, as friend,
For her bloodless travesty was again at hand.

Now down from the plain Storm did come,
Unto those cities wherein was no sun.
There with whirlwind she did rip and scour,   65
For those souls of whom she could tear and devour.

She comes to seek the living and the dead,
Those who were frightened, those with no dread.

Thus upon those she did acclaim,
"I am the Mistress of the living and the slain."   70

O' haunting Spirit of this land,
Taker of life, maker of the damned.

DOUGLAS M. LAURENT

Chapter One Valley Footnotes

Chapter 1 introduces us to the unseen ground between Earth (aka Midgard) and classical Valhalla, or the Deadlands '*Halla* proper. For the first time, we mortals are privy to the fact that abominable spirits, acting as mercenaries or as part of their own dark nature, slip through the world's *veil* to prey on humans and lesser spirits. Here we see them boiling out of the Netherworld, and are introduced to one of the main characters, Dark Storm Rising. Storm is tall for a female spirit, with long jet-black hair and a queen's regal beautiful face. However, she wears her hair over one side of her face to hide an evil red scar on her cheek that changes hues according to her emotions, given to her no less by Angel-Heart, the squint-eyed *bladepackin'* icy duelist.

1. *Tempestuous plains tell the tale.* In order to translate these otherworldly images as close as possible to our own familiar imagery, the contextor has utilized the Badlands of South Dakota and the vast prairie that surrounds them as the earthbound comparison. The horizon in this sparse area is so wide one can actually see the curve of the Earth. For those who take their time, because it is an uncluttered environment, they can 'feel' the unhindered spiritual power of nature. Thunderstorms in the Badlands are tremendous, both beautiful and formidable. In phrase of fact, this poem functions as an austere, stark, minimalist Japanese Zen garden and is designed, like the stern Zen garden, to be a active, yet true non-reversing, highly polished bronze looking-glass for meditation. ZGs consist of finely raked sand, strict rocks and very little in the way of cheery greenery. The concept that 'less is more' is thematic-rampant in these ascetic gardens where gardeners of the mind work the arid less to yield the lush abundant more. Readers would do well to spy out pictures of Zen rock gardens such as at *Ryōan-ji* to get a feel for the bleak Spartan poem and their own *poiēma*, their own literal and figuratively made "fabric of soul," properly entering the unflinching formidable mind garden and contemplate its many strata of unrealized hidden wonders.

6. *Dark Storm Rising in the pass.* *Storm* is the mega-villainess of the poem. Described around classical story motifs, she is a female war-spirit of pre-Valkyrian era persuasion. Little is known about her background, although the text affords intimate glimpses into her past. Some say she is half human, half pure spirit. Her profession is primarily that of an opportunistic self-ordained, hired mercenary.

7. *Ageless Spirit seeks the path.* The text in this case speaks of Storm as an Earth-and-Deadlands bound wicked spirit. This lends credence to the idea that she may be a fallen angel. According to the tenth century *Irish Monastic Script* and other accounts from which we draw our materials, spirits were formed without reference to time and are immortal. Time as we understand it has little meaning to these great celestial beings.

13. *Burning Prairie.* Like the spiritual realm, as when spirits are coming together and churning, our text is a bit hazy. It does however make it apparent that there are two wicked spirits in operation here. One is Dark Storm and the other, Burning Prairie, a subordinate. Prairie is also a strong, feminine, war spirit. In the Deadlands, just as in C.S. Lewis' *The Screwtape Letters*, weaker spirits are usually absorbed extensions of the wills and desires of stronger spirits. Many live within each other for empowerment.

15. *Ahhh, with bowstring does she fly!* Burning Prairie is an archer. However, the Earth adage, 'to bowstring someone' also refers to strangulation. This seems to be one of Prairie's 'preferred' methods. *Ahhh* expresses her looking forward to relieving her *intentsions* thru the released bowstring and getting out of an intense situation. Seems the lady if we can say that, has an idea or two in her mind as she 'strings along' with her 'pal' Storm. To *string along* means to keep company with someone or a group as long as it is convenient and profitable for a particular individual.

19. *Reaps the harvest of the Age.* Those victims made ripe by their willing adhesion to the dark mortifying, soul-numbing values found in the planned times, or eras (*Ages*) they inhabit.

24. *Spirit of the Age rises again. Age* in the Greek is *aion*. This term does not mean physical time. The German term *zeitgeist* is useful here. The word literally means "the spirit of the times." These are all the transitory moods, attitudes, tastes, fashions, trends, beliefs, philosophies, opinions, arts, pop-ideas, literatures, politics and so forth that are found in, dominate and shape a particular decade. All these are the pop-cultural fads of a particular era, for example, the 'Roaring Twenties' of 1920s America. *Zeitgeist* is a carefully planned and controlled commodity manipulated by

the *viler* side of the poisonous black as November "Powers that be." The passage implies that Dark Storm is a mastermind of pro*pagan*da, shaping the banal thoughts and feelings of commoners for her own convenient sinister use, giving us another glimpse into her immense talents and background.

29. *Giants grapple in the Earth.* *Giants* are spirits found in the Deadzone. From *Genesis* Six, they are called *Nephílim,* a Hebrew term meaning "fallen ones," rendered as our "giants," and from the Greek *Gegenes,* which probably means "earth-born." Biblical and Middle Eastern scholar Nigel Hawkesford suggests that both terms speak of freaky pre-Flood demonic-human offspring of tremendous evil and power, renowned for their prowess. As centuries passed and history convoluted into pop-folklore, by the time Norse mythology rolled around, the giants inhabited the city of Jotunheim, and were the deadly ogre-like enemies of all that was good. They were also the enemies of Asgard's gods, the Aesir, *i.e.,* the *Asians,* a term telling of ancient migrations. The tale of bad blood between the Nephílim and the Asians may have its roots in the ancient Middle East. The early Israelites were afraid to attack a certain area because the Nephílim were once again being propagated (Numbers 13.31-33). In the end-time battle, *Ragnarök/Ragnarøkkr* 'Fate/Twilight of the Gods,' the giants believe they will win; at least, that is what their 'propaganda' says. Both Frost and Mountain giants are depicted as the brutal powers of nature. Giants are known in histories and mythologies and are usually seen as much larger than men are a description that fits well with the old pre-Flood Nephílim.

38. *Leads men on to bottomless pit.* The Greek term for *pit* is *abyssos,* or 'abyss.' Here we find a dramatic 'misnomer,' or applied wrong name that nonetheless suits our translation well. The abyss in biblical literature is a place of temporary confinement reserved for wicked spirits, that is, fallen angels or demons. Humans never have or will go down to 'the Pit.'

42. *Black funeral pyre.* Burning a body on a funeral pyre was an ancient *pagan* way of burying royalty or great warriors, sending their spirits off to the next world. Dark Storm wants to kill and use the pyre for her own diabolical purposes, collecting souls for her to rule over them. *Pagan* is an uppity Latin word that describes 'country

dwellers,' the regular hayseeds, sophista-hicks, rubes, *i.e.*, the common, regional working class.

46. *A storm-wracked Fury. Wracked*, or 'wreck,' *i.e.*, very destructive. Dark Storm has many like-titles that attempt to describe her and functions in this play. Virgil, the great Roman poet, placed the *Furies* (Gk. *Erinnyes*) in the Underworld where their chief task was to punish evildoers. Other poets felt that they pursued sinners on the Earth. In either case, Storm's purpose is a self-righteous one. *Fury* also describes Storm's inner feelings.

47. *This bleak Northern wind.* Dark Storm is like the ranker, wilder elements—a bleak, cold wind, another look into her personality. 'Wind/breath' or *pneuma* in Gk. denotes 'spirit' as well; hence, Storm is 'a bleak spirit, a breath of bad air.' The Greeks thought that spirits were fiery and wind-like. Even more, she is quite a phantasma, a spectre, an incorporeal visible spirit with a terrifying nature, a deading idea, a source and object of great dread and horror. To cut a long story, she is an *eidōlion*-image of something extremely unpleasant, menacing and ferocious (*cf.* 1Peter5.8). An *eidōlon* is an image that reflects and confuses, said of crumb-bum spirits. This psyche-sucking *spiritpire*, somewhat of a Gk. *kakódaimōn* "evil genius," has a *kakós-ponēros* 'malignant evil character' that corrupts and then causes others to labor in wickedness, pain and sorrow (on their now own corrupted accord). Truly, for her kind she is quite the Spectracula. (*See* Ch. 18 note # 193 for spirit and soul-pires, spirpirs and solpirs.)

54. *All yore wants.* Storm speaks of long-standing wants and desires from a person's past. These wants of *yore*, or 'yesteryear,' are what people build illusions and happy thoughts around. She intends to use people's dreams as traps to consume them.

64. *Unto those cities wherein was no sun.* The sixth century *Upsalan* translations, as do other folklores, all heavily imply that the *cities* of man are dark places where there is no true spiritual, moral or intellectual light or understanding whatsoever.

TWO: SONG OF DESPAIR

On whitewashed walls stood they guard,
Flat realities of their former glowing charge.
Trapped essences, to which none could relate,
Existed for mind décor, to entertain the initiates.

Faded mighty leopard adorned thin used wall,   5
With paper tigers, their caricatures menaced—
Oh. How awful.
Capturing this tiger, one can only paint the skin,
That spirit of the bone none sees (*there* the secret lies 'in).

Low flying dragon hid its 'guised face behind the cloud,   10
Crane looked determined with its trumped-up battle caw.
Blanched images, black and white overall,
But *the* snake who illustrated them—
Was ʔoiling on the floor.

His hungry soul hid behind the *façade*,   15
A cardboard creature that stood between man and God.
His star-studded kingdom reached unto the skies,
God help 'the man' who hid behind *those* eyes.

A Nhero now of celluloid fame;
He lived that image, he played the game.   20
An idol of millions on the big silver screen,
He excited the children; he lived off their dreams.

His empty soul of no regret,
So arrogant a man with zheros respect.
Fought movie villains by the dozen and score,   25
The children awaited him outside his starred door.

VALLEY OF THE DAMNED

Hollow man waited and looked his best,
Had his secretary tell them all the rest.
Little faces saw him boldly stride
(*"Just tell 'em anny-thing*!!" to bide his time).   30

Disinfected man he threw the kick.
He got their applause, he knew the trick.
Told them all how to be good:
"Martial arts are life,"—
They pretended to understood.   35

And the sweet lies *ohhh* he did tell,
Of lofty morals and conduct (all for the sell).
Scribbled he off an autograph or two,
God help the man—if they only knew.

'The man' prated and continued to rave,   40
Pirouetted pretty kicks; he felt no shame.
As he turned, glanced he out the door,
Deep spirit brooding; night of the Storm.

The mighty teacher with exalted ego,
Practiced the art for external glow.   45
Those with minds he duly cut down,
To accept 'what is'—the winner's crown.

Kick kick kick kick—eternities shaped by a moment's bit.
Kick kick kick kick—repetition dulls the immortal wish.

Students toiled under florescent sun,   50
Mimed those motions of the *Non*
(Spirits suppressed think they are free,
Under the *façade* of pretty martial philosofee).

They did their kicks; they did their bows,
To that man-idol they committed their vows.   55
Colored belts showed the way,
Of fragmented minds in disarray.

Learned the art so very pure, starved their spirits, to be sure.
Came to believe, accept the lie, that what they trained for was to learn to die.

Pajamaed students all in a row,   60
Followed O-sensei; but nowhere to go.
Movement moved without its life,
Art with no meaning; internal strife.

Bodies moved, followed the chore,
Circle step and punch (they knew no more).   65
Truth of movement painted o'er with words,
The height of wisdom—ʕto believe the absurd.

Moved they far into the blacking night,
Discussing philosophies of the moral fight.
Destruction of others revealed instead: 70
Strength only mattered to make others dead.

Struggling students renew the attack,
Never knowing of the truth (denied behind their backs).
Struggled to gain the sought for point,
Body and mind deliberately kept. In 'aɪ̈ɛ→_"ĵoyn̥ɪ̠ʎ.   75

Strike strike strike strike—pain increases with illusions of strife.
Strike strike strike strike—false wisdom ensues giving no light.

Performed did they their caustic forms,
Knowledge lost through the need to conform.

This for the sake of their leader's pride.   80
This for the sake of *that truth* to hide.

Minds grew dull, yet increased in respect
Told to do with little time to reflect.
Looked down upon them, the man entertained,
"Follow my teachings—   85
And you'll be like me someday."

Little students worked with great purpose–
Turtled images in their heads, it was all so superfluous.
When he heard this the man inwardly *sneeered*,
Knew how trite it all was yet it played ↭ on his fears.   90

(All types were at this bogus, bloated seminar—
Those who lived off these putrid martial fumes by far.
From wanna-be *Norrises, Caines, Ninja's, Daniel-San's* and *Lee's*,
Some were with ponies and phony accents; their egos just to please).

Still, persons diminishing was the teacher's goal: 95
Enter the Void, to make drones of them all.
Faces so eager to fulfill their tiny need,
For that desire, he would make *them* bleed.

Self-made man so puffed up,
Body full of steroids, mind full of lusts.   100
Led the kids in kata forms just for show,
Congratulated himself on the way to go.

Buzzed the numchuck round his head,
Impressing even him self–*heh*, they were so easily led.
Used a samurai sword to cut a melon in ha **v** lf,   105
Punched through pine boards to make impressions last.

The applause died down, he stopped *this* show,
There was more to be made, it was time to go.
The door was opened and cold wind curled in,
Touched the man behind his eyes—   110
Touched 'the man' of sin.

Block block block block—actions pass with sweep of the clock.
Block block block block—time winds down on winnowing mock.

Stretch limo stood it across the way,
The man shivered deeply in nightning grey.   115

Above, Dark Storm brooding, belched⌐her rage,
D'ead bolt of lightning marked its way.

'The man' screamed his mind was ¡sp ⚡LIT*!!*
A million volts hurling him into fiery pit*!!!*
Down fell he into mawing dark.   120
A soul consumed (it left no mark).

Dead Yet Alive (the man) felt himself lost,
Going know not he cried and tossed.
Hit he the pavement far, far below—
〰ÍMḾ!!!〰*PACT*!¡!〰   125
≈And he felt his soul expl•de≈∼⌒∿.

VALLEY OF THE DAMNED

Chapter Two Valley Footnotes

In translating, we are using a very personal side to the American martial arts scene as it existed from the 1970s–today. The commercial side to these noble arts reveals the sordidness that goes on behind them. At this point, we are introduced to the second major character, shallow 'karate' movie star Mark Theman, known as 'the man.' He is well developed, dashing, yet has animal-like characteristics, especially around his eyes. He is greedy and arrogant, a perfectly ripe soul to be targeted by 'collectors,' *vile* spirits who trawl the earth for 'garbage souls' human waste, those who have wasted their lives, fit for their version of waste management. The unwitting Theman, unbeknownst to him is a source of immense power in the Deadlands. A wretched human as such with a multitude of fans to follow in his wake churned up by his powerful screws, can only help but fuel a spirit's personal ambitions and power. That is why Storm blasts him into the Deadlands *via* a lightning bolt. She wants his soul!

2. *Flat realities of their former glowing charge.* The text's early archaic language is suggestive of extremely amateurish works of art. These drawings are so cheesy that they themselves are 'ignorant,' ignorant cartoons that reflect no meaning of once formidable means and ways of life.

5-12. *Faded mighty leopard . . . black and white overall.* This section chronicles the pop-downfall of the 'Five Animal' (*wǔ xíng*) system of *Shaolin* Kung-fu, the mainstream ancient mother of many modern arts. According to Oriental historian and martial arts adept Dr. Peter Hsu, the martial arts as we know them today were said to have originated at the famed Shaolin Temple in China. Fitness/Fu exercises there were grouped around five major fighting animals, *ch'uan-fa* here meaning "fist-method/law"–white crane (*bái hè quán/ch'uan*), dragon (*lóng xíng quán*), leopard (*bào quán*) snake (*shé quán*) and tiger (*hēi hǔ quán*) each having a specialty or emphasis of exercise such as limberness or strength. For example, tiger forms today use motion for heavy muscle and bone development. They encapsulate heavy springing motions with the legs and powerful pulling (ripping) and pushing handwork. The motifs rendered in these poetic stanzas, observes Hsu, reflect the superficial and commercial 'instant gratification' attitude many people in the pop-martial arts have. This atti-tude is a direct result of the artificial 'modern educational' learning mode people unwittingly labor under. As these animals now are only 'noises on paper'–*i.e.*, *paper tigers* (Chn. *zhilaohu*), they reflect short and long-term types of learning. Short-term learning is logical, rational and is, as a matter of course, soon forgotten. Intuitive long-term learning, aimed more at the body than the mind, *via* action, is always with its possessor.

7. *Oh. How awful.* This deadpan, expressionless line tells it like it is. These illustra-tions, trying to portray the 'mighty martial spirit,' instead give their onlookers, so used to tired *clichés*, a cheap, stereotypical 'expected' thrill, much on the level of a mother showing her child a cartoon of a 'scary' lion for the first time.

8. *One can only paint the skin, that spirit of the bone.* Dr. Peter Hsu explains that this line can best be understood in reference to the Chinese proverb, "In painting a tiger, one can paint the skin, but not the bones." *I.e.*, external superficialities do not cut to the heart of a matter, which is what is needed for mature understanding. In light of our text, it is a warning to us mortals about the main character(s) and the story in general. We must decide what is real or not.

10-11. *Hid its 'guised face behind the cloud . . . trumped-up battle caw.* Dr. Hsu cites that all these great martial animals are ashamed that they have been degraded into meaningless pop-forms. The non-rhyming *trumped-up battle caw* implies sub-standard falseness, a squeaky fake croak, not even a real 'battle-call' from the white crane (*bái hè*). These animals suffer from shame, their spiritual images having to put on pre-tences of the old fighting spirit as if they are at a freak side show at the circus, playing down to the low-budget expectancies of shallow, wheezy, rabble-ridden audiences.

12. *Black and white overall.* Things are colorfully described in the Hallan Deadlands. In this chapter however, which takes place on Earth, the absence of color speaks of Theman, his bedazzled followers, and the class seminar as a whole as having a severe *black & white* cartoonish quality about them. This is a facetious statement on the state of the arts, their grip on people and their pop cardboard star representative.

13-14. *But the snake who . . . was ꞇoiling. Lit.*, "coiling." The translation, using an interesting meld of ancient *Lu* symbolism and modern American jargon, plays on our stereotypical expectations. This fifth animal from Shaolin must cry the most because, in a reverse Garden of Eden sort of fashion, its image (not humankind's) is fallen. The noble Shaolin snake (*shé*), in this seminar, is now an insulting snake-in-the grass symbol. It is used to introduce the even lower, unsavory character, Mark Theman, 'the man.' Let it be known right here and now that if push comes to shove, Theman, the all-American plastic celluloid kung-fu movie star, couldn't "punch his way out of a brown paper bag" as the saying goes.

15. *His hungry soul hid.* Theman is a self-made creature, full of pride and arrogant conceit. The text suggests that this character type is 'designed for destruction.' However, his forward attitudes are fronts that hide much. On the inside, he is very insecure, afraid that someone will discover what he is truly like. '*The man*' is a term used that is indicative that this person has no real deep-rooted identity at all, both a victim and perpetrator of such realities. For convenience, this borrowed concept from Dr. Greta Hastings stems from her psychiatric studies of cinema where the protagonist is so alienated from himself and society that he functions autonomously for his own self-interests, in this case, deceitful ones. Theman is not, however, an anti-hero type that in the end is a hero who bucks the system. He is just a *cockalorum*—a 'petty small-minded man' who thinks he is big—that tries to pull the wool over everyone's eyes.

22-24. *He lived off . . . with zheros respect. Lived off.* Like a *twisperv-o* junkie, 'the man' utterly was turned on, *i.e.*, '*got off*' on the dreams of his young 'drain-ages.' Zero + hero + her + eros. Also, a stalky predator full of lust, Theman, the 'hero,' has little respect for himself or his female fan-victims.

31. *Disinfected man he threw the kick.* The text uses the concept of theatrical circus arts to make the point that a buffoon is clowning around to amuse a boisterous crowd. For us, these are flashy, non-workable, film-style kicks, usually worked in the movies for dramatic effect. 'Flashy' kicks in America have become as, Dr. Peter Hsu observes, a symbol for a type of 'cool' attitude found in the pop-culture surrounding formal martial arts. From the standpoint of pop-culture, to be able to throw a kick at someone's

head means the kicker is 'with it' or 'macho,' or at the very worst, a 'successful' martial artist. To combative experts like Hsu however, flashy kicks imply ignorance of the real fighting arts and a foolish, arrogant, unrealistic 'untried' attitude.

34. *"Martial arts are life,"—they pretended to understood.* The bogus teacher is parroting a popular phrase used in teaching martial arts. This is what he has heard but has never taken to heart. However, for the diligent practitioner, the study of the arts offers a superlative vehicle for self-growth and discipline. *They pretended.* This is not a garbled translation but a literal one. The line is something young children might say, they 'chopping up' their English. The line is apparently meant to convey that the children did not understand what Theman was saying at all. It reflects how young children might respond to adults who give advice to them that is way over their heads—by nodding blankly; *they pretended* to know what they are talking about. The text is making a fool out of the hollow character who for us is our movie star who thinks he is suave and communicating well.

38. *An autograph or two.* This phrase is indicative of a whippy, slick, fast type of uncaring, unthinking mindset that runs rampant in popular martial arts. Theman has been trained to do things for expediency and showmanship, without any real value, care or concern.

44. *Mighty teacher with exalted ego.* Due to watered-down, dishonest training, Theman's mind and spirit are warped, albeit well adapted to the commercialism of the day that feeds his selfish nature. The submission of the *ego* in real humility goes a long way toward *teachability*, the prime requisite for true learning. If one is not teachable, one will not learn. True education in the arts only comes when one is ready to submit, learn and be taught. The essence of the arts—learning how to become human and civilized, can only be grasped after going through this process. Becoming a truly humanized and cultured individual is the greater, martial teaching.

47. *To accept 'what is.'* According to Dr. Hsu, accepting *'what is'* is a very common teaching in the arts. It denotes the idea of accepting the *'now is-ness'* of a situation as a sophisticated form of truthful philosophy. It reflects a certain level of 'maturity' and understanding in the arts. Again, Theman appeals to his follower's vanities, that

they are somehow 'the privileged few' who are cool and 'in the know'—one major sign of a false teacher and a cult, as cults often use the pretext of 'secret' or 'special' knowledge to lure their victims in. Theman is an expert at manipulation.

48. *Eternities shaped by.* One of the major realities of the Deadlands we will discover is that there are eternal ramifications to seemingly insignificant acts. As the child-rhyme runs, 'For want of the nail the kingdom was lost.' So, little things mold and shape a soul forever in the 'Halla. An analogy might be the flowing oddity known as the Colorado River, Arizona. The 'trickling remains' of whatever primal forces scoured out the Grand Canyon; it etches its profound character forever deeper into stone. But if the Colorado etched out the canyon, where is its floodplain with what should be an immense washout? It is not there! Something else made the Canyon, the river being just a 'remnant.'

49. *Repetition dulls the immortal wish.* Things repeatedly acted upon in time without an eternal perspective dulls and replaces the truer desires of the heart. Deep hearted *knowing* desires are swapped with choppy distorted illusions toward one's self and the temporal life. Solomon looked at this sad state in *Ecclesiastes*, OT. An extreme rarity, this strat of a gem-book works backwards giving great hindsight before foresighting future actions occur, and the *readerought* to know by now that "hindsight is greater than foresight" as the old adage runs. Theman knows practice does not make perfect, *but makes permanence*, and trains his followers in this, his *vain* to use them. By training them wrong from the start, and then slowly and 'kindly' correcting them, it will take them twice as long to play catch up having to overcome mistakes *then* get things right, all the time the soulpire sucking up their time, profits and energies into his soft cell tyrannical zone of control and marred, crinky egoo. This chicanery Theman sets about him appeals to Storm, he, the '*it*' man striking a harm'onious chorrd within her. (Note # 56-57 below, 'tribal knowledge' and Ch. 24 note # 101-103 for *trap-door* concept.)

50. *Toiled under florescent sun.* Modern lighting often reflects an extremely sterile, void-of-spirit, colorless environment, much like this and many schools have.

51. *Motions of the Non.* The 'Void' is in mind. According to Taoist and other Far Eastern traditions, to enter the 'Void' is to become so much attuned to nature one naturally blends in 'becoming one' with it. This, says Dr. Hsu, is to understand the mysteries of nature in a deep and abiding sense, with all its rhythms and ways. It is to live harmoniously with natural principles. Theman only uses the jargon of these lofty concepts to promote his own schemes as any ruthless executive would. The word may also be construed as 'None,' meaning that Theman knows that what he is doing is absolutely and utterly worthless (Ch. 3 note # 32).

53. *Pretty martial philosofee.* Just as in the old days, the modern American view of martial philosophy promotes, in theory, good morals and conduct. The term *pretty* however denotes greedy thinking about a marketable ideal that permeates the commercial end of the arts. Martial art philosophies in America, for a few, are a true living experience. However, a casual glance at pop martial magazines and the like shows a gross, glossy 'packaging' of these noble ideals to sell, appealing to the plebian masses. *Philosofee* is self-explanatory. *Philosophy* "love of wisdom" is a commodity to be sold and bought as part of a package business deal, much like a slick 'Honest John's' used-car sale does. The following denunciation for this type of activity in the martial arts can be found in the *Ground* Chapter of famed swordsman/duelist Miyamoto Musashi's (1584-1645) classic work, *A Book of Five Rings*:

> If we look at the world we see arts for sale. Men use equipment to sell their own selves. As if with the nut and the flower, the nut has become less than the flower. In this kind of Way of strategy, both those teaching and those learning the way are concerned with colouring and showing off their technique, trying to hasten the bloom of the flower. They speak of 'This Dojo' and 'That Dojo'. They are looking for profit. Someone once said 'Immature strategy is the cause of grief'. That was a true saying (p. 40).

And:

> I think it is held in other schools that there are many methods of using the long sword in order to gain the admiration of beginners. This is selling the Way. It is a vile spirit in strategy (p. 88).

56-57. *Colored belts showed . . . Of fragmented minds in disarray.* Peter Hsu relates that in many arts, the promotions of students are shown with colored belts (*e.g.*, black belt). Originally, early students of the arts had one belt that got dirtier over time, becoming a 'black belt,' showing how long they had put their time in. In modern schools, an old frayed black belt is a symbol within a symbol as well. It begins to turn white again from wear, returning to original purity, thus further indicating how long senior students have been involved in their arts. More so, to reach black belt level in classical Japanese schools mean that the person is now accepted as an 'official student,' or *dan*, as in *shodan*, the first beginning ranked black belt. Before that, students simply do 'not exist.' In many unscrupulous schools belts are given out as promotions that are meant to keep students, whether they earned it or not—and their money coming in. Some schools even 'guarantee' for a certain amount a black belt within a specific time.

Of fragmented minds in disarray. This phrase has several interpretations. One of the more interesting, taken from the eleventh century Icelandic *Heliaspur Saga*, is "Fragmented minds led the disarray." This alludes to teachers. Another alludes to both teachers and victim-students alike being in disarray. Overall, the line implies that in many schools, martial knowledge or knowledge in general, as the *Saga* claims, is fragmented and piecemealed out. This is sometimes due to traditional teaching, but more often than not, fragmented information loss is the product of defective teaching. At this level of the power game, this is known as *tribal knowledge*, which is having no policies or procedures whatsoever, everything being passed down by word of mouth, *etc.* This is what, for example, Rome *did not have*. Rome had standing orders for every conceivable situation that when executed automatically made them great. Tribal knowledge, squeaked and trickled out a little at a time, shows a very low order of trust and educational ability as it seeks to retain and centralize power for the top guns. In these matters, unwitting students are led to believe that what they receive is the full and truthful knowledge of a certain art at a certain level–but they don't. A strategy apt Chinese proverb captures this idea, "Never break your rice bowl." This means don't chuck out information all at once, if one wishes to make a living off of it. It has to be spooned out and spoon-fed to underlings a small dollop at a time in order to regulate knowledge, prestige and power. On a more positive note, this is done all the time to ensure quality control over a product and for the betterment of students who need to digest information slowly in order to enact its proper use. However, this too is dual-edged, many arts and secrets dying off because of mistrust and stingy teachers withholding data. Definitely, *wisdom hidden is wisdom wasted*. But yes, sadistic Theman enjoys 'belting' his 'marks' all right with residues owed him, or perhaps rather them—*'just because'*—just because they are so dense he can't stand it or them leaving their souls as 'black'–and as blue as his.

59. *Accept the lie*. Classical Japanese martial philosophy dictates a denial of self or resolute acceptance of death for a cause or leader. In an underhanded way, Theman is manipulating this ancient principle. He is bloating the student's vanities, making them feel superior, god-like, by adhering them to a lofty, or 'manly-man' cause, so that he can maintain control over them. On a deeper level, this 'lie' parallels the Garden of Eden story. Lucifer promises Eve that she, like him, can become god-like not as in God's graceful character but in power and social position, knowing both good and evil. For our text, Theman, the devilish martial 'man-god,' knowing both good and evil and the manipulations thereof, promises his students god-like power and prestige if they will accept his *ego*-enhancing lie(s) and follow him.

60. *Pajamaed students all in a row*. Karate students wear baggy (peasant) uniforms called *Gi's* in Japanese. A symbol of humility, they are white, but *pajamaed* here reflects the American zeal to add flash to all things. *Gi's* in America come in all colors, styles, including gold and the U.S. flag. Here *pajamaed* means a well thought-out, *'zeitgeist*-designer' trend-setting, era-fashionable sanitized approach to the arts. It is an unscrupulous attempt to make the ancient peasant killing art of karate chic and tasteful to the mass consumer. Peasants used to wear *Gi's* in the old days, but the art of Japanese jūdō took over the wear and turned it into a sign of humility, like the black belt, or dirty white belts the plebes also wore. Later these were passed on to the karate guys.

61. *Followed O-sensei*. The *O* translation used here is Japanese for 'Great Teacher,' as in the head master of an art or system. Other texts, most notably the seventeenth century *Book Haiku*, however, use a like-term in a sarcastic sense. From *Book Haiku*, *O* tells of Theman's vacuous mind in an evil, anti-Zen sense. There is truly 'nothingness' in it. That is, there is nothing noteworthy or of any value in his *vile*,

vanity-ridden mind. Theman's students have been short-changed. Under him, they really do have *0*, or 'zero,' *nowhere to go.*

62-63. *Movement moved without . . . no meaning.* The difference between a 'real' martial art and its 'shell' consists of intent of mind. Gichin Funakoshi, founder of Shōtōkan-ryū karate, captures the essence of realistic training (*Nyūmon*, p. 43):

> Each and every punch must be made with the power of your entire body behind it, with the feeling of destroying your opponent with a single blow. You must believe that if your punch fails, you will forfeit your own life. Thinking this, your mind and energy will be concentrated, and your spirit will express itself to the fullest. No matter how much time you devote to practice, no matter how many months and years pass, if your practice consists of no more than moving your arms and legs, you might as well be studying dance.

65. *Circle step and punch.* Circle stepping in the arts has many functions. One of them is to go around, or skirt obstacles in a fight to avoid clutter or being hit. Contextually however the text appears to be saying that the circle is symbolic in that it is 'void' or 'emptiness,' the symbol of the circle implying a never-ending journey and return to origins. Hence, as Dr. Peter Hsu observes, the students are doing symbolic motions but do not know their meanings, such as hitting 'on the nothing.' In particular, what this means here is to move off the line of force where an opponent's blow is coming, thus avoiding the full solidity of an opponent's strike. The opponent's action creates a hole. The student then counters through this 'nothingness,' empty hole or *suki-gap* (*see* Intro.). 'Avoiding the full and striking the empty' is a source of much meditation in the arts. This is in line with the philosophy of Du Mu, colleague of Sun Tzu, famed Chinese general of two thousand years ago whose book, *The Art of War*, is still required reading at military schools the world over. In Chapter 6 concerning tactics rendered toward *Emptiness and Fullness*, general Mu says that successful militarists "avoid the full and strike the empty" (p. 100). In all, this lack of a fuller 'full-circle' of teachings is just another statement reflection on the student's lousy instructor Theman who side-steps, 'skirts' or 'circles about' many issues to avoid revealing just how little he really knows.

67. *The height of wisdom—ƨto believe the absurd.* According to Hsu, true martial teaching enables practitioners to return to the humble basics and a clear understanding of the art's nature—an ordinary life or living experience. This returning full circle however is only after an immense amount of jargon and intellectual flack they go through as part of the training. For those who do not outgrow this point, they are forever lost in false ways, going off on *pseudo*-spiritual and intellectual tangents. For those who successfully trod this path, enlightenment comes when they come to see the 'ordinary' as it truly is—the simple and elegant height of life, beauty and reality, of learning how to live truly in peace with self and others. (Note: For our studies, *irony punctuation*, a backward question mark ƨ before a sentence is useful to alert readers that they are entering an irony or sarcasm zone. The Fe-punct indicates a statement or a word's bite or intent before they read on. Irony states that initial surface meaning is different from its secondary or more intended meanings. Modern written English does not exercise the vitamin-rich ferrum punctuation point although Laurentian, a major dialect of 'Hallan, does.

The text however describes Theman as deliberately manipulating his followers with *dis* ('hell-false') information. He tells them grandiose things. On a deeper level, *to believe the absurd* in the arts is sometimes taken to be the normal thing, the *height of wisdom*. Theman knows people are very gullible and are willing, desperately willing, to believe in something larger than daily life. That is why he tells whoppers. The bigger they are, the better, as they are more believable. Yarn spinning is common in the arts as legends are larger than life. A quote from the 1962 *Paramount* film by brilliant John Ford, *The Man Who Shot Liberty Valance* starring John Wayne and Jimmy Stewart (Theman would know this one) says it all. Upon telling the sobering truth as to how Valance (Lee Marvin) actually died—not by his own hand, Jim Stewart says to Editor Scott (Carleton Young):

> *Ransom Stoddard* (J. Stewart): You're not going to use the story, Mr. Scott?
> *Editor Maxwell Scott*: No, sir. This is the West, sir. When the legend becomes fact, print the legend.

Stretching the truth empowers Theman. He preys on his student's gullibility, everything designed to bolster their *egos*. Another aspect *to believe the absurd* concerns the bastardization of a Zen concept known as the *kōan*. Much misunderstanding in the arts' philosophies can be traced to here. *Kōans* are non-rational *riddles* given to students to force them to use their intuition and contemplate, the purpose of which is to create an 'epiphany of maturity' and awaken a greater awareness of their selves and their place in reality in order to escape their petty-mindedness and erstwhile biases. This has been taken way out of context and has been badly misrepresented in the West, making the Zen scene look absurd. Anyhow, gullible, believing stupidity is a dangerous bridge to cross in the teachings, the uninformed getting lost.

A further point can be made on the "*to believe the absurd*" theme. Hsu explains that words and rational logic cannot effectively explain the simple fluidity of motion. This means that rational explanations of motion, based on observations from a 'static' non-moving viewpoint are poor educational tools, taking on absurd descriptions. To overcome this educational block, the more accurate philosophy of martial motion rests upon *doing*. This is where the mature philosophies of the arts reside, *in action* 'beyond words' as it were. The trap to overcome in honest training, Hsu cites, is to get beyond mentally sticky technical jargon and get back to basics, where humanity resides, in the simple doing of things. The trap facing Theman's students however is that to 'return to the beginning' may imply, especially from their unwitting perspective, Theman's continued and controlled regurgitation of sly acts as scams to further benefit his sinister ambitions. The great and wonderful movie cross-starred Mark Theman is keeping his dim-witted underlings on a never-ending exhaustive squeaking gerbil tin wheel treadmill; a caged stupidity. This cage is of their own making, he only 'lending' a helping hand because they wanted to be led so. Cults perform this little operation, one should know—putting a smile on their victim's face while exhausting them, making them like *Scrawny* wet paper towels, pliant yet tough enough "to get the dirt out," and accept their teachings; such a schmoozer Theman is.

70. *Destruction of others.* As recorded in ancient times like today, in many martial art schools, there is a pleasant atmosphere and a veneer of morality and right conduct. Underneath though, one inevitably hears the bravado of people about what they 'would do' or 'have done' to people, reflecting the bestial, hidden *genetic* side to the martial arts based on fear, competition, rivalry, envy, strife, anger and

greed—a nice package of spiritual fruits. *Genetic* here is defined as "man-made, creature-centered, devilish and sensual—of the earth" (James 3.15). Geneticism is what shaft-drives humankind onward to survive, where the *acquisition of power* on this planet with its multi-any forms is all. Remember though, we are being reminded of illusory *eidōlons* here, 'reflected images that deceive and lie,' such as an idol inevitably is. *Eidōlons* are not only defined formally as "reflected images that confuse," they can be evil "spiritual entities" as well, the eidōlon concept covering false, confusing deceiving imagery, idols, their ever-predictable worship and hidden heinous spirit phantoms. They all tie nicely together in the war zone of god Mars. Illusions, no matter what forms they take are keys to understanding the realm of humankind and the plane of the spirits if our eyes can penetrate such things (*cf.* James 3.13-18).

73. *Never knowing of the truth.* With a limited curriculum, observes Hsu, it is very easy to keep people in ignorance, as the curriculum can be designed to control and funnel them and, in many cases, prevent individual creativity and thinking. The term for this is *stultify* or *stultification.* It means to be "trained or made stupid gradually by degrees," which many educational systems do, making their people's thinking and actions narrow and limited. *E.g.*, one may be a terrific runner but if they are put into a weight training class, they may be okay at lifting, but never reach their full genetic potential as if they were 'born to run.' Thus, the appealing 'learned' training program itself is actually frustrating, hindering and denying them—calculated, deliberate, cold-hearted designed failure is the main gist here—economies of the rich and powerful depend on it and many graduated 'wise-fool' *sophomores.* A 'cult' is a perfect word for this type of 'keep 'em in the dark' fly-by-night martial art school, such as Theman is running.

72-75. *Struggling students . . . deliberately kept.* In ˈäĭ ˈz—ˌˈĵoͩͯn̂ʹt̪ Theman well knows the martial doctrine and concept of self-balance. He further knows that coming from all walks of life students struggle for balance in their lives. But many of them are messed up, that they are by-products, *dis*-oriented by hyper-energized modern pressure cooking pop-culture and thus are *dis*-balanced, dis-jointed äĭ ˈz⇌ˌˈˈĵoͩͯn̂ʹt̪, 'out of joint'—and he intends to keep it that way, milking them for all its worth.

77. *False wisdom ensues.* Taking 'blows' under a false martial system is often a very carefully controlled event or commodity by the hands of an unscrupulous teacher. Once 'blood' or bruises are drawn, it is designed to prop up the student's *ego*, making him or her 'feel' they are part of the group, having 'earned' their place in the school as it were, in those 'terrible' throes of mortal combat. Theman pulls this trick off very well.

79. *Knowledge lost through.* In olden times, acquiring martial art knowledge was a personal quest gained *via* experience. Mass conformity and importation of the arts to America began in the 1940s, when many American service members returned from the Orient. To both import the art *en masse* and Americanize it meant an exceptional loss of truer combative knowledge's and philosophies that only could have been gained through the intimacy of one-on-one relationships with teachers, *the* formal way of training. The history of martial arts is replete with this fact.

82. *Minds grew dull.* Overwork of the mind and body dulls the capacity to interpret things correctly, and is a tool used by many cults to stultify and condition the weak-minded. This is such a deliberate and subtle action on Theman's part that it goes unnoticed by his all too willing suckered followers.

88-94. *Turtled images . . . phony accents.* In translating difficult passages, we can utilize parodies of all the pop-movements found in American martial art history. Although some of the great martial practitioners are listed, *e.g.*, *Bruce Lee* (1940-1973), and *Chuck Norris*, fictional characters such as *Kwai-Chang Caine, Daniel-san* and the *Teen-age Mutant Ninja Turtles*, capture the hodge-podge and glitz of the American pop-martial scene from the 1970s to the 1990s. *Ponies* (pony tails) and *accents* refer to pop martial stars of the late 1980s and early 1990s.

96. *Enter the Void.* *I.e.*, the 'Void' is the true natural-spiritual dimension of the arts in its mature state. This signifies in part a return to the ordinary life. Understanding this simple point is held to be the great secret behind all things. In the text, though, Theman is suppressing the personalities of his followers instead of uplifting them. By promising them enlightenment, he further enslaves his dupes to their detriment and his gain.

DOUGLAS M. LAURENT

The m-arts, representing and spear-heading societies in general, are caulked full of *contronyms*, also called *Janus words*, named after the two-faced Roman god portraying biblical Cush/Nimrod. *Janus-contros* are singular words or phrases that can have two meanings. Frinstance, *strike* means *to miss* while attempting to hit something or *to hit actually* something. As for the phrase *martial arts*, what can be said? Can slaughter and butchery truly be considered a *fine* art form, one that is *excellent* or *acceptable* or merely *good enough?*' Or is the wording simply a justification and defense-mechanism to help shield our fragile consciences from obvious horribilities? Deeper, could it be that we are being conditioned to be hard-hearted and accept such atrocities nowadays as 'normal?' Scan the history of TV and cinema. What was visually innocent at first, nowadays you see lust-ful people even on commercials getting blown to bits just having a *Twinkie* for a snack while zombies, terrorists, aliens, hidden agenda operatives and mutated dinosaurs; evils all, are clawing on their doors dying to get in to rip their hearts out, gush their blood and get at their Twinkies! Say, who and to what end is somebody pushing these buttons and envelops for? For us poor and downtrod-den plebes, for our welfare, or perhaps we should say our whellfare?

Perchance one here could confer with Gen. 6.11; 2 Tim 3.2; Matt. 24.37-39 and v. 12, where in the concluding times "the love of many shall wax—psychō?" ¡*Psychō?!*—*Ooops*! The scribbler meant to write *cold* in there, but *psychō* is the major root word here).

In all, being theatrical, perhaps it is just merely a case of "Suit the action to the word, the word to the action" that Theman has learned from *Hamlet* (III. ii.). As Hamlet exposes his murderous uncle by shoving a mirror in his face in the form of a play that re-plays his dad's—the King's murder, it just may be that the highly touted *fine* martial "art does indeed imitate life," nature, after all, and not the other way around. How deadly dreary, dull and droll—we being put to sleep and made thick through the boring repetition of massive *cliché* brain-less images while at the same time being excited, pumped and wide-eyed while stuffing popcorn into our gullets at the movies, getting 'fattened up.' Yes, this masterstroke of subtle war art is to be appreciated as it most certainly looks like the work of dark Nether-masters such as Storm and her associates as they deal out our fate from the bottom of the deck. The "Powers that be" and we

80

scrambled and hard-boiled Midgarders must like our eggs, as there is an awful lot of it on our faces.

101. *Led the kids in kata.* Since ancient times, *katas*, a Japanese term, are the classical exercises or 'forms' in the martial arts. Like a file cabinet, these forms contain combat knowledge but much of this information has been lost due to modern instructors teaching with no practical combative experience whatsoever. The *kata* encapsulates the study of the mind, body and spirit (Draeger, *Classical*).

103. *Buzzed the numchuck.* Or 'horse-bit.' Our translation uses the pop American term for *nunchaku*, the Okinawan flail-weapon that became famous *via* Bruce Lee in the late 1960s and early 1970s. The nunchaku is two pieces of wood united by a short cord, allegedly inspired by a horse's bridle. Cinematically, Lee created a visual style for the *screen*-weapon that consisted of whipping it around his torso at tremendous speeds. He also had bright colors taped to the end of his weap in order to catch the audience's eye, he calling it "retina retention." The public noticed this eye-alluring 'screen reality,' now believing that this was *the* method of combat for the weapon. In reality, it is more so used for locking, pinching, blocking, throwing and choking. Nunchaku whipping patterns in combat are rare because many times it causes one of the sticks to *reverb*; 'bounce' off its target disorienting its operator due to the disruption of its pattern. Strategically, the nunchaku, used at close quarters, surprises opponents after an initial encounter by 'opening up' (for whipping), doubling its distance, giving the user an advantage. The difference between screen *numchucks* and real nunchaku use is easy to detect. On the screen, force is generated by the arms, making the weapon go fast, but with relatively little power. In combat, the whole body torques into a blow. Hence, Theman knows only the pop-superficial method.

105. *Cut a melon in ha/lf.* As cited in Greek, Roman and earlier histories, boxers used to break and cut objects. For us, cutting melons was a very popular demonstration technique of karate skills in the 1960s where a blindfolded karate man, using a sword, chopped a melon in half on a person's stomach. Initially pioneered in the U.S. by Tadashi Yamashita (1942–), famed Shōrin-ryū karate and kobudō weapons master,

this technique was designed to demonstrate the concentrative abilities of karate and kobudō. Shōrin-ryū is a structurally fast empty-hand art stemming from Okinawa. Kobudō is the islands fighting art that uses five main farm implements as their choice of traditional karate peasant weapons (staff, nunchaku, tonfa–grindstone handle, kama–sickle, and sai–steel shaft with two-prongs along side of it). These plus the 'empty-hand' *kara-te* was originally designed to deal with maverick samurai who used long swords. Contextually, the text is implying that Theman is living off old routines.

106. *Through pine boards*. This is yet another very popular crowd-pleaser. These light boards are easily breakable. *Tameshiwari*, 'the art of breaking' however, is a complex science, and adherents train for years to break rocks, bottles, wood, concrete slabs, ice and so on. This technique was fist popularized in America by Mas. Oyama (1923-1994), famed Kyokushin karate master, during the 1950s-1960s.

112-113. *Actions pass . . . winnowing mock*. Small actions affect eternity. To *winnow* means to "weed out" something. *Mock* is self-explanatory. Theman's time is running out.

122. *Dead Yet Alive*. Another title for Mark Theman, 'the man.' This phrase reflects his still *Yet Alive* status (from our point of view) but to be in the Valhallan Underworld, one has to be dead! For this reason, Theman's rare 'dual' nature allows him passage into the Land of the Dead while yet retaining his 'living flesh humanity,' a glowing yummy property highly prized by the all consuming deadlanders.

THREE: MARKET OF THE SOUL

A tumult of voices made him awoke,
Dry wind blowing made him choke.
Crowds of denizened citizens moving through the din,
The man opened bleerie eyes to the market of *his* sin.

Breath lurching out tearing from his heart,   5
He led captive by that she-beast from the start.
On leather throng was the man long he dragged,
By Dark Storm Rising's sole demand.

The dead man looked and saw the great host,
Deadly deaded spirits from all nations' posts.   10
Silently brooding, some murdmured their craft,
Fatally sealed in where spirits breathed their last.

Horrendous vision crashing through his eyes—
A market of the dead deprived of their lives.
Ancient warlords of every blistwring fate,   15
Sought fulfillment; their appetites to satiate.

Watching, cavernous dread seized the man's mind,
Like-spirits as himself, deceived in like kind.
A hundred hands tore at him to offer him the way,
Each to his own truth, never procuring *that* light of day.   20

The man blistered into maddening heinous spell,
Sought for an answer—there was only pure Hell.
A babbling mass of damned spirits bold,
Who desired only soulace—
Where spirits were bought and sold.   25

Some were more solid than others to see,
Rotted phantoms (little perceived) told of fallen majesty.
Wailing mightily that their echoes would be heard,
Dreaming of lost glory, the dead hearts conjured.

And on and on through *this* viscous ectoplasmic mass,   30
The man dryly wandered, his heart made to gasp.
Innumerable spirits conversing to each or to the none,
In the market, inanely performing deeds they had done.

These spirits, danced they rituals to each and everyone,
Those with more body moving through *those* who had none.   35
Lamenting rites, the tales that were in secret told,
All to find peace where they were bought and sold.

Moving now, performing dire martial feats,
All hollow, empty, futilely mired in defeat.
Screaming, attempting to tell of their 'rent powers,   40
Strength had deserted them, nothing in their dower.

Wracked bodies, these murdering one another,
Bodies passing through each unto the other.
Techniques of the dead, gone warriors there pondered,
To tell of their lives they brutally squandered.   45

Modern masters the man saw from every Wasteland,
Judo, karate, kung-fu and small ninja'd bands.
There were boxers, fencers and thai kickers few,
They all offered sweet poisons to pick and to choose.

Half-rotted limbs; these skulled warriors fought,   50
Kick boxing each other 'til their guts were lost.
Dressed in Gi rags lost karateka did stand,
Throwing punches with ghostly empty-hands.

VALLEY OF THE DAMNED

Swirling dervishes, spektral fevered delight,
Of aiki warriors circling in dismal dusklight.　　　　55
Swordsmen playing with ghastly, illumined blades,
Cut through their bodies, relishing the grip of Hades.

The man, thorr asunder, his guts began to spew,
Animal, plant and machine forms, offered in decaying view.
These once-men had become *those* infernal idols of their art's lack,　　60
It was his soul they pawed for, wanting their own lives back.

(*Its*, things, were there too, so vile and unhumaned,
Fallen morning glories; now pale and unpruined).

Most able-bodies wallowed in their animal forms,
To their bestial image were they now conformed.　　　　65
Men, now spirits, now becoming vindictively less,
Caught in the rage of the beast for their fullest redress.

And those whose ways were of the green,
Twirled like dead leaves, ghosts near unseen.
Now plum, now willow, now cotton and lotus fist,　　　　70
Spirit remnants rustling unto the great abyss.

Spirits whose minds craved that universal way,
Lost their persons to her mechanical foreplay.
Lost their birthright to exist beyond eternal end,
Lost sight that human souls must at the last—　　　　75
Make amends.

So many arts, methods, styles to choose,
The art of the lie; systems of confuse.
There were those revenants of freeish eclectic bent,
Ghosts' hording fragments; truths once dearly spent.　　　　80

All values offered to lone wandering eyes,
To glut the spirit, *to make it joyously die*
(There are ways that seem right to men but only end in death,
All told, Truth voided leads to *that* final damnedness).
A hundred, nay a thousand truths were wantonly heard,   85
All whirling spirits performing katas of the dirge.

Many masters performing at their festering pace,
Offered him their art, if only he would take their place.
More spirits (though hardly noticed) performed weapon's feats,
And those nearly gone with high ideals wisped ethereal conceits.   90

Many were the horrors of these masters of the night,
Impulsed by their own craft to lose their lives in fight.
Disembodied wretches who grappled in unbelief,
Seeking fullish answers, never to find relief.

These were the damned, the finest of their kind,   95
Part of that faithless crew Losecipher led behind.
Shrieking horrors, their lost glories gone fast,
Their techniques now moving, but meaning well past.

Damned were many, humble quite the few,
Shadows in denial, now trying to lose,   100
Memories of they as men once been and had,
Among those joyous living, in Earth's bountiful land.

And shades' trying to rekindle life's lost light,
Love and their senses, once given in delight.
These barren squalid souls they do brazenly burn in thirst,   105
To drink the (cup of) life immortal past their mockeries birth.

Poor etched souls from beyond deep grave's way,
Seeking lost loves, only to be driven more insane.

Disjointed fingers reaching out for filling love,
To scream in remorse, for there was found none.   110
The man, sweating salt-vomit and blood, thought of a daring, swift escape,
Yet unwilling was he to contend with the corpse behind his captor's loathsome face.
Dark Storm from steed jerked and threw him unto sharp cutting ground,
The price was fixed and in hot chains, the fallen star was bound.

DOUGLAS M. LAURENT

Chapter Three Valley Footnotes

In our world, we are so used to heroes and storybook happy-endings. Here though is the failed, down side to heroism, the fallen un-heroic flotsam of the Ages. This 'Soul Market' characterizes those lost human beings and otherworldly spirits who have followed false, self-prideful ways. They could have chosen to be heroes at one time or another but turned their backs on such self-sacrificing opportunities only to serve their own selves, using their unique skills and knowledge to their own gross advantage. The market is a vast 'bizarre' wasteland of lost souls and despairing vacuous arts.

3-4. *Denizened citizens moving through the din . . . his sin.* *Denizened* means "denied Zen," or "self-enlightenment." These souls turned away from the truth of their honorable capabilities to aid humanity only to be shipwrecked upon their own futile selves. *Din* is a compound. The market is a chaotic, riotous place, but also very hazy and dim. *Sin* (Gk., *Hamartanō*) in the basic sense simply means 'to make an error,' or more formally defined, "to *miss* the mark and so *not share* in the prize." It is much as a determined archer, though aiming well, would nonetheless miss the bull's-eye or set standard, losing the contest. By default then, we all sin in one way or the other, 'missing the mark' of higher spiritual laws. Even in ignorant sincerity, such as one finds when they turn down a wrong street to find an address, this would be wrong behavior, and so imply defection from any of the Divine's all-healing spiritual directions or standards, as recorded in *1John* 3.4. In short, this horrid place and the state of mind therein is a completely lawless, insane, mentally diseased one (Ch. 18 note # 31-32).

11. *Murdmured their craft.* Murder + murmur. Not only had these spirits' ways so enslaved them to their craft, now their only audience to that activity was what remained of their own car*cassed*-like spirits. These spirits had hung onto their arts so tenaciously in life, or rather, the parasitical arts hung onto them, that like jealous lovers, the arts got the better of them and had murdered the better part of their human host's personalities. These spirits' remains (not full, healthy spirits) were now murmuring in Dantean-like (*Inferno*) numbing repetitive confusion, trying to relate to their own domineering art for comfort and escape, a *diechotomy* they can never overcome. As a *hole*, instead of

being the honorable offspring of noble Kung-fu animals, these meshed remnant bestial *et al.* style-spirits had decomposed into less than 'in the limelight' creatures such as breying asses and devout scavengers. Deep down inside these non-human no more spirits are wanting, yearning and dying to avenge themselves upon the Powers that drove them double-fold 'into within themselves,' ultimately ripping their own shoules open, knowing they 'did themselves' and now are nothing but mass confusion—a peeping, grunting *dis*dainful religion made of their own squirming, beliefs—where "the worm dieth not." And what massters there are all over yet.

16. *Sought fulfillment.* These wretched spirits pursue empty pleasures that never, ever satisfy.

19. *To offer him the way, each to his own truth.* Recognizing Theman's semi-*Dead Yet Alive* status, the dead would gladly trade even that miserable portion for their own worse ones. Contextually, they are offering 'the man' their brand of truth or reality. Unfortunately, relativistic truth in the Deadlands creates a treadmill-type affect, 'allowing' its slaves the action-illusion of continually seeking for an absolute truth, but never finding one (*cf.* 2Tim. 3.1-7). In the Nether, lost souls always seek but never find because they are stuck with, and cannot get out of their corrupted selves. This is of interest. One of the rules that we will find here is that there are no fence sitters. In Valhalla proper, one is either for or against the "Powers that be," namely, good and evil, and everything that pertains to them, although from our limited view, these lines are sometimes blurred. This treadmill reality is a fitting 'punish-ment' by the higher powers of the Deadlands as these spirits deliberately chose their own courses of self-damning actions. Unlike on Earth where justice may take a while to catch up and so foster arrogant lawlessness, in the Dead, every action one makes has a near-immediate impact, carrying its own form of searing, immanent justice fostering the direct reality of pain and terror. One thing we Midgarders can learn here is to be aware of philosophical and knowledge systems that claim to be gloriously 'open-ended' but in reality are closed and *entropic* (Gk. 'in-turning,' 'col-lapsing') in the sense they don't produce freedom, but more enslavement under the guise of seeking truths. Some Greek factions were very much like this, this view yet existent.

26. *Some were more solid.* According to chthonic ideology, one rule of the Nether is that the more 'solid' one is the better. This means two things. One is that a more solid spirit is a 'survivor,' not being cut into smaller bits, and secondly, it shows that it is in the upper hierarchy of more capable spirits. Thus, the more beat, hacked and shriveled a spirit is, generally the more depraved it is as well. That is why in the Netherscape, one sees dark blobs moving about. These are the sintering low-life losers of the Deadzone. The more battles they win the better looking they are, lacking a transparent or corpse-like look. This rule depends mostly on their state of mind—will, moral, intellectual and emotional, as some spirits take tremendous beatings, but their interiors shine. In old Greek, a term that might describe these killers and all others in the Mortuus nethers is *phasma*. Phasma if you will, are ghosts or phantoms that haunt the living. Some are souly bodiless whilst others are corporeal keeping their physical bodies—or what we think passes for them. Recall that descriptions from the *Valley* are Midgard-bound metaphors, a thick and poor tool at best that attempts to capture, describe and relate to us will-be flatliners what is going on in realms intangdefinable. In Dark Storm's case, she is very beautiful but extremely wicked, the top of her line. Having suppressed her more 'humangelic' passions in the pursuit of gain, she is a machine-like predator, a mind of complete discipline (she thinks) that has thrown out lesser forms of evil within her. This, in part, is what also makes her both tough and beautiful, according to Deadlands standards.

30. *Ectoplasmic mass.* The number of dead spirits in the market in some places is so great it is like sluggishly wading through thick condensed masses of floating jellyfish.

32. *Conversing to each or to the none.* Spirits do talk to each other, but they are so wrapped up in self, it seems that no other ever hears them. They only pay dim attention to what is said when it is important to their own self-interests and advantages. Concerning *none, see* Ch. Two, note # 51, where *Non* or *none* in this footnote may also be understood as a gross perversion to the doctrine of the union of mind with nature.

33. *Inanely performing deeds.* These spirits try to recapture 'lost glory' by endlessly repeating 'shadows.' These shadows are remnant, hollow scrap memories of them acting out their greatest deeds, thus becoming for them, like a fire at night in a 'refuse' barrel, a burning punishment of empty folly.

37. *All to find peace where they were bought and sold.* These heavily dead spirits repeat their acts, hoping to fill their empty souls on the slowly diminishing returns and vapors of partial memory, not the full memory itself. As memory dissolves over time, it means to have no more memory, to be inert and weak, easy prey for stronger spirits. It is imperative for the ones who still have strength left in them to 'feed' on other souls, in order to retain their memories in general. They can also live on through another spirit's memory. There may be parallels to this on Earth. Sometimes folks see things, peoples and events from distant times, but the memories may not be their own (perhaps demonic or *pseudo*-memories—fallacy-tenants of re-incarnation). This market also serves as a slave block where lesser spirits are absorbed by entities that are more powerful.

40. *To tell of their 'rent powers.* 'Rent implies 'transparent,' or 'false powers.' It also means to be "torn" and "ripped." As cited in the thirteenth century *Kel's Yellow Book*, it seems that these spirits know they lost their powers to change for the good, to help others, to be 'human' as it were, but would not face up to that fact. They themselves ripped the power of good out of their own hands with their own self-murderous lusts. From this they also know they are forever empty, futile and therefore damned. This makes them howl all the louder.

42. *Murdering one another.* As these spirits are already quite dead, the fullness of killing, murder and martial techniques can be endlessly acted upon. This shows explosive rage and inner, ultimately impotent self-torment as they are eternally 'set' in their depraved state of doing, growing more and more self-wretched as time goes on. In this plaza, to murder and be re-murdered is a common 'pastime' activity. For many, it is the ultimate, hollow perverted ecstasy of trying to let out immense unspeakable frustration with no fulfillment. This is why their acts are always growing more violent—there is never any relief, only vain repeated emptiness that tries to fill a soulish void.

46. *From every Wasteland.* The false, despairing martial art systems found in the *Nether-realm* of their minds, aka 'the world.' These systems had promised these spirits fulfillment, but used their practitioners as living canon-fodder, promoting their

systems over personal being, spirituality and freedom. Many unscrupulous schools in our world as well, observes Dr. Peter Hsu, defines the 'genetic worth' of students by how much they can service the school and keep it going. This statement reflects a great controversy in the modern parallel martial arts, that is, how much conformity or freedom should one strive after in the arts? Bruce Lee was the most vocal of the 'freedom' advocates in the late sixties and early seventies, when conformity to ancient traditions and classicism was heavily in vogue in America (and still is). As classical martial arts, with its Eastern mindset of filial and social obedience (Confucian and military-based) were becoming very popular during that era, students giving their all to a master or school was coming under the fire of 'Yankee karate' that was and is highly individualistic. In the *'Halla* however, this sort of eclectic freedom is just another disguise of self satisfying, self-binding illusion.

47. *Jūdō, karate, kung-fu and small ninja'd bands.* Using modern terminology and history to translate the properties and occurrences of the once-and-future Nethertexts, here we can use a rough chronology of what was important during (*zeitgeist* era-fashion market manipulated) certain times in American pop-martial art history. In order, there was jūdō 1950s–1960s, karate-dō 1960s–1970s, kung-fu in the 1970s and ninjutsu in the 1980s, *et al.* Readers might look at modern martial art magazines to see what is the current, manipulated *zeitgeist* trends in the arts are.

49. *All offered sweet poisons.* False arts with their emphasis on over-indulging the vanities of mind and bodily appetites easily impress themselves upon weak human souls who only want power. For these lost spirits, following their carnal hungers led them to a sweet death, a 'willing submission' to arts that often brought them the 'accomplishments' they desired in life, although these alleged successes were exactingly fleeting, empty and passing away with their *diminishing returns.* In the midst of these hollow achievements, false arts, like jealous overlords, suppressed these people to become their slaves with their conformist (mental, physical, *etc.*) political needs and other *genetic* lineage concerns. Such concerns, for example, would be making money for the system and promoting the arts 'cultic,' cultural influence. So painfully desperate are the spirits in this fallen realization, they want to trade away what they have for what little Theman has.

52. *Karateka did stand.* *Karateka* is Japanese for 'karate practitioner' or 'player.' It denotes an expert who is so good at their craft he or she can 'play' with the art at its high end, and not be encumbered by technicalities as a beginner would.

53. *Ghostly empty hands.* "*Kara-te.*" The term *karate* signifies not weaponless hands as popular notions suggest, but a philosophical hand of emptiness, *i.e.*, implying a Zen-like natural way. Originally, *kara-te* meant 'China-hand,' but was changed in the 1930s by master Gichin Funakoshi of Shōtōkan-ryū karate as the art, having been splintered, was reorganized around modern Japanese, not older Okinawan needs. Historically, Okinawa-te was the peasant fist art that merged with the more sophisticated Chinese arts of kung-fu. Supposedly, it never had a Zen base to it until the 1930s when the master and others attempted to give the arts a more sophisticated and acceptable philosophical gloss for modern times in order to compete in Japan and the rest of the world as a 'mature' art form.

55. *Of aiki warriors.* *Aiki*, Japanese for 'spirit-meeting.' In the Japanese martial art of *aikidō* "the way of harmony with universal energy," practitioners integrate themselves with their opponent's movements based on natural laws, primarily those of the sphere or the spiral such as found in a hurricane. Morihei Ueshiba (1883-1969) founded this art in 1940s. Aikidō is a non-combative, non-aggressive spiritual path (*dō* art = a spiritual path, *jutsu* art = a combative killing method). In context to the poem's passage, *aiki* represents the older, more brutal type of understanding based on ancient combat jutsu principles (formerly, aiki-*jutsu*, signifying "technique of harmonious spirit"). Summarily, these are *aiki* warriors who had 'gone sour' they using their formal noble craft for dire ends. In addition, since they were doing exercises like modern aikidoists, it reveals the hypocritical fact that these spirits really had forsaken the ancient, truer aikidō way and had retrogressed in their own spirituality and understanding of the arts. To practice edited arts, such as retrogressing from combat to modern sport arts means to cut information, having less than what was once of old. As original information and meaning is lost, alternate ideas and applications spring up, fusing into the remaining old ones, filling the gaps. This process is called *syncretism.* This is like losing the primary application of a combative art and turning it into sports martial arts or just performing the outer form of kata

without knowing the interior movements or actual functions, as seen in tournaments. Master Funakoshi ciphers (*Jutsu*, p. 27):

> Likewise, in times past swordsmanship was taught only through *kata* since a *shiai* [competitive match], whether using real swords or wooden swords, was always fought at the risk of one's life. Subsequently, today's face masks and wrist guards were developed, and although this brought about a certain amount of degradation of kendō, it allowed it to become that much closer to a sport rather than a martial art.

59. *Animal, plant and machine forms.* This translated list is inspired from Dr. Francis A. Schaeffer's (1912-1984) *Escape From Reason* (1968) where lost man, having forsaken Divine knowledge, looks down on a fallen world rather than up for inspiration, only to land second best. Because the Divine knowledge had been obliterated for these wretched spirits, it shows their folly of adhering to a descending order of empowerment as found quite readily in nature markedly less than what they originally were, being once 'made in the image of God.' Looking down on things less, they feel this somehow is the 'height of wisdom,' which the arts greatly advocate. Unfortunately, this is literally true for their case, because this is all they have.

Their animal/plant/machine names (plus terms, phrases and metaphorical descriptions found in the arts) plus their underpinning philosophies/imitative ways, like spiritually 'becoming' a beastly lower tiger-spirit in practice inspired from corrupt nature tells it like it is. Despairing martial philosophy only leads to death or the mind-numbing acceptance thereof, as seen in many martial views such as that of the samurai's *hara-kiri*, or ritual disembowelment. Another hidden aspect of this passage has to do with the *second law of thermodynamics*, or *entropy*. A Greek term, *entropy*, from which despairing philosophy arises, implies 'in-turning' and 'self-collapse' as available energy within a closed system in time decays and burns out to nothing (new cars rust, we grow old and die, civilizations become extinct—such as the martial Lydians of Asia Minor, fifteenth-fourteenth centuries B.C., who were famous as archers, *etc.*).

Martial philosophy foments this major despairing entropic *line of despair* as it peers down upon *fallen* nature (from an *entropic*, inwardly 'self-collapsing' viewpoint) for motivation and not up to a personal Creator God in whose non-entropic, non-collapsing image man was originally made. The fallen martial view mimics deposed nature's designs and encapsulates them into styles as in whirlwinds. E.g., jūdō and aikidō are based on swirling circular principles, animals like 'leopard fist' (bào quán) style, plants 'plum-flower fist' (méihuā quán) style and bio-mechanistic forms/philosophies such as found in wing-chun kung fu and modern sports like western boxing and fencing and Bruce Lee's jeet kune do ("the way of the intercepting fist"). These later machine-like endeavors are all based on the linear mathematical efficiencies of the thrust for ultimate inspiration.

Thus, these spirits are in a gross state of lust—which is an undue entropic fixation of their dwindling minds, attentions and hopes on things in time that are in a self-collapsing state of corruption such as the martial arts are. In this instance however, they have passed from time into the eternal, their very souls having been corrupted and contaminated in a permanent fallen state due to their previous temporal lusts. As an aside, we will also find the 'animal, plant and machine' formula a hidden, 'descent of man' theme in George Orwell's masterful novel Animal Farm (1945).

60. *Those infernal idols.* The worst punishment for these wicked spirits is that they have become their own gods, *i.e.*, they are stuck with their own selves for eternity with no opportunity for growth—shut off from light and love—a course they deliberately chose. Permanently fixed, these spirits can experience much on a horizontal plane, but they are irrevocably trapped on this self-same level. *Entropy* is again at work in this passage and helps explain an amazing quirk found in the Nether. From *the second law of thermodynamics* that speaks of entropy, the available energy within a closed system diminishes. Hence, these fallen ones are a product of their own retribution. It seems a paradox, but their very spirits are in a state of decay, becoming more degraded, and yet at the same time, being immortal, they do not decay! Their personalities are subject to degradation and so decay, but they will always retain the full measure of their ever-hollowing vaporizing personalities. This weird apparent contradiction of degradation explains why some spirits are more *vile* and wicked in the wastes and yet retain their punch.

64. *Wallowed in their animal forms.* The spirits in the wastes have descended to a lower form of Nether-nature—that of mere animal remnants. Animal forms are immensely

popular in modern martial arts and are derived from masterful observations of nature, a source of inspiration. Past masters studied animals to learn the secrets of nature, but they retained their great dignity as human beings. In the Deadnether though, these spirits have traded in the totality of their human spirituality and literally chose to turn inward, collapse into themselves and become less, to become in the Greek, *psychē spaghion thērions*, "soulish slain wild beasts," *zōion pnéumas*, "animal spirits," grotesque two-legged monstrous remnant-entities. "As natural brute beasts" they were "made to be taken and destroyed," speaking and performing evil of the things that they understood not, utterly perishing "in their own corruption" (2Peter 2.12-13; Jude v. 8-10). In *Wisteria Lodge* and *Hound of the Baskervilles*, Sherlock Holmes cuts the line clean, "There is but one step from the grotesque to the horrible," and, "The more outré and grotesque an incident is the more carefully it deserves to be examined." Indeed, such atrocities and crimes against one's very own soul are grotesque and horrible; let us take heed. *Yah, yea*, more than *verily*, there is in this choosing business the danger of being forever fixated in a certain state of mind; becoming less than a heaven-ordained man or woman-spirit—or avoiding this trap altogether:

> And you, young warriors, you are free, in your minds, you think—allegedly.
> Spirit cannot be killed, that is what the harbingers say,
> Only filled or spilled—and that alone on your appointed day.
> 'Tis an harrowing hour, when naked souls stand in blazed or putrid breeze,
> To gain the prize immortal or to the gates of hell must flee.
> To till or to mill, that is the key. Choose the path of the way to be. . . .
> —*Dark Sword Midnight*

Certainly, these spirits knew all this, but chose the quick and easy way to power without reviewing its *black piranha* eternal 'chomping-power' ramifications (Ven. *vassago* "servants of the dark lord," the "tooth-fish" black piranha have the strongest bite in the creature world—30 x's their own body weight). As there are many bizarre markets in the Deadlands, the feeling the spirits have about this particular market is one of little remorse. To be found here means spirits have known the potential good that could have come out of their arts—they should have realized Heaven, but have willfully rejected it.

As it stands, these debauched spirits are now only parasites to the true arts both in being and in practice. Perhaps a more accurate assessment is that these are not parasites to the true arts, but are twice removed—parasites to their fragmented view of the greater truth, and taking their hacked remnant view, made it into their idolatrous god. This false fractured idol-god eventually gave them the cold shoulder. Hence, they are not 'vague shadows' of the real art, but second-string shadows to their once-removed false god-art, a deplorable state to be in, to be sure. Vague shadows in the real arts are the barely visible undercurrents. They are inklings of dark thought found within them, that all good practitioners come across from time to time, *e.g.*, the self-centered 'politics of the school situation.'

What initially happened to these spirits is quite a common occurrence in the arts. As master practitioners of the arts are said to *be the arts* themselves, they lend their own unique interpretations and stylizations to their chosen art forms. Thus, the black undercurrent trends in the arts eventually struck a common, 'already there' dark chord within their souls and took hold of these spirits, overpowering them, they now being absorbed under the darkness of their 'made in their own image' idolatrous art form. *Idolatry* defined $=$'s "worthless, vanity, nothingness."

These shadows were, in popular *Star Wars* lingo, seduced by the dark side of the force. Even more so, they were seduced by their own cracked fixated entropic lusts that convoluted them and their arts into a gross fragmentary perversion of truth. To the deadlanders, this implies for them at least an absolute in the arts, there was, long ago, an original standard of goodness that these miscreant spirits rejected. In Valhalla, the simple fact is that goodness rejected does not produce an opposite and equal reaction, namely evil, but a lesser, broken down counterpart of evil. For this ghastly Underworld, it is right to say that good must first exist in order for evil to defect from, to go against. This substantiates the more accurate Earth idea that evil is parasitical and ultimately weaker than good. Evil is not co-equal to good (like *yángyīn*, an entropic view holds), as evil must first have a standard from which to default from, signifying good came first.

73. *Mechanical foreplay.* For spirits in the Deadzone to become 'mechanically oriented' since they view the universe as a mechanical object and that they are merely

by-products of it is to obliterate the better part of their spiritual personhoods. In turn, they become a 'thing' or an 'it.' Based upon Nether-groundless naturalistic heresy, it is the selling out of their spirituality to become less. As an equivalent, in the Nether as on Earth there are no records whatsoever of how a spirit or personality could ever evolve founded upon exact 'scientific' principles. Defined, true science (not *pseudo* or 'false' science) is established upon things that are *observable, measurable and repeatable* Only, a very narrow tool indeed in which to interpret the whole wide universe! Scientifically speaking then, one cannot 'prove' they had breakfast this morning, as this would require historical documentation! True science then is in the realm of *the Present, not the past or the future*, a point that many spirits apparently need to learn about. Like the ancient Northern Europeans, the deadlanders believe that the universe is a living being, one that requires stewardship and harmony with it, not personality obliteration because of it. This to the more alert spirits implies a strong choice of belief—whether to succumb to their besmirched Deadlands intellect and sensibilities and become the mechanical universe's cog-slave or to see into spiritual matters deeply, becoming nature's sovereign stewards.

77. *Arts, methods, styles . . . systems of confuse.* Borrowed from controversies from earthly arts, the translation reflects a very popular argument in the martial arts as to which art is better than another. Some advocate classicism and tradition over those who, with freer intentions, desire to make eclectic their art. In the Nether way, the 'righteous' spirits, those 'in their right minds,' want commitment to a noble ideal or cause (*e.g.*, good *vs.* evil) simply because it defines one's loyalties, showing a person's truer nature. Actions toward one of these ideals are a major form of identity.

In the Zone, there are no fence sitters (mugwumps), but if there are and can be found, they are highly despised. There are also no petty grievances arguing which art is better. The main idea is, 'either you are with them, or us, period,' the true art in the Deadlands is to kill efficiently or be killed—each to their own way. Everything else to these spirits is mere intellectualization fit for pantywaists. Like the old Northerners, the dead ones like everything up front. Even mercenaries here are known for their political stances, although they like to bend the rules.

To the boys in the dead, motion is the final standard and arbiter of all things. As a matter of interest, their martial systems at a more 'civilized' level tend toward things of the mind, abstractions that drift toward the political and social arenas, rather than life-deciding ones. This is the true mainstay of their strength. This in time however, forces a loss of their truer fighting capacity, it becoming 'civilized,' prone to moral and divisive rationalistic debate as to whether to strike or not. This problem is not only an ancient one, but a modern earthly one as well, causing the fall of many a civilization. It displays the changing 'perception values' of old and modern societies the martial systems being merely 'symptoms' of the times. For example, in modern society, all things are based on *mathematics*, or true original science. *Pseudo* or false science, that which is gropingly speculative, is highly destructive. In old societies, their view of life was based on a philosophy of motion, of life, not numbers or living based on false premises and partial truisms. A quote by Genshin Hironishi, Shōtōkan master writing of karate may serve as a point of understanding here (Funakoshi, *My Way*, p. vii-viii):

> The origin of karate remains impenetrably hidden behind the mists of legend, but this much we know: it has taken root and is widely practiced through-out East Asia, among peoples who adhere to such varied creeds as Buddhism, Mohammedanism, Hinduism, Brahminism and Taoism. During the course of human history, particular arts of self-defense have gained their own followings in various regions of East Asia, but there is a basic underlying similarity. For this reason karate is related, in one way or another, to the other Oriental arts of self-defense, although (I think it is safe to say) karate is now the most widely practiced of all. The interrelationship becomes immediately apparent when we compare the impetus behind modern philosophy with that of traditional philosophy. The former has its roots in mathematics, the latter in physical movement and technique. Oriental concepts and ideas, languages and ways of thought have been to a certain extent shaped by their intimate connection with physical skills. Even where words, as well as ideas, have undergone inevitable changes in meaning through the course of human history, we find that their roots remain solidly embedded in physical techniques.

The sum of this stanza is that the speculative sciences, systems and methods of the arts are fine for Monday morning armchair practitioners of the *vea pugnus artia lex*

(Lat., "the way of the fist-art law"). Taken to extremes however, they are a form of spiritual clutter and bondage that, like the *Gordian knot* Alexander mind-*cut* through, needs to be razored to the max in order to see motion in its pure state and what it is capable of doing. This 'doing' biz is not merely confined to physical actions, but affects the perceptions, sensibilities and life-views as well, developing, for example, rarified powers hardly used on Midgard. The extraordinary kung-fu master Bruce Lee writes, "Jeet Kune Do avoids the superficial, penetrates the complex, goes to the heart of the problem and pinpoints the key factors" (*Tao*, p. 12). His teachings and skills are a brilliant testimony to this.

86. *Katas of the dirge.* *Katas* are the formal exercises that many arts have and serve as filing cabinets, repositories of self-defense information, giving an art its particular look, feel and philosophy—its particular 'kick.' The ones that are performed by these damned masters are spiritually dead with no functioning meaning for the past, present or the eternal. A *dirge* is a song of sadness and lamentation, often accompanying funerals with music, making these katas non-edifying, ab-*soul-lute*-ly despairing in their nature. These katas of the damned cannot help those who practiced them at one time with such youthful vigor.

94. *Seeking fullish answers.* Foolish + full. These lost masters want full and soul-satisfying answers but under their own canopy of despairing logic, with its seeming mature 'answers of no answers' (which is considered a high mark in earthly martial philosophy), they seek for and ask (and get) only more mind-spamming wheel-spinning irrelevant questions that go nowhere.

96. *That faithless crew Losecipher led behind.* Lucifer. The great gnawing, file-tongued Prince's political spin machine is keen on spreading ciphery 'mysterious' information and 'special secret knowledge' about to induce others to lose themselves in his catchy programs. Of the Cherubim class, he is said to have once guarded the throne of God. To be *led from behind*, or from a position of apparent nothingness or weakness is a shrewd act, tyrannical leadership appearing in the guise of humility. He led a third of the angels in rebellion against God early on in human history, the rebellious angels numbering perhaps in the

billions (*e.g.*, the nation of India boasts of having at least three hundred and fifty million 'gods' alone). For further info on this corrupt, eclipsed Machiavellian ill-bedimmed sooty illuminous masterlessmind war leader, *see Isaiah* 14.12-17; *Ezekiel* 28.11-19; *2Thessalonians* 2.1-12 and *Revelation*. The Deadlands are full of 'fallen' and 'redeemed' spirits (so to speak) whether they are angelic, human, demonic or otherwise. In kung-fu axiom-land, the phrase, "From the dragon we learn to ride the wind" implies most certainly to lead strongly but, paradoxically this through the *façade* of 'following meekly.' This means yielding suppleness and the ability to adapt, as when, feigning a defensive breach, the opposition shoots a punch and the defender avoiding it 'rides it back' to its source with a blow of his or her own, very much surprising the attacker. True *meekness*, if one digs around, can be whittled down to the notion of 'strength under control' in many ways.

Here is another general rule for interpreting the spiritual dynamics of the Netherzone. Many times the text functions as a *euhemeristic* mirror so that angels, heroes, humans, gods, demons, demigods (half-human, half-god), *etc.*, may be interposed, left for us to interpret who is who and what is what. *Euhemerism* is from the Greek philosopher Euhemerus, fourth century B.C. He believed that the myths of the gods were in actuality tall tales, editorial cartoons and embellishments of real people and their exploits greatly exaggerated, much like movie stars or political figures are in the yellow journalism supermarket tabloids today.

For example, the father of the Greek nation is said to be the mythical god-hero *I(y)apetos/Iapheth* (*Japetos*), who had sons—Prometheus, Atlas, *et al.* We know him as *Jā'pheth*, son of biblical Noah. Settler of Europe, the 'great one' is known as gods Roman *Jupiter* (*Iu/Ju-pater* 'god-father Jove'), Ind. *Brahma Prajāpat(h)i*, Chn. Miautso *Jap-phu*, *Yafes* of Turkey, *Sceaf/Iafeth* of Britain, Proto-Indo-Aryan *Iapeti/Djapatischta* ('chief of race'), Idn. *Perapatisi*, *Majapahit* of Java, Skt. *Dyáuspīta/B(v)raspati* ('chief prayer giver'), Hin. *Brihaspati* ('god-priest'), Scand. *Seskef*, Sumerian *Atab* and Proto-Indo-European (PIE) **Dyeu(s)-petēr* ('god/sky-father'). Yeah, there is more. Myths find their basis in real historical events and persons all we have to do is know what we are looking for and hunt them down. *Euhemerism* is a vital tool for studying, as the *Valley* translations make much use of it. It enables us to see many levels of possibilities within the text all at once.

106. *To drink the (cup of) life immortal past their mockeries birth.* This is an allusion to the blood cup of eternal life offered by Christ at the last supper. *Mockeries birth* implies the lies these spirits live, to which they are now fully compelled to indulge in and are ensnared by. This is the result of having become what their dark hearts really desired—to shut out the eternal light and have a self-centered form of power and nothing else. 'You get what you deserve' is a grand principle in the *Valley*. However, our text runs a bit deeper. These 'sealed in evil' spirits wishfully dream of being sealed in goodness like the elect, unfallen angels.

FOUR: ANGEL-HEART

Four black shades stepped rightly forth,
To bid on the remains of that human mort.
A great prize in deed for their master was he—
A *Dead Yet Alive* man still alive to be.

Dark Storm settled she the bleak account,   5
Filling her coffer came bloodgold a'fount.
Sold the man-beggar to those grimed spekters,
Took their gold–it was all for the better.

Grossest characters of rankful nature,
Sunken eyes that lusted for that living treasure.   10
Desperate criminal shades to possess the man,
Creatures who sucked at *that* vital light he had.

In great leaden chains they drove the man out,
More the animal now living his truer part.
Slung over the saddle of a great red phantom beast,   15
Desired to turn the human in that they might feast.

Journeyed they unto the forest in starkened gloom,
The man writhing knew of his forthcoming doom.
"Hey friend," one rattled to the human in his tow,
"Know that you are worth much, as far as things go."   20

"Too bad you won't see one red cent," the voice quietly said,
The shades stopped abruptly, a lone warrior stood ahead.
"Down," he said softly, and unlatched he his blade,
"Sorry to kill you, but *um*, you're just in my way."

Long silence as the shades hard stared,   25
The man watched on, was all he could dare.
The four dropped lithely to the black ground,
Spread themselves thin—
To make the killing more profound.

Eyes met eyes, more silent depraved stares,   30
Hands sweated to swords barely visible there.

"Who are you„ one skull craȼk·∹∤əd in deep gut'tral voice,
The warrior smiled, he was their terror by choice.
"Who am I" the tall spirit cleared and softly said,
"An Angel with heart, of course—   35
The one who'll make you more dead."
The man's swelled jaw fell open dry and wide,
The Angel of Death drew his blade hand aside.

High-pitched whine coursed their ears,
Dead blood pumped, producing so much fears.   40
Hands creypt closer to tangs of their blades,
Ready to fang with the speed of damned shades.

Explosioning of motion, swords out screeching,
Demons denied life, instantly gashed; ectoblood feeding.
Cutting through the ghosts with no rushed concern,   45
Wisps of blue flame, their bodies burned.

":–Know what?" the Angel from Thule said to the man,
"You're worth twice as much living now than dead."
"Unchain me, damn you!" the man let hot volleys fly.
The slingsworder knocked him cold with hardening sigh.   50

As the phantom warrior rode forward with his chattel,
Dark Storm Rising smirked, having purr*veyed* the battle.
Laughed to herself and slapped back in her sickle-blade,
Deprived of her double-cross and now, plans waylaid.

DOUGLAS M. LAURENT

Chapter Four Valley Footnotes

We are introduced to the third main character, Angel-Heart. His other names include 'The Claw,' 'Brackish (k)night' and 'Thulander.' *Thuleland* to the ancients was the unknown northernmost part of the world. Hence, this name gives a brief geographical glimpse of this spirit's origins. This is not to say though whether Angel is a full spirit or human. We do know however, he is an amoral ruthless opportunist. Tall and lanky, he is lightning-quick, a notorious swordpacker/bounty hunter/duelist in the Valhallan realm.

2. *That human mort.* 'Mortal.'

12. *Sucked at that vital light.* Lesser spirits crave the humanity or alleged 'angelicity' they lost. It is not uncommon in the Deadlands to find lesser spirits hunting in packs like wolves, surrounding stronger spirits and trying to bring them down to gain their power, prestige and life-force. If they succeed, they 'become' that stronger spirit by absorbing its person with all their traits.

15. *Red phantom beast.* The splint'ered bones and glowing red animal is reminiscent of the fiery second steed of the Four Horsemen of the Apocalypse in *Revelation* 6.4. Everything about this broken 'Second Seal' Horseman judgment tells of bloodshed, *i.e.,* "another horse *that was* red," "to take peace from," "that they should kill," and "there was given unto him a great sword." *See* also *Disney's Night on Bald Mountain* from his masterpiece animated film *Fantasia* (1940) with its 'ghostly warriors' for a more than creepy visual aid to this poem.

38. *Angel of Death.* Angel is not *the* Angel of Death, although he could probably apply for the job, but this tag describes him well.

39. *High-pitched whine.* The genres of the Samurai and Western films by Akira Kurosawa (*The Seven Samurai,* 1954) and Sergio Leone (*The Good, the Bad and the Ugly,* 1966) are primary tools for translating this poem. As in the case of Leone's 'Spaghetti Westerns,' high-pitched musical tension was employed to heighten forthcoming action. For editorial interest, in order to convey the chthonic impressions

found in the poetry, this story, based on strong visual descriptions, has been cut into a modern 'movie' format, where stanzas or lines represent film cuts designed to focus our attention onto particular poetic aspects of events in question.

45. *Cutting through the ghosts.* Miyamoto Musashi, the famed sword-duelist samurai from the 1600s, writing out from his *Water* Chapter of *A Book of Five Rings*, specifies for us the difference between *cutting* and 'slashing' as being primarily a 'spiritual thing' (*p. 61*):

> To cut and to slash are two different things. Cutting, whatever form of cutting it is, is decisive, with a resolute spirit. Slashing is nothing more than touching the enemy. Even if you slash strongly, and even if the enemy dies instantly, it is slashing. When you cut, your spirit is resolved. You must appreciate this. If you first slash the enemy's hands or legs, you must then cut strongly. Slashing is in spirit the same as touching. When you realize this, they become indistinguishable. Learn this well.

Cutting in Angel's case attests to his terrific skill level.

53. *Sickle-blade.* The 'switchblade' sickle is Dark Storm's chosen instrument. It has the quality of death, harvest, and a 'Grim-Reaper' type of attitude about it. Master illustrator Frank Frazetta inspires many of the impressions used in translating this poem. *See* his *Woman With A Scythe*, to get an idea of this mercenary *wurting* 'fate-spinner.'

FIVE: DEEP FOREST DREAD

Enter the 'Halla of deep forest dread,
Down to the land of the living dead,
Down to the blace of the searing soul,
Down to that land where heroes do go.

Tortured land of vulcaned darkness blows,   5
Of quiet forest ravagings and battle-plained throes.
Ages of spirits live in your swarmed domain,
Imprisoned spirits are all *that* you contain.

Hacked jagged lands hold forgotten truths—
Those loving their haunts in love and battle-pursuits.   10
A quiet thunder of many kindred tongues,
Eternity still looms when each day is done.

The sandstorms *a'wombing*, that bristling plain,
Tell of lost secrets; tell of found pain.
Spirits damned in lost eternal chains,   15
No lies are lived; their truths go unfeigned.

Ghosts and shadows of once mighty men,
Now haunt the mountain, now haunt the glen.
A land worthy of her exalted span,
Land of Light—   20
—And the Valley of the Damned.

So haunted and twisted a rugged 'scape,
She tattered the man with her rage and *his* hate.
A true land where strength was the stay,
Turned many toward the night or to the day.   25

VALLEY OF THE DAMNED

So hallowed a place that all spirits respect,
The riddle of land reflecting minds of no regret.
Where iron sharpened iron and conflict took its toll,
The land of steel that cleansed—or murdered the soul.

Indigo-black suffocated the fear-tearing night,   30
Greying mist fingered the hollows, tangling their flight.
Now past those boundaries where stone gods stood guard,
The undaunted 'slinger brought his lunaticked human charge.

It was in this wilderness the man was made to walk,
No more boasting like a fool, no more idle talk.   35
The land took delight in healing or giving pain,
She knew the spirit; souls she did repay.

Past a harvest of bodies flowering on the hills,
Fertile memories of recent battle; so many spirits tilled.
Broken weapons and remains strewn along wayside,   40
Thaunted unspeakable horrors—
The damned lived and re-died.

Soon in the distance upon low, browish hill,
Stood a great Hall that tugged at all wills.
Like a moth to that fire the man was made to go,   45
To enter the Hall where great spirits do show.

Dragged was he before warriors of blazing light,
Took they him from The Claw of the brackish (k)night.
A trial was set to hear the (yet another) dull, simple case—
Of a plastic warrior from that upland human race.   50

Angel was paid off for his bold and might,
The mercenary drank then rode out of sight.
Another soul claimed and set to the side,
The man's reward was his, his power to abide.

109

DOUGLAS M. LAURENT

Chapter Five Valley Footnotes

Here we find Angel and Theman, 'the man,' descending into the bowels of Valhalla proper. It is a bleak land of tremendous spiritual and physical power—just right for nurturing hardy souls.

1. *Enter the 'Halla.* 'Valhalla.'

2. *Down to the blace.* Black + place. This describes a black and brooding area, a place of great dread.

6. *Battle-plained throes.* Plain + pain. It is a wide place of great conflict, turmoil and pain.

8. *Imprisoned spirits are all.* The Deadlands are an interesting mixture. In the case of its citizens, whether they are good or bad, they are working out their own life-equations, in a 'purgatorial' sense. It all depends on their state of mind. The lands of the dead are prisons to some, paradises to others. Still, classical Valhalla is a place where the righteous dead go and therefore constitutes a Heaven of sorts. Within the play's context however, all those in the Dead are 'marooned' there (allegedly). The place functions something like a landing platform to higher states of reality (but always within the confines of Valhalla). All here can move on to better things, but some stay eternally wicked due to internal corruption or just prefer to stay rotten for gain, taking their chances of being dwindled down. Others, like Angel, prefer to sharpen their 'hunting' skills. In Angel's circumstance, it is his way of improving himself.

12. *Eternity still looms.* There is no time here. Every 'day' is a continuous *now.*

15. *Spirits damned in lost eternal chains.* This despairing passage indicates that all carry their own weight in the Deadlands in light of an eternal finality. This finality is so bad that not only are the spirits lost, but their chains are *lost,* long gone as well—their own vacuous minds, not their once physical chains keeping them in eternal fetters of bondage. This is like putting a heavy chain on a baby elephant so that it gets used to it. By the time Dumbo grows up to be a jumbo creature, all one needs is a thread about its neck to lead it about, the elephant being that conditioned to be directed around almost

by nothing, it's 'never-forgetting mind' being so trained to be less than what it could be. All the gargantuan elephant has to do is snap the thread and it is free. Hence, the metaphorical notion of being locked in a cell with the key thrown away is the main gist here, the inmates being the ones who, in their corrupt fallen belief, toss the key. 'You are your own reality' might be an apt saying the dead have, their mental constitution making or breaking them. They hold onto or loosen their self-made bonds. There is wishful thinking in the Deadlands as well as on Earth and in Hell proper.

20. *Land of Light—And the Valley of the Damned.* This note is a good example showing how terms are used interchangeably as particular areas may be known by various names. It just depends on who is doing the interpreting. *Valhalla* is a general term, a vast Nether-geographic area and a state of mind that is divided into many regions of one's own making. The *Land of Light* for example, is one of many stronghold regions where the good rule, while there are many areas controlled by the wicked, for example 'Sullen' and 'Contention' Valleys. All names and areas however, being metaphorically the same, can be applied overall. They are based on a spirit's state of mind. Names are the result of how they feel at a certain place or time. They may curse or love a place, naming it appropriately.

23. *She tattered the man.* Feminine attributes are used for translating many motifs. The land in Valhalla, as in ancient Earth times, is depicted as being female. To the Vikings, the Earth was a living being, not the 'it' of modern scientism, but a 'thou.' The land 'knows' the spirits of those who trod her and deals with them accordingly. The land 'dealing' with people is a main symbol in the work. The land either naturalistically nurtures or destroys those with good or adverse morals, indicating that spirits who inhabit the Deadlands are intimately tied to the land.

27-29. *Riddle of land . . . iron sharpened iron . . . land of steel.* Like "the riddle of steel" of Conan the Barbarian fame, the riddle of the land fosters stoicism and wipes out regrets. The land is unlike the earlier visited *Market of the Soul* (Ch. Three), where there is no hope at all. *Iron sharpened* is taken from *Proverbs* 27.17, "Iron sharpeneth iron; so a man sharpeneth the countenance of his friend."

32. *Stone gods.* These are tribal boundary markers indicating ownership and warnings.

35. *Boasting like a fool.* This is a borrowing from *Macbeth* (IV. i.). There is a dual meaning here. Theman wants to become organized and 'get his act' together in order to survive, but his vain life and theatrically educated earthly thoughts, the only media he can think and relate through, portend, like Macbeth's thoughts, further destruction.

37. *She did repay.* In the Deadlands as on Earth, one decidedly reaps what they sow.

44. *A great Hall.* Valhalla. In myth, this seeming miles-long banquet Hall is described as glorious with many doors indicative of lives coming and going. It is made of the finest weapons. The roof is made up of shields; the support beams are like giant spears. The doors are significant because they aided warriors as to where attack was coming from so they could defend that post.

48. *The Claw of the brackish (k)night.* These are other names of the swordslinger Angel. They however also describe very inhospitable environments that are found throughout the Deadlands, especially at night, when the powers of darkness are at their height. *I.e.*, the sharp-clawed night with its ripping environment, can hack a weak spirit into greater death. It is only then that the toughest go out and this terror-Angel is undeniably "tough enough to crack *hickory nuts with his toes," as the say towards the south. This does not reflect poorly on those heroes who wish to stay the night at Valhalla central. When the fit is upon them, many do go out at night. Some apparitions like Angel prefer to hunt rotten spirits at night and kill them just as easily as they would in the daytime.

> *Hickories are symbolically known for their patience, strength, flexibility and their great ability to absorb shock, telling why its wood is prized for tool handles. It also smokes meat and fires the grill well. So much the metaphors for Angel but does the following info give us a glimpse of his murky background? After all, he does like wood and whittles it. According to Seneca Indian legends, the hickory is a connect to quickening the dead. After being cannibalized, the bones of the dead are placed before a hickory, and as the tree is pushed upon the screaming command, "Rise up or the tree will fall on you" is shouted and the dead come back to the land of the living (Curtin, J.).

50. *Of a plastic warrior.* This is yet another insult to Theman, the hollow movie star and his bilge of pop-cultured *cliché* martial ways.

SIX: RASP

Into that well-darkened chamber went dreaded she,
To tell him of foul truths and bright apostasies.
Dark Storm Rising to meet her snake-tor'mentor—
Horrid Rasp, disgusting 🕷 spider at the center.

"I have some information to report.   5
Some that is pleasing, some with resort."
Rasp looked upon her with baleful eye,
'Twas callowed yellow from eons of lies.

This demented force of great power and fame,
Was sealed in evil, yet weakened and lamed.   10
Storm spoke, "the man you seek is now at Val,
Behind its towers and accursed walls.

But *it* must not have been as corrupt as you say,
For four 'good' shades came and took him away.
As for me, I *ehh*, killed him quite dead   15
(This she said while tapping fingers of lead).
Yet he survived, I'll finish him, this I pledge."

"Go on," the old battle-lord in a quiet fit *wheeeezed*,
"For that I have spoken, I will give you as I please."
He writhed Dark Storm payment in moist blood gold,   20
All to help killing that human man soul.

"You did fine," the wizened spirit knew,
"For all the spirits that for me you slew."

"Why's he so important, this little man-shade?
He's not yet dead—you're still going to fade."   25

Rasp hacked, sp—ate⌒red, he bilently choked,
Hid the truth behind his soiled stained cloak
(At last impatient her hair did she stroke).
Dark Storm throttled hard her hand to his throat,
"'The man' will lead millions astray," Rasp did gloat.   30

Dark Storm Rising fanged her cold shark eye,
Let Rasp go with a str*angel*ed-stifled cry.
Knew that *Dead Yet Alive* men were great power stores,
With millions for him to lead——*heh*, all the power more.

"I'll fuel Hel's fires for me," Rasp gurged, laughing slow,   35
"When he dies 'martyr,' he will bring in quite a flow."
Dark Storm hesitated, smiling coy as she thought 'bout that,
Twist*her sick*ill——
Then punctured Rasp through his putrefried fat.

"Not anymore," the vicious one said,   40
"I will make *it* one of my own living dead.
Dead-Yet-Alives mostly find their puny souls,
He'll be given *the* chance, no doubt, I must 'console.'"

Dark Storm grinned then tipped her hand,
Ravened locks dangled round her goregeous head.   45
Yellow pus oozed from Rasp's taut, blue frozen lips,
Face of terror embraced, death's loving grip.

VALLEY OF THE DAMNED

Chapter Six Valley Footnotes

Dark Storm confers with her most recent 'boss,' *Rasp*, a very old, wicked spirit, a crime godfather of sorts.

4. *Spider at the center.* Rasp is not a spider, but like a greedy one. He sits dead center in a web of his own intrigues and conducts a great deal of evil activity. But the old fool has overlooked something. He has taught the Dark too well she not needing him any longer. It may be a literary *cliché*, but a lot of times in such circumstances, evil apprentices true to form predictably knock their masters off. Perhaps Sir Arthur Conan Doyle's description of the evil Professor James Moriarty from the lips of detective Sherlock Holmes can help sum up this rotten character. From *The Final Problem*:

> He is the Napoleon of crime, Watson. He is the organizer of half that is evil and of nearly all that is undetected in this great city. He is a genius, a philosopher, an abstract thinker. He has a brain of the first order. He sits motionless, like a spider in the centre of its web, but that web has a thousand radiations, and he knows well every quiver of each of them. He does little himself. He only plans.

10. *Weakened and lame.* Rasp is hacked, weakened, which in the Deadlands is indicative of the fiend having taken many sound beatings. Additionally, in Sergio Leone's Westerns as in many genres, evil bosses are usually afflicted with some disease or physical atrocity such as a scar, limp, *etc.* Or they may have an iron claw, serrated knives or small flame-thrower for a missing arm—a rotten, scheming gimmick to heighten the melodramatic finale, they using it to fight the hero unto their demise, as part of a *just dessert* type of retribution-mechanism.

26. *He bilently choked.* Bile + violent, indicating how sick Rasp was. As we often categorize evil persons as being ugly or physically twisted in some way, a clawed hand, hunchback, *etc.*, the same goes for this ancient land. We have to remember here that being ugly, as in Rasp's case, or torn apart in any way sometimes tells us that a spirit is very wretched and debauched.

30. *Lead millions astray.* This line is a motif running through the play, whether wealth or the souls of people, Theman's potential for bringing in power is enormous.

34. *All the power more.* In many ancient societies and still today, to kill, subordinate or consume an enemy (like a cannibal) means the acquisition or absorption of their 'powers' and the extension of one's own, spiritually, mentally or physically, as in the simple case of getting others to do work for one's self. Indeed, the prevalent policy in Midgard, just as it always has been, is the 'acquisition' of power no matter what form of power that acquisition takes. Like a broken mirror with its loads of splint'ry shards, however, power takes on many ways, shapes and forms. What is truly wanted, notwithstanding, is the mirror in its wholeness, the Divine. Recall, the fogs of deception a prized s'kill, is fundamental here and thereabouts.

45. *Ravened locks . . . goregeous.* These are compound words. The *Raven* portends evil, and is black, like Storm's hair. Storm is beautiful, gorgeous, but so ferocious a mercenary, that she is steeped, gorged on bloody, gory deeds.

46. *Blue frozen.* According to the linguist Jonathan Mycroft, a consonant shift in the language has occurred affecting this phrase. Later manuscripts read '*blue prozen*' instead of *frozen*. What this means is that the term "*pro*" is in favor of something. If the interpretation is correct, the passage could be translated as a somewhat pro-Zen 'doing' action-construct. Instead of *fro*-Zen (inert Zen), it is *pro*-Zen. This implies that Rasp was a victim of Dark Storm's very efficient pro-Zennish 'no-thought' heightened state of 'doing' mind-killer technique. This has more meaning. Storm left her mark, not only that, she 'read his lips.' They suggested some part of him was 'asking for it,' being in favor of being killed. Whether this was a desperate plea or a sarcastic comment is uncertain. Storm simply read these deeper intents and depravities of his mind or perhaps read into them what she wanted and killed him because she did not like what she saw and did not trust him anyway, he having been known to dispose of his subordinates, not to mention tombing him was going to help her pick up an immense soul-fortune. Clairvoyance, among other powers, is common among the stronger spirits in the Dead.

SEVEN: DEAD RIGHT

Passed they now stables of great steeds of war,
Who champed at their bits for danger's store,
To bear their masters bold into harrowed warfield,
To take on the Legion, the victory to yield.

Weapons were polished with deadly glint,   5
Of impending carnage, they gave no hint.
Swords, spears, battle-axes to wield
(Death to the wicked in those blood-let fields).

Instruments of war they do solemnly glean,
To kill the evil in their righteous sheen.   10
Silent steeled weapons of that wondrous lot,
Sang somber melodies that victories begot.

For Ages have they done their grim cutting chore,
To guard Hel's gates, and entry to Heaven's door.
Patiently await they at lone sentry post,   15
The final solution to death's riposte.

Now as far as the man's eyes could spread,
A banquet Hall filled with the nobility of the dead.
Warriors from every clime and epoch of life,
A gallery of heroes that had conquered their night.   20

Armor, regal, in its vaulted glistening jaded stores,
And on the shoulders of greats from every kindred shore.
Many were they *these* adventurous guests,
Perfection of humanity—their noblest quest.

At many an honored master's sides were there,   25
Hounds and falcons whose wings swifted through the air.
War-creatures trained to kill darkness' mates,
Talons and fangs of hellish dissipate.

Among these splendid, there was no question of fight,
They practiced daily, their blades dancing in light.   30
Righteous minds are those committed to the blade,
They practiced for love; their spirits never fade.

Saw the man clans and tribes from far distant lands,
Dressed in the war-gear of their time-honored bands.

Highlanders with their great claidheamh-mors,   35
And Samurais with their virtuous swords.

Mighty Kshátriya of India stood the guard,
While Berserks and Dog soldiers discussed deeds afar.
Daring Zulus of African fame held prestige,
Planned with Odysseus fortifications to besiege.   40

Tuaregs and Romans mingled much,
Greeks and Huns boasted as such,
Crusaders laughed with old Muslim foes,
Tales of love and victory they did show.

Boadicea and Amazon queens were there,   45
As Joan and Scatha with stories to tell.
Ng Mui, Wing-Chun showed their proper form,
Before battle, before the coming storm.

Many faces more were seen in this crowd,
Most unknown, yet those who could astound.   50

Excellent Prince Thomm was there as well,
His only desire—to give Lord Mars Hell.

Saladin, Richard stood as best friends,
Fighting side by side until the day's end.
Arthur laughed with noble Lancelot Du'Lac,   55
In life, rivals, now they led many attacks.

Sun-Tzu and Eric talked of brave strife,
How to instill love now, yet more so life.
Beowulf and Red Cloud drank the brotherhood cup,
While Musashi, Cuculain and Roland talked of sun up.   60

Yoshitsune and Benkei spoke of far Eastern creeds,
And listened to El Cid of mighty Spanish deeds.
Gideon and David roared with their host,
Along with Goliath, Egyptians, Cossacks and Visigoths.

Many more discussed at fine banquet tables—   65
Of nations no longer, and those that were able.
Of Hatti, Scythians, Cimmerians and Gauls,
Of Aztecs, Sumerians, Phoenicians and Mongols.

More than one to match the lofty powered sky,
O' to be of that company *that* gloriously died!   70
From every nation and tongue yet undone,
Many more came at the setting of the sun.
In all, a roaring of shades high-spirited,
Bedecked in light because of the truth they exhibited.
Warriors in arms for the good that they stayed,   75
'Gainst the evil swell their games did they play.

Alexander and Julius now filled the fair,
Both sitting down in great judgmental chairs.

Warriors gathered, a thousand eyeing stares,
Looks of discernment and of tender despotic care.   80

The man's eyes beheld this heroic unseemly mix,
Knowing not where to go—knew he was unfit.
And not knowing where to run or to turn,
He crypt down along side of one buried deep in concern.

The stranger then said, "amazing, is it not,   85
These are the dead whose souls in eternity did not rot."
After long pause, the man finally spoke, "eternity?
They look to me familiar of my former industry."

"Nor are these," the stranger said to him,
"That followed the ways of *that* fallen Cherubim.   90
Neither are they, who fell to nature's deepest lie,
To become as the gods, for them to dwell On High."

"Where am I?" said the man growing in frostrate disbelief,
"Is this a dream? I have appointments to keep!"
A look of hardt pity poured from the stranger's face,   95
So much so, that it made the man feel like an ingrate.

"Your mortal life has been shortened by the enemies of your kind,
But Fate is impartial and has decreed your life that you should find.
You are to be tried and more likely found wanting in the balance,
More to the good, I think, that has occurred in your marked absence."   100

"Who are you?" the man finally broke,
His senses now attuned, as if from a dream he awoke.
"I am Li, former of that intercepting destiny,
Taken in life by a bitter pill, now I have my battle-fill."

At round tables they all sat, names upon their chairs,   105
These showed they were enabled; that these mightily cared.
One the man noticed had his own carved name,
A seat in pre-destiny, calling forth his post-fame.

"This table is almost empty, the one at which we sit—
Because *that* nation of liberty has produced few humble—   110
So many are unfit.
These who sit here are from her few and far between,
Having drunk of the milk of her discipline, forsaking the libertine.
And now witness the outcome; many a seat stands naked and empty,
Having sold her virtue comes that lost defense, her 'manifesting
destiny.'"   115

These things said Li, then added in kind reply,
"This stand is yet reserved for those of 'our' tribe.
You who will sit here must be told,
To earn your place, the deed must be shown."

"How can I earn it?" the man heatedly said.   120
"That is true," said Li, thumbing his nose—
"For you are not yet dead."

The whole host roared at what appeared a joke,
They knew the man had yet to take that solemn oath.
Li waving, quieting down his riotous company said,   125
"Your enemies wish to kill you; it's your leadership they dread."

The man browed his uncomprehending eyes,
Sage Li read them with empathetic sighs.
"Those of the other camp they dare tread,
The Land of the Valhallan unrighteous dead.   130
They are the ones, who live the sham,
Willing sojourners in those valleys of the damned.

You have arrived at such an opportune time,
On the eve of a great battle, all has been defined.
This battle will separate many a cloven soul,   135
To decide they must; into light or Hel they must go."

With that, the man smirked, thought he was one of them,
But upon looking at their faces, changed his countenance instead.
Terrible silence fell over the luminous, rowdy court,
The man met with sharp glares that loved to exhort.   140

"You peacock," said Saladin as calm as could be,
"What do you know of life, tragedy and divine destiny?"
The man turned to Sage Li, not knowing what to say,
For their looks upon his person did they heavily weigh.

"Show us your worth," a samurai was heard to shout,   145
"If we don't like your wares, we'll throw you out."
Many a warrior then asked the man's name,
"Did you win that in battle?" he fell silent in shame.

(The spirits of the Netherworld always know the truth,
He had not won it in battle, but had a stage name from his youth).   150
Li smiled and told him to worry not, that all was well and good,
To earn a name was the high-Mark; that was to be understood.

Round the center the man was then made to perform,
Gave an account of his life, to their wishes he did conform.
Watched him wide-eyed as he tried a feeble movie kick or two,   155
They burst out laughing, knowing him a fool.

The man desperate, showed a kata with its rigid filmsy form,
The warriors of old sat bemused, their humor greatly warmed.
Finally, an old Kris knight said, "my son, kindly sit down,
You have much to learn by tomorrow, if you are to win *that* crown."   160

"Brothers and sisters," Sage Li said waving casually to them,
"Be calm before this mortal, for he is not yet 'baptized in red.'"
With that the mighty throng roared and sat back relaxed,
But the man did not, fearful of attack.

A Viking came forth, guffawing; the man knew not his name,   165
He had fought many a battle, to high glory, he staked his claim.
"You see, my friends, the heroes they make in the world above today,
A green-horned creature of disrespect, who knows not the true way."

All laughed and Shaka stood, gave the man a toast,
"Let us drink to him my brothers, our enemy's do him loathe.   170
Let us drink to the man thus, that we may at a later time boast."

With that the crowed fell back to their loud and cavorting ways,
Telling of tales of love and life against the coming day.
Time long paused before the 'littled man spoke, again turning to Li,
"What is it that these noble have, that they are so against *me?*"   175

Li said, "The living live illusions much more than we dead,
For the fullness of technique here means cutting off a head.
We are those who through corruption are no more to be ruined,
Expenditure of full motion here is the only true solution."

The Turk, proud and bold threw down his winding hookah pipe.   180
"Who will teach this young idiot, that he may vhowel with us and strike?
For tomorrow's battle has already been procured,
If he is not with us, our loss will be ensured!"

The mobbed then jeered and barked at the man,
Called forth their judge so the little one could stand.   185
"Let him," Julius decreed, "learn of our virtuous ways,
Bring in the Valkyrie; let her teach what she may."

DOUGLAS M. LAURENT

Chapter Seven Valley Footnotes

Here is an inside glimpse of that fabulous, mythical Hall of the righteous Valhallan dead. As the Nether-realm is of mind and soul, of constantly shifting shadows and shapes, it is indeed a spectacular, glowingly curious place. For our earthly comparisons, we can use familiar figures—the Hall packed with the heroic dead from all Ages and tribes, a unique family in the annals of the Underworld. Keep in mind that this particular Hall, although the greatest, is just one of many where the righteous congregate. The wicked dead have their own town Halls too.

4. *To take on the Legion. Legion* is a collective name for a demonic division from Hell. When Christ cast the demons out of a man, *Mark* 5.9, the leader of the pack said their (and his) name was *Legion*, for there were many stuffed inside the man. At that time in Earth history, a Roman legion consisted of anywhere from three to 12 thousand fighting soldiers with an equal number of auxiliaries and other non-combative functionaries. This passage gives us an indication of how many enemies are in the Deadlands, innumerable—and how many can be packed into one body, human or otherwise (Ch. 26 note # 226).

12. *Somber melodies.* Victory often brings jubilance, but also sadness and sobriety over killing others. Some here reflect on their deeds from long past and the daily Nether-battles.

14. *To guard Hel's gates.* In the old North, *Hel* was a place for the dead. In this mind-play, it is one of many places in the Deadlands. It is a term used for the 'real-dead' of Valhalla, that is, where exceedingly 'bad' dead spirits go who are 'killed.' Apparently, to die in the Nether means either to go to a disgusting spot of torment or to be self de-generated even more. Perhaps the distinction between the two is not all that sharp, both being the same. In any event, the constitutor has rendered the term *Hel* and the biblical Hell pretty much parallel to each other in the work, and use them interchangeably. It is important to note that certain characters, like Dark Storm Rising, use the term *Hel* rather than Hell. It depends on a character's cultural beliefs and backgrounds

16. *The final solution to death's riposte.* Using our Far Eastern mortal perspective, weapons are said to be Heaven's last resort to thwart evil. A *riposte* in Western fencing is where fencers make linear thrusts with their blades toward the opposition and the opposition *parries* them, 'bouncing off' of the blade and thrusting their own blade back into the initial fencer. The *riposte* in this stanza reflects the fact that death and evil are always sneaking around, re-attacking or riposting, and so require one final countering action on the part of Heaven's weapons, or the good guys.

20. *Conquered their night.* The term *night*, like 'darkness,' implies 'moral, intellectual and spiritual depravity.' The heroes having overcome *their* own base natures and *vile* enemies, spiritually, mentally and physically, have earned their rightful place in Valhalla.

24. *Perfection of humanity.* (Or angelicity in some cases). This is the highest quest for heroes in Valhalla. They use the extremes found within this powerful environment to temper themselves burning off their baser dross to be as excellent as they can be.

32. *They practiced for love.* The Greek term *agápē* for *love* is used here. This is the highest state of love, one that sacrifices the self for another.

35-77. *Highlanders with . . . Julius now.* This section is mirrored through some of the greatest warriors and martial innovators our world has ever seen. One such notable is *Ng Mui*, the Chinese Shaolin priestess whose art of kung-fu, *Wing-chun*, is now world famous through Bruce Lee, practitioner of this art. Some characters are more familiar to us than others are but more are completely unknown, such as *Prince Thomm*, who is only known by other writings found in the remarkable anachronistic work, *Letters From Mars* (Laurent). *Julius* is Julius Caesar (100-44 B.C.), Roman general, dictator and conqueror. The *Amazons* were said to be fierce female warriors, their greatest queens being Antiope, Hippolyte and Penthesilia. Other females listed are *Boadicea*, queen of ancient Britain who fought the Romans, *Joan of Arc*, and *Scatha Buanand*, a famous Irish warrioress, said to have run a very famous school of martial arts in Scotland. It is thought Scatha left a very deep impression on the martial ways of ancient Ireland, as nobles sent their sons to her for instruction.

35. *Claidheamh-mors.*   The term is Gaelic for *claymore*, or 'great sword,' used in ancient times by the Scottish Highlanders.

69. *More than one to match the lofty powered sky.*   According to St. Paul's *Letter to the Ephesians* 2.2, Satan, aka 'the Adversary,' the most powerful and interesting kingpin on Earth, is known as "the prince of the power of the air." This phrase speaks of Lucifer's kingdom extending over the whole Earth as well as the 'first' and 'second' Heavens as well. According to biblical thought, there are 'three' Heavens. The first is the Earth's atmosphere, the second the stellar Heavens, and the third, the actual abode of God. Accordingly, those who are righteous and are of the light are always more than a match for the contemplative dark-glowing Machiavellian prince and his followers.

85. *The stranger then.*   Jun Fan Lee or Bruce Lee. This amazing artist became an international superstar noted for his tremendous fighting ability and cinematic choreography as well as his provocative philosophical views on education and the arts. Having won his place in the righteous Valhallan Deadlands, he acts as a counselor for Theman. This is a curious shot. Former movie star and true combative expert Lee stands out in sharp contrast to the superficial movie star Theman.

88. *Of my former industry.*   To Mark Theman the 'big' film star, all these warriors look like they are stereotypical costumed characters out of a cheap summer 'B-grade' adventure movie.

90-91. *That fallen Cherubim . . . deepest lie.*   Lucifer's great stretch of the truth was that all who followed him could be like God not in likeness or character, but in power, prestige and control, the same thing he wanted. Lucifer is a despot, using a convenient '*Me*-first' philosophy among fallen angels and men in his on-going attempt to try to usurp God's throne. A *Cherub* is a very powerful angel, one of at least seven classes of angels we know of. They are said to guard the throne of God. Since Lucifer was created in the perfection of wisdom and beauty, *Ezekiel* 28.12, guarding the throne of God, the only way for him to go, he more than likely felt, was up. Besides, biblical text suggests that humans will eventually outpace the angels, so, why would he want to kowtow to and baby-sit, lowly dust specks who would one day 'have his job' as it were? Anyway, Lucifer's decisions led to a disastrous career choice at best since the Divine's essence is said to be love, creating everything in love for love. For the Creator not to run the show is an odd argument since His character of love is part of all things created. A created being such as Lucifer is, although he claims not to be with no small wonder, could never rule in love absolute. To have a creature of time on the eternal throne would only mean eventual chaos, as the effect of lawlessness, or sinful 'missing the mark,' is certainly devastating and chaotic as we see in our world today. There are many battles but only one war. There are many faces but only one foe. There are many guises but only one enemy of humankind. The battles on Earth are the result of one creature's intent proclaiming its desire to rule overall. Perhaps the few last lines of W.W. II General George S. Patton's (1885-1945) haunting poem, *Through A Glass, Darkly* (1918) will help us see Mr. L's life and career work better:

> So as through a glass, and darkly
> The age long strife I see
> Where I fought in many guises,
> Many names, but always me.
> And I see not in my blindness
> What the objects were I wrought,
> Bur as God rules o'er our bickerings
> It was through His will I fought.
> So forever in the future,
> Shall I battle as of yore,
> Dying to be born a fighter,
> But to die again, once more.

93. *In frostrate disbelief.* Frustrate + prostrate. This compound indicates that Theman is very frustrated and mentally beat, worn out, at wit's end, on his back, *etc.*

98. *But Fate is impartial and has decreed.* As in our medieval era, *Fate*, or 'Lady Fortune,' was likened to a gambling wheel that would eventually bring a person high or low.

103. *Intercepting destiny.* Bruce Lee is particularly famous for inventing a very efficient fighting art that he coined "the way of the intercepting fist," or *jeet kune do.* Dr. Peter Hsu explains that, more of an ideal or perception, the main tenets of this view postulate freedom of motion and thought for its adherents, becoming an 'artless' or 'selfless art,'—a Zen thing. This was opposed to being rule-bound by systems of thought and/or movement that produced mechanical responses. Lee's high point was that his view promotes the individual's intimate personal growth beyond fabricated rusted classical systems of forced learning such as an earthly martial system is, something that they can never do.

104. *By a bitter pill.* To combat a headache, Lee inadvertently took someone else's prescription medicine, which allegedly caused a major allergic reaction, causing his death.

108. *A seat in pre-destiny . . . post-fame.* All are called to high glory, but it is uncertain whether many will attain it. It all depends on their decisions in life, manifesting their hearts through actions. Theman's empty seat shows that glory can be had.

109. *This table is almost empty . . . libertine . . . manifesting destiny.* Apparently, this section alludes to the nearly empty 'American' table in Valhalla. The only ones sitting here are the deceased fathers of American karate, such Ed Parker, Robert Trias and Joe Lewis. The Table has yet to be filled, but the chaotic society of the American nation is noted more in Valhalla for its decadent divisiveness, pop-culture superficiality and the abandonment of true spiritual mettle, therefore its inability to produce 'quality' martial artists. Theman himself is an acute testimony to this fact.

Manifesting destiny is an Americanism. It refers to the idea that God gave the Anglo-Americans (from the tribes of Japheth, son of Noah) 'the mandate' to colonize North America. According to the historian Rodger Atterbury however, a more accurate assessment of this statement is that God *used* the Anglo-Americans to colonize North America on an intellectual and industrial level. This was in order to back up the re-emergent Israel, which heralds the coming of Messiah, and help prepare the world for Christ's return. Apparently, all this is supposed to happen soon as biblical *Eschatology*, the 'doctrine of last things,' implies.

VALLEY OF THE DAMNED

Throughout history, the Divine gave special talents to the three sons of Noah. To Shem, the modern S(h)emitic Arab, Jewish and Muslim peoples, He gave them charge of spiritual leadership concerning the 'One' monotheistic God. To Japheth, the modern Europeans, Americans, Canadians and Russians, He gave the ability to expand upon things intellectual and philosophical, improving on what others created. To the sons of Ham, the Asians and Africans, He gave the grand ability to be great stewards of the land, inventing physical items so that man may live well. (Genesis 9.25-27. Understand that the archaic term 'slave' implies not degrading slave ship but honorable stewardship over the care taking of the Earth.)

In any event, Li is saying that the 'lack of (spiritual) ability' America has is another form of 'destiny' that is being shaped right now. *Libertine* refers to dissolution, immoral and licentious activity. The trading of true liberty for the corrupt abuse of those privileges that liberty brings, leads to poor martial artists, those in spiritual, mental and physical bondage.

Scottish historian Alexander Tytler (1747-1813) cites 'eight successive steps' to the rise and fall of a democracy such as America is, and that on the average a democracy lasts about only two hundred years, and is inevitably followed up by a military dictatorship then a monarchy. This is because a democracy can only exist until "the majority can discover it can vote itself largess [patrons giving gifts in generous or showy ways] out of the public treasury. After that, the majority always votes for the candidate promising the most benefits with the result that the democracy collapses because of loose fiscal policy. . . ." (From *The Decline and Fall of the Athenian Republic*— no actual record of this book has been found. Apparently, most of Tytler's works have been lost. However, *see Wikipedia/quote* on the Internet for this author.) As history definitely repeats itself, America is in the 'seventh stage,' so go figure. A democracy goes from 1) bondage to spiritual faith; from 2) faith to great courage; from 3) courage to liberty; from 4) liberty to abundance; from 5) abundance to complacency, from 6) complacency to apathy; from 7) apathy to dependence; from 8) dependence back into bondage. Many, many souls in the Nether are the products of these eight steps, most notably the last few. This is because of the *naturalism*-based inherent self-activating 'despairing philosophy' thought-system that is the 'closed loop' de-energizing foundation of the arts. This product know less, comes direct from atop the downtown pyramidal offices of Tower Babel. Turn off, tune out, drop in.

Interestingly, and Theman would know this, the kung-fu and karate world is loaded with references to 'eight-step' arts as in superstar Jackie Chan's 1978 smash hit movie, *Eight Steps of the Snake and Crane* aka *Snake and Crane Arts of Shaolin* (*Shé Hè Bā Bù*). If the reader wishes to view brilliant choreography known as 'old-school' style (incremented motion, not modern fast-paced blu*rr*ry screen action that does not allow one to see the finer points of the kung-fu arts), this movie is an excellent piece of work. Sifu Chan's genius in the field of cinematic martial choreography is indisputable. Other notable early works of the master are *Shaolin Wooden Men* (76), *Fearless Hyena* (79) and *Drunken Master* (78). As to this business of eights, both East (*I-Ching* trigrams) and West (medical symbol *caduceus*—the dbl. or single *snake* climbing a rod, the wing's on top are those of a *crane*) can be traced to Noah's octad family, especially through the martial arts seeing they go way back.

121. *Thumbing his nose*——. Bruce Lee was famous for *thumbing his nose* at his antagonists in the movies. Here it is meant to be an amusing, yet warm-hearted rebuke to Theman, as Li has already ascertained his dour character. Li is playfully 'thumbing' his nose at him, at which the whole audience laughs. However, the audience understands his gesture all too well as it is double-edged. To them it means that Li already has in mind that he might have to fight Theman someday, making the thumbing more meaningful.

133-135. *At such an opportune time . . . this battle.* Every day in the Deadlands is an opportune time; practically every night is the eve of great battle. Li parodies the situation, but reflects the fact that yet another conflict is a great opportunity to sharpen oneself.

135. *Many a cloven soul.* *Cloven* is the past tense of 'cleaved.' In addition, some parallel manuscripts such as the thirteenth century *Kel's Yellow Book* show "*c'loven*." Both terms however suggest actions that literally chop or decide a person's fate. Some examples might be the severe splitting away or gain of true and eternal love, being for or against good or evil, *etc.*—the usual bottom-line decisions. All battles—spiritual, mental and physical—are character tests, showing persons and those that observe them, who and what they are.

147. *Asked the man's name.* In many ancient and modern societies, a person's name was and is often a source of great prestige and power.

149. *Spirits of the Netherworld.* One of the observations of Nether-realm is that spirits there have somewhat of an ESP-type of ability. Perhaps keen discernment, honed after centuries of practice, is a better definition for this ability. They can see right through Theman all the way to his wavering jellied backbone.

157. *Its rigid filmsy form.* Film + flimsy. A movie 'kata' form is intentionally illusory to fool the camera and so the audience; hence fighting on film is only for show and entertainment, not combative reality. Theman's technique to the Valhallans, therefore, is not real. It is amusing, ridiculous, phony and it stinks making them know of his character.

159. *An old Kris knight.* The *Kris* is the famous wavy-bladed sword Indonesian warriors carry.

160. *To win that crown.* This is the 'crown of life,' *i.e.*, victory, enlightenment, *etc.*

162. *'Baptized in red.'* Theman has had no practical battle experience, especially in the actual spilling of wicked blood, which would effectively initiate him into the ranks of the righteous dead. *Baptized* in Greek is *baptismo*, meaning, "To be plunged under." It indicates the depths of purging Theman needed to undergo in order to have new birth from his old peacock ways in order to gain a clear perspective of the realities of battle, life and death. The underworlders suffer no illusions.

168. *A green-horned.* This term is an Americanism for 'rank amateur,' one who is still 'wet behind the ears.' The term *greenhorn* (fifteenth century) literally means "horn of an animal freshly killed," also "young horned animal." It implies 'recent, fresh, new' a nickname given to new soldiers and eventually applied to any inexperienced person, the term carried out to western cattle country.

169. *And Shaka stood.* This is Shaka Zulu, great tribal chieftain (*ca.* 1787-1828), founder of the Zulu Empire in Africa around 1820.

174. *Before the 'littled man spoke*. 'Belittled.' Before the great battle veterans, with his 'karate' antics, Theman is being made fun of.

177. *The fullness of technique*. Only the dead can truly know and 'appreciate' what it is like to give out and receive the full reality, the final measure of an action or technique—death. They see their actions, ideologies and lives from 'the other side,' quite a mature, balanced view compared to Theman's shallow, limited one-sided human perspective.

179. *Full motion here is the only true solution*. Doing an action in a total sense is the only thing that truly takes care of business; that is, destroying both ego and/or opponents. A line from Lee's work (*Tao*, p. 13) is helpful:

The tools, your natural weapons, have a double purpose:

1. To destroy the opponent in front of you – annihilation of things that stand in the way of peace, justice and humanity.

2. To destroy your own impulses caused by the instincts of self-preservation. To destroy anything bothering your mind. Not to hurt anyone, but to overcome your own greed, anger and folly. Jeet Kune Do is directed toward oneself.

And:

Punches and kicks are tools to kill the ego. The tools represent the force of intuitive or instinctive directness which, unlike the intellect or the complicated ego, does not divide itself, blocking its own freedom. The tools move onward without looking back or to the side.

187. *Bring in the Valkyrie*. Old Norse *Valkyrie*, *lit.*, "Chooser of the Slain." These were the female war-spirits of northern Europe, particularly of Germany and Gaul. They were Odin's attendants, said to select beforehand heroes who would fall in battle. They would then take them to Valhalla. Early in their history, they were painted

as extremely war-like and bloodthirsty, hovering around the battlefields drinking the blood of the dead. Later, they were portrayed as beautiful women with flowing hair wearing shining armor and riding fine animals, but warriors still believed they were bloodsuckers. Mythologist Etta Jörgens cites that there are some links to reality here, as throat-cutting priestesses in old Europe were said to accompany armies into battle and select how prisoners of war would die. Not a very lady-like career to choose it seems.

EIGHT: ST. KARI OF THE BLADE

Who but the brightest and the brave,
Who else but Kari, Saint of the Blade?
His eyes cast upon her, and were not deceived,
A mere wisp of a girl that he alone perceived.

A pleasant maid girl, yet a satin in snow,   5
Led up to the plain of battle, she bid her people go.
How she got the name, the man scarce not knew,
'Pon the field of honor her steeled legend did grew.

Long before she was found at Satan's right hand side,
To head his army of the night, to live by it or die.   10
Now purged of black deeds, a new path she treads,
Kari, lovely Kari had turned—
Past the Valley of the Damned.

Yet for a thousand years she lay fettered in *that* prison house of pain,
Ministering to those souls in solitary and practiced night and day.   15
Odin's flame-daughter quenched, her evil was forbade,
Until she was 'miss stress'–known as Kari, Saint of the Blade.

No dark powers were hers to command,
Only in those ecstasies of swordplay did her respect demand.
None were her equal so they said that day,   20
Unparalleled with blade or dagger, thousands she did slay.

Sweet St. Kari of the Blade,
Flaming brandished sword tells of your crusades.
Deep somber spirit of that Northern wood,
Destroys those who inflict; takes lives she should.   25

Carried she a fine edge with an indebted past,
And cut her enemies down with deadly impass'.
A spirit pure, now seen the light,
To not tolerate evil was her chosen right.

Her cold eyes cut; an angel's face shown,   30
Illumined in light, yet so terribly alone.
Well-beloved, there was none whose love did not lack,
She smiled to all—then gave the plan of attack.

Afterward, she was asked to teach,
All to lend ear so that the man she might reach.   35
As the poet implied, "A man's reach should exceed his grasp,"
To grapple to the end the full of Hel's blast.

DOUGLAS M. LAURENT

Chapter Eight Valley Footnotes

This section introduces the fourth major character of the story, *St. Kari of the Blade*. She is one tough Valkyrie, but in appearance is somewhat lanky with a basic, somewhat athletic girlish face. In fact, she is a teenager, the only one of her kind in the entire Deadlands. Some scholars place her appearance 'age' anywhere from fourteen to seventeen years old. A spirit with a past though, she is another top mercenary. *Kari* in Norwegian means "Beautiful Rose." Her other name, *St. of the Blade*, indicates her exceptional sword prowess. Taken as a whole, she is an interesting mix of early classical Christianity and paganism, just what we would expect to find in the old North and Valhalla. *St. of the Blade* is also akin to the *kensei*, or the 'sword-saints' of old Japan, like Miyamoto Musashi, who went about dueling other weapons experts such as staff masters and chain-and-sickle specialists. Musashi dueled to the death over sixty men, thirteen times using a steel blade, the rest with a wooden sword. He is well known for the beautiful works of art he left behind including pen and ink paintings and wooden sculptures and was an adept of Zen.

5. *Satin in snow.* Satin + Satan. This passage has compound meanings. Looks are deceiving here. Kari is pure, like satin and snow. She is pretty in a female country sense, a bit skinny, yet ruthlessly deadly, a nuisance, a 'devil' and a holy terror to her opponents.

14. *She lay fettered.* According to the sixth century *Upsalan* text, Kari is a former convict in Valhalla's 'House of Pain,' one of the many prisons or rather insane asylums for the unruly found in the Deadlands. It is uncertain, but scholars such as Jonathan Mycroft suggest Kari may have been in and out of many prison *helks* in her time, the text allegedly reflecting offbeat references to them, although these may be metaphors coming from her troubled mind. In old times, the *helk* was the lowest, stinkiest, dingiest, squalid part of a dungeon—a real hole where the nightmare worms spawned, hyper-worse than the historic "Black Hole of Calcutta." Some suggest that the word *prison* is actually 'prism,' that reveals the glistening, delicate fractured schizophrenic mindset of Kari. Like Hamlet's father though, Kari, by Valhallan edict, is forbidden to speak of such places, although her interments are well known.

16. *Odin's flame-daughter.* Odin is a major father-deity to the northern Europeans, leader of the gods of Asgard, the Norse Heaven of the Vikings. But, this personage

has his true and diabolical mythic caricature and origins in wicked King Nimrod of *Genesis*, Chapter Ten (Ch. 26 note # 6). *Flame-daughter* is another term for 'Valkyrie.'

17. *Until she was 'miss stress.'* Kari is not only a supreme master, or mistress of her arts, she is also known about the Hall as 'Miss Stress.' Apparently, she is so intense and fanatical at times she creates much stress to friend and foe alike.

19. *Swordplay did her respect demand.* Demandead + damned/maddened. "Never odd or *even*," Karina the kid kills (*de-man, i.e.,* 'dead them') many, leveraging respect and fear from all, and quite fluently at that.

21. *With blade or dagger.* Popular weapons used in conjunction in old Europe. Kari's skill is such that she does not need to carry a shield to protect her. Her blade motion does the work for her.

24. *Spirit of that Northern wood.* This gives us a glimpse of Kari's ancient background and homeland, possibly ancient Germany or Gaul, powerful descendants of the tribes of Gomer, son of Japheth, Noah's son (*Genesis* 10.2).

27. *With deadly impass'.* Impassion + impasse. Kari is very impassionate, that is, fervently emotional. The term *impasse* means sort of a "bottleneck," "standoff" or "jam." This does not means she is ever blocked or frustrated in her ways, it alludes to her immensely disciplined yet psychotic mindset that does not allow any breaches or quarter, she always jamming and stopping the other guy.

33. *She smiled to all . . . plan of attack.* Kari's sincere sweetness only covers her immensely complex *geniaced* ('genius-maniacal,' or 'maniac genius') troubled mind that hyper-excels in strategy, tactics, literature, poetry, theology and the 'lore & logic' of intuitional motion amongst other notable things. She does not think in terms of past, present and future in chronological thinking linking's but these three in the super-compressed realization of them in an instantaneous compacted hyper-*now*, and all that these condensed atomic factors mean and affect.

35. *All to lend ear.* This is a biblical phrase and a dramatic one. Whenever Christ taught something of immense importance, he would say something akin to he who has an ear, let him hear, while in Shakespeare's play, *Julius Caesar* (III. ii.), we find Mark Antony asking the audience to lend him their ears. The passages indicate a call for intense scrutiny by all.

36. *As the poet implied.* Poet Robert Browning (1812-1889), the poem, *Andrea Del Sarto* (line 98). The original line runs, "Ah, but a man's reach should exceed his grasp, Or what's a heaven for?" In light of our text, the main idea seems to be that a man or a woman's virtues must make them reach beyond the ordinary to challenge their persons constantly.

NINE: THE TALES OF THE SEVEN

The sainted girl of framed stained glass,
Fragmented together from her deceited past,
Told now she ledgends from the old Valhall,
To impress all brave minds for that conflict *fine* all.

Aridescent spirit former of the prism-house of pane,   5
Wandered dry places for a dwelling place to gain.
The play of dark colors still bedazzle; break within your breast,
Shard images of visions impure do you in rupture protect.

She looked at the orangered-glassed cathedraled wall,
Leaded lines showed footwork of men's mortaled falls.   10
She thought of her *nemysis*, goddess Kali,
That stick and dagger *artiste* of greatest folly.

"To sit and convey truth 'tis our rightful progression,
To share *eaches* burden is for us our soul expression.
To extend our rite hand of fellowship before disastrous war, 15
Seals forever in the pact of love causes that are born."

She turned and smiled, pointing with asphodel sword,
Knew the man's name discreetly and settled with accord.
"The living don't know what it is to be accounted of the dead,
Much less lead them into battle, the fullness of their passions fed." 20

This, said she, while clutching her cold steel shaft,
Extolling those enlightenments of her lonely cutting craft.
Softly spoke she with a requieted silver tongue,
And upon the golden tales she in resolute begun.

DOUGLAS M. LAURENT

Chapter Nine Valley Footnotes

The *Tales of the Seven* are the first major speeches given by a lead character in the series known as the *Seven Short-Story Poems*. Inspired by *The Prophet* by poet Kahlil Gibran (1883-1930), they are moral tales of valor, as we would no doubt hear on any Valhallan night. To help us understand them, translations are taken from earthly cinema, drama, history and the glossing over, or mythologizing of actual events. Kari weaves the stories to teach in an entertainment-educational way as oral story-telling and tribal schooling was back then.

In these sketches, Kari uses two unique sources of spiritual information. The first is the seven spiritual attributes of God found in *Isaiah* 11.2. These attributes are wisdom, understanding, counsel, might ('strength'), knowledge, fear (M. English 'respect') and the Spirit Himself. 'Wisdom and understanding' imply intellectual and moral understanding, 'council and might' refers to the power to mastermind plans and carry them out, while 'knowledge and fear' mean accurate familiarity with the Divine's known will and the unbendable determination to carry it out come what may.

The other set of spiritual values she uses derives from the *Code of Bushidō*, the ethical samurai warrior code of old Japan. Kari, trailing from ancient Indo-European lands, would know these virtues as:

Bushidō Virtues	*Indo-European Wi-ro*
Benevolence	Deu
Courage	Kerd
Honor	Spek (respect)
Justice	Reg (rectitude)
Loyalty	Leg
Politeness	Gher (courtesy)
Veracity	Ker (sincerity)

With the two classic, fruitful lists from *Isaiah* and *bushidō*, the sword-saint firmly wields her perception of the world of the warrior together with that of the world of the eternal spirit. It is a direct reflection into our own.

VALLEY OF THE DAMNED

1. *Framed stained glass.* Here Kari is described as one would observe a stained glass window that is disjointed and fragmented but as a whole is beautiful. This motif enables us to see into part of Kari's troubled psychological profile.

4. *To impress all brave minds for that conflict fine all.* Linguist Jonathan Mycroft suggests that the line *all brave minds* is a distortion of the Italian word *allabreve*. It is musical notation of 2/2 timing where the half note gets the beat. It also translates as 'cut time.' This may mean either Kari was about to deliver a series of quick speeches, or more so, the passage refers to the contents of the speeches, how things in tight places need to be speedily done cutting straight to the matter. *Fine all* is 'final' (*fē'nā*), Latin, *finis*, or 'conclusion.' It is also Italian music notation for 'the end.' Apparently, the reference is alluding to a major, final battle. As accorded in the tenth century *Irish Monastic Script* this is the great and future battle characterized, so imply Christian, Jewish and Muslim scholars, by the up and coming revived Roman Empire (the European Union, or *E.U.*). In its final phase, the Anti-Christ's confederacy will be a ten-nation union that will pit itself, under Lucifer's guidance, against Israel, Christ and His elect. For us on Earth we understand this to be *Armageddon*, while to the Valhallans, *Ragnarök* 'Destruction of the powers' (*see* Daniel and Revelation).

6. *Wandered dry places.* In *Matthew* 12.43, Christ tells the story of a demon that wanders dry places finding 'no home,' and coming back to the man he once possessed, takes up his 'home' residence once again, only this time with seven spirits more wicked than himself. This interesting curse-judgment is due to the man's warped neutrality on vital spiritual matters. After being kicked around and possessed, he did nothing to improve his spiritual state of being by getting right and walking a straight path. In Kari's case, the analogy may reveal another glimpse into her questionable, checkered past (Ch. 19 note # 51).

8. *In rupture protect.* 'Rapturous.' Broken, ruptured Kari, like a predatory raptor that yet loves to hunt, is ecstatically zealous about guarding her past history.

9-12. *Orangered-glassed . . . leaded lines . . . greatest folly.* Orange + range + anger + red. This passage is most peculiar. Kari is seeing colors in the stained glass that are inciting a bit of anger in her, the emotions having a range of red in them, implying the color of blood. *Orange* is a color important in brilliance yet painful and sharp to the eye at times, and as an off-kilter or penetrating color, pops up now and again as a motif in the text. *Leaded lines* are indicative of triangular footwork patterns taught in some schools of martial arts, such as Renaissance fencing or Filipino *kali* (*lit.*, "*ka/mut-li*/hok: hand-movement"), a major sword, stick and dagger art. When pieced together, the lines, like stained glass, form a beautiful pattern of multiple triangles in a square. Kari sees this in the window and it invokes a memory as to how many have fallen in battle because of these simple lines she has used.

11. *Nemysis, goddess Kali. Nemysis,* 'my sister.' Kari is being flippant when she uses the phrase 'my sister.' It is probable that, because there is animosity toward East-Indian goddess Kali, Kari, as a Valkyrie, has had some dealings with her in the past. The term *nemysis* does not refer to blood relations, or belonging to the same order, but essentially sarcastic ill will, as in 'my dear sweet sister in ill-fortune,' as if these two were thrown together somehow in an antagonistic sense, they sharing a common bond, making them rival 'sisters.' As both are military artists, perhaps their contention was over European and Indian combative stylistics, political affiliations, or that even they once worked together. According to popular writer and historian Hector Kyle, there is evidence to suggest that because of Kari's dislike toward Kali, she may have been in India previously (Ch. 18 note # 93).

13. *To sit and convey truth 'tis our rightful progression.* Kari, like others, has a tendency to use archaic contractions when nervous, agitated, or using loftier language. This shows an older, more anachronistic use of language.

17. *Delicate asphodel sword.* Kari's sword is both ghostly and underworldly. According to Greek mythology, the Underworld palace of Pluto, or Hades is roundabout surrounded by vast gloomy wastes "Wan and cold, and meadows of asphodel, presumably strange, pallid ghostly flowers" (Hamilton, p. 43, *et al.*). Asphodels are a funerary plant of ruins and cemeteries. The soil was barren, void of all living mortal things and black poplars were sparsely scattered about. Willows too were present, but they never bore fruit. Although razor sharp, Kari's straight cross-hilt sword in its construct is well-suited to the Deadlands, being insubstantial like a ghost both

as light as a feather yet solid as steel able to cut through all. Its flowery description speaks of its delicacy.

20. *The fullness of their passions fed.* Those living have no true idea what real battle is like. Only the dead do. They do not suffer delusions of heroism or glory from some trumped-up political ideal cooked up by some greedy fat old Nether-plutocrats tucked away in some cigar-smoke filled back room who want to make money off war. The dead only share the anonymity of countless unknown graves. When the Valhallans originally died on Earth and die on Nether-battlefields everyday thereafter, the height of reality for them is that dying means the fullest expressions of their passions, whether those passions are full of courage, anger, remorse, *etc*. We can see a parallel to this with the samurai of Japan, whose resolute acceptance of death was standard procedure. Here we view the reverse angle of this effect, passionate resolutions being played out from death's side to the fullest extreme.

23. *With a requieted silver tongue.* Required + quiet + requited. Apparently, Kari is giving the necessary, 'required' daily pep talk that is very reassuring although it appears she may be a bit nervous addressing a crowd. She speaks eloquently, quietly, directly, with an 'edge' in her voice that hints of urgency and settling personal matters, of 'taking care of business.' She is a great story-teller however. Her command of the language is extraordinary, full of expressionisms, *onomatopoeias* (imitation words that have no formal spelling but are made by imitating the natural sound associated with the object or action involved, such as '*buzz*,' '*duh*,' '*mm-mmm*,' '*pssst*,' '*huh?*' and '*oooh*.' Kari also uses a great deal of body and hand gestures. To hearfully comprehend the needling collection of cháophōnic Nether-*onos* found lustered throughout the poem, readers are just going to have to practice and *ono-it* for themselves. C.S. Lewis' Screwtape would enjoy this. He proclaims the glories of noise in Hell and decries the music and peaceful silence of Heaven. "Noise, the grand dynamism, the audible expression of all that is exultant, ruthless, and virile—Noise which alone defends us from silly qualms, despairing scruples, and impossible desires. We will make the whole universe a noise in the end." Screwtape's description of the writhing sound effects in the Nether is a noxcid portrayal of virulent spirits, ironies, foreshadows portents, *etc*.

TEN: THE MIGHTY SEVEN

"Wisdom and justice were theirs of that day,
The mighty seven had gone out of their way,
To deal a firm hand when none was to be found,
In a lonely farm village with four graves dug 'round.

They went forth these intrepid seven samurai,   5
From many concerns their mission did tie.
To join hand-to-hand in that common cord of war,
To kill those bandits with the edge of their sword.

"Masterless," the warrior was heard to say,
And a farmer went with them to help save the knaves.   10
With bold hand and wise mind did they with battle rite,
In the sight of Heaven do justice in her sight.

The mighty seven spread through windswept village,
Preventing rapine, plunder and godless pillage.
By unreasoning men, nay, animals gone insane,   15
With greed and lust—their evil portrayed.

Throughout the season they readied their troop,
To display courage, with wings it would swoop.
Nothing but righteousness would win the awful day,
To preserve life innocent would be their only way.   20

In far field and village green one by one fell,
Divine wisdom decreed that each death should quell,
The rising tide of blackness that wisdom sought to kill,
And in the end, four graves dug 'round on top of lonely hill.

The mighty seven were men of little-known estate,   25
Unknown to none but us, yet forevermore great.
Unhesitant duty to the highest, most lofty of calls,
Wisdom and Justice brings—
The righteous to death's unclosing halls.

By council fires they sat and stirred their brilliant plan,   30
To defend the lonely village, to turn it to a stand.
One by one the walls went up each with a guardian,
And one breach in the fort to let those mongrels in.

Wisdom's highest art is achieved only when minds are set,
To bear the greatest burden and justice never rests.   35
For through wisdom all things are made circumspect,
Divining deep secrets; showing love's great subjects.

In the end the battle was won, but at *that* costly price,
The samurai moved on like the wind; farmers planted their rice.
Round about the land was glut, for she had her say and fill—   40
Four graves of lone warriors stood, with sword hilts on the hill."

These things the star-man of infamy knew,
Yet for all their worth the truth away he did threw.
Pondered the man silently on to himself,
For in mortal life never he upon them dwelt.   45

DOUGLAS M. LAURENT

Chapter Ten Valley Footnotes

In translating *Valley* poetry, many earthly parallels are used to make comparisons. Kari's remarkable narrative is 'exceptionally similar' to Akira Kurosawa's masterpiece film, *The Seven Samurai* (1957), and so is used to convey meanings within this micro-poem. Scholars are at a loss as to how she would know such a story, but given her vast battle experience, perhaps it is nothing more to her than art imitating life, designated history conveniently being repeated. A tale within a tale, the story embodies the finest elements of the ethics of the samurai, or *bushidō*. This particular tale concerns itself with wisdom and justice.

10. *A Farmer went with . . . knaves.* Cicero (*Kikerōn*, 106-43 B.C.) believed that farmers made the bravest heroes, a point made undoubtedly clear in Kurosawa's film. One of the seven samurai, we find, is a peasant farmer (actor Toshiro Mifune) who wants to be a true warrior. As might be expected, he is possessed with uncommon zeal and courage that reflects the true heart and strength of the warrior land. The professional samurai on the other hand, who are so used to hellacious violence and bloodshed are realistic and sad over war's vast fact, do not share his idealistic boyish zeal. In a heart-wrenching scene from the movie, the farmer-samurai cries. He blames the warriors for the miserable, cutthroat conditions farmers are forced to undergo daily at the hands of sword-wielding men. This oppression made the farmers both protectors and defender-killers of what little they had. The official samurai government of the times would no doubt agree with Cicero's observation on farmer-warriors, for in 1661 and 1668 it stripped them and the merchant class, forbidding them from having firearms and swords. *Knaves* refer to the peasant farmers.

24. *Four graves dug 'round.* In the epic classic, four of the seven samurai die as heroes—all from gunshot wounds—a statement of classic times and noble virtues versus sterile, secular modernization. In the end, only the samurai's graves with their swords sticking out of them are seen, a testimony to their sense of duty.

26. *Unknown to none but us.* Here is an amazing reality found in the Deadnether. As taken from the introduction of this chapter, the question arises as to how Kari

would know of this Earth tale. Historian Gustaf Von Hauser and Mythologist Etta Jörgens suggest reasons for her awareness of it. They claim that: the popular notions or urban myths they de-bunk are that characters in films are actual 'living spirits.' This pop ideology is due to cinematic special effects and script writing, writers always upping the ante in films as to what spirits are. It is only logical to say that, as an extension of our own psyches and myths, they would come into their own.

Exempli gratia, in the 1956 *MGM* movie *Forbidden Planet* starring Leslie Nielsen and Robby the Robot, the mad scientist's (who else?) own *id* comes to life as a big crabby invisible monster that leaves deep footprints, makes mayhem and kills everybody. This is about one step away from reality as you can get. What is an *id*-unit? According to Freud, the *'id,'* Latin for *"it,"* is pure instinct and fun, some think—wants, desires, impulses, pleasures, bodily needs, drives, *etc.* The *id* likes to 'let loose' as it were, questing after the beastie 'pleasure principle,' that is, to hunt out and act upon any instant gratification impulse it sets its little sights on. Mr. *Id-It* likes avoiding pain or un-pleasure (not displeasure) which simmers up by an increase of its instinctual tensions or perhaps even *intentsions*, like poor *id*-driven Burning Prairie of Chapter 1.

Allegedly, these so-called spirits live out their reality through the film 'medium.' As they are interior, or 'real' aspects of our souls, and images of our mind's eyes, the energy they produce enables them to take on 'life,' and so enter the Halls of the Dead. This is one common thought as to how Kari gets her 'Earth' ideas.

Another, perhaps more 'realistic' and riveting Netherworld interpretation the scholars focus in on is that unseen spirits, who have access to our world, are re-enacting or re-cycling mythologized events to justify their existence and semblance of honor. This would give them a *face* and a *raison d'être* ("reason for being, of existing, purpose") as they feed upon and perpetuate what they like to hear about themselves—the myths of their 'doing,' tales of their exploits. This is not a difficult premise to believe, cites pop-writer Hector Kyle. He claims this is a known phenomenon in our world, pointing out that 'historical persons' are asked to regularly appear in dramas (*cameos* in movies, *etc.*) to tell their tale. He only points out that we should ask ourselves who or what is the real person or thing behind the 'face' of the historical person.

The consensus among scholars however is that it is most likely that Kari has 'insider information' to tell her tales, our world melding into the mindscape of the Nether-zone. This means that the constant regurgitation of mythology in our mortal sphere are the spirit's ways of shaping, moving and controlling our world to their ends. The re-cycling of mythological stories is a subtle conditioning tool and outlet for, as psychiatrist Dr. Greta Hastings observes, establishing, and continuing a sense of identity, dictating behavior and thought, and ultimately, control. It shows a *progressive indirect* millennia-old game plan of attack. She claims that there *has* to be heroes and villains to bounce against each other to play the spirit's epochal story out, of good versus evil down through time. In many life scenarios that consist of one central theme, the names and faces change through time to accommodate different human audiences and their shaped views but the central core is always the same. As for us mortals, tales from the thirteenth century *Kel's Yellow Book* and the recently translated *'Halla* texts allows us to have the spiritual eyes to see into this sublime reality (*see* St. Paul's letter, 2Timothy 4.1-4).

ELEVEN: MAN IN THE BREACH

Wise Li looked at the man with expressive, wedged eye,
Saw through him, right through his tarnished self-lies.
"Where do you stand?" seemed he to the man to say,
The man choked a tear, unaccustomed to display.

Then a dusky voice called out,   5
"Speak to us of knowledge, let us not doubt."
Kari smiled and thought of many mindful things,
Many pains to be shared with sincerity and feelings.

"Sincerity is the greatest virtue," her strong voice shot in,
"With it the Romans built her virtues, not wholly corrupt sin."   10
Noble Horatius smiled, then bowed with great solemnity,
Kari spoke of his knowledge, of fate that forestalled calamity.

"O', pure industrious Roman virtue,
Builder of empires, leader of *the* rising future.
Sincerity and virtue, 'tis what made you great,   15
Attributes of strength, lead all through thy gate.

Sincerity of mind is what gives a warrior his edge,
To go into battle and strike clean, to give up self for dead.
It comes from the pure knowledge that is from On High,
And to those who work it much, *ahh*, in the end their gain is to die! 20

Alerted to invaders at the elder's hurried request,
To guard Imperial Rome at the bridge that Hell itself would rent,
One bold spirit took he the mighty Legion on,
Kept Rome from rapine, safe from destruction's harm.

Against all odds did Horatius confront,   25
The mighty Etruscan army in its invading blood hunt.
Stood he alone of the far side of treacherous Tiber River,
With spear in hand, he was Rome's sole life giver.

While the great enemy host gained access to his city,
He, above all, knew the secret of love and her ability.   30
His pure soul now fully girded and romanized,
Knew he had to hold the bridge, or be utterly cast aside.

Only the greatest of those who know the true way,
Can face insurmountable odds on the battle-judgment day.
This day must fall upon all whose spirits are secured,   35
To stand against the evil and in the end, to have endured.
Mighty Horatius at the far and away bridge,
Favored of man and gods at death's brilliant edge.
Sincerity and virtue was his true heart strength,
Held at bay *those* hellions, an iron soldier zeal thus makes.   40

Shook off the invaders while bridge was being cut down,
Wounded in battle, his life's blood flowed sound.
Sacrificed his life for the Imperial cause,
Perished in the Tiber, for him let us pause."

The warriors looked at their comrade with gleam in their eyes,   45
Smiled at the hero who saved so many noble lives.
The man watched abashed from his small pointyed view,
Curled his legs underneath him, his heart now askew.

Chapter Eleven Valley Footnotes

Horatius of Rome (*ca.* 508 B.C.) is the subject. He with two others, according to some accounts, defended a strategic bridge to Rome against enemy invaders. His heroism stands tall as proper Roman virtue. This passage applies itself to true knowledge and sincerity.

10. *Not wholly corrupt sin.* Much is said about Roman decadence, but great virtue was noted among the early Romans as well.

14. *Leader of the rising future.* Kari's poetry works forward as well as backwards and vice-versa. As a result, she can poeticize future events that have already 'taken place,' as if she has in the future already 'been there.' Her life and work, therefore, is *Apocryphal* in nature. She is referring to the imminent rise of the European Union (*E.U.*), the final form of government which will be a ten-nation confederacy that will, prior to the second coming of Christ, rule the world based out of the Roman territories of old, particularly from the cities of Brussels, Rome, Jerusalem and possibly a re-built Babylon in modern-day Iraq.

33. *Those who know the true way.* In Medieval times, a clean and righteous life was believed to enable one to perform astounding deeds of courage and valor, as was said of Sir Lancelot Du'Lac of Camelot, King Arthur and Knights of the Round Table fame.

35. *This day must fall upon all whose spirits are secured . . . endured.* Great temptations come to those who wish to live purely. As a comparison, this stanza parallels the 'fight of good faith' against evil spirits and their schemes as outlined by St. Paul (*Ephesians* 6.11-13):

> Put on the whole armour of God, that ye may be able to stand against the wiles of the devil. For we wrestle not against flesh and blood, but against principalities, against powers, against the rulers of the darkness of this world, against spiritual wickedness in high *places.* Wherefore take unto you the whole armour of God, that ye may be able to withstand in the evil day, and having done all, to stand.

40. *An iron soldier.* Horatius was indeed a great 'iron man,' but this also is a borrowing from Daniel's vision of four great world empires and their meaning in biblical prophecy as relating to our world. It started when Babylon's King Nebuchadnezzar (*ca.* 630-562 B.C.) had a dream of a statue made of a golden head, silver chest and arms, bronze thighs and two legs of iron. These represented the four empires that would act as milestones pointing to a definite history with a definite conclusion. These four were the Neo-Babylon (gold), Medo-Persian (silver), Greek (bronze) and Roman (iron) empires. Rome would grow to be a mighty power—past and future— and would be characterized by the symbol of iron and ultimately iron mixed with clay as seen in the feet of the statue, signifying that at the end of the ruling ten nation confederacy that has yet to be, it would be very strong yet very brittle. The Greek Hesiod (*ca.* 700-900 B.C.) also recorded this 'empires made of metals' scheme, apparently popular in the ancient Middle East. Both share a common, Babylonian origin telling of creation—and conclusion (Hamilton, pp. 86-87):

> According to another story, the gods themselves created men. They made first a golden race. . . . In this account of the creation the gods seemed bent on experimenting with the various metals, and, oddly enough, proceeding downward from the excellent to the good to the worse and so on. When they had tried gold they went to silver. The second race of silver was very inferior to the first. They had so little intelligence that they could not keep from injuring each other. They too passed away, but, unlike the gold race, their spirits did not live on after them. The next race was of brass. They were terrible men, immensely strong, and such lovers of war and violence that they were completely destroyed by their own hands. This, however, was all to the good, for they were followed by a splendid race of godlike heroes who fought glorious wars and went on great adventures which men have talked and sung of through all the ages since. . . . The fifth race is that which is now upon the earth: the iron race. They live in evil times and their nature too has much of evil, so that they never have rest from toil and sorrow. As the generations pass, they grow worse; sons are always inferior to their fathers. A time will come when they have grown so wicked that they will worship power; might will be right to them, and reverence for the good will cease to be. At last when no man is

angry any more at wrongdoing or feels shame in the presence of the miserable, Zeus will destroy them too.

In this tale, it appears that the Greeks have two headings, the early and mean 'brass' Greeks and the later enlightened Greeks (godlike heroes, Odysseus, *etc.?*) making the Romans the 'fifth' iron race. This could also mean that this tale records both the old classic Roman Empire and its revived counterpart, suggesting the ancients knew of older Middle-Eastern biblical prophecies. (*See* Daniel 2.31-45; 7.——; 11.36-39 "forces" and Rev. regarding 'power worship' as cited above in the myth. The dates as to which version of this story came first are disputed.)

47-48. *His small pointyed view, Curled his legs underneath him.* Point + pointy + eyed. Theman, the movie star, is a small-minded pinhead that never has gotten the 'big picture' (pardon the pun). *Curled his legs.* In front of these masters and in opposition to an onslaught of righteous thought, Theman is so distraught he is starting to feel the immense pangs of self-shame and conviction and begins to assume a defensive fetal position to protect his bent-dented psyche against the overwhelming feeling of panic-attack insecurity he is having.

TWELVE: THE MAN OF VISION

Celaine of the tribe of Amazons
Then raised her voice to say,
"Tell us of honor and understanding,
That our minds may not stray."

With that, Kari smiled and looked she to 'the man,'   5
Passion flowed from tinted face, in her loving stead.
"Honor has no peers that they should upon it check,
For in the union of love, honor is reverent respect.

Understanding and honor is the crown of a king's head,
Placed on the brow of a warrior—virtues are gallantly led.   10
Yet 'twas written of those of long ago,
That honor should be "as long as grass shall grow."

In battle honor is a fearsome beast, no man can contain,
In the strength of his own self-heart, it brings him only shame.
Yet honor from On High bounds far beyond mere and mortal man,   15
Brings freedom to his earthbound soul, as he does what she commands.

A mighty warrior of the plains was he,
Crazy Horse—Tashunka Witco, of Sioux battle creed.
Given to the ravages of noble, savage war,
Against his enemies he vaulted to the fore.   20

Peering down from his lofty mountain hold,
Crazy Horse in a dream—the warrior was already of old.
Wore a smooth stone and red hawk feather, strength inured,
Talismans of power—his spirit's harbinger.

The promises *they* were broken one by one,   25
Until only war unbridled could be hardtily done.
Understanding and honor was not for those weak,
Only the evil Long-knives now he eagerly did seek.

Long-knives came to steal, to plunder their land,
To kill the sacred mother with marauding, guilty hands.   30
They had no regard even for their own swelling words,
With lust in their eyes their greed greatly stirred.

From southern lands came noise that Longhair did kill,
Black Kettle's camp on river Washita, their blood he had spilled.
Longhair destroyed all; dastard agent of the evil strife,   35
Deprived them of their children and their bountiful life.
Yet this lone, brave holy man stood in Longhair's way,
Crazy Horse, man of vision, his plans were well framed.
His command rode north hard to that destined battle,
To meet wicked Longhair—to dash him from the saddle.   40

Fate led him on to the Little Bighorn,
Where warriors of the sun met with sacred horn.
A hellish dry place of calamitous battle,
Found many a soul hearing death's final rattle.

The Long-knive snakes scouted for the great camp,   45
That morn' they set their fateful, forked-tongue attack.
They raised their sabers, waved them strong,
Entered eternity, their deaths foresaw.

A sea of pilfered blue engulfed in crimson red,
Amidst a swirl of feathers sacred of the motherland.   50
Through the carnage, The Horse did lead his men,
Beyond the battle, to the place where legend began.

Up that hill rode the bold Crazy Horse,
With a thousand others to show determined force.
To engage those Long-knives at their last stand,   55
Striking them down until dead was every man.

Great Gall and Crazy Horse led that righteous attack,
Against the forceful Custer, whose plans did not lack,
For 'twas he himself who boasted and *heh*, wantonly said,
"I will become a great chief, if my enemies I fill with lead."   60

With righteous honor as their sacred ally,
Holy arrows that day they did let swiftly fly.
Crazy Horse met the Longhair in battle forever stayed,
Defeated mighty Custer; his corpse on the field in state.

Upon *that* fateful day, on sage choked sandy plain,   65
Spirits clashed with spirits, for the sacred domain.
Unconquerable, indomitable this sacred warrior heart,
Leads many against the evil now, for this righteous court.

Thus The Horse brought the valiants into stark raved battle,
Battle scarred by holy wounds delivered by the blue devils.   70
Yet he would not relent, this honorable man of gifted vision,
But peace came through the lie; his life ended by steel incision.

Breathing out his last, quiet honor came his way,
"Bring my heart home, the Great Spirit will find my way."
Thus 'tis with all whose understanding shows what may,   75
Honor leads righteousness to death, ask they of that claim.

War spirit vigilant with mighty spear and bow in hand,
Leads those Great Plains spirits, under his gallant command.
His spirit never conquered lives it to this good day,
Among the heroic mighty, let us his spirit proclaim.   80

In the hour of travail, honor can be finely seen,
Leading multitudes unto battle, their hearts boundlessly free.
Understanding charts her pure course for all true warriors,
For without perfect clarity, honor does not heed the call.

Thus, understanding with honor is a battle-shorn gift to see,   85
A thousand encounters a'born them, in that crucible of destiny.
Cowards can never know the freedom of the plains and wind,
Or how she musters a soul and the courage found within.

Honor as such, is the gift of humble divinity,
Without which spirits cannot in visions wholly see.   90
Born in deep commune of Earth and Great Spirit above,
Understanding and honor flow from hearts of true love.

One without understanding is a fool said at best,
One without honor is a spirit that never finds rest.
O' majestic Horse of the relentless plain,   95
The mountains ring joyous with thy sacred name.

Many more tales could be now told,
But the Ancients among us, they do withhold.
Of myriads of warriors from far flung lands—
Know they end in death for all who honorably stand."   100

With this, the man of Earth was quite aghast,
He could see now that he had no living past.
A hollow man, *that* truly was his trade,
A comic-book hero, of no real fame.

Chapter Twelve Valley Footnotes

The great Sioux warrior-chieftain-visionary, *Crazy Horse* (ca. 1841-1877) is our world model here. A leader of the Plains Indians, Crazy Horse for many years fought against the U.S. His victories culminated in the Battle of the Little Bighorn (June 25-26, 1876), a battle that saw General George Armstrong Custer and the Seventh Cavalry wiped out. The battle is also popularly known as 'Custer's last stand.' This story tells of honor and understanding.

1. *Celaine of the tribe.* This spirit's name is short for 'Porcelain,' another glass motif.

12. *"As long as grass shall grow."* Using a famous Americanism for our translation, this line was part of a treaty-promise given to the Southeastern Native Americans when they were forcibly resettled in Oklahoma from the 1820s to the 1840s. This treaty, like all others, was broken. Here, St. Kari uses a kindred idea to indict the evil of broken honor.

22. *Crazy Horse in a dream.* Crazy Horse, the holy-man warrior received power and visions through dreams and as a result, believed himself to be invincible. He wore the talismans found in his dreams—a smooth stone and a red hawk feather.

26. *Be hardtily done.* Hard + heartily. The concept for this line is in *Hamlet* (III. iv.): "I must be cruel, only to be kind; thus bad begins, and worse remains behind." As a war leader protecting his people and sacred lands, Crazy Horse indeed had to be cruel in order to be kind.

27. *Honor was not for those weak.* This cites the U.S. government who went back on its word.

29. *Long-Knives.* U.S. soldiers, particularly the Cavalry. The name denotes their sabers.

30. *To kill the sacred mother.* The Earth.

33. *That Longhair did kill.* A term used for Custer.

34. *Black Kettle's.* This is the famed Cheyenne chieftain (*ca.* 1803-1868) known for his peace efforts. His village on the Washita River, Oklahoma, was attacked by Custer on November 27, 1868. While trying to escape he and his wife were shot in the back. Many died that day.

44. *Death's final rattle.* The rattle of sabers and war-dance rattles personified as death.

46. *Forked-tongue attack.* This term refers to 'liar.' It is said, perhaps stereotypically, that the Native Americans used this phrase against the white man.

55. *Their last stand.* This is another Americanism for 'Custer's last stand' where Custer met his match.

60. *I will become . . . with lead.* Custer, according to popular historical data, suggests that he was an *ego*maniac who sought the Presidency. It looks as if he felt that one great victory over the Indians would give him enough prestige to launch his campaign in Washington. Scholar Nigel Hawkesford points out that "Pride *goeth* before destruction, and an haughty spirit before a fall" (Prov. 16.18 *kjv*). He relates this passage to Lucifer's five "*I will's*" as he attempted to usurp the throne of God. Both Lucifer and Custer are (and were) very proud individuals, pride leading to both their bitter downfalls (Isaiah 14.12-14).

64. *Corpse on the field in state.* Native Americans mutilated dead enemies in the belief that their dead spirits would be so cut up in the afterlife that they could not enter 'Heaven,' an apropos concept for entry into the Deadlands. They say, however, they respected Custer enough after the battle to not desecrate his remains.

72. *By holy wounds . . . blue devils . . . steel incision.* The gallant warrior Crazy Horse received many scars from battle by the blue devil federal soldiers, but

was apparently was bayoneted to death at the U.S. prison at Fort Robinson, Nebraska, 1877.

84. *For without perfect clarity.* According to the deadlanders, a righteous war with a clear vision is the only winnable kind.

87. *Cowards can never know.* Again, the temperament of the land fosters men and women of great ability and fortitude.

92. *Hearts of true love.* This is devoted, sacrificial love. It is the type of love one person has for another and is spiritual in nature. Greek *agápē* is the term for *love* here.

103. *A hollow man.* An allusion to Theman's potential of becoming one of them, that is to say, a 'Halla man—especially on the wrong side.

104. *Comic-book hero.* Comic book heroes do great deeds but are not real; much like the buffered fantasy life Theman lived.

THIRTEEN: THE FORTY-SEVEN

A warrior now spoke, illumined he bright,
A veteran of onslaughts that nightmared the night.
"Tell us of high council and loyalty,
To help us see o'er cowardice to duty."

"To extend arm and eyes before the battle is already settled,   5
To never forsake peers or command is the test of one's mettle.
Concerning loyalty," Kari said, "there is always heartfelt meditation,
For in her council what is spoken of is acted upon without hesitation.

And we, who hold the truth so dear,
Should ever make it to the world so clear,   10
The tale of those Forty-Seven honored men,
Masterless samurai, known as *rōnin*.

Upon the eve of a great parlay,
Their Master, Asano, attacked Kira, the attaché.
In defiance of standing rigid court order,   15
Drew he his sword and boldly cut forward.

In a fit of rage the Emperor knew,
To keep the peace Asano must shew,
That the ultimate in life was loyalty—
Commit the *seppuku*; fulfill his destiny.   20

Yet for many an unjust etiquetted reason,
Asano the slain was taken out of season.
For his sword had cut in righteousness,
But upon his crown was laid falseness.

Forced to take his life in unhonorable way,   25
Disembowelment let fly his spirit away.
And upon doing unrighteously so,
Stained his clan in the way of Bushidō.

In dark of night Lord Asano's men did plan,
To avenge dishonor, leaving it to the conscious of each man.   30
In the end, Forty-Seven dauntless stayed behind,
Immortal rōnin of that single honorable warrior mind.

The council was simple, so it stood,
They for a season would wander through the wood.
Mighty warriors living wasted lives,   35
So their sacred mission that they might hide.
Some became drunkards and were spat upon,
Some left family and wandered one by one.
And in time the official Kira did cease,
To make inquiries of their sotted decrease.   40

Fine men of renown reduced to but rags,
Leaving home and hearth for their driven plan.
And after the season again they did awake,
Rekindled their spirit—their revenge to take.

Entering castle one fine December night,   45
Humiliation unleashed its terrible sight.
Snowstorm and fury of falling silvery blades,
Killed that perpetraitor Kira unto his grave.

Battle was never seen like this,
Men fought in frenzied, righteous bliss,   50
For loyalty was avenged according to *the way*,
Men now as samurai—those who had stood the day.

Their cause was soon known, but did they run?
Nay, they came forward calmly, unto the Shogun.
With what serene and deliberate warrior mind,   55
Gave an account of their reasons defined.

The court had no choice, but to honor *the* code as well,
Ordered them to kill themselves, committing them to Hell.
One fateful day they all sat, calmly in that line,
To remove their lives slowly, by belly cuts so fine.   60

Today, there are Forty-Eight graves that by each side lay,
Of loyalties charge, once done, there is no more to say.
The last grave, 'twas dug for that man who proudly spat,
For upon learning of their mission, was humbled in that act.

Now, their loyalty is acknowledged forever more,   65
Owed to their samurai lord beyond death's iron door.
These Forty-Seven knew they had to make the stand,
Against unrighteousness that had stained their beloved land.

Now dear friends, *sniff* they are with us, this emblazoned crew,
One of the immortals of we, *they* of the chosen few.   70
Drink to their health now, and remember their day,
Of loyalties conviction, and where ultimate duty lay."

The man, at loss for word in need to understand,
Turned sullen eyes to Kari, her truths he could not withstand.
The Forty-Seven, they were the shining and living proof,   75
Of pure souls committed, their lives do behoove.

DOUGLAS M. LAURENT

Chapter Thirteen Valley Footnotes

This particular earthbound story also concerns itself with council and loyalties. *The Forty-Seven Rōnin* ('rōh-nin'), or 'wave-men,' (so named because they were like turbulent waves of the sea looking for adventure and errantry) that is, masterless samurai. There were many rōnin wandering about due to the unification of Japan that threw them out of 'work,' they no longer being able to serve local warlords. These masterless samurai are those whose master was dishonored before the high court of old Japan and so decided to do something about their status and honor as classical warriors. Adhering to the ancient ethical code of *bushidō*, the men, led by Oishi Yoshio (some texts specify Oishi Kuranosuke), sought to avenge their master and their tarnished clan's name. In the course of their action, they used the weapons of the classic warrior—the sword, spear, naginata and the bow. This choice reflected their deep heritage and commitment to the high ideal of chivalry. This triumphant comeback-vendetta occurred in 1702.

12. *Known as rōnin.* 'Masterless samurai.' Japanese literature abounds with vibrant tales of these adventure-seeking men, who, having been freed from the constricting bounds of feudal society, were at liberty to engage in glorious exploits that were not afforded to those belonging to constrictive clans.

15. *Standing rigid court order.* It was a great offense and an insult to draw one's sword on castle grounds.

18-39. *To keep the peace Asano . . . official Kira.* This refers to officials Asano Naganori (1667-1701) and Kira Yoshinaka. Asano and Kira were commissioned to entertain government representatives of the Emperor. Kira held a high office and apparently, it was expected of his colleague to give these state envoys gifts as an act of politeness as he was to receive their advice. When he failed to do so, Kira criticized him day and night, until finally, Asano, in the presence of the Shogun, drew on Kira and wounded him in the head. Asano was banished and forced to commit *hara-kiri*. *See* below.

20. *Commit the seppuku.* Better known as *hara-kiri,* or 'disembowelment,' the ritual slaying of oneself for some grievous moral dishonor by cutting the belly open from left to right then up, then being beheaded by a second man, who was often a friend of the victim.

31. *In the end, Forty-Seven dauntless.* Or 'hauntless.' Actions performed nobly, with a noble purpose allow the conscious to be clear. In the Dead, weaker spirits are 'haunted' by other spirits, memories, guilt, *wouldashouldacouldas* (a despicable, despairing soulwaste region where *no one* in their right mind ought to ever enter, haunted by thistles, stickers and prickers of pain and indecision that fasten deep), and other spiked pit dead-fall trappings of the mind. These samurai spirits fought with a righteous heart. They had no regrets as to their duties toward their creed, master and loved ones.

33-34. *The council was . . . the wood.* The plan of these disgruntled samurai was simple—to become derelicts, wayward drunkards and ne'er do wells for a couple of years to ward off suspicion then re-gather to exact the appropriate samurai 'revenge.' *The wood* here is Dante-like (*Inferno*), signifying dread, calamity, misjudgment, and danger. *Wood* further implies that these samurai were about to go into the world with all its prevalent spiritual misgivings. Historically, this probably was a great challenge to them as time, pleasures and other concerns no doubt tried to sway them from their fanatical die-hard mission.

45. *One fine December night.* December 14th, 1702 was the time of their revenge on Yoshinaka.

51. *The way.* Or '*dō.*' The term, *dō* implies a spiritual pathway to enlightenment, whether it is for martial, religious or artistic purposes. It is the moral code and social path of the samurai closely tied to *budō,* "the *way* of combat," without which the martial arts would descend into just a barrage of mere killer-technique.

57. *The court had no choice.* As any institution does, writes Dr. Peter Hsu, this one had grown apart from its former roots in terms of warrior ethics of the samurai

ideal. Yet, these rōnin behaved so much like samurai that the court had no choice but to enforce the full penalty of the law for their actions in order not to give in to the idea that the officials sanctified vendettas. Loftier samurai, conversely, did not exactly go about exacting 'revenge.' Zen would not allow it, as it would clutter the mind. Revenge, therefore, had a higher ethic, it was a detached 'business response,' of making things right. It was their right as samurai to 'respond' accordingly and righteously. On February 4, 1703, by order of the Shogun, The Forty-Seven committed *hara-kiri* en masse in front of Asano's tomb. This act of the Forty-Seven has since become immortalized in Japanese history as one of the greatest displays of *bushidō*.

61. *Forty-Eight graves.* The Forty-Seven are buried at the Sengaku-ji Temple in Tokyo. The man who spat on one of them, out of shame and honor is buried alongside of them.

FOURTEEN: THE TWO-FACE

Next Kari spoke, a cooler face by some,
Told of a man's splintered life before his day begun.
He was cowardly, now the 'bravest' of the brave,
Both resided within, yet the weaker had dug his grave.

"Fear and respect are two branches of one tree,   5
Twins of the other, prompters in the hands of duty.
In an (ass as sin's) grip, who knows what they shall be?
Dagger to a friend's heart—it tells the truth to me.

Yon' star was felled by he with lean and hungry look,
Once foe, now friend, did him by this treachery brook.   10
Mighty Caesar laid bare at foot of statue Pompey,
The monarch stabbed to rest by his 'friend's' jealous fray.

Cassius, triumphant, of the Syrian campaign,
Alighted with Lord Pompey for the Empire to gain.
Defeated by the noble one, yet pardoned throughout,   15
Respect burned to fear, hidden murder he did pronounce.

Yet generous Caesar heaped up royal rewards,
Upon friends and foes alike, his empire to be restored.
Still, the well of bitter envy flooded Cassius' heart,
To dispatch that tyrant—his ambition from the start.   20

"Pardon Caesar; Caesar, pardon" his last words to that tyrant said,
Now with seven guilty others quickly knifed the man-god dead.
Then, with *that* exalted gore still red upon his hands,
Cried, "freedom, and liberty!" to all Rome's distant lands.

In the throes of his blood lust, did he smugly condone,   25
"How many ages hence shall this our lofty scene be acted over→
In states unborn and accents yet unknown!"

His own heart debauched, it curdled to stone fear,
He died much less, like he did to Caesar, so dear.
"Caesar, thou art revenged," said he, at self-thrust of death,   30
"Even with the sword that killed thee,"—a soul gone unblest.

This Cassius, this hellhound, this Judas who misled,
His voice is not with us, murders he now with the dead.
A brave warrior, yes, the coward among us, no→
So 'tis for all those who fear—   35
Their souls with them shall go.
Thus, a blade is an awful thing, this two-edged fang of death,
Yet within the single stroke there abides both fear and respect.
For fear turned outward and running its wayward course,
Causes a man to flee battle, making him worse than a corpse.   40

Yet fear turned inward is to make a warrior see,
The strength and tenacity of the swordsman's mentality.
The way of the blade is seen then in the ways of two men,
Who, both as one, stand on the brink of eternity's far edge.

For in that final stroke there can only be but one key,   45
Great veneration for life, opponent and mutual destiny.
A sword stroke can never be more than judgment herself,
Because in the cleaving act, there is discernment of the self.

It takes a strong hand to divine what at the moment of truth one shall be,
A coward or a full man, once done, its judgment forever b'ceived. 50
Once fear reigns in the heart 'tis a false and wicked thing,
And love finds no voice upon which to brightly sing.

Thus a forgotten grave is for those of Cassius' ilk,
No laurel crown or oaken leaf for those who wallow in like filth.
The slab already lays for them all the days at their turned backs,   55
Respect then, and not fear, rides on the wings of righteous attack."

Now the star man remembered dark acts—
Those that bought him more,
How he had denied love, and had lost its vital store.
As he mused upon these thoughts his eyes did meet she,   60
Volumes spoken without a sound, the saint in deep sympathy.

Chapter Fourteen Valley Footnotes

This is the tale of *Gaius Cassius* (died 42 B.C.), one of the assassins of *Julius Caesar*, who was murdered March 15 (the Ides of March) in 44 B.C. This translation of the tale borrows heavily from Shakespeare's play, *Julius Caesar*, but Kari's story is concerned with fear and respect. Here, fear and respect function as a compound: "The fear of the Lord is the beginning of knowledge," *Proverbs* 1.7. In this context, *fear* means "reverential respect," "awe" and "trust." Thus, Cassius' jealously induced fear, doubly warped and not of this nobler respectful kind, is the most heinous. As this scene borrows heavily from the illusory theatre, it functions as a floating story within a story. Like the tale of *The Seven Samurai*, both are not real histories *per se*, but dramatic renditions of it. This is indicative of the many illusions, good or bad that deadlanders live by—one of the many undercurrents found in their world (and ours). As a matter of standing, *Valley* is flooded, deluged with mesmerizing reflecting ponds, cascades, backwaters, black water rapids, riptides, thermal and tidal pools, sounds, straits, coves, brackish standing waters, slime puddles, run-off, maelstroms, sickfalls, flash-floods and *eddies*—huge uncanny oceanic whirl shaped shapes—underwater twisters and of course, dams. Although very captivating some of these dimensions are easy to detect while others are not. The weaker soul-portals exist as full or partial *italicized* words and some look plain, the eyes easily skimming over them as ordinary words, but through these plying *eye-lies*, the soul receives quite a different subliminal message. Even more knotty and fringed, some words are *polysemous* in their knurly & gnarled nature (Gk. *polysêma* "many-sign," the capacity for a sign like a symbol, word or phrase to have several meanings, thus different but related senses or levels). These mind-traps exist in fragments, oddments, word and line forms just waiting to suck us water-loggers below into their briny unfathomable fathoms of torrential mind and soul unknown. In the Nether-fields, the dead live illusions or truths out of their own making. For a darker tone to this thought, perhaps a line from the film, *Demetrius and the Gladiators* (*Twentieth Century Fox*, 1954), starring Victor Mature and beautiful Susan Hayward might allow us to see the 'edge' by which the underworlders live. Hayward as the scheming Messalina tells Demetrius (Mature) that, "When the truth is ugly, only a lie can be beautiful."

3. *The 'bravest' of the brave.* Here, a sarcastic comment.

7. *In an (ass as sin's) grip.* That is, *assassin.* This compound word conveys Kari's cool thoughts towards treachery. Like C.S. Lewis, to her, evil is unimaginative and stupid. Killing Caesar, therefore, was *all* that they could do, what they could *only* do, and by that time in history, murder was extremely redundant, banal, dull-minded and unimaginative and from a spirit's point of view, almost boring.

9. *Yon' star was felled by he with lean and hungry look.* This is a reference to Caesar (III. i.) who equates himself as being "constant as the northern star." *Lean and hungry look.* While talking to Mark Antony at the games, Caesar (I. ii.) spies Cassius, a jealous rival staring down upon him from a balcony. He tells Antony that he would prefer chubby little old men surrounding him as Cassius the man-eating *microphage* ("small diseased consumers with excessive appetites") looks too much like a *Velociraptor* ready to order a gut-filling *entrée* paid for expressly at the expense of him (abridged):

> *Caesar*: Let me have men about me that are fat; Sleek-headed men and such as sleep o' nights: Yond Cassius has a lean and hungry look; He thinks too much: Such men are dangerous.
> *Antony*: Fear him not, Caesar; he's not dangerous; He is a noble Roman and well given.
> *Caesar*: Would he were fatter! But I fear him not: Yet if my name were liable to fear, I do not know the man I should avoid so soon as that spare Cassius. He reads much; he is a great observer and he looks quite through the deeds of men: . . . Such men as he be never at heart's ease whiles they behold a greater than themselves, and therefore are they very dangerous.

11. *At foot of statue Pompey.* In the play, Caesar is stabbed to death and dies at the foot of the statue of Pompey, an earlier, more 'virtuous' Roman leader than Caesar allegedly could ever be. Caesar, with Pompey and Crassus, ruled the Roman Empire as a triumvirate. After Crassus as well as Caesar's daughter Julia, who was Pompey's wife died, Pompey's jealousy over Caesar's victories in Gaul caused a falling out and civil war.

13. *Of the Syrian campaign.* Cassius in his early career defeated the Parthians in 51 B.C.

17. *Heaped up royal rewards.* Caesar had pardoned both Marcus Brutus and Cassius after the battle of Pharsalus, in which Pompey was their leader, yet these two were the ringleaders in Caesar's assassination. It is said more than sixty people died as conspirators in retribution. "With a spot" Antony damns them (IV. i).

21. *"Pardon, Caesar; Caesar, pardon."* These lines are spoken by Cassius before he kills Caesar (III. i.).

22. *Seven guilty others.* The other assassins, according to the play were Marcus Brutus, Casca, Trebonius, Ligarius, Decius Brutus, Metellus Cimber, and Cinna.

24. *"Freedom, and liberty!"* In the play, Cassius shouts these lines. They mean to be set free from the growing tyranny that was Caesar's (III. i.).

26. *"How many ages hence."* While stooping to bath his hands in the blood of Caesar, Cassius speaks this immortal, riveting line, "How many ages hence shall this our lofty scene be acted over in states unborn and accents yet unknown!" (III. i.).

30-31. *"Thou art revenged . . . killed thee."* In Shakespeare's work, Cassius has a friend run him through with a sword to avoid capture by Octavius and Antony (V. iii.).

32. *This hellhound, this Judas.* *Hellhound* is from *Macbeth* (V. viii.), in which Macduff calls Macbeth out for killing the King and Macduff's family. Judas, of course, refers to the one who betrayed Christ. Judas, Cassius and Brutus, traitors all, are also to be found being forever munched on in the *muy grande* three-way 'Hell-Mouth of Mouths' Lucifer at the end of Dante's *Inferno*, who just so happens to be permanently frozen in waist-high muck signifying his impotency, the lowest and most ironic fitting end for these four symbolic traitors. Here Lucifer has three faces, a pervertwistortion of the Trinity, a black, red and yellow one (guess this outdoes folks who are called 'two-faced'). In each maw, he makes eternal s'mores out of the traitorous men, Judas in the middle and Cassius and Brutus on the sides. Being frozen here

implies the great sin of coldness whilst politics and religion are viewed in the three men traitors. According to Dante, this is the worst of the worst, these Judas' all; very deserving to be tough, chewy rump roasts cuisine or filet o' fools in Satan's forked-tongue filed-toothed fire and pie hole for eternity (*see* Ch. 16 note # 44 on the diet maniac Mr. Hell-Mouth.)

33-34. *Murders he now . . . a brave warrior.* It must be recalled that we are observing reality from the 'good side' of the Deadnether, a precarious position at best, because all in the Deadlands are, to their own opinion, 'in the right.' However, Cassius, it seems, is on the bad side, but this does not mean that the bad people are not bold, brave and famous there either. There are many 'greats' on that side as well.

40-41. *Causes a man to flee . . . worse than a corpse. Yet fear turned inward.* The Chinese believe that to have a divided mind on a battlefield means instant death. Being divided or worried about one's own life, one cannot concentrate and perform one's duty adequately. Being unfocused and vacillating means one is an obvious target. That is why the Chinese say a battlefield is "a field full of standing corpses." *Inward.* This is intense introspection, as in the cinema where the hero looks into a mirror, into his or her eyes to reckon up exactly what kind of man or woman they are. An excellent cast of this impression can be found in the 1976 *MGM* film *Rocky* with Sylvester Stallone as he is about to confront the preening, malicious devastating champ Apollo Creed (Carl Weathers).

44. *Who, both as one.* Cowardice and bravery abide in the same person, again affecting destiny.

46. *Opponent and mutual destiny.* There is a compound meaning here. Christ speaks that if one lives by the sword, he will die by it, *Matthew* 26.52, while St. Paul writes to take up "the sword of the Spirit, which is the word of God," *Ephesians* 6.17. In context to this seeming paradox, Christ is speaking of the violent man eventually doing himself in, whereas Paul speaks of the daily defense of the faith. This is coupled with the idea of a *mutual* slaying. In old Japan, swordmaster's there were so excellent that many times they felt the best they could do was to kill their opponent—only at the

same time being killed themselves (known as *ai-uchi*). This in turn created a mutual, 'duel' destiny. In context, those who in the Deadlands slay their enemy are in actuality bearing their own soul to all, somewhat of a violent self-slaying or 'dying to self daily' type of thing. This is kind of like a negative or opposite anti-Christ sentiment where He says if one follows Him, one needs to die to the self daily. The same concept applies to the character of Dracula. In the novel by Bram Stoker (1897), in a negative polar symbolic 'vein,' Drac drinks blood to keep him eternally alive, much like the Church drinking the 'blood of Christ' as a positive symbol of eternal life. In the Nether then, killing further compounds one's destiny. It depends on the motives, good or evil, these being sacrificial Greek *agápē* 'love' or self-centered interests. As such, the use of the sword here means the two combatants become a unit, creating a personal history or destiny, ultimately affecting them both.

47-48. *Judgment herself . . . cleaving act.* One lives or dies by their sword and abides by her true dictates. The sword shows people who they really are. The *cleaving act* alludes to a mirror-like quality; the swordsperson's soul is laid bare for all to see in that one single absolute stroke.

50. *Its judgment forever b'ceived.* Believed + conceived + received. Jonathan Mycroft cites this word as a compound of three concepts: judgment is born and rendered in the very action of the sword cut. The person judged by it believes or receives its 'verdict-cut,' in this case in the form of cowardice. In other words, the final act of cutting with a sword during a duel reveals whether one is brave and a 'man,' someone who is willing to give their all, or a 'coward' afraid to fight and possibly die; someone who wants to live and is out for self-centered preservation (a *suki-point* mental gap). The conclusive stroke of the sword, *the moment of truth* tells of one's bravery or cowardice in the split-second life-giving or life-ending act, affecting fate as the combatants discern themselves as to what they truly are on the inside.

FIFTEEN: LONG SWORD OF YOUTH

As she sat teary, another story arose,
Young and full of vigor hewed with manymany*many* years of repose.
"Comrades" she brightened, "listen again to my tale,
Of courage and power, and how evil can never prevail.

'Tis true that as a youth he was young and brash,   5
Couldn't take orders, he was foolish and rash.
Because of this, many skilled young men were killed,
His arrogant eyes, fam'is shed, did see much blood that spilled.

Then *it* came to this proud warrior one day,
That courage and power were one in the same.   10
Yet courage and power untempered did pass,
As cowardly weaknesses in the heat of battle-mass.

For this reason the man who cannot control his soul,
Is one who is weak, he shan't never attain *the* goal.
I know this spirit, honored Kojiro by singular name,   15
Whose courage was unflowed, yet his power was unchained.

Though his youthful quest of life in the final did yield,
A match with swordmaster Musashi, his actions were sealed
(She smiled at the two, now the greatest of friends,
Who fought daily back-to-back to the always ever end).   20

Bountied in success the youthful Kojiro yet fell to his shame,
On that dawn soaked morning, his unbridled strength to blame.

He had trained for years for this great endearing match,
But his life was ended in *that* shearing, *horrific* ⋛〰 *PP Flassssh PP* 〰⋜
Yes, all for the want of a more glhorious, eternal name,   25
Yes, to test his skill paid he d'early for his en*grav*ened fame.

Yet this proud youth had beat many a man,
Many opponents were with him unable to stand.
Hence, power unchecked turns one into the fool,
Courage is for necessity; life can be so cruel.   30

Thus in his final bout with *the* double-blade master,
He found peace with himself, *after* untimely disaster.
Now he abides as one of us——
Sasaki Kojiro of the eternal trust."

Silently the youth bowed and slighed back into his seat,   35
He smiled at Kari, his best friend at the keep.
With a polite and quiet show, nod he to all,
Unused to the honor, he humbly left the Hall.

As the leading man of fame listened on and on,
A strength was ignited, *it* began to dawn.   40
Seeing for the first time the hidden desire in himself——
The possibility of a man now, and not a cartoon mask.

VALLEY OF THE DAMNED

Chapter Fifteen Valley Footnotes

This samurai tale chronicles the famous duel between *Sasaki Kojiro* and *Miyamoto Musashi* who advocated two different styles of swordsmanship. Sasaki's method was known as the *Chujo* style, and his favorite technique was the 'swallow-counter,' inspired by the swift action of a swallow's tail in flight. Musashi's way, the *Ni Ten Ichi Ryu*, or 'two-sword' method, not only implied using two swords in mass combat, but also carried the concept of making the fullest use of one's weaponry (mental, strategic, spiritual, physical, *etc.*), no matter what one had on hand (note # 31 below). In contests with masters, Musashi always used one sword, and more often than not, a wooden one. In order to avoid the law that forbade duels, the combatants met on an isle in the Kammon Straits around eight a.m., April 14, 1612. In actuality, the duel was of such a public nature that the provincial governors and other powerful patrons of the arts covertly sponsored it, betting big on the contestants. Both men had trained years for the match and Sasaki lost. For the contest, Musashi had whittled a long sword from a boat oar, said to have been equal in length to Sasaki's own long sword. Musashi in his career went on to kill at least sixty opponents in duels. Kari uses this earthy tale to tell the deadlanders of the wonders of courage and power. *See* the movie *Samurai Trilogy* starring Toshio Mifune (*Toho Productions*, 1954-56) directed by Hiroshi Inagi for an excellent portrayal of the above poem. The movie is based on the novel *Musashi* by Eiji Yoshikawa.

1. *As she sat teary.* As Kari is a flawless storyteller full of passion, her emotions sometimes get the better of her. As can be said of her from the many acquaintances who know her intimately, her bark is worse than her bite. A heart of gold, she is full of "tough love" (Gk., *sklirí agápē*) being the basis of her many moods and so *acute* akimbo *inspirangular* mercies (inspire + spiral + angular). Not only is Kari "a-cute" negatively sharply bent mental angle, she is canny, incisive, astute, penetrating, drastic and quite melodramatic. Further, she is dangerous, complex, nimble, dexterous, volatile, sagacious, razor rapier-witted, piercing, severe and keenly wise for her teen-age and times. Summarily, being unique of her kind, she is a *helluva* insightful individual, the tri-dented *inspirangular* term referring to her mind-blowing dissymmetric abstract poetically motional inspirations and off-beat ways that often

take huge spiraling circuits within circuits to pull something off. It also speaks for her quirky off-angled 'respect and mercy' getting swordpoem play. *Akimbo* are the hands on the hip with the arms bowed out position. It denotes many meanings *via* body language such as readiness, aggression, preparation to take steps, to perform, to take part in, to take charge of, to step forward, to discipline or threaten a subordinate and *to defend against those who overstep their bounds.* If bits and pieces of psyche fragments can ever be greater than the sum of a person, well, she is the poster child for such a study. Notwithstanding, having been as Captain Ahab re-spliced together on many occasions, overall she is hard-edged on the outside from the thick coats of shellacking she has had. Kari has to be tough, yet she is, as the Celestials (old Wild West term for the Chinese) say, like "iron and silk," the definitive *yin-yang* example of pure martial integrity and ability. Like Orpheus who went into Hades to retrieve his true love Eurydice by singing so eloquently that, everything and everyone in 'the Pit' stopped to listen, so Kari exists in the darkest of places. Here her tales, poems, theatrics, proverbs and songs many a evening "Drew Iron tears down Pluto's cheek, And made Hell grant what Love did seek." Such is the power of her oratory. (Hamilton, p. 141 quotes John Milton, *Il Penseroso*, line # 105, 1631).

2. *Manymanymany. Lit.*, "many men + any man." As the accent is on the third 'man,' what Kari is saying is Kojiro in his youth took on a lot of good men in combat to instill his reputation, and wasn't above killing anybody who stood in his way of fame and fortune to become Japan's number one fencer-duelist. Only Musashi stood in his way.

8. *Eyes, fam'is shed.* The passage implies that Kojiro's eyes were 'famished,' lustful, or hungry for glory, yet at the same time the word usage suggests that the term indicates 'fame is shed,' meaning that upon killing, his fame was shed and spread abroad, he becoming a 'house-hold' name and hero. Lust is highly addictive and its skeleton password key phrase is 'I want—*gimme.*' Lust is the vice-like illusory super-glue that a corroded mind degenerates to inflate itself for more power, which is but a fleeting, graspless illusion. Here it fixates and attaches itself, with blinding un-inspiration mind you, to *D*rab, average, regular, tedious, humdrum, *V*anilla, arid, deadly, everyday, run-of-the-mill objects that in time are in a state of corruption

and like their devout adherents, passing away themselves. Economically, this de-composting demoncratic bourgeois pedestrian manure yields great crops of bland, pasty, sugarless Wh*eaties* in the Nether for souless.

9-12. *Then it came.* Here, Kojiro has a 'sudden realization,' or *epiphany*, in regards to unbridled courage and power being useless and brash, even *cowardly*, if it went *untempered* undergoing refinement in *the heat of battle-mass.* A Kari-ism, Kari, relating the story, adds *mass* to the term *battle*, reflecting not only the idea of 'full' or 'mass battle,' but her own sacred fervors as to her 'worshipping' battle as sort of a religious service. The term which best describes her wording might be in the ancient Germanic/Indo-European dialect 'faith-service' or *bheidh-slougo* in regards to going to a *domos apo deu*, 'House of Worship.'

17. *Life in the final did yield.* Book Haiku helps translate this line into English as "life in the final did Mars field." What this means, some hold, is that world-god Mars played ball with and 'fielded' Kojiro's life. Mars, through his Japanese war-god branch office did indeed bring the young man great glory, yet he *beefed* the youth, killing him off on the royal red 'field of battle,' better known to us western interlopers metaphorically as *Campus Mārtius* the "Field of Mars." The stained Field was the old arena area in Rome where many games of blood were played out. As to why Mars and other world princes nonchalantly go about bumping off famous up and coming promising young men and women like Kojiro, consider this thought. These sorts of actions are blinds, clever strategic ruses; a combination of war and politics that fall under the auspices of the unseen propaganda ministry of the forces of evil. To keep their world dominions running, such as what the global wall-to-Walmartial conglomerate is, they need to continually fuel and make sacrifices of select well-groomed martyrs unto this infernational Hell-Mouth macro-martial system of theirs. (1John 5.19; Eph. 6.12; *see* our Ch. 16 note # 44 for Hell-Mouth and Cleary's *Japanese Art of War* on deception.).

For example, bear witness to the ill, star-crossed "martyred" fates of the incomparable Bruce Lee and his son Brandon, Jimmy Dean, Marilyn Monroe, John Lennon, Honest Abe, Elvis, *etc.*, they all serving as revered draw-play siphoning-off idol-icons now. These are beautiful folk, dedicated professionals and heroes all, who forever youthful and locked in time, became iconic inspirational representations that the common herd gladly rallies around. By continually regurgitating the pop-culture that surrounds such symbolic figures, the massive, night-crawling, theo-torodozing darkly-oiled, scheming Martian juggernaut and World-Image machine's imachinations irretrievably and irrevocably keeps on pushing. Its ironic grinding ball-overbearings intimidate and coerce—soft-violently disposing of all oppositions along the way. How does the reader think these karate and kung-fu magazines, movies and the like stay in business? They use their iconic pet figureheads to promote their causes and so sales, to keep them and those unseen thrones, dominions, principalities and powers who rule the planetoid afloat. ➤ This is the savage, exotic beauty of being educated and stultified in the fine art of deception, brainwashed folks just meandering about like a clumpish convocation of *automatons*, deceiving on auto-pilot, not even alert to the fact that they are deceived themselves, being played out as pawns in a much bigger game, the end result—*auto-elim* (2Tim. 3.1-*13*). At its best, this is what the old Greeks called *arthro hōraios ponēros*, "the beautiful evil, flourishing in effect and influence." The spirits love it!

The idea of heroes runs, like still waters, very deep. Without a doubt, every-body seems to enjoy and admire the concept of the lone rugged hero, such as *Rambo*, who against all excruciating odds battles scores of baddies and overcomes the impos-sible singlehandedly. Even so, is this not a question of someone else's condition-ing and advertising, of propaganda, we are *trained* to buy into? From whence does this idea come from? The hero gig comes from the very powerful and conniving King Nimrod of *Genesis* 10.8-9. Nimrod was a mighty hunter of animals and human souls. His name means, "Leopard Subduer," "Valiant One," "Let us Rebel," and in the Chaldean idiom *"He-roè."* He was the lone rugged rebel dude who bucked the system as it were. He, along with his father Cush and Grandpa Ham rebelled against goodly Patriarch Noah and successfully took a massive chunk of the world system with them for their own. That is why the rugged and stalwart hero motif still rings out, it setting a massive archetypal precedence that resonates yet today.

21. *Bountied.* That is, 'bound.' Although Kojiro was made rich in life by killing war-riors for power, prestige and rank, nonetheless he was 'bound' to the trade of kill-ing. His ego became so intense, *bound* and *tied* up in self and circumstances, it cost him his life at the hands of Musashi.

24. *That shearing, horrific—* ⋛⤳ *℘℘ Flassssh ℘℘* ⤳⋛ This is the only instance in the entire play that a quad of *interrobangs* (‿) are used (they are mostly used for exclamatory rhetorical questions). A very rare punctuation mark, it is a combination of an exclamation point and a question mark. What the rarified symbol implies is that everyone expected the favored young sword-prodigy Kojiro to win the duel with Musashi but were shocked and stunned when the kid was cut down to size.

25. *More glhorious, eternal name.* Glorious + horror. Kojiro sought great glory by selling his soul and sword skills in order to ensure that his name would be venerated in the annals of Japan. Kojiro, as top-sword, and feeling rather w*horish*, was becoming slowly aware of the atrocities and *horrors* of the murderous bloodshed he was committing, even though it was under the guise of *bushidō*, the 'code of the samurai,' and knight-errantry.

29. *Power unchecked turns one into the fool.* Even sour *crème de la crème* rises to the top. As historian Lord John Action (1834-1902) said, "Power tends to corrupt, and absolute power corrupts absolutely" apparently turning one into an absolute corrupt *fool* (*cf.* Psalm 14.1, *nābāl*, a "stupid, wicked, impious, *vile* person."). Portending to the future, possibly as an investment, Kari fully realizes Theman is in the same boat, a product of corruption absolute, and like a luxuriant evil tree in its own rich native soil, in the Nether he can only but take one its further dark, corrupt characteristics, she knowing the tree by its fruits.

31. *The double-blade master.* Master Musashi was not only a brilliant swordsman/duelist with the single blade, but he was able to fight many opponents at once using two swords, his method called *Ni Ten Ichi*. The name itself is also a metaphor. It means to make the most of what you have available otherwise you will die a dishonorable dog's death. In the *Ground* Chapter of *Five Rings*, the *Meijin* (master) calligraphs:

> Students of the Ichi school Way of strategy should train from the start with the sword and long sword in either hand. This is a truth: when you sacrifice your life, you must make fullest use of your weaponry. It is false not to do so, and to die with a weapon yet undrawn (p. 45).

32. *After untimely disaster.* Kojiro found peace with himself upon his demise. Dying so *untimely* young appears to be 'disastrous.' The term *disaster* is a compound of dis + aster. *Dis* implies a negation while *aster* is a type of daisy that has bright rayed petals, so named after the stars (Gk., *astérs*). What this is saying is that it was considered a *disaster* that Kojiro died in the flowering of his youth as his 'star' was rising, or shall we say inadvertently setting, so to speak.

40. *It began to dawn.* Like Kojiro, Theman has an *epiphany* about himself and his situation. He could conceivably become better and improve his circumstances.

42. *Not a cartoon mask.* Theman realizes that he can become a real man, and not just a bogus 'living cartoon' that everybody sucks up to.

SIXTEEN: KURSCH CHERVÅL

The Turk again now stood and pounded *a demand*,
This, a hard soul who lost his life long before *it* began.
"Tell us of 'love and benevolence' my sweet killing dear,
So that *I*, to its light, may draw to its warmth so near."

Kari *hmmmd* the ways of spirit-men all too well,   5
She could tell at a sharp those bound to Heaven or to Hel.
"A consuming love," said she, "is all that one would need,
For her jealous fires take in all that she can see.

No force can oppose love in Earth or Heaven above,
No, not even *the* damned of Hell can stop relentless Love."   10
Kari eyed the crowd of gloried, enraptured souls,
Hand on hilt, a two-edged swordead tale she now began to unfold.

Still, with hesitance spoke she; flutterance in fragile voice,
It was not a lore she longed for, being envious by discordant choice.
For all that she was, a reed of a girl, untried in the ways of the Hall,   15
Compared to her most 'accomplished' guest—
A flower who lived and died; yet ne'er did fall.

Yet Kari pressed on, telling the ballad open, true and wide,
Of Kursch Chervål, a certain lad-prince and of those whom she 'cid.

"Unique of her kind, this Cossack warrioress,   20
Alone she stands; no peers of regrets.
Her sword, 'Symphony of Destruction,' gleaming at her waist,
Blues notes dripping off, catching the morning's somber lace
(String-bladed instrument full of wiles and grace).

183

Green piercing eyes, green ringed with eternal fires,   25
A blaze unquenched—and *so fuull* of all spirit's desires.
And long and luscious that ashen lithe, blonde hair
(That dark haired maidens whisper jealous in their saddest of despairs).

Indeed her locks floated upon gentle west zephyrs,
Shim'ring in the sun; haloing upon her.   30
Red rubied lips pouted the wisped winter air,
And kissed the cold and embraced—as if she had a lover there.

With shad belly coat and her black whip in tow,
Fair breasts a'gleaned, *'gleaned* 'gainst the whitened snow.
Her name a legend throughout the hushed pressed land   35
(A warrior vixen to be sure—that no spectre could withstand).
Her name only whispered on lonely crossroads,
Her deeds fantastic; (legends bid it so).

And beside her, great *Bursheen*, companion—that ravened-
steeled s'able steed,
Enjoined her in battle amidst red carnage's darkest creeds   40
(Aye and roughshods sundered Styx's blackest weeds).

An unspeakable companion in the rite of death throes fight,
Lightning hoofs of flint and steel *a'sparkin'*; spirits fleeing in the fright.
An ancient team they were, right from Hell's Mouth start,
She and the Hellion-stallion lived each other's tempoed beating hearts.   45

She played the cur for his deadly warhorse dance,
Her stallion *breaching/bucking* in lethal *dressage* parlance.
Cur Airs above the misty cold damnpened ground,
He knew them all—all horrific ancient battle-trumpet sounds.
A treacherous a fighter than ever was bloodlet called.   50
A *Dressier*-in-arms—many did he in hoofen battery fall.

VALLEY OF THE DAMNED

A contrast, yes her golden tresses and his lustful midnight mane,
Eternally bound to the battle, from On High they were together twain.

Kursch Cherval, warrioress deeds too numerous to be redressed,
Yet upon oceans vast and lands beyond her compositions are addressed.   55

Now, the king had summoned in long dead of night,
Her and her spirit for a mission without mortal light.
—To bring the lad-prince safely through,
Through desperate wildernesses and snow that flew.

The clan in trouble; the last of his dynastic line,   60
The prince to sanctuary to a Temple Divine.

The prince she had to deliver both safe and sound,
To go forth alone—no one was to be found.
Many were the trials of the mission accepted,
Sloughs, bogs, plains and deserts; hardnesses attested.   65

Then came the snows, the terrible snows,
Wind whips cold; desperation throes.
A mountain pass; visible bare seen,
To but cross yond'; the prince would be free.

But then the Horde released the mighty wolves,   70
Weremen by day; their appetites predacious, not full—
To track the prince and slay *that* Kursch Cherval,
To gain the clan and jaw-crush the bones of her all.

Wind whistles shrieks and moans,
She heard them coming and strummed her sword bow.   75
Neatly strung the boy tightly to her back,
Prepared for 'The Battle' Overture so that none would come back.

'Sword of Destruction' now in hand,
Played it gently then by *grave de-mand*.
A mournful kakophōny of rhythmed music thus,   80
Made the arrangement—on symphonic *thrust*.

Sword well-ro'sinned now but platinum made,
The diva stepped in; crescendos to be waved.
And then they came, twelve in all,
Weremen but wolves; their feast to fall.   85

Kursch Chervȧl in center of ring,
Heard their growls; a most desperate nocturne thing.
"Give us the boy," one snarled and saliva dripped and snapped,
"And we'll let go you, appetizer, *you* as yet."

Her eyes barbed, then with slight smile,   90
Red their score with a knowing beguile.
"There are twelve of us and only one of you," bared the toothful Were,
"We'll make it short and sweet, 'save you fatigue,' that is, if you come
    to our lair."

"If you were twelve or 1200 it would not matter still,
You see, I've ariaed your howl before, just for *the* kill."   95
Were's eyes gleamed in sudden dissonant inspiration,
The Movement had arrived; 'Death by Blood-fanged Dis-unction.'

*Bloodingicingswhi*rrr*rrlingcolorrrrk-*fuuuulingm*êléeing*,
Symphonic record; notes de-furred, Were's heavy-metalled; waylaid.
Sheaved like slanted razors in the sonorous, bleak winds,   100
An elegy of execution; malodies was to her sword of sin.

An arrangement in blade, fervor to tell,
A chamber*ed* orchestra fit (—*bass, cello, viola, violins*—),

For the bloodspring *pits* of Hell.
Notes fell like lead maces on blood snow *rrr*ifting,   105
Snarlsscreeches died off; the wind doth si*fiff*ting.
Wild music true to its baying call—a sonata all to slay,
Made the impassioned melancholy as the Were's in heaps did lay.

The opus was her sword; virtuoso; played she so very well,
A song she violinced, wailing as it did, her enemies knell.   110
Her edge, no less, she called it her most unchained 'pet,'
That no enemy should boast; it killed in dischord unrelent.

Still resounds the deed on the mountains they say,
And snow and rain falls to commemorate the s'playing day.

Then to the Temple to deliver the boy,   115
The clan was spared to all a great joy.
Honors were heaped upon Kʉrsch Chervàl,
Mistress of the 'slanted light'—(yea: *both wicked and small*)."

Kari lift sighed eyes, knew the woman, resonant,
Yet a hero's tale overall; she would not recant.   120
"Kʉrsch Chervàl, I'll say it again, unique of her kind,
Beware her only, for her harm'ony upon you, you will one day find."

DOUGLAS M. LAURENT

Chapter Sixteen Valley Footnotes

The tale of Kʉrsch Chervàl, last of the *Seven Short-Story Poems*, is, strangely enough, the only one that includes a Valhallan character. Without reference to time, many have tried to decipher as to why such a character should so end the tales and many have died trying. Perhaps it is because tales of heroes transcend time and culture or that our own consciousnesses concerning myths and heroic archetypes eventually merge into the likes of the Deadlands proper taking on cosmic proportions.

Notwithstanding, this charismatic commanding leader apparently hales from the Black Sea region (last known address) and is of Cossack lineage. However, for her bladework she prefers to use a larger version of the *khopesh*. This is the famous curved sickle-sword of the Egyptian gods, pharaohs and their armies. Derived from the Canaanites, the historic *khopesh* "leg of beef," about two feet in length, comes in twin varieties. The first khopesh has a hooking end for snaring and grabbing the enemy or his equipment. It also has a blunt tip used for beating. The other brand has a point for stabbing. Both varieties are sharpened only along the outer end of the forward single-edged curve making for severe hacking and slashing tactics. A stout and reassuring infantry weapon and an icon for nobility authority, the tidy, but bloody weapon, derived from earlier crescent-shaped axeplay, was employed in pitched battle for wholesale slaughter. Chervàl's blade is an excellent hybrid of the two sword types and is inlaid with "green gold" (*electrum*), a natural alloy of gold, silver and copper, its iridescent reflections ranging from pale to bright jewel-tone yellow. The only one in the Nether, her khopesh also has the unique distinction of serving as a stringed instrument upon which she composes her high-strung heavy metal classical malodies.

This unique in kind sword is *harmon*ized to Chervàl's psyche, enabling her to compose astounding destructive masterful compositions while in the midst of combat, notes and melodies attuned to cutting strokes, parries and so on. A veritable powerhouse in her own right, there are many tales yet to be disclosed of her. The story told, simply enough, tells of her exploits in saving an unnamed child-prince for a warrior clan. Kari is hesitant to tell the tale because of Chervàl's accomplished immodesty as a woman of the world compared to her being a plain teenager. She knows her true character very well; the two have often been in competition with each other.

However, this tale of many tiers is the consummation of the *Seven Poems*, and is about ultimate love—a sacrificial *agápē* love that takes numerous forms and guises, like impressions from a looking glass, and is barely visible except to the keenest of eyes. Chervál is known to play many roles in the Mortuuslands (Deadlands), her seeming 'narcissist badness' often is a veneer for 'good,' however she and we and our loving friend the poem defines this, despite Kari's feelings towards her.

3. *Tell us of love.* Kari knows the Turk is being sarcastic. Out of a shortening impatient 'steeled' kindness toward him, she tries to teach the remorseless killer anyway.

7-8. *A consuming love . . . for her jealous fires.* The ultimate nature of the spiritual cosmos is love. Depending how one goes about expressing that love characterizes one as being either good or evil, evil here being defined as taking questionable paths against the establishment in order to obtain what one wants, not particularly needs. Here the line is metaphoric, like that of a lover's love being a consuming jealous well-meaning, protective fire. In Chervál's case, she is extremely passionate, jealous (one can suggest 'hard-loving'), willing to take chances and cut corners bucking the system, 'resisting much and obeying little,' as Walt Whitman (1819-1892) in *Leaves of Grass* (1855) might say, so one may possibly define her as evil, although these attributes may be used for the final good. We must decide what she is. However, because the spiritual universe is grounded in love, it eventually consumes or absorbs all things, good or ill, either drawing all things to its 'soul' or repelling them for the ultimate good. This can be said of our own hearts as they harden or melt like clay or wax under the same "sun."

12. *A two-edged swordead tale.* As Kari plies the tale, there are many 'duel-edged' levels to it she contending with Chervál all the way. The word *swordead* entails a great adventure-action story where there is a hero and much blade work. But she tells it in a sort of way that tinges upon sordidness, that is, she implies on the very rare occasional use of a word that Chervál's actions were ultimately 'unsavory.' *I.e.*, she really was not too worried about saving the prince; that she is really self-serving and ignoble, arousing a slight moral contempt for all who really know her. This is Kari's own biased view of course coming through the text, but her choices of words and tone, which we can read and hear, reflects her

feelings towards this 'creature-creature' woman as Kari might say. This darker strain of Kari's personality slipping through a few words here and there in her story shows her immaturity and many realizations that come to her along the telling. She knows a lot more about Chervàl than beats the eardrum or cares to think about, she considering the whole engagement concerning her a waste of time and effort, but nonetheless, the matchless teen fires on.

14-15. *Not a lore she longed for being envious . . . reed of a girl.* Although a true genius and mature in her own right, that is, being a literary-sword savant, exemplary shrewd, Kari is nonetheless eternally fixed at being an immature teenager and so she doesn't understand a lot of adult things. She is jealous of Chervàl who is a masterful warrior and woman of the world and can never compete with her in her womanly prowess.

17. *A flower who lived and died; yet ne'er did fall.* Being of royal Cossack blood, Chervàl never stained her honor in any way, shape or form.

19. *And of those whom she 'cid.* That is, 'cut, kill,' from Latin *caedere*, as seen in the terms 'virlupicide' (killing of werewolves), 'hosticide' (killing an enemy) and 'monstricide' (killing a monster), all three of which Chervàl has conveniently done in times past.

21. *Alone she stands; no peers of regrets.* Being masterfully trained in the ways of royalty and a brilliant commander, Chervàl has made little or no mistakes in her long and action-packed colorful career. Therefore she has no regrets.

26. *—and so fuull of all spirit's desires. Lit.,* "full + fool." Kari's magnificent use of the language on multi-levels tells us that not only are there many spirit's *full* of desire to, in a manner of speaking, love, *desire* and so 'possess' Chervàl, but they are *fools* as well to want her so. The kid is pretty tricky with her tongue!

39. *And beside her, great Bursheen.* The root proto-*Valhallan* term *Bursheo* literally means, "Fire of [in] the Soul." Bursheen is a huge black shiny Frisian war-horse, a veteran of many battles.

41. (*Aye and roughshods sundered Styx's blackest weeds*). Here, the great Nether-Frisian Bursheen runs *roughshod* over their enemies, breaking, severing them into pieces, they becoming *sundered* or 'under red,' *i.e.*, all bloodied up underneath the mighty animal. The phrase, *Styx's blackest weeds*, is troublesome. Some translations render it as *Sticks as black as weeds*, that is to say, *evil's blackest weeds and/or deeds*. However, the tighter interpretation is truer to its word in that it is a reference to the River Styx of Greek mythology. Since Styx is the "River of Hate" and was so well-respected by both the gods and heroes who pledged unbreakable oaths over its very name, it seems likely that the phrase means something to the effect that Bursheen and Chervål trample underfoot even the most *vilest* of deeds, *i.e.*, *evil's blackest weeds* overcoming them.

44. *Right from Hell's Mouth start.* A 'Hell-Mouth' is a depiction derived from Medieval and earlier pictures of the opening of Hell. They are characterized by a huge demonic creature or god with a tooth-distorted gaping yap so rotten that a cosmetic dentist would love to study it just to write an article on it, and volatile breath reeking so bad that it fire-flashes up human combustion. Within the sputumy, drooling Hell-Mouth's gaping cavity are swarming packs of chewy granola-style long-lasting dead shrieking souls *on the cusp*, the 'tooth biting edge,' the 'point in time that marks the start of something.'

    There they will be for a very long time, as Mr. HM, as Shakespeare's *King Richard III* (II. iv.), "could gnaw a crust at two hours old." And besides, Mouthy is a slow gluttonous gut-packer as well, and likes to 'diene' on his daily bread. On a good day, even when Hell-Mouth is pleasantly cooking with his "Class K" fire-grade kitchen oils and fats, his cui*sine* of souls is oft accompanied by blowtorches of howling torture, squealing misery festering firenado's (temperatures up to 2,000 degrees F), and screechings of ghastly soul-geyser eruptions. Often *die*ting, he yet enjoys listening to the ill-joyous sounds of his charbroiled cacophonic hellenly pyoir beating their *marrow-bones and cleavers* that are really a hot commodity these days. Hell-Mouth is a regular molten soul-blasting insinerator sort of fiend. And not being bulimic, he never, ever visits the fabled *vomitoria*, as a goodly binge-purging hard-partying Roman might do even if they had them. In lieu of this nonsense, both Chervål and Bursheen have fiery hellish consuming temperaments. (On "marrow-bones and cleavers," study the rowdy *Skimmington* (ride)-style parade designed to humiliate people, *ca.* 1796.)

46-51. *She played the cur . . . lethal dressage . . . Cur Airs . . . Dressier-in-arms.* Bursheen has been well-trained in the art of *dressage*, French for 'to train,' the battlefield war-horse art. He is known for his brilliant maneuvers, horse and rider complimenting each other perfectly on the battlefield being of one accord. *Cur* is French *curvet*, a move made in response to a rider who leans to one side of the horse's body to curve him into action. *Cur Airs* is a classical move in which the horse jumps up and kicks out, leaving the ground.

57. *A mission without mortal light.* That is, a suicide mission, one of little hope of return.

68. *Visible bare seen.* Apparently, this phrase can be rendered several ways. One as in the mountain pass is *barely visibly seen* through the thick snows, or *visibly*, it is just a raw, *bare scene*. The phrase can be read like pounding a hammer, each word being hard and accented, or it can be read in a flowing manner, depending upon which continuity we choose to interpret it. Both renditions are acceptable however and can be mulled over for a greater poetic affect.

70-71. *But then the Horde . . . Weremen by day.* This may be possibly the Mongol Horde, although the text does not state it. *Weremen.* The ancient term *werewolf* means 'man-wolf' and implies a shape-shifting quality. People like this are psycho. However, there is somewhat of an Underworld devitwistation occurring here. These Weres were not exactly *were* or 'man-wolves,' but on the contrary, these were wolves that turned into men, and not just this, they only transformed during days when there was no full sun! So looking kindasorta like 'men' most of the time—or what marginally passed for men, they had incredible beyond Dire wolfish senses and behaviors and were viciously bestial to the core. Although not cited or described, it is well known in the Lands Dread that werepigs often act as auxiliaries to the Weremen clans so it is assumed several were on hoof to assist their masters here. They are usually omitted from formal Netherscripts because they are so disgusting and deemed 'less than human.' Chervàl definitely has her hands full. (Ch. 33 note # 347-348 for Dire Wolf.)

79. *Then by grave de-mand.* Grave + rave. *Grave* is a musical term to denote that the movement is to be played slow and serious. However, built into the word is *rave*, meaning that even though Chervàl initially played slow and serious warming up, her music began to *rave* in anticipation of *de-man*ning or killing off the opposition.

81. *Made the arrangement—on symphonic thrust.* As Chervàl composes with her sword, 'Symphony of Destruction,' she masterfully crescendos her piece to the thrusts of her blade, hence the whole battle is punctuated and 'cymbalized' by sharp, succinct sound and movement as a coordinated whole. She is an exceptional master. A kindred Midgard spirit to the very commanding Chervàl, although no less fiery is *Cyrano de Bergerac,* swordpoet dueling soldier *par excellence*. While at the theatre, he is threatened by a jealous rival. After composing a complex ballade, while dueling he recites it perfectly to accompany his masterful swordplay rhythms, ending the conflict with the in-motion immortal fluid line, "Then, as I end the refrain . . . —Thrust home!" He proclaims this exacting phrase precisely as he skewers his rival, to the enraptured cheers of the crowd. (Edmond Rostand, 1868-1918, *Cyrano*, I. *See* the 1950 *Kramer Production* starring José Ferrer. He is supreme.) Musashi, with your 'Munen Muso' bit, eat your heart out! (Ch. 22 note # 121-122.)

82. *Sword well ro'sinned.* Chervàl metaphorically ro*sins* up her 'sword-bow' as they do with stringed instruments so that it will play exceptionally well. She is well known for her complex compositions, that are 'sinfully' wicked, or 'bad,' that is, a brilliant medley from classical to heavy metal.

97. *The Movement . . . 'Death by Blood-fanged Dis-unction.'* Not that 'the moment' had arrived, but the symphonic *'Movement'* had, meaning that there was about to be a symphony of bloody violent chaos about to be performed upon Chervàl—at least, that is what the Weremen thought. The same concept appears in line # 77, where Chervàl prepares for the opening sequences of *'The Battle' Overture* she is about to compose

and play on her adversary/victim Weremen. Defined, *unction* is a "fervent manner of speaking or behaving." *Dis* here is rendered as a negation hence the Wereman beast is speaking hellishly, guttural-like, fervent and misbehaving very badly. His distinct rhythmic otherworldly dialect is only a lead-in *prelude*—a short piece of music that begins a more substantial composition—to the 'Symphony of Destruction' Chervàl will mete out with her finely-tuned musical blade of the self-same name.

98. *Swhirrrrlingcolorrrrk-fuuuulingmêléeing.* The visual imagery here is all a blurry motion, as one would see in battle. In order to understand nether-concepts better, colors, like the descriptively angular off-beat fused wording ('twistorted'), normal words whether revealed with *italics* or not that have words within them (*e.g.* 'heat'), re-arranged words (devilered), stanzas, focuses, twists, and their inherent rhythms must be viewed as 'in-motion,' as our mind's work. In Ch. 5 on *Force*, Li Quan, *Art of War* Sun Tzu's pal says "nothing is fixed in the art of war."

99. *Heavy metalled; waylaid.* Chervàl's blade, playing excerpts of heavy-*metal* music, *led* the *way* to her enemy's destruction, way laying, or ambushing them. In sum, she heavily 'met-all.'

101. *An elegy of execution; malodies.* An *elegy* is an instrumental lament praising the dead. 'Mal' as in 'bad' or 'evil' + melodies. Chervàl's fevered racked tunes are melodic yet terrible in scope to hear. She is a sight to behold, a blur of music and motion becoming one.

110. *A song she violinced . . . her enemies knell.* Violin + violence. Chervàl's composition is macabre, energetic and violent, that is full of passion. By composing her nightmarish song, she writes the score to her enemy's death *knell*. A paradox, a *knell* is a bell rung to announce a death or a funeral. It also precipitates or indicates death and destruction. Sounding mournful, it is an ominous warning as well. Apparently, some of the 'movements' within Chervàl's little arrangement indicates these qualities whether performed fast or slow. A variant of this stanza is cited as well through the phrase, *her enemies quelled.* 'Quell' is to put one's enemies down forcibly, suppressing them, and in this stanza killing them

off. Both phrases and words work. By quelling her enemies, Chervål performs funeral music for their knell.

118. *Mistress of the 'slanted light'—(yea: both wicked and small).* As in cinema where a character stands in the light of a window with slanted curtains, the effect is to give the character a questionable disposition, telling of their clouded personality and situation. Here, the line renders Chervål's character as dubious. She could be good or bad depending on circumstances. But Kari knows her well enough to whisper the line *both wicked and small*, meaning she knows she is tall in stature among her peers but short in height as was Napoleon, and more scheming than good. It is a slight against Chervål.

SEVENTEEN: THE WINNOWING OF VALHALLA

As Kari breathed her last, door ⌇🪓¡BUR←R→RSTING¡🪓⌇ Open Wide!¡!
Hordes of shrieking creatures rushing, gaining the desirous Inside!!
Valhalla, beloved great Hall, under sieging attack!
Damned apparition's pouring in, war-axing men's backs*!!*

Depraving spirits in carnivality *a'slaughterin'* the nobles,   5
Who, falling back, with them took they many a soiled opponents.
Bold courageous countering attacks, it was not enough,
To hold back contagion's plague from *its conspiracy of destruct.*

In through the boiling *mêlée*, Black ✳ Sun came crushing in,
Along with Dark Storm, who had incited the rioting therein.   10
For she, having breathed covetous lies into Sun's vaperous mind,
Fanned the ether and body celestial, to use her in her good time.

As she cut down souls, Dark Storm remembered the long phobic night,
How she toiled with Black Sun, unto Sun's sinister deadlight.
Told her of feverished secrets that lied in wait wor herd,   15
Dark Storm, yes, she remembered, the lies that she in wanton whored. . . .

(. . . Storm rode strong into the camp of *the* vast and cavernous dead,
Sliced lowly spirits back for depraving her in their eager stead—
Found Black Sun at council fire, her mind with hates thus fed.
Flames flickered, drenched all in red dashed stains,   20
Their charred hardts hardened, their evil forever ingrained.

VALLEY OF THE DAMNED

Their weapons oiled o'er sleeked, insensed the night,
Under dull moon waxing, lycanthroping for fight.
Wolf-hounds baying, sounding the troubled alarm,
Wicked spirits pricked their ears, seeking to do harm.   25

Spek'tral horses grhazed in dismal sub-light,
Splint'd saddles with bones all pulled out of joint.
Great she-wolfs tugged at adamantine taut chains,
To seize and tear the prey, to murder their *chi* away.

Weapons smithed with *that* powerful curse,   30
Thirsted for blood from wounds they'd coerce.
Charged instruments, with those powers of Hel,
That spirits should inhabit, their steel indwelt.

Self-hate was *their* tribe's gross pestilence,
By which they hoped to purge themselves of good's eminence.   35
But hate fused their souls to fanaticed base amends,
Into the bane of their existence, their souls sealed in.

Wraiths and dervishes of every shape and size,
Great horned creatures with glowing black eyes.
Spirits hunched about consuming firelight,   40
Weapons of battle clutched in their clawish gripe.

And mighty men of renown known more for their name,
Which empties their vesture upon entry to the grave.
The wicked, *always* charged from wrathful humanities store,
Sheol, dribbling blood, never ceases for wanting the more.   45

They peeped, muttered and sharped their idol gods of war,
Red blades *a'hissin'* as they warshipped their executors.
Spirit's eyes lost deep in dark and brooding thought,
Of the life they once had and now forever lost.

Accursed demons and spirits of the appalling night,   50
Sought their vic'try through deception's groping blight.
Spirits o'war wail through the drearful land,
Plotting destruction far below—in the Valley of the Damned.

As they squatted around their smoldry, witchy pots,
Dark Storm spawned seditions to kill the entire noble lot.   55
Smoke poured forth, wretched of its murky, greasy din,
Hushed voices brash, spoke of killing victims.

Dark Storm surveyed this, this repulsive, helish camp,
Hands on hips; how they drooled, shout and stamp—
The inhabitants sang, nay, were compulsed to chant: 60

"Woe to those of mortal kin,
Woe to those, whom we find therein,
Woe to those, whom fall to our device,
Woe to those whose souls we sacrifice."

As they sat, a brazen cup was off'd to all to rudd,   65
Gorged Black Sun she on that sacra'mental blood.
Chaliced and blessed by souls a'damned,
The deadly draught—of cursed spirits and men.

All of nature was disposed to grope,
With branches bent over the red-hot coals.   70
Trees and night creatures, they listened in,
To Death's council of the final, immortal sin.

Many renowned led the ghoulish ghastly array,
Moredread, Grendel and Death herself told of Hades' display.
Lord Mars abode in the grisly camp too,   75
He came often, yet on Earth still had much to do.

Mawort Ars and Vlad the Prince lead many a debased shade,
From helbound spirits to Nephílim to those fresh from the grave.
Great ones from river Euphrates were to lead them to their knell,
The Four and Apollyon to deliver them to their master—   80
Waiting at the chops of Hell.

Unhumaned, unheroed, unangeled, ungodded—
They were all there,
Down in this–this Valley of Living, Eternal Despair.
Souls no more unhumaned than destiny decries,   85
Sword in hand urges them to battle again ➢ another day to die.

And at the heart, the twisted black heart, there upon stood,
A great gathering of champing Valkyries ready for *their* food.
Feminining war-spirits of longhaired, jawed majestic evil intent,
Seeking to revenge themselves upon enemies for whom they had
grim bent.   90

These were *they*, who had forsaken the righteous battle-call,
Mercenaries of unmentionable horrors of *that* unspeakable fall.
These who left their first estate for fame unto their self's,
They were of that tribe of the damned, doomed to never rest.

How many nations and men have you led to their doom?   95
Of riches beyond the hinter and have given the damned to ruin?
O' thou powerful spirits of the deep forest Germany,
Odin's men you have lied to, they are never let free.

Leaders without equals were these wicked feminine few,
Fe-demons of Teutonic steel from the Black Forest sloughs.   100
Unparalleled in battle their enemies they disdained,
They were Odin's mistresses, accursed—'Choosers of the Slain.'

It was *they* who filled Valhalla for the *status quo*,
Far beyond all spirit powers, toward good or evil they did not blow.
Evil twice, nay thrice over for never once taking sides,   105
Felons from Dante's prison, their mercenary judgments did abide.

Yet such fierce warriors were they, the dead did pay them well,
They paid for the Valkyries' honor, to lead multitudes to Hel.
And although they ministered to these dead and profane faithless crews,
The Valkyries knew bad and ill—   110
That in the end they would destroy them too.

Dark Storm smiled as she viewed the grim, disgusting lot,
An incredible subterfuge in her mind she had already longed plot.
Beyond the din of the Valkyries her dirge was under way,
A plan unholied, designed for the innocent to betray.   115

She offered Black Sun information to gain,
The land of Valhalla and all that it became.
To fill her coffer, and to destroy her enemies,
To rule the land entire in blasvenomous monarchies.

"Take what you wish," Storm said, *heh*, "for the damned's sake,   120
But that man's prize-soul is mine, she recalled, ready to take . . .").

Now wounded she a lighter who intersected her path,
Demanded the man's name, then in rage, loosed him from her hack.
Stalking her victim laughing she recalled her amusing task,
Of seducing that Sun fool to do her call and beck.   125

(. . . The stately one had arose, she with long dark hair,
She, the regal of the Eastern empire's affair.
With long flowing robe and besmirched kabukied face,
Her naginata in hand to shed blood of *the* race.

How she came to the Valkyries, they all surely knew,　　　　　130
A sisterhood of fe-spirits, this was the 'soul' clue.
Upon agreeing with Storm, Sun, war-spirit of old Japan,
Only then searched derisive faces out, as to how to blame the man.

Yet, "all of *Valhalla*," Sun thought, deeply concernedly she,
"And all Storm wants is to keep a soul apart *from diabolic me?*　　135
Spah! 'Morrow's battle may find Dark Storm no more,
An accident, perhaps, and I will have him cored."

"Sisters" said Sun, "let us not vie,
High council has ruled that St. Kari must die.
For she was once one of ours, now gone astray,　　　　　140
She sits on council seat with our enemies across the way"
[Aye, dark 'Kyries do not care for those who openly take sides,
Too much good in them; like a stick in Sun's basilisk evil eye].

Vlad the Prince, looked o'er the weapons' tiers,
Pole implements to imbed, excited him in fier.　　　　　145
'Sharp keys to Hell,' these long devices were,
Spear, naginata, bill, and the mutilating halberdier.

These shunned from the place of noble weapons formed,
Found their home as he spit enemies, bodies suspended, in scarlet adorned.
Regarded by many as unfit and rank for a hand born high,　　　150
"Yet with each turn of the skew," he thought, "and their souls
　　shall be mine."
These nosferrius edges told not for whom they came,
Silent as church bells at midnight they summoned thee—
Whilst their bedeviled steel rang.

Vlad, Sun's vizier, then *whisp-her-red* to say,　　　　　155
"Tomorrow in battle when Kari goes to that fool's aid,
He will turn the stake upon her, and impale her on his blade."

201

Around a thousand council fires the Valkyries gathered,
Searched the furnaced flame for *the* ideal that mattered.
The vast throng pondered the Impaler's thought for a tarnished moment, 160
Then disdained to deliver their own to those dead for increased torment.
But dread outweighed black reason; her penchant for resurprisal,
Killing her would gain the name; it was better than lying—horizontal.

The razing of the Hall yet had aroused the rest of that motley band,
They would take the home of the righteous and consign it to their hands. 165
The conflict of the Ages would finally be complete,
Victory would be theirs and *their* conquest at last replete. . .).

In the midst of the Hall battle they did finally meet,
The Dead Yet Alive man and that evil she-seed.
Eyes locked on each other, the man remembered her face,   170
Knew he was her prey, and from the wall ripped a mace.

Dark Storm smiled knowingly, and with sickle taking aim,
"Put it down," she said smoothly. "All I want is your name."
The man gazed at her in puzzlement, furned his maced shaft,
She slicening her way through the swarm, squaring to attack.   175

Eternity in the moment when bodies do freeze,
To reconnoiter danger, to fight or to flee.
Hands *vice*-gripped weapons; the man's sweaty palm,
She tapped her fingers; his feet of lead sutured the ground.

Dark Storm hackening a path to the little movie man,   180
Who rushed toward her from his anemic killing stand.
Brushed Storm aside falling bodies with iron imbued,
Engaging she warriors of whom many she slew.

"*The* name," she demanded, raising dripping blade,
The man attempted parry, but it was a move feigninged.   185
She 'sixing' a leering line upon his bloody human head,
Marking *it* out as one of her own, one of *her* future dead.

"Your name," she grimaced laughing, enjoying her slashes,
The man staggering back, unable to engage or smash her.
Impatient, she knocked the man and placed her hand on his heart,   190
—A force tore between them; it was Li who wrenched her apart.

"Fall back!" a far command was heard, and the air roared with pain,
The man getting to his knees saw legs in smoky haze.
Arms picked him up and placed him on his feet,
The man, he rolled his head, Li was there to see.   195

"What was that?" the man said to Li,
Li smiled, thought his friend was of the ancestry.

"She is the one who denied her king,
Who sold her birthright for past flesh off'rings.
Storm Rising was she who on Earth her art was great,   200
Who denied *the* self-less mandate and is now reprobate."

"She wanted my name," the man gasped to Li,
"What did she want it for; for God's sake tell me."

"We are one of many clans that patrol the Valley's of the Damned,
Eternal warfare is ours, to live and die; our exulted command.   205
The longer one lives the more powerful and wanted they become,
If you lose, it's over—on the last rung you'll again have just begun."

The man knew now his name was *the* commodity,
That his soul was his, a power to bandy.
"Come, Theman," said Li, "the battle is not yet taken,   210
The righteous must win, or all will be forsaken."

Off into the night rushed the man and noble Li,
One to fulfill his grand martial destiny,
The other, to engage in battle and find the mystery,
Of his life's meaning at the hands of his enemy.   215

VALLEY OF THE DAMNED

Chapter Seventeen Valley Footnotes

After a fine evening of entertainment and Mark Theman 'the man' getting an ear full of high talk and ethics, those of the dark attack Valhalla in a sneaky underhanded scheme to destroy the good, capture Theman for Dark Storm and wipe out the current Valhallan leader, Kari.

1. *As Kari breathed her last.* A portent.

5. *Spirits in carnivality.* Carnal + carnival. Linguist Jonathan Mycroft renders the idea of one of gross indulgence on the part of the wicked as they act out their animal natures in a riotous and gleeful-like atmosphere.

9. *Black ✳ Sun.* Pronounced 'Swun.' This is another evil war-leader of tremendous power. She is not however a mercenary as is Dark Storm, but a chieftess. She is a Valkyrie-type creature gone renegade from a far and distant land-dimension—old Japan. It is said that Sun wore an eight-pointed crown on occasion to purposely infuriate and disbalance Kari, who, for some unknown reason, was said to be *októphobic*.

11. *Sun's vaperous mind.* Vapor + viper. As gathered from other fragmented ancient accounts such as the eleventh century *Heliaspur Saga* and the tenth century *Bough of Conleif*, we may conclude that from Storm's point of view, Black Sun is vicious, but not much in the brains department. However, to be a great chieftess in the Deadlands is a big thing, so we can see how much sharper Storm really is as she gets this air-head 'viper' to do her bidding.

15-16. *Lied in wait wor herd . . . the lies that she in wanton whored.* For +war. Storm is lying to Sun, not that Sun was going to get something out of the deal. Jonathan Mycroft suggests the phrase *wor herd* be taken as one word. If so, *wor herd* implies the 'peddling of the flesh,' just like its rhyming sister counterpart speaks. Promoting and being *for* this particular up-coming *war* battle, Storm cleverly has laid a trap for Sun, *her(d)* and is literally selling her out by getting her to buy into the idea of going to battle. In fact, one might even say all wars are acts of whoredom, in that gluttonous power-mad fat old Plutopimps hawk the lives of younger men and escorts out on the streets by getting them to go screw people over and kill them psychically or physically—and in return they getting paid a pittance for it. *Wormongers* have much more powerful addicting street drugs to 'hook' their property on to do their lucrative bidding—fine sounding stirring words. So what's the diff between a gutter strumpet and a battle trumpet? Words. Even the "p" in words such as hockey 'puck' and boxing 'pugilism' show consonant shifts over time, yet retain the meaning of 'to strike.' *Herd* implies that storm is manipulating Sun, *her*, the evil 'kabukied' spirit. In the illusionary *Ukiyo* "floating world" of the *Kabuki Theater* of old Japan (amongst other questionable places), characters often caked their faces with white make-up, giving them a ghost-like appearance. Spooky Black Sun then is as white as a sheet with a ghostly appearance of jet black hair and an alabaster, ghastly, waxen ivory pasted face, her bright red lips making her appear blood glutted, the total effect being unworldly. Kabuki was a type of 'heroic' bawdy theatre in medieval Japan, popular with commoners and samurai. Officials, however, frowned on it in its early stages of growth as they felt it not fitting entertainment for the samurai class.

21. *Their charred hardts.* Heart + hard. These are twice over exceptionally hardened hearts.

22. *Their weapons oiled o'er.* Black oil is the thought here and under the dull moon and firelight, it gives off a dark, eerie, glistening evil-looking sheen. This sickening, twisted nimbusing aura of the evil master's oozones off these tools of Hell. This brings up the concept of *glosses, vapors and remnants*. All actions of the mind and body leave characteristic 'imprints' or 'signatures' on reality and in the Nether this is exponentially magnified. Barely discernible, these 'trace elements' are found all over in the occulmartic arts there—word phrases, postures, hand positions, eye movements and preferences, likes and dislikes of all sorts. Paralleling, in the Midgard arts, all classically rooted systems have 'weapon vapors,' or 'glosses' 'imprints' or 'signatures' on their empty-hand play and body posturing, *e.g.*, a deep horse stance, at first used for holding long heavy weapons like a *quan-do*. Later the horse translated to empty-hand combat. These remnants, once noted, allows at least two things to

happen. One is we can reconstruct past action. *E.g.*, we see heavy-handed iron-hard "pounding" blocks from Hung gar kung-fu that reflects heavy weapons use (staff, sword) in the past. With this bridge, we may then "see" into the "philosophical mindset" of the artist or opposition, as the mindset (attitudes, perceptions, outlooks and ways of doing things) is usually handed down fairly intact, even though the physical aspect of an art may degrade. In terms of self-defense, the phrase, "Tell me what you eat, and I will tell you what you are" by French Epicure Jean Brillat-Savarin (1755-1826) is useful here. A person simply moves and behaves according to their life philosophy, experience and training along certain routes of action. Seeing these characteristic vaporous leftover imprints and faded signatures allows one to be up on matters, a vital necessity to spirits in the darker regions of soul, mind and dimension—always at war with itself.

22. *Insensed the night.* Insensible + incensed + incest. According to popular science writer Hector Kyle, the notion here is that since these are 'false' weapons, that is, being used for dark purposes, they have lost their true way and cutting virtues, having been cut off from their own true nature. The original intention of any weapon, it seems, is to be used for the general good. The result is that the weapons have a self-centered spirit and great rage, much as their masters do. They are insensible, their elemental spirits seared or hardened for their evil *vile* tasks.

It appears that certain weapons in the Deadlands have a 'primordial knowledge' of what is right and wrong, in the beginning least ways, and this can be said to be true of weapons forged in righteousness. In this section of the text, these are weapons 'born bad'; denied their 'birthright' of goodness there being the connotation of incest here as well. These particular weapons are illegitimate offspring of the dark unions of spiritual wickedness (the darklanders creating these weapons knowing what they will be used for) and of violent, hexed forging techniques.

In light of this, mythologist Etta Jörgens sees in this personification a subtle law being worked out in the Nether. Weapons, which are regarded as having rudimentary spirits, become the shadowy reflections of their master's worth. These weapons like grim evil and the work thereof. World history, as found in Japan and Iceland, tell tales of good and bad weapons, and their spirits. In Indonesia, swords were known to 'rattle' in their sheaths to warn their owners of impending danger.

23. *Lycanthroping.* These are spirits acting as drooling 'berserk' wolves in their fit to fight. In some ancient societies, such as old Iran, 'wolf,' or *vraka* societies of soldiers followed the tactics of the animal in battle. (*See* Ch. 18 note # 110 for berserks.)

28. *Adamantine taut chains.* This is extremely tough material.

29. *To murder their chi away. Chi.* Spanish for a form of 'stew.' Also, in classical Chinese cosmology *ch'i* is a personification of the soul, the mental/psychological structure of a person, their mind, vital energy, breath, power, *etc.* In context the beasts desire to rip away and devour the souls of their enemies as they would a delicious stew.

30. *That powerful curse.* In many instances, charms and hexes are put on weapons to give them extra power. It is thought in the old North as well as the East, that weapons 'had souls' and in Icelandic literature, we find feminine war spirits (the *Fylgjukona, Fylgja, etc.*) guarding family swords down through generations, even helping out those family members who possessed a particular sword, thus the idea of a sword being indwelt or having magical powers. Here we see the Nether-dynamic of this behind-the-scenes type of activity.

34. *Tribe's gross pestilence.* As on Earth, wicked spirits are known to cause diseases, *Matthew* 9.32-33, *Luke* 8.27-29. In our text, this pestilence is more like a spiritual disease or derangement. Like war and poverty, in the Etherlands, emotional and spiritual afflictions are part of the programmed 'commodities' that are circulated among the wicked for control and gain. These dark commodities are used to maneuver the masses into doing a more powerful spirits bidding. Jealousy, rage, despair, hate, *etc.* in the Valzone, therefore, are the merchandises the wicked 'traffick in,' foisting off these 'products' on the unwary and weak for percentage gain. In this instance, not only is this tribe a victim of such circumstances, but also its originators and perpetrators—they have taken the poison unto themselves and are now trapped and addicted by it within their own persons.

40. *Consuming firelight.* The fire was exposing and eating these evil spirit-souls alive, or rather dead, a dark antithesis to God's fire-like all-consuming Love.

41. *Their clawish gripe.* 'Grip.'

42. *Mighty men of renown.* This is a biblical phrase for the pre-Flood *Nephílim* giants. *See Genesis* Chapter Six. However, in this case the text is referring to the bad side's 'heroes,' such as the earlier mentioned Cassius. This descriptive passage suggests that even great people lose their identity upon entry to the grave, and a fading memory is all they get as their 'big reward.' The pop-phrase, 'he who dies with the most toys wins,' is a very misleading statement. The quest for temporal gain at the expense of the eternal soul should be reviewed accordingly, after all, what does it profit a man if he gains the world but loses his soul?

44. *Charged from wrathful humanities store.* These bad spirits are always and ever supplied with what they need from the festering ranks of swollen humanity—these being all too willful to join in.

45. *Sheol, dribbling blood, never ceases.* *Sheol* is the Hebrew term for the unseen world, the place where the dead go. The term is often rendered 'Hell,' 'pit' and 'grave,' which is what our text is alluding to.

46. *They peeped, muttered.* This is a condensed amalgamation of small dark mutterings and cursing which is what one would expect to hear from many rotten disgruntled soldier-spirits. One can hear shades of this in Dante's windstorm, *Canto* Five, *Inferno*, indicative perhaps of lost loves and dreams.

51. *Sought their vic'try through deception's groping blight.* This refers to a half-baked, fractured *trying* attempt at victory. *Deception's blight.* Blight + light. This speaks of a diseased, fungal lie that deceives with false light.

52. *The drearful land.* Dreary + fearful.

58. *This, this repulsive, helish camp.* Words fail to describe here. Even Dark Storm finds this vast camp of wretched spirits disgusting. In fact, entering the camp she has to kill a few of the more rambunctious spirits who insult her and want her

soul. This gives us a glimpse that even the villains in the Nether have their prefer-
ences and own levels of morality. Some spirits, simply put, are more debauched
than others in this Land of the Dead. *See* poem line # 18, *Sliced lowly spirits back for
depraving her in their eager stead—*, meaning these spirits had no respect for trying
to deprive her of her depraved life.

66. *That sacra'mental blood.* The powers of darkness have their own deranged anti-
light rituals arrayed against goodness.

72. *The final, immortal sin.* The idea is 'goodicide,' the wiping out of all that is good—
namely the elimination of good angels, human folk, the creation and anything else
that sides with these.

74. *Moredread, Grendel.* This spirit while on Earth was Modred, King Arthur's bas-
tard son who sought to usurp Camelot from him, while *Grendel* is the poeticized
'demon' who fought the hero Beowulf. Cooper (pp. 150, 238) cites that Grendel
was in fact an extinct species of lizard that lasted into recent times and gives more
than fifty named descriptions of similar beasts:

> By the time of his slaying the monster Grendel in AD 515, Beowulf himself
> had already become something of a seasoned hunter of large reptilian mon-
> sters. He was renowned amongst the Danes at Hrothgar's court for having
> cleared the local sea lanes of monstrous animals whose predatory natures had
> been making life hazardous for the open boats of the Vikings. Fortunately, the
> Anglo-Saxon poem, written in pure celebration of his heroism, has preserved
> for us not just the physical descriptions of some of the monsters that Beowulf
> encountered, but even the names under which certain species of these animals
> were known to the Saxons and Danes.

This perhaps explains why the Vikings had dragon figures on the prows of their long
boats—to keep the real ones away! But there is another interesting point to all this:
these 'sea reptiles' must have been real, just as Beowulf was. This is because what-
soever a society places value on, the more descriptive terms or names that object

has. This process of labeling allows for a more thorough scrutiny, application and discrimination of that object across a diverse cultural area. Master Japanese garden designer David A. Slawson pens:

> Names are an important key to what a society values. Anthropologists recognize naming as 'one of the chief methods for imposing order on perception.' What is not named in a culture very likely goes unnoticed by the majority of its people. The converse is also true: people pay greater attention to things that have been given names. Names tend to cluster in those areas of human life that are highly valued, because with valuation comes the need and desire for greater discrimination. Consider the number of words that we in the United States have for money—the 'Almighty Dollar.' In other cultures we are struck by the number of names people have to distinguish varieties of snow, or bamboo (p. 133).

75. *Lord Mars*. This is the Roman god of war. Here though, he is more of a mercenary type.

77. *Mawort Ars and Vlad*. *Mawort Ars* is the ancient Indo-European term for 'martial arts,' here personified as being wicked. *Vlad* or 'Vlad the Impaler' as he is known to our history, is the dire spirit of Dracula. In this case, like so many others, his remains is not a 'ghost' as we would understand the term, but a ghost's hideous, disproportionate 'remains,' so he's a real baddie for now. Dracula, by the way, is a curiosity in the Deadlands. He is dead, a spirit-remnant, but he is also an 'undead,' a *Nosferatu*, a sickly weird Nether-combination to be sure.

78-80. *Nephílim . . . great ones . . . the four . . . Apollyon*. *Nephílim* are the alleged crossbred offspring of fallen angels and humans, those exceedingly wicked creatures God wiped out in the Flood of around five thousand years ago, *Genesis* Six. The *great ones* are the four mighty angels presently bound at the river Euphrates (modern Iraq sits on this spot) who will lead a two-hundred million man/demonized army from the Far East to the battle of *Armageddon, Revelation* 9.14. Today China boasts of a militia of over two hundred million men. *The four* refer to the Four Horsemen of the Apocalypse—War, Famine, Pestilence and Death, *Revelation*, Ch. Six. Greek *Apollyon, lit.*, "Destruction," is the captain of the angels of 'the Pit,' or the abyss, *Revelation* 9.1-11. These too are to be let out at *Armageddon* to wreak terrible destruction upon the Earth before the second coming of Christ. Christ is the 'second Adam' and He will come to reclaim the stolen Earth from Lucifer who ripped it off from the first King of the Earth, Adam.

82-83. *Unhumaned . . . all there.* All categories of bad folk are lumped together here, regardless of class, distinction or creation.

84. *Valley of Living, Eternal Despair.* As with all regions of the Mortuuslands, names are metaphorical in nature, corresponding to the inhabitants (and our) own shifting minds, perspectives and feelings. Thus, this is just another name for the Valley of the Damned and its surrounding areas.

91-94. *These were they . . . never rest.* This stanza does not appear in later translations of the *Upsalan* texts after A.D. 700. *Left their first estate* derives from the *Letter of Jude.* It speaks of the angels who forsook Heaven rejecting their original station that their Creator had given them. This gives a hint as to the Valkyries' possible origins. If they were previously angels, Lucifer took a third of them with him in the great rebellion, *Revelation* 12.4

95-97. *How many nations . . . Germany.* Ancient Germany is the major home for the Valkyries. Odin is known to be a liar. He promises great things like victory, honor and booty, but he gets men drunk and then gets them to promise outrageous things in front of their buddies for a coming battle, they only ending up horribly maimed or killed. History reflects that many crippled soldiers denounced Odin afterwards for being false.

100. *Fe-demons of Teutonic steel from the Black Forest.* This line refers to bad feminine war-spirits whose old haunts were Northern Europe in the Germanic regions.

102. *Odin's mistresses, accursed—'Choosers of the Slain.'* The formal translation for *Valkyrie* is 'Chooser of the Slain.' The text implies that since they are in the camp of the wicked these are renegade, mercenary 'dark' Valkyries. The passage hints at

sarcasm as well, these Valks being so-called alleged *Choosers*, both a title and honor from which they have fallen. *Accursed* tells of *a cur*, or an aggressive dog or one that is in poor condition, especially a mongrel, thus a double sarcasm.

103. *The status quo.* The Valkyries supplied classic Valhalla with the dead.

104. *They did not blow.* The Greek term is *pneuma*, or 'spirit,' 'breath' or 'wind.' These spirits, unlike the wind, were strong enough not to have their loyalties blown about by petty alliances and trappings. They are negative in the sense that they only serve their own self-centered interests, which for them being initially noble, is now an especially low thing—especially in the eyes of other non-Valkyries spirits, even the evil ones.

106. *Dante's prison.* In *Inferno, Canto* Three, some of the first spirits Dante meets are those who took neither side in the great rebellion of Lucifer, but were for themselves. They were not allowed back into Heaven because of her perfect beauty, and Hell could not receive them either, lest the damned feel some measure of superiority over them. The text suggests that these particular Valkyries, having the same parallel mindset, apparently evaded or escaped that Dantean prison but somehow ended up here.

110. *Bad and ill.* Lit., 'Good and well.' Darkened minds think in reverse and, being negatively charged themselves, often reverse the polarities between good and evil, *Isaiah* 5.20-21.

119. *Blasvenomous monarchies.* Blasphemy + venomous. Extreme irreverence for all that is good or holy, and very poisonous, like a killer snake. Such is the height of Black Sun's wicked ways.

122. *Now wounded she a lighter.* Dark storm 'kills' a lesser evil spirit here, one who has more light than she, meaning he wasn't or isn't as rotten as she is, she being all the darker of a shade.

127. *The Eastern empire's affair.* This female spirit, Black Sun, whose present occupation is that of war, came from old Japan. Hints from the *Autumn Mirror Chronicles, ca.*

500 B.C., suggest that she may be a *Yuki-onna*, a 'Snow Woman,' a female mountain spirit terrifying yet beautiful. It is certain however, that Sun is of Valkyrie caliber but here she looks like a crazed gothic-style *kabukied* corpse.

129. *Her naginata in hand.* A *naginata* is a Japanese battlefield weapon, like a spear only with a long curved blade at the end. Women martial artists in Japan practice the weapon to this day. *Shed blood of the race.* This refers to the human race.

144-145. *Weapons' tiers . . . in fier.* The weapons are damp with night air, but they are also mixed with the slime of hands and blood, literally, their "tears." *Fier* is a combination of both fear + fiery, but the hidden text indicates sexual excitement in a strongly lustful, sadistic sense.

146-151. *'Sharp keys to Hell' . . . these shunned . . . skew.* While this passage on the surface appears to be scanning Vlad's thoughts, underneath there is a plethora of meaning. The first phrase is rendered as a famous saying. When the combative fighting arts of old Japan were undergoing transformation into spiritual ways (*jutsu* to *dō*), the sword, the *katana*, being the 'soul' of Japan, took precedence. The spear, naginata and nagamaki, a long-bladed short-staffed halberd, were *shunned*, regarded by many as unfit for nobility, those whose hands were *born high*. These weapons were still considered lower instruments of war under their battlefield synonym, '*sharp keys to Hell.*' *Bodies suspended* refer to Vlad's preference of impaling people on long poles and leaving them to die slowly as a vicious reminder to his once-Turkish enemies. In order to give some modern analogy and clarification, *turn of the skew* is an inserted word play on Henry James' story, *Turn of the Screw* (1898), in which a governess battles ghosts for the souls of the children she watches over. In this case, by driving the weapon in deeper, the skewered victim's souls would be controlled and belong to Vlad.

152-154. *Nosferrius edges . . . steel rang. Nosferrius* is a compound of nefarious + ferrum (iron, referring to the weapons) + Nosferatu, implying the undead, as Dracula is. The term indicates wicked, undead weapons that are vampirish, seeking blood. *Told not for whom . . . bell.* This line is taken from John Donne, the metaphysical poet (1571-1631). The original phrase runs, "And therefore never send to know for whom the bell tolls; it tolls for thee." For our text, this indicates that the weapons themselves never give reasons to their victims. They just show up and kill. *Silent bell.* Our reference here is to a high level of 'Zen' martial training in that the adept's movements are coordinated to fit perfectly in with that of their teachers. During the course of training, masters may *kiai*, or 'spiritually shout' at certain intervals of movement. But then to further train their students, masters may 'not shout' at the appointed time—the 'roaring' silence throwing off trainee's timing causing them to move and stumble, because they expected the sound and are conditioned to react to it. To react adversely to the silence means to the master that more training is needed. It shows that his student's minds are not yet that well disciplined.

In context to the phrase, the silent bell is like one that overlooks a bone orchard (Wild West graveyard) at midnight. The 'deafening' eerie silence easily frightens and draws weak minds that 'expect' to hear something but there is nothing, the *'expectation' being the *mental draw*, the hole, the *suki* (*see* Intro.) in one's defense. As for the weapons, their silence, like that of the silent 'non-shout' of the Zen sword master, 'summons' victims, pulling victims toward their mental cutting edge due to the instability of their victim's weak minds. In other words, weaker minds are attracted, drawn to the thought of being murdered due to the dark allurement these weapons generate. Finally, *summoned thee whilst their steel rang* reveals that these dark instruments actively seek out certain victims in action. Here we may parallel *Macbeth* (II. i.). Macbeth, upon hearing his wife sound the bell as a signal to kill King Duncan, utters, "The bell invites me. Hear it not, Duncan; for it is a knell that summons thee to heaven or to hell." A general axiom in martial arts as in life is that "A stronger mind will always lead a weaker one—always."

*The expectation is the bell's dark allurement. Another manifestation of this negative energy is seen when kids or wannabes pick up toy swords. Here multitudes are instantly transformed into Zorro's or other pop-icon sword masters. The latent, inherent, dark tendencies in the weapon and what is projected *cult*urally onto it not to mention the fact that the weapon represents and acts as a mask, a mind-focal device that when 'put on,' brings out people's violent tendencies that are then amplified and *via* misdirected enthusiasm, 'take over.'

DOUGLAS M. LAURENT

Pretty convenient tool for the Dark Powers. Thus, by increasing their undisciplined id-ish egos, their weapons turn inward (entropy) they becoming their own casualties as it is said, their own weapons 'bite them.' (Laurent, *Faces*.)

161-163. *Disdained to deliver . . . penchant for resurprisal . . . lying—horizontal.* Even these creepy, hardened mercenary Valkyries are hesitant to deliver one of their own, Kari, over to baser spirits. But caution pre-empts this consideration. Mulling things over the Valkyries are lying to themselves over honor and do not want to end up *horizontal*, or 'dead.' Kari, who has a tendency to surprise-retaliate, is a pest, a bloody red terror to all and killing her would be a good thing for every one that opposes her.

166. *Conflict of the Ages.* Between good and evil. This is reminiscent of Darth Vader's words to Luke Skywalker in *The Empire Strikes Back* (*Lucasfilm*, 1980), that, with their combined power, they could end this destructive conflict in the galaxy, and rule together as father and son.

186. *She 'sixing' a leering line.* Storm marks 'the man' with a slash that is partially reminiscent of the Devil's number—666. She did not quite finish the job though.

198. *Denied her king.* God, or any of a number of her sovereigns for that matter, until Dark Storm came into her own as a self-realized entity.

199. *Flesh offerings.* Jonathan Mycroft suggests that the text should read "spirit offerings," but from our earthly point of view, we can understand the concept of flesh being 'handed over' to its own lusts through increased conditioning in its own sordid devices. The same can be said to be true of a pure spirit. However, this phrase acts as a mirror. Storm has used people as an extension of her own will, much as she is now trying to use Mark Theman, 'the man.' Further, this passage does not say Dark Storm was ever a human although we cannot know for sure. The text is merely reflecting the concept of *Euhemerism* that runs throughout the play; that the stories of the old gods are actually exaggerated caricatures of real humans. Greek Euhemerus (fourth century B.C.) interpreted myths based on the idea that all myths—mythological heroes, *etc.*, were embellishments, political portraits, propaganda and

'editorial cartoons' of real people. In sum, they were tall tales, over-blown traditional accounts of actual *history.

However, this particular case also speaks of demonic possession. Possession is the process whereby parasitical indwelling spirits live vicariously through human bodies going from one to another down through time, most notably through family lines. For example, a royal genealogical family tree line a mile long may show the record of demons holding onto their earthly power through time, the power of royalty helping to create governmental policies and laws that allow them to entrench themselves further in the world and extend their influence (Psalm Two). Demons use the families (and their bodies as vehicles) whom they consider their property as their hosts, feeding off and living through their flesh activities in a covert yet hypersensual/destructive manner (glimpses of their past memories, perhaps, being the truer source of our 'reincarnation' memories).

The following information (Dickason, pp. 182-186) is particular to the particulars of demonization. "Suggested definition. Demon possession is a condition in which one or more evil spirits or demons inhabit the body of a human being and can take complete control of their victim at will." Below are eight distinct symptoms of possession observed of the demoniac from *Mark* Chapter Five:

1. Indwelling of an unclean spirit (v. 2)
2. Unusual physical strength (v. 3)
3. Paroxysms or fits of rage (v. 4)
4. Disintegration or splitting of the personality (vv.6-7)
5. Resistance to spiritual things (v. 7)
6. Hyperaesthesia or excessive sensibility, such as clairvoyant powers (v. 7)
7. Alteration of voice (v. 9)
8. Occult transference (v. 13)

➤ The last four *do not qualify for psychiatric illnesses*. Other symptoms may include the projection of a new personality, moral depravity, deep melancholy, spells of unconsciousness, ferocious or ecstatic behavior, idiocy, passion for lying, impure thoughts, strong sensual cravings, phobias, great cursing, rejection of council, study and the inability to pray or renounce Mr. Nasty Pants *El Diablo*.

DOUGLAS M. LAURENT

This is more insight into Storm's past. For these particular mercenary types of spirits, one must look on possession as a 'job' or necessary evil to them, as part of their profession of manipulation and intimidation. Storm's record indicates that in the past she 'farmed' groups of people, patrolling certain territories like local neighborhoods at certain hours of the day. Doing so, she would know when so and so was performing a particular aberrant deed (*e.g.*, being abusive, getting drunk *etc.*) and using those people's weak minds and bodies, their habits and predilections to foster and encourage degrading habits spiritually, mentally (emotion, intellect, will), physically, *etc.* This was so that she could control them even more and reap their souls in the end—all the while creating stores to recharge her negative batteries.

*Take the *Criosphinx*, the lion-ram. This was an Egyptian beast with a ram's head and lion's body. Guarding souls and temples was its bag. This does not sound like too bad of a vocation until we find out that the CS was created by god Amun and was a personification of the god Ammon. Who is he? Well, he is the Egyptian equivalent to Jupiter or Zeus. In old Egypt, the head of the ram symbolized the 'universal soul,' and so iconized Ammon (Amon/Amun) who was the Egyptian bigwig god. Peeking through the mythic *veil*, he was originally one of the eight original founding deities of Egypt. He is also found in the Hermopolite creation tales of antique Greece. Later in his chequered career, Amun became the one true chief *El Jefe* of old Egypt. What does all this mean? Broken down, we find that *Genesis* Ten Cush's symbol was the Western Criosphinx lion-ram of the ancient city of Lagash, Iraq located northwest of the junction of the Tigris/Euphrates Rivers. Its god was Ningirsu-Ninurta, Cush's heir-apparent Nimrod (Pilkey, p. 133). Crio-Cush was well acquainted with the extremely powerful hard case solar deity Sekhmet; daughter of god sun god Ra. *Foithamore*, Cush's dad is rotten Ham, Noah's son, aka (H)Ammon-Ra, the big sun-god of Egypt, which explains his closeness to Sekhmet. Not just this, but Cush shared the power/political level of Jupiter/Zeus, his son the supremely powermaniacal Nimrod whose offices were equal to but controlled by Ham, his granddad, thereby explaining the allied equality of Ammon with Jup/Zeus. So yes indeed, Crio-Cush was created out of (H)Amun who personified his dad Ammon who was none other than (H)Ammon-Ra who gave

218

him power and the Criosphinx motif to play with. Ham most definitely was one of the eight founders of the post-Flood world, who was a big shot in Egypt, which still bears his name, the "Land of Ham." Cush today is also known as god Hermes in Greece (Hermes being a synonym for "son of Ham"), early on being the main tongue-twisting confuser at Babel not the noble interpreter of the later Greek gods. Nimrod was his military counterpart at Babel. —*Got Myth?*

201. *Is now reprobate.* Reprobation implies a mind entrapped in its own base nature, no longer able to discern right from wrong. It is given over to the enslavement of its own re-cycling degenerating blinding lusts. Because of this, the *reprobate* mind is highly destructive to itself and to others. Reprobation occurs in many forms, from being plain ol' stupid and mediocre to downright conscious hand-rubbing fiendish depravity. All are dangerous.

206-207. *The longer one lives . . . If you lose.* By conquest, warriors gain power over others. One of the rules of the Mortuuslands implies that if one is killed, one has to start out again on a lower rung, which means only the best are on top.

208-210. *Knew now his name . . . "Come, Theman,"* Names are a lucrative commodity in the Deadlands. If through any means available one defeats or owns a person and their name, great power and prestige comes one's way. *Theman.* In this case, Li is as sharp as Kari is to figure out 'the man's' real name. As an added interest, in ancient days, great fighters may have 'hired' themselves or their names out, lending prestige to the buyer. This was done for example in old China, where famous fighters would be escorts to trade convoys and what not. But it even went deeper than that. Whole towns or even provinces were famous for their empty-hand and weapon combatives and thus the need for travelers to keep silent lest passing through they would insult the local kung-fu masters. Draeger and Smith write:

> It is said that one district in Hopei was so famous for its *hsing-i* that convoys passing through did not show their flag or call out the names of their guards (a practice to intimidate would-be bandits) for fear of insulting the district (p. 40).

EIGHTEEN: THE BATTLEFIELD AND THE ROSE

Come near, come near and hear the tale bold,
And know the haze that covers the shredding of one's soul.
That the gods in their Heaven have loftily said,
"That justice and liberty must be kept from the dead."

Thus, the battle raged on all through the night,   5
The tide turned against the dark ones and their ignoble plight.
Marched they back unto favorable fallen domain,
To the land that was theirs, their kingdom to proclaim.

They had ridden hard back then in the nighting deep,
Grim mutterings sounded in their blackened scorched keep.   10
Of groans grotesque and muffled cries despaired,
Of damned souls—*knowing*—going nOwhere.

Now a clink of armor, now a cloven booted hoof,
A vast mounted army of worn, helish troop.
Eyes blooded, swollen and burning plasma red,   15
Great beast's *a'cursin'* at her profaned head.

Coiling through forest night under cold lunar orb,
They appeared in the expanse, this riding black horde.
A million eyes hardened to the butcher's chopping task,
Dire purposes again–about to be unmasked.   20

Passed they in the night to do their sterile evil bidding,
Silently tearing, swift with no soft heart pity.
Shadows hid the obsidian blushes that they did in visage make,
Wailings they left behind in their blood-sotted 'tesque haste.

Mutely enthroned on their steeds embalmed,   25
Glint of the dead, the storm before the calm.
Going to battle this long-twisted snake,
Breathing in cold at midnight's last wake.

Past iced lakes in winter morning glow,
Unto the battle constrained they did to go.   30
To render judgment on *that* final argument,
Of free spirits apart, from their master spent.

To fight those noble ones who gave that high decree,
That the gods and men should go forever free.
The Land of Lightness to be finally last lost,   35
Against darkness' sons, and all their great host.
Mist covered hills they eyed with mal-glee,
This silented land gave them the strength of misery.
And desperate soil played to their furrowed degeneracy—
Held she a sadistic hand in shaping their seeded atrocities.   40

Knolls spilling over fell onto the plain,
Where trees scraped low and grass blades pained.
The lay of this land was their sinister strength,
Her contours and shape prophesied their fate.

St. Kari, alone, stood facing them on *that* plain.   45
Black Sun, she smiled of her enemy's forthcoming pain.
Numbered they like the sands of the vast swollen seashore,
Kari's golden hair fluttered as in the coming storm.

Battalions of shrill screams cut the silent air,
Spirits gathering for battle, their courage fore beared.   50
Dead souls joined ranks in the classical formal style,
Prepared to s'wipe their enemies out with the greatest of beguile.

Dark Storm knew; watched the forming battle disaster,
She tilted her eyes at the girlie swords master.
Smiled, she did at St. Kari of the Blade,   55
Dealt with her before, in business' betrayed.

Dark Storm then eyed the over confident Sun,
Her dupe before the teenager from the Hellicon.
Advancing in formation they crossed the barren steppe,
Kari unsheathed Ravenblade for Heaven to bless.   60

Sang she now her battle-death song,
To show the Lover to whom she belonged.
A song of power, a tale of woe,
Divines the portion where true ones must go:

"How wonderful 'tis to be a saint,   65
Not of Earth, but of Heaven's fate.
No fame and valor from here below,
But from above do blessings flow.

Make me not a statue of men,
That they should pray, and I give amens.   70
Let me be a one unassuming and small,
Who walks through the back of kingdom's hall.

Do not remember me from the Earth,
Or make me a hero for irreverent commerce.
Let me rather be remembered by The One,   75
When the day is over, and the work finally done.

No jeering, glowing crowds for me,
Just Heaven's fields where I am free.
Like an eagle's silent flight, on Heaven's wings soar do I,
And leave the realm of man, and their visions pitifully styed.   80

No mighty name follows after me,
Just memories by a few friends, is all that I please.
No throngs to chant my wondrous name,
Except His voice in a whisper——'tis not to my shame.

So no battles now where men may lift me high,   85
But carried to Heaven, on the wings of angels I'll fly.
No crowds to greet me when I come above,
Just friends to see me to His throne of Love.

I used to be honored as if in a sundog dream,
But 'tis all the better they cheer Him, and not me.   90
It must be nice to be made of men a saint,
But His love for me is more than I can take.

Though I matched wits with the Empire of the skies,
I seek His face, what greater than He, the prize?
For all that I did was nothing but flesh,   95
And in the end, I was laid to rest.

So let me go into my Father's house above,
With reverent respect and nothing without love.
In quiet humility I will knock at His gate,
He will come to open, 'tis never too late.   100

O' to be a saint numbered among men!
It is His doing; it is not from *them*.
No wild, earthy crowds for me!
It was for freedom's sake——
The Almighty set me free.   105

Thus, a rose in the field is what I shall be,
A fragrant aroma, pleasing to just He.
O' Love, thou who made this beautiful Earth,
When will she be ready to receive thy saint's worth?"

Now packs of berserked phantoms broke formation,   110
Charging, lusting to kill the bystanding sainted maiden.
Desiring to take the swordgirl's head,
To give it to Sun, to revel in her—dead!♄!

Kari smiled sweetly and with wave of gentle hand,
Brought forth her clans to do battle with the damned.   115
Who would question their noble's worth,
Up to battle lines they fatigued and lurched.

Up, up to the flatlands did they go!
Innumerable company of a mighty host.
Under command of that glorious one,   120
Outwardly shining, inwardly spun.

They stood upon the brows of rolling dried hills,
Looked down upon Black Sun and all her ill wills.
A grand throng, of the most a'blessed of souls,
Swooped they into the Valley, to joyful death do they go!   125

Ceaseless wind tore through massing battle ranks,
Grey cold sun above marked *the* timeless date.
There they clashed; titanic indescribable force,
Giving no quarter, having no remorse.

Multitudes, multitudes in *the* Valley of Decision!   130
Lives in the balance, ended by steeled precision!
Writhing souls on agonizing field *a'gatherin'*,
To try each one—the place of eternal plutonian testing.

Spirits bellowing out, shouting their name and line,
To find an opponent worthy, their blades to profind.   135
Each to their own, to work out their life equation,
To confirm each spirit—in their loyal consecration.

Under driving rain now came the contention unchained,
To win the relentlessing battle, the field again to gain.
There was never any talk of taking lost hostages,   140
Only a diatribe, to fill vindiction's rampages.

The Turk fighting the corps side by side,
Yet begrudging the others when in cruelty he spied,
Blamed he the luck of the ponderous battle,
Upon the Dead Yet Alive—*that* disgusting human spectacle!   145

Staccatoing whining blades, bodies' percussionin',
Blurs of slicening motions with actions a'slurryin',
Colors blending horses upending bodyings gwrapplin',
—A thousand quick horrors to the man a'drenalin'.

On the field of blood the task was nearly undone,   150
The man with great claymore now facing the Black Sun.
In the night he had chosen the cold metal (an idol he could see),
To be the damning god of his pathetic eternity.

Kari saw the man in the moment of blinding light,
Decisions needs be made to turn him left or to the right.   155
Embraced she a chain fighter cutting his neck with a swatch,
Wrapped into his *whirrrling* chain, vortexing the dispatch.

Past tall mantled spear fighter seeking to engage,
The sword saint parrying her thrusting, inflicting her eager blade.
Coolly went she down the 'scape to guard his blinded side,   160
Crashing headlong with Black Sun on her plunge to idicide.

In shock, the man saw a red line arcing through her back,
Sliced to metal's grain, inflicted by the demoniac.
In pain Kari turned and to him solemnly bade,
"Ne'er a love made that was slashed clean through by the labor of a blade." 165

Attack by the draw Kari deathly knew,
Would only compel the unmercied 'kabukied' shrew.
Fain weakness, dropped she Ravenblade down,
Black Sun shrieked, bringing her 'Damocles' 'round.

Bold Sun bared her snap-fanged naginata,   170
Curved edge moistened from the day's *anáthema*.
Kari enfeebled, her guard cast low,
Black Sun cut, guillotining with sev'ring blow.

Kari's fore was prime, ready for the next target met,
In one stroke, she brought her blade under Sun's hack'ed spent.   175
Lifting over the heavied motion in sickening heaving ride,
Hot passions met; St. Kari daggering deeply into Sun's open side.

Sitting aloof from the heated battle, Dark Storm in she walked,
Choppening four down with sickle, while Kari and Sun *tête-à-tottered-talked*.

The despicable Turk hacking over to embattled zone—   180
Driving to engage the man—*for a victim of his own.*

From afar coming Dark Storm with a snake's bead saw,
The loathsome Turk and his scimitaring curved sword.
A fine Damascus, yet in battle clash the Storm arrayed,
To determine herself 'tween 'the man' and this disgusting shade—   185
(To take a hack from the troublesome dour little man,
To set him up—to cover her scheming conniving plan).

She yanked this lower spirit in by a twisting angle away,
Deluded Turk's scalding metal, he striking the space of day.

The man's blade then sliced to the Turkspirit's shocked harm,   190
Convulsed he, this Turk, with cleaved geysering half arm.

Caught Storm the man's jaw with the shaft of her reaping shear,
And put her hand on his breast to suck forth his spirit with a leer.

Stealing forth the man's spirit, she put it in a box,
Saddlebagged it to her horse, and key-torqsioned the lock.   195
Tipping her head at the dazed man she left her battlefield,
'The man' stripped of his person left to feel *the* true Valhallan evil.

"A man that is halved," Dark said, "is a man undone and fold',
I may possess his name, but I must have his body and soul.
The more he does, the stronger he is wont to become,   200
And in the end his life shall be my bountiedful sum."

Therefore Storm purposed within her dark, adderish self,
"I will lead him by following, and bait him in my trap.
Ha, his own soul will be the prize he unwittingly seeks,
Use him against himself, my energies I will keep."   205

Steel head chunked, vomiting into ground,
Eyes widening! Sun; spatting; *loooping* wildly around.
Hair moving flowly amidst the sloe battle drop,
A slow deathing dance for the fallen kabukied demigod.

Meeting war-axing, Kari dashing the head down,   210
Verticaling her straight edge she loosing a hand from an arm.
Walked over to Black Sun, shook her head at the nightshade,
Felt for the dark slain creature, but smirked at her poor aim.
"Ne'er a philosophy made that wasn't cut-clean through by the art
of the blade."

Her glance now caught a form moving fast on the raw cut horizon,   215
Riding hard over the stretch; that grisly myrmidon wanton.
The battle then shifted and there for a paused moment,
Kari came to 'the man,' despite his raging foment.

"She took something from me!" ripped he hysterically,
"Yes," Kari said calmly, "your soul to keep, undeniably." 220
"I'll kill her! Ill kill her!!" the man frothingly said,
"It is I who'll put her in the ground, I who will shape her end¡•!
"That so?" said Kari, staring through 'the man,'
"Think twice Theman, don't go; for she is a seasoned damned."

The man looked her over with disgust and glare in his eye, 225
Cinched he a horse and mounted, spun it about to fly.
"I don't care what it is!" the man barked at St. Kari,
"She stole my spirit outright, this one I'll kill for free!

If I am to be prisoner here, wherever the hell this is,
I'll do things on my own time, don't you ever dare come near!" 230
Drove he the steed forward through the distanced war lines,
Kari smiled knowingly, a fool to *her* ambition, asinined.

Looked she now to ridge of yonder distant hill,
Two bold spirits toward him, galloping to the kill.
Walked to her charger and unfurled her sack, 235
Looked over her weapons that glimmered in the pack.

Swords and bows, long and short, neatly laid in leather bag,
With dirks, handstones, darts, spears, javelins and war-axe.
Fit she elegant slender javelin shafts into her compact atlatl,
Harpooning the fiends clear at two hundred yards— 240
For 'the man's' coming battle.

On pursued the man past the rocky out crest of the hill,
"An appointment in the 'Samarran style,'" sighed Kari—
"*Ehh*, he will come to *nil*."
Turned back her attention now to the meandering, waning fight, 245
Sang she, and sought for her lines to cross, to continue in their right:

"Hell is a'one made forever, yet her lies duly forestall,
Infernos swallowing their owners, belching to torture them all.
Forever, forever fighting the ever-branding flame,
The soul is not quenched, and contests ne'er gained.   250

The flame, 'tis the battle and is the spirit of man,
Element of the cosmos, wrought for immortal ends.
Man of dust, man of clay, yet sparked with life divine,
Caught betwixt Heaven and Earth, thy countenance so defined."

Spasm'd Turk on the ground, rolling and he bled,   255
Cursing eternal vengeance upon *that* man he swore cowardly fled.
Swearing native tongue; saw him ride toward the great and evil Dark Storm,
And rav'ed in his lunaticked heart that the two were now conformed.

Chapter Eighteen Valley Footnotes

This great battle, one of many in the Nether, is unusually violent, due to the sneaky underhanded attack of the wicked the night before on the Valhallan Hall. In response, the righteous war-spirits are out to 'set things right.' This calls for an open confrontation, the only honorable way of fighting that they know, not like the wicked spirits who use every dirty trick in the book to win.

2. *Shredding of one's soul.* As a 'type' of morality play, this line is aimed *directly* at the reader. The genre of the morality play hales from Medieval and early Tudor theater. An allegory, the protagonist is met by personifications of various moral attributes who try to prompt him or her to choose a devout life over one of evil. These plays were very popular in the fifteenth and sixteenth centuries. As the battle between good and evil rages on in our own lives even today, which way will one go in life?

3. *That the gods.* The closest we can get to the meaning of this phrase is taken from the Hebrew word *Elohim*. The "*im*" ending refers to a plurality, taken to be an allusion to the Triune God, Father, Son and Spirit.

4. *Justice and liberty.* The meaning is that fallen spirits had their chance at glory but rejected it and are now, like a heat-sealed twist-tied *Baggy*, shut up in evil.

12. —*Knowing*—*going nOwhere.* Conscious of the eternal war in Valhalla, even in the midst of it, these spirits are aware of their own burdens. There is literally nowhere to run, and all are compulsed to continually fight as a way of life and survival. Sometimes this one thought is overpowering, maddening, even to the worst— and best, of spirits. Fixed in good and evil, right or wrong, spirits in the Mortuus Deadlands also live a paradox. They are fixed in their spiritual state, but there is room for improvement to the good or bad in a 'purgatorial' sense. From what can be understood of this strange Underworld, this 'fixedness' seems to depend upon a spirit's state of mind and purpose at the time, although this may change. Again, it all depends on personal virtue and action. In addition, some spirits like Dark Storm relish the place immensely as it affords a great laboratory for the 'practice' of

sharpening their personal attributes and skills of spirit, mind and body. *Knowing*—. Bruce Lee said something to the effect that knowledge was 'stuck,' but knowing was growing and alive such as we are in 'living' learning relationships. Says he, "*Knowledge* is fixed in time, whereas, *knowing* is continual. Knowledge comes from a source, from an accumulation, from a conclusion, while knowing is a movement" (*Tao*, p. 16). The point is these spirits are growing in the horror of 'living *knowing*' moment by moment. It is not a "fixed" knowledge where as they are finished with their atrocities and horrors and can now take a break, 'resting on their laurels' as it were.

13. *Cloven booted hoof.* Some spirits have cleft feet, indicating cross unions. Demigods, half human and half 'god' are known to dwell in the Nether-regions. Not all of them have cleft feet.

15. *Eyes blooded . . . burning plasma red.* In an attempt to translate the fantastic imagery the poem conveys, we may draw inspiration from artist Frank Frazetta's fantasy illustrations. *See* his excellent painting, *The Death Dealer*.

16. *Great beasts a'cursin'.* Even the dark leaders are miffed at their failure of the night before, *muttering curses* under their ectobreath. *A'cursin'.* Cur + sin. *Curs* are mutt dogs that are hostile or in poor form, especially mongrels. In a larger sense, these wicked spirits are aggressive, wild incurable *yellow dogs* (yhell + low *i.e.,* low hellish mutterings and who are 'contemptible, cowardly, and despicable').

18. *They appeared in the expanse.* Out of the trees and onto the vast Valhallan plains.

24. *Blood-sotted 'tesque haste.* 'Sotted,' as in 'drunk on blood' butchers, this evil army went about destroying everything in its path. '*Tesque*, as in 'grotesque,' or 'grow-tesque.' Not only were they blood-drunken lushes, they were growing more grotesque every minute pursuing their red lusts and criminal passions. In *Wisteria Lodge*, Sherlock Holmes adroitly observes, "There is but one step from the grotesque to the horrible" (*cf.* James 4. 1-10.). While in *Baskervilles* he concludes, "The more outré and grotesque an incident is the more carefully it deserves to be

examined, and the very point which appears to complicate a case is, when duly considered and scientifically handled, the one which is most likely to elucidate it." The conditor inserts these quotes to kindle careful thought and examination on the part of the Midgarders. Midders should well realize that these guys are out there and therefore just based upon "the grotesque to the horrible" scale, warrant their careful attention and looking into for they are "coming soon to a planet near you" for the big showdown.

26. *Storm before the calm.* Even at relative rest, this vicious army was turbulent. *The calm* refers to their future defeat.

30. *Constrained they did to go.* Like eager racing greyhounds waiting to chase the fake rabbit at the dog races, the deadpraved were under evil compulsion to go, not so much of an external necessity, but of an inward instinctual drive. Among their foul ranks, the battle-field haunters, the dark-winged blood-feeding fanged and taloned *Keres*, crave their ectofood. They are the very horrid female spirits of cruel or violent death, including battle death, by accident, disease or murder. They work for and are the hit fe-spirits for the Fates. The usual psycho-pathological *modus operandi* of the Keres are to feast upon blood after tearing souls out of warrior's dying bodies and packing them off to Hades. Like thick hacking hail, thousands lacerate through massive battles and fight like scavengers over the dying they mow down. Having no power such as their Fateful bosses wield, the *Keres* nevertheless push the envelope, forcing certain ends for their victims to their own blood-bloating advantages. The Olympian gods often shoo the Keres away from their chosen favorites who were wrenched out in battle, beating back the slathering, sharp-clawed evil-eyed wicked female spirits. Hesiod (*Hēsíodos*, ca. 750-650 B.C.) speaks of them as being called *nosoi* ('plagues' and 'sicknesses'), *lugra* ('banes'), and *kakoi* ('evils' with a capitol 'E').

31-32. *That final argument, Of free spirits apart.* A tremendous 'loaded' theological problem is presented with ramifications in the political, action-oriented and Midgard arena. If angels were created with a free will, were they not free to refuse their Creator? Would not this be their God-given right, or do angels being created, have rights? As free agents with free wills, God, their Creator, expected angels to banter things about with Him, as they do grow and learn (*e.g.*, 1Peter1.10-12). The scholar Hawkesford cites that this argument is faulty however, in that the concept of God's all-pervasive love is missing. As Creator, He loves his creation dearly, not willing that any should depart from Him and to be separated from His Spirit in any way means death, the creature finding its highest glory and worth in union with the Creator. This reality is apparently manifested for us mortals in the work of the Son on the cross, whoever trusting in His work for them personally should not perish but have everlasting life. The bald-face and very, very, dark, glistening subtle concept of sin implies "error-making," and "to *miss* the mark and so *not share* in the prize," separates one from a holy God. What seems to be not mentioned therefore is the lack of love attitude these spirits had according to that relational situation, not the political ramifications. It was this hardened self-serving attitude that caused the great rebellion and separation between God and his angelic sons. John Milton's *Paradise Lost* (1667) catches a glimpse of some of this reality (our Ch. 3 note # 3-4).

33-34. *Those noble ones . . . gods and men.* This is a reference to the Creator God of *Genesis*, Chapter One, celestial beings, that is angels, and humans. The term 'gods' in Hebrew refers to the *bene-Elohim*, or 'sons of God,' the angels. Only three groups of individuals may qualify for the *bene-Elohim* title. Directly created angels, humans who are regenerated through the new birth Christ speaks of, *John* Chapter Three, and Christ, *the* Son of God.

35. *Land of Lightness.* Apparently, Heaven is in view here. These spirits remember that terrible battle when they were ousted.

36. *Darkness' sons.* This is a reference to fallen angels.

37-40. *Mist covered hills . . . their furrowed degeneracy— . . . seeded atrocities.* This stanza reiterates the idea that the contours of the she-land have a hand (as in this case *held she a hand* as in poker, a winning one at that) in shaping souls and destinies. For us, the study of geography is the study of how the physical world shapes the arts historically, culturally, physically and morally. For instance, arts played out on hard ground or in wetter regions are worked differently. This is why it is said of the Chinese martial kung-fu arts, "kicks in the north; punches in the south" (*běi tī nán quán*). *Cultural geography* deals with looking at the ways language, religion, economy, government and other cultural phenomena vary or remain constant, from one place to another. The samurai sword for instance, with its slightly curved blade, is the product of cultural geography, shaped by the land and history of Japan. *Furrowed . . . seeded*. The evil ground is ploughed into 'furrows' or lines and sown with the 'atrocious' *vile* 'seeds' of wickedness.

44. *Prophesied their fate.* This was to their good, or so they believed.

47. *Sands of the vast swollen seashore.* This is said of an innumerable, uncountable host.

49. *Screams cut the silent air.* Battle cries (*e.g.*, Japanese *ki-ai* or 'abdominal spirit-shout,' or 'martial scream') are well documented on Midgard as well as in the Zone. They are to build courage and terrify enemies. They momentarily freeze (Jpn. *bonno*) the opponent's ability to act. In ancient times, musical bands, for example, playing Scottish bagpipes, marched ahead of their armies to scare the enemy and drown out the enemy's battle noises.

50-52. *For beared . . . in the classical formal style . . . prepared to s'wipe.* Bear + red. Coming on as enraged bears, the baddies were going to 'swipe' at and 'wipe' out the good guys. In the many Netherzones, armies fight in the ancient *classical* military ways.

56. *In business' betrayed.* Businesses + hisses. Storm has had business with Kari before and practically hisses at her through the pronunciation of the word.

58. *The teenager from the Hellicon.* The *Helicon* is a mountain in south-central Greece, elevation 5,735 feet near the Gulf of Corinth. It is said to be the home of the nine Muses (Gk., *mousai*, most ancient PIE **men*, or 'think'). Apparently Storm is snidely referring to one of the many areas which the 'gracious' but hellish Miss Muffet Kari

received her massive education, while sitting on her tuffet (toughet), in this instance under the guidance of the brilliant Muses and then some. Named by the poet Hesiod the Nine were, 1) Erato/love poetry, 2) Euterpe/flute-lyric poetry, 3) Clio/history, 4) Calliope/epic poetry, 5) Thalia/comedy-pastoral poetry, 6) Terpsichore/dance, 7) Polyhymnia/sacred poetry, 8) Urania/astronomy and Melpomene/tragedy (*Prologue* note # 5 for Osiris).

60. *Unsheathed Ravenblade.* St. Kari's sword portends an exacting and judicial death. It is judge, jury and executioner all rolled into one beautiful sublime piece of 'poetic-justice steel.' 'Poetic justice' is a literary device in which virtue is ultimately rewarded and evil/vice punished, often in modern literature by an ironic twist of fate intimately connected to the character's own conduct and behavior. Too, many times villains are portrayed with some sort of psychological or physical quirk, like mania, twitching, limping or a gimmick such as a false hand that can be switched out for an iron hook or sword, bronze fist, spike, *etc.*, in order to fight the hero in the end. Dark Storm has a scar on her beautiful face she hides with her hair. Often, super-villains in such stories have to have a 'gimmick' along with their malady as well. In cinema, they can't just fight with one sword, they have to fight with two, but that isn't good enough. Soon both swords are set ablaze and the valiant hero has to fight two flaming swords—just the right stuff for heroes and legends.

61. *Battle-death song.* World and Deadlands history are filled with tales of warriors composing deaths songs before great matches or battles. Before engagements, they would sing their personal songs to their gods, paying homage to those deities, and telling of their (the person's) accomplishments and failures—their life stories as warriors.

62. *To show the Lover.* God. Kari's eeridescent darkly imprismed broken-color soul can best be summed up with a fragmented line from the poem *Ordained* by 'the poet; unknown': "A poem for a beautiful day and a lost Love, can a poet ask for anything better—than a broken heart ordained from above?"

65. *To be a saint . . . fate.* Historian Rodger Atterbury cites that sketches and tales of Joan of Arc (1412-31) from the *Orleans Manuscript*, dated 1553 were used to convey

earlier translations of this particular passage. *Fate*. From 'before the foundation of the world,' things have already been decided.

89. *In a sundog dream.* A *sundog* is a bright spot in the sky appearing 'beside the sun' on either side of it, often accompanied by a luminous ring or halo. This is a compound phrase. A sundog is also known as a 'parhelion' (Gk., *parēlion*), 'mock' or 'phantom' sun. What this multi-tiered passage is telling us is that Kari, *honored* and famous for her warrior prowess (*sundog dream*) trails her enemies like a dog, fights as a 'pair of hellish lions' and that she is a mock or phantom sundog-shadow whilst going about her business of battle. Native American Indians thought it was a sign of good fortune of an impending hunt. This thought lends further credence to Kari's never-losing streak while 'hunting' her enemies down. As icy Kari is victorious she wears, metaphorically speaking, a saintly halo.

93. *Empire of the skies.* Satan's kingdom is said to be in the upper atmospheres of this planet, *Ephesians* Chapter Two. This passage may also indicate Kari's past dealings with goddess Kali and her association with the East-Indian *Maruts*, or 'war gods.' This Sanskrit term describes these gods well. They are the 'martial ones' found in the 'upper atmospheres,' but 'below the Heavens.' It is said that they fight their enemies, what they 'call' the *asuras*, or 'demons.' It is interesting to note that the word *asura* is much like *Aesir* (Asia) both meaning gods of some sort, giving hint to the historical reality of ancient migrations from Asia into Europe. Linked Indo-European literature from Iceland to India attests to this fact as well Kari has had dealings with such ectofolks before (Ch. 9 note # 11).

95. *Nothing but flesh.* This does not refer to Kari's alleged 'Earth' life because apparently she is a Valkyrie. More than likely, it is an allusion, from a human point of view, to Kari's own past with its regrets. To do battle without regret was the high mark for warriors in many societies.

108-109. *O' Love . . . saint's worth.* This last line of Joan is a translated borrowing from George Bernard Shaw's (1856-1950) play, *Saint Joan* (1923), compounding Atterbury's view, "O God that madest this beautiful Earth, when will it be ready to receive Thy saints? How long, O Lord, how long?" As to where the rest of Kari's song came from, like poet Robert Browning when asked what a certain line meant in his work, the writer can only reply, "God only knows."

110. *Berserked phantoms.* From *berserker* or *berserkr*, that is, 'of the bear cult, those who wear the bear, or brown shirt.' These fighting fanatics lived after the method of the bear, fighting like it in combat. Entire cults were formed around this venerated beast from Northern Europe to East Asia. In fact, being berserk was a question of *werebear*-ism. Native Americans have a term, *skin-walkers* that tell of incredible shape-shifting qualities, the only thing is that in order to transform, one has to be wearing the skin of the animal one wishes to morph into. This is another form of the 'masking principle.' The bear to the Native Americans is the closest kindred spirit next to a human. The Nordic berserks were furious in battle. There is some discrepancy however over the term 'bear shirt,' some contending that it meant to be naked. There are indeed stories of berserk Viking warriors being amped up on stimulants running amok into battle buck naked biting their shields and swords as they went forward in a frenzied bloodlust sort of way and attacked as initial shock-troop battering rams to break up enemy formations. Once inside, the berserkers would kill many, making headway for the regular troops until they dropped from exhaustion. Curiously, like a snapshot into the past, the exotic twelfth century walrus ivory-carved washed ashore *Isle of Lewis* chess set shows a medieval Nordic army where shield-biting Viking berserker warriors replace the rooks, paralleling the frenzied berserk mindset (Williams, pp. 20-21). Hitler's Nazi party members wore brown shirts to commemorate these war-crazed fanatics—and to skin-walk *werebear* themselves into the powerfully efficient predators that they were. (*See* Frank Frazetta's masterful work, *Berserker*. Also, Ch. 17 note # 23 for more berserkfast surreal and Laurent, *Faces* for masking.)

126-127. *Ceaseless wind . . . massing ranks . . . Grey cold sun.* Death is in mind, and the fact it was a cold day for the battle, but one well remembered in Valhalla. *Massing ranks.* This ritual of battle to the deadlanders is almost hysterical-religious (*massing*) in scope (given the circumstances), hence, the descriptions connotative meaning.

127. *Marked the timeless date.* There is no time in Valhalla as we earthers reckon time. Valhalla, a state of spirit, mind and reality is an eternal ever-present *now*, with no past or future.

129. *Giving no quarter.* Only the fullness of technique and ability was the 'soul' test of all Valhallan warriors, good or bad, which gives us an intimate glimpse of the ethics in the Nether.

130. *The Valley of Decision!* This is from *Joel* 3.14. The valley Jehoshaphat, yet to be created near Jerusalem *via* a massive earthquake when Christ again sets foot on the Mount of Olives, is said to be the place where God judges all those who are left alive after the battle of *Armageddon.*

134. *Shouting their name and line.* As in old Japan, warriors first announced their names and lineage in order to find a 'worthy' opponent on the battlefield. Only then did they fight. There is a subtlety here. Aristocratic warriors were so well trained that even enlisted soldiers with years of hardened battle experience were no matches for these masters. So to defeat an underling meant no stature acquisition in terms of honorable conflict. The same goes for the Deadlands. To fight 'lessers' means no real advancement in prestige or power, unless, of course, it was for practice or if there is a price on the opponent's head.

141. *Only a diatribe, to fill vindiction's rampages.* Die + a + tribe. Vindication + vindictive. A *diatribe* is a 'prolonged speech,' usually bitter or abusive in nature. In the Nether, there are no formal talks between the two armies on taking hostages in mass battle. In our text, *diatribe* implies, because there is no hostage swapping, that they literally "die-a-tribe," meaning annihilation. The only people left after Valhallan battles are the current now dead, or survivors. Hostage taking, or kidnapping, however, does occur on occasion for the 'games' mercenaries play. The compound *vindiction* suggests that there is no love lost between these armies. They go at each other furiously, seeking justification in a 'settling the score' spiteful sense. Both sides know the battle is and will be tough, with hard ramifications for the losers.

142. *The Turk fighting.* This warrior is from the previous night at the Valhallan Hall who addressed Kari sarcastically. He blames the misfortunes of battle on the movie star Theman, 'the man.'

152. *Had chosen the cold metal.* The headstrong actor had made a very stupid, self-centered choice in the night. The *cold metal* he had chosen was the *claymore, lit.,* "amore." In other words, Theman fell in love with the exotic Scottish weapon through its glittery film and literary hype, its 'coolness.'

161. *Black Sun on her plunge to idicide.* Id + cid, the 'killing off of the *Id*,' the lustful, sensual, pleasure-seeking instant *get now* gratification part of the human psyche, and a big fat misshapen one it is, *i.e.,* Theman's. More so, '*The Id*' (short for "idiot") is one of many snotty insulting nicknames the spirit's in the evil camp use for the bloated x–starred Theman. In fact, Sun de-<u>cid</u>eadly went out of her way to de-liber*ately* waste Theman because she is a bit of a revengeful revenant (Lat., *reveniens,* "return-ing"). A true *gynpneumata* ("female seducing, deceiving, unclean spirit"), her type of etheric revenant is particularly vicious and dangerous. Supposedly, an animated corpse or visible ghost come from the grave to terrorize the living, in her case this undead kabukied creature survives by feeding upon the energy of the living such as Theman is. 'Tis no wonder this *vile* soulpire wants to suck the Idiot's vitals and his Dead Yet Alive light from him.

165. *Slashed clean through.* A Musashi-ism. Musashi believed that slashes were weak in the spirit while cuts were strong. In context to this passage, the slash is weak, spiritu-ally, and there is no slash powerful enough (or blade for that matter), that can stand up to or slice through the highest form of love–the Greek *agápē* love of self-sacrifice.

166. *Attack by the draw.* This form of attack is one of the five major ways of attack. The other four are attack by the 'combination,' by 'immobilization,' by 'indirect progression' and 'simple direct' attack. The translatable materials for these notes are derived from the studies of the late kung-fu master geniac Bruce Lee, which are now world famous (*Tao,* pp. 194-199). After having scanned hundreds of martial arts and their literatures, Lee broke down all attacks into these five basic categories,

giving him incredible insight into the physical and psychological nature of combative offense to which he excelled.

169. *Her 'Damocles' 'round.* This is as in 'The sword of Damocles.' Damocles was a member of Dionysius II's court who ruled Rome from 367 to 433 B.C. Apparently Damocles was a big mouth and a flatterer. Roman Cicero complained to Dionysius that the braggart talked too much about the King's questionable successes, which may have been construed as somewhat dangerous. Therefore, in order to teach young Damocles as lesson, Dionysius invited him to a party and when he was seated, Damocles looked up only to find a huge sword dangling by a single hair thread directly over his head. The moral of the story is that 'Don Vito' Dionysius was telling the youth of the 'dangers' that went along with a fragile life, wealth, power, leaked info—and a big *bazoo.* In the context to our story, the *naginata* moving in an *a'roundin'* circular motion, always hangs over Kari's head, metaphorically symbolizing great danger and power, even though she is not a whistle blowing snitch or braggart. Although they do say she knows, based on millennia of accumulated experience, countless covert secrets concerning many skeletons in many royal cupboards from any number of undisclosed resources.

171. *The day's anáthema.* The day's 'curse.'

176. *Lifting over the heavied motion.* According to martial exponent Peter Hsu, passing, or boosting a 'live' angling-in blade to the side from underneath is a superior work, as there is no weapon between the attacker and defender. Hence, there is nothing to protect the defender except timing and distance.

184. *A fine Damascus.* Some of the finest blades in the world were produced in ancient Damascus, Syria. Two other notable areas of great sword making were Toledo, Spain, and Japan. As is well known, in many parts of the world weapons were buried with their masters to accompany them to the Underworld. Here we see proof of that. Even the dead Turk has his favorite weapon with him, as all the deadlanders do, and in the midst of battle, Dark Storm appreciated its great artwork, another insight into her personality.

188. *She yanked this lower spirit.* This line refers to Storm jerking the evil and disgusting Turk off his attack line during the battle.

189. *Deluded Turk's scalding metal.* Delude + elude + deluge. This three-fold interpretation allows for a deceiving, eluding 'water principle.' In the *Ground* Chapter of *Five Rings*, Musashi explains water's combative virtue:

> With water as the basis, the spirit becomes like water. Water adopts the shape
> of its receptacle, it is sometimes a trickle and sometimes a wild sea (p. 43).

In Storm's situation, she literally adopts the 'water principle' to suit her combative needs, she 'dousing' the Turk's 'hot, watery-like' metal.

193. *Suck forth his spirit.* Stronger spiritpire entities in the Deadlands have the ability to drain the spirit out of a weaker soul. A reasonable parallel is in C.S. Lewis' *The Screwtape Letters* in which stronger spirits absorb or feed on weaker ones, as they, along with their verminous human spirit counterparts do every day on Earth. There are only slight differences between *spiritpires* and *soulpires* and the terms are interchangeable. Known as *spirpirs* and *solpirs* in the Nether, they focus on different things. *Spirpirs* prefer to dine upon the rational human soul, mental dispositions and vital principles. *Solpirs* tend upon more of the *Zōé* ("life"), the 'animal sentience' level of the immortal human soul and its vitalities. It appears that each aspect of the psyche has a different flavor and nutritional value, but interestingly, because of socio-ectonomic conditions, both classes reflect social bias and occulturally acquired tastes. The terms *soulpire* and *solpir* are derogatory, as solpirs imbibe on lower-shelf psyche spirits. The terms are used by the elitist spooks as snobbish comments to castigate and look down upon what they consider the *bourgeois*, the plebes, bodies, mortals, the trogs, the lower classes of phantoms—the '*boo*'zers. With these downtrodden come strong criminal elementals so it is no wonder those higher up on the food chain sneer at them. Because competition in the Mortuus is fiercely spiricidal, this they do all the while, they, being dead to the world, hypocryptically inhaling and soaking up their own swills, essences and other unfortunate *aqua vitae* (Lat., "water of life"—brandy on steroids, but in their case 'water-life's'; humans).

From what the dedicator can gather, the difference between the two groups is that of sipping a fine French wine on the romantic Riviera at midnight or chugging some ripple out of a crinkly bag at 3 a.m. in some dingy back alley in Watts. Oh yes, there is quite a difference and *spirpirs* do tend to use straws.

197. *To feel the true Valhallan evil.* 'The man,' stripped for the moment of his humanistic and civilized aspects, begins to feel confusion, panic, dread and his baser natures coming to the fore. In the dark light of the battle, he begins to feel what the wicked deadlanders feel all the time.

200. *The more he does.* Like a battery, spirits in the Nether store energy through deeds. Goremet spirits like Storm know when someone is marinated ('mars-ate') and pounded up enough in their evil ways for their gr(ill)ing and *de*(vi)licious consumption.

205. *Within her dark, adderish self.* Adder + add + at her. Not only is Storm like a poisonous *adder*, she is out to get Kari, to get at (ad)-her, adding her to her list of victims.

208. *Hair moving flowly . . . the sloe battle drop.* Slowly + flow. As Black Sun is cut down, her death is shot as if in slow-motion. *Flowly* describes a slow, flowing, sensual poetic motion. *Sloe* is an archaic term for 'black,' or 'pitch dark.' Here it means "great darkness"; that the battle took place when it was 'black as midnight/ November/thunder'–phrases related to 'black' and *sloe*. Other associated words for *sloe* include 'swarthy,' 'swart,' 'somber,' 'ink-like,' 'ebon,' 'coal,' 'sable,' 'obsidian' and 'onyx'—the reader gets the idea. Everything is as black as Hell. Check out a list of synonyms for 'black.'

214. *Cut-clean through.* Another Musashi-ism. No argument of philosophy ever was made that was not proven wrong or destroyed by the *cut* of the blade, indicating the blade's high spiritual purpose and the finality of truth in action.

216. *That grisly myrmidon wanton.* *Wanton* implies a cruel, unprovoked, deliberate, violent, despicable action. In this context, Kari views Storm as a disgusting

subordinate *myrmidon* who "wants" to execute her own ambitious orders without thought or remorse. *Wanton* is also a term applied to women who are lecherous and lustful. Kari must really despise Storm to think of her as such, or it just could be she knows a lot about her. And given the fact she is a spirit such sensualities of the flesh must inevitably transfer to the intangible ungraspable, meaning Storm is probably enjoying this battle on several different 'exciting' levels—really turning the Valkid's stomach.

224. *"Think twice Theman; don't go, for she is . . ."* Kari knows of Theman's split nature, that is, his pending split personality. She is not referring to his 'Dead Yet Alive' nature. In addition, Kari is trying to work 'the man' to her own purposes.

232. *A fool to her ambition.* Even the 'good' in the Deadlands aspire to manipulate events to their own advantage.

239. *Shafts into her compact atlatl.* *A(h)tlatl* "spear-thrower." The ancient Aztecan Nahuatl device, acting as an extension of one's arm, functions as a lever, adding tremendous power and range to a spear throw, increasing its distance immeasurably.

243. *Appointment in the 'Samarran style.'* This is a borrowing from the play, *Sheppey* (1933, III.), by W. Somerset Maugham. This phrase is used of Death, who was surprised to find an old servant of a rich man in a Baghdad market, because that night he had an appointment with the old man in Samarra, a far away city. The old man earlier had seen Death in the local market curiously peering at him, and in his fear the man ran away seeking to avert his own death only to find it—unfortunately, by fleeing to Samarra. In light of our story, Kari has great foresight, knowing 'the man' is running to his apparent destruction.

246. *Lines to cross.* Kari is going back to her battle line, allegedly.

247-250. *Hell is a'one made forever, yet her lies duly forestall.* According to the text, Hell is of one's own making. But here, Hell is also personified—she does not want anyone to know she actually exists in Earth-reality, that is, until they arrive at her doorstep (or her big Hell-Mouth) and then it is too late. *Ever-branding flame* is a sarcastic comment, meaning "ever-lovin". *And contests ne'er gained.* There are no victories in Hell proper, which reflects Kari's Valhallan ethic.

252. *Element of the cosmos.* (Gk., *kos'-mos*). *Cosmos* is 'an orderly, ornate arrangement or adornment.' Here Kari points out while singing during battle that man is an element of the *cosmos*, the *hoch punkt*, the 'high-point' 'adorned arrangement' of nature fashioned by the gods *for immortal ends*, his spirit being an eternal *flame*.

253. *Man of dust, man of clay. Genesis Adam, lit.,* "Dirt," or *"Man of Earth,"* made out of *dust.* Ancient Chinese texts also indicate that Adam may have glowed like a lightning bug or an angel would, the glow being tinted in red. "In summary, before Adam sinned and disobeyed God, the Chinese characters portray his body as being covered with a glorious light, as having a fiery appearance. . . . Adam and his wife were made in the image of God, pictured as a covering glorious fire (possibly also red-tinged). Since the Hebrew name 'Adam' means not only 'ground,' but also 'red,' it may have been this imagery of a fiery covering that made both the Chinese and the Hebrews describe him as being red" (Nelson and Broadberry, pp. 35-36).

258. *And rav'ed in his lunaticked heart.* Raven + raved. This refers to an insane attitude portending, like the raven motif that runs through the poem, the nasty Turk's death.

NINETEEN: MESSENGER OF DEATH

The air scorched the buttefull day,
Canyons cracked open in noon display.
Black orb overhead, lumined dark sunny land,
Desert whipped wastes that tortured and de-*man*ned.

Junipers split, boulders fractured round—   5
Enter the Nekropolis where the Angel was found.
Slid he down from his horse all frothed and foamed,
Into the ghost town did he cat-saunter and noiselessly roamed.
—Sought for *El Capitán*, with a price on his head,
To take him to Valhalla, or serve him up dead.   10

They played quiet languid notes, the music drifted by,
Angel listened inwardly, and feeling, he sighed.
Pleasant strings on such a tough business day,
Made him appreciative–then he went on to slay.

Squint eyed, entered he into dark den of iniquity,   15
De-lights of soulless flesh square about are all he did see.
Dry wind stirred strong, rearing brown *swirly* coarse dust,
Unlatched Angel he his blade, ready for *that* must.

Approached the lone headman, an abrasive felon at best,
Cold eyes met colder ones; strong wills to contest.   20
"Where is he?" the tall one with quiet impatience said,
A hundred stares around him, all desiring him bled.

The decayed minion's hand nerved away from his Spanish buckle and belt—
Those hot flashing pangs of being cut down from Angel's cool face pre-felt.

Nodded he his noggin with a nod of his no chin,   25
"Room six—to the left, be sure to go straight on in."

Angel watched him slowly then to the splat'red stairs went he,
The minion motioned five others to complete the treachery.
With hand on blade, silent, Angel stood before the old scarred door,
Intensing pitch pierced the air, glittered nerves *auroar*.   30

"Come in," a husky voice firmed and Angel cocked back,
Opened the creaking door slowly readied for attack.
"It's been a long time, Heart," *El Capitán* offered him a cup,
"We've both come quite a ways, when last you looked me up."

Angel's dead eyes peered about the oppressing heavy room,   35
Shades lounged about in the thickening crimson overgloom.
"You won't take me," laughed *El*, "like you planned to today,
No, I have some information for you, if you'll, *heh*, 'spare me your blade.'"

"You were always good for that," Angel said, relaxing in his stance.
"It's about that man you brought in"; the shade stared over Angel's back.   40
Angel watched him, an unkillable predator cat curious to know,
He would listen to his enemy—to see how far he would go.

The shade, *El Capitán*, smiled and paced about the room,
His boots thunkscrape the dry wood floor; dust raising in the tomb
(Knew he would kill *this* pain in the Angel in time just as possibly soon).   45

"It's about a certain battle that went on yesternight.
Precious Valhalla was laid waste, it lies in ruinous blight.
Too bad, a pity, you find that interesting I do detect,
You should keep abreast of things; it's your one defect."

As the *Capitán* shade spoke the room slowly filled,   50
With seven more evil spirits to bar the swordslinger's will.

VALLEY OF THE DAMNED

Angel raked about, gaunt hands dangling at his hips,
Calmly readied for finality's action—the dogs of war to slit.

"And 'the man'?" Angel spoke, with drawled deliberate voice,
Calmly stroking his chin now, ready to deploy.   55
"You mean, *'The Mean?'*" *Capitán hehehed* to say,
"Well, *gringo*, he survived His first battle—
But the Dark One has taken his prize away."

"And where?" said Angel smirking, appreciating Storm's robust hel-zeal,
"I don't mind telling as you'll be dead in a moment,"
said the *El Capitán* of evil.   60
"She's taken it to the Mount, to those recesses of the North,
There you will find the Dark with all her malignant cohorts."

"And now, sweet *adiós*, my friend," the shade spirit did explain,
"It's time to deck you out; your corpse on a platter will lay?
(*Sí*, it's for you to push up daisies, you'll make a pretty bouquet *dis*-play).   65
—You hear? They are already playing funeral music now—just for you,
Pity the poor spirit who at death does not have a requiem, and so, *adieu*."

Angel smiled, thought for a moment then looked him in *the* eye.
"You're right," he said smiling, "it is about that time to die.
But I think you have it backward, it's *uh*, not going to be me,"   70
Slowly he looked to his tang, arm readied to snap it free.
His bead swept to the nearest damned, and spoke uninvitingly.

"They'll make swift work of you, of this I can guarantee—"
"Don't think so," said Angel, lithe fingers tapping his weathered hilt,
"Well? I'm waiting to finish off your demonic fallen guilt"   75
(Never one to send a spirit to Hel on a growling empty belly,
Angel made sure *El's* shot was full, as he got his whiskeyed ready).

247

Flushed spirits looked about, air charged in negativities,
Incorporeal hearts pounding, speaks of their intendencies.
Feet and limbs; *a'breat-thin'*, anticipating what was in store,   80
Gripped the ground; faces; music; tensioning for gore.

Lonnnnnnnnnnnnng————————————**PAUSE**

Hot sticky hands jumping to their icy callous grips,
A Harpy seizing Angel's swordhand, preventing its flighted apocalypse,
Angel turning in; drawing short blade, he through the air let slipping,   85
Pealed loosening hands, his foes' killing skills he eclipsing,
Blades gushing forth, hissing to stick deep their fangings,
Whipped he the demon across his belly, his sword a'slanging.

The small room holding its vast up surprising,
With it, *Angeling* was openly angling, brazenly allying.   90
Chasing his enemies round about in fast crampening room,
Cuttingly left and right, weaving them to his loom.

Bodies amassing; cornering in *this* adhesive collecting,
Raining runny blades down, vicious dead vivisecting,
Bodies and limbs rotating slow prolonging in dust-hewn air,   95
Intensing motion–ballad of deadly actioning despaired.

Hades razorings *whirrrling* through spiraling bloodspace,
Angel cuttening shades down with *that* poetic-like grace,
Bodies tumbling steeling arcings rip cross *zagzzzigging* cut m'eat,
Angeling harrowing through motion as wind mows through wheat.   100

Blood painting walls, spat'ring fragile gorying lines,
Supreme abstract of the impressionistic master ⇀ artwork so refined.

El Capitán wounded on all fours now hurriedly gasped out,
Angel stood over him with dielate eyes, without a trace of doubt.
"You were right," he said, placing his sword on the shade's stiff neck,   105
"This should have saved you, but my price is finally met."

"*Bastardo*!" *El* wretched to Angel, "from me depart,"
"Right again, old *amigo*," and his head from his body he part.
"*Adiós*," Angel wryed, spatting calmly on his old 'friend.'
A great bounty to collect, and '*The Mean*' once more to rend'   110

DOUGLAS M. LAURENT

Chapter Nineteen Valley Footnotes

Here we watch Angel-Heart pay a visit to his 'old friend,' *El Capitán*, 'The Captain.' The two apparently had worked together before, perhaps at cross-purposes, but now Angel is out to collect some dividends. He comes to the *Capitán* to gain information concerning general events, Dark Storm, Kari, other mercenaries, bounties and 'the man.' *El Capitán* knows what he is there for—to kill him, and so tries to buy him off with the information Angel wants. Failing this, he plans to kill the swordpacker himself.

1. *The buttefull day.* Beautiful + butte. This is a fine day in an area of rocky deserts and buttes. The dark sun shines wonderfully on this 'sunny' day.

6. *Enter the Nekropolis.* (Gk. *nekrós*, "dead body," I.E. *nekro*, "perish, "disappear"). This Greek term implies "city of the dead."

9. *El Capitán.* This is a powerful town boss of Spanish origins.

11. *Quiet languid notes.* Here we catch a glimpse of one of Angel's interests. He is partial to music.

18. *Ready for that must.* Some subscribe the line as being *ready for that cut.* However, in context here the meaning is plain. Angel will naturally cut, but it is much more than that. His psychological and physical preparation does not lay so much on cutting, but on the relishing of *that must w*hich courses through him like an addiction, the psychology of it far outweighing the mere physical blade cut. He enjoys the feeling-tension of pre-killing, *the must* of it all.

33-35. *Long time, Heart . . . the oppressing heavy room. Heart* is one of Angel's nick names, short for *Angel-Heart*, a nether-snub, as in 'he's all heart.' There is nothing sentimental about his name however. Everyone knows this spirit is a killer. *Heavy room* or 'heaving room.' The room itself is so thick with tension it seems to be panting and sucking in air unto the point of angry heaving vexation.

45-47. *Pain in the Angel . . . in ruinous blight.* Knowing Angel so well for such a long time, 'perhaps' *El Capitán* is thinking of squelching the pains within him, sort of as an act of mercy, but this is speculation and we Midgarders know what they say, "actions speak louder than edited text." Blight + light. The *Capitán* thinks Valhalla is rotten and useless from his own viewpoint. Being an old West-style gangster, He hates the heroes there.

51. *Seven more evil spirits.* According to biblical literature, when an unclean spirit decides to leave a man that it is indwelling, it goes about wandering, looking for better action. When it finds no better options for its own sordid gain, it returns to its 'home,' the man who is considered its property. If the man still wishes to remain neutral about spiritual matters, living in the same deplorable spiritual conditions where there is no growth or allegiance to God, the rotten spirit has permission to re-enter him and is obliged to share its residence in the man with seven other spirits more wicked than itself. This serves as both a legality and judgment in the spiritual realm as a recompense for the hard-hearted person who desires to stay willingly and spiritually ignorant and neutral about extremely powerful spiritual realities, *Luke* 11.24-26 (Ch. 9 note # 6).

53. *The dogs of war to slit.* This line is adapted from Shakespeare's *Julius Caesar* (III. i.). Mark Antony, vowing revenge against the murderers of Caesar, shouts, "*Cry 'Havoc!' and let slip the dogs of war.*" *Havoc*, a battle cry, literally means "total slaughter." In Angel's case, he is going to kill these dogs by slitting them apart.

56. "You mean, '*The Mean?*'" This is the first time Mark Theman's name in the poem has surfaced as '*The Mean.*' Theman, 'the man,' has changed, revealing his slow, darkening transformation.

61. *To the Mount, to those recesses of the North.* From *Isaiah* 14.13. The epic poetry of Canaanite Ugarit often refers to the 'Mountain of the North' or *Sapunu*, as being the abode of the gods, where they held their high councils. As a powerful spirit, it is only logical that Dark Storm would metaphorically utilize the vast wilderness area to the north of the Deadlands as part of her domain and arsenal, and as the biblical

passage suggests, Lucifer boasted of his five prides there, in the north so to speak, portending his eventual destruction—and perhaps Dark Storm's. *FYI*, Ba'lu is the Canaanite god of the North mountain Sapunu/Saphon/Casius. But this deity god is no other than Ba'al the Phoenician and Babylonian all-round baddie King Nimrod of *Genesis* Ten who in time morphed into Zeus Kasios and Jupiter Casius.

76-77. Growling empty belly . . . his whiskeyed ready. Empty belly recollects the tale of R. Clay Allison (1841-1887) a Wild West gunfighter who calmly sat down to dinner with his enemy Chunk Colbert, a killer of seven men, and while they were dining, Chunk drew a pistol that struck the under table and Allison unperturbedly pulled and shot him in the head. When asked why he sat down to eat with a man he knew was going to try to kill him, Allison coolly responded, "Because I didn't want to send a man to hell on an empty stomach." *Whiskeyed* or *'whisk-eye.'* As Angel whisks his eyes about the room, he keys in on and gives *El Capitán* 'the look,' 'the eye,' 'the stare,' 'the vibe.' Angel, intense and alert, knows everything that is going on around him.

80. Limbs; a'breat-thin'. Dead spirits do not exactly 'breathe.' *'A'* in the Greek is a 'no,' or negation, thus these dead living 'eat(en) thin' spirits are stone cold still. This is in opposition to Western genre expectations where everybody, except the super-hero, is panting right before explosive action. The grim silence adds tension to the scene (explore the concept of what the *a-musement* 'no-thought' park we send our kiddies to is all about 'in dark' of the ployish soul-snatching Deadlands).

84. A Harpy seizing. This is one of *El Capitán's* disgusting hench-spirits. A Harpy is a malignant creature from Greek mythology. It is part woman and bird, sharp-clawed and very predatorial, giving us a clue as to what this spirit-criminal is all about. They liked to torture, seizing souls and children and were into tormenting with evil vices and wicked obsessions. *Flighted apocalypse.* Greek *apocalypse, lit.,* "revealing," or "show-ing." Angel's brilliant sword work 'enlightens' his enemies as to their destruction.

85. Angel turning in. There are techniques in the Japanese sword art of *kenjutsu* for effective counters if an enemy grabs ones drawing hand. Apparently, Angel, being a master swordsman, knows many. He is not caught by surprise, baiting and utilizing the initial attack to set up his offense. The phrase *turning in*, however, suggests the linguist Mycroft, is also indicative of Angel being bored with the action overall, 'sleepy' almost one might say, further telling of his prowess.

89-90. *The small room . . . Angeling was openly, angling brazenly allying.* The secret to Angel's brilliantly confusing bait-and-switch techniques are such is that they *all 'lie'* in motion. For him the *small stifling room* was wide *open* in terms of cutting-edge possibilities and applications.

91-92. *Chasing his . . . cuttingly left and right, weaving them to his loom.* This is yet another Musashi-ism for actions done for mass combat. In the *Water* Chapter of *A Book of Five Rings*, Musashi explains the technique and spirit of *There are Many Enemies*:

> 'There are many enemies' applies when you are fighting one against many. Draw both sword and companion sword and assume a wide-stretched left and right attitude. The spirit is to chase the enemies around from side to side, even though they come from all four directions. Observe their attacking order, and go to meet first those who attack first. Sweep your eyes around broadly, carefully examining the attacking order, and cut left and right alternately with your swords. Waiting is bad. Always quickly re-assume your attitudes to both sides, cut the enemies down as they advance, crushing them in the direction from which they attack. Whatever you do, you must drive the enemy together, as if tying a line of fishes, and when they are seen to be piled up, cut them down strongly without giving them room to move (p. 65).

In Angel's case, this is a tried and true reality with him. *Weaving them to his loom. Loom* here means appearing as a "shadow," especially one that is 'large' or 'threatening.' It is an expression of a vague and often exaggerated appearance of an object as seen in darkness or fog, like being at sea where one at first with trouble sees 'the loom of the land.' Here the metaphor is combined with Angel's talents to 'weave' with his sword motion a 'tapestry of mayhem,' being a shadow that looms up unexpectedly like a rock in the gloom to cut his enemies down in the seeming vagueness of his Nethermotion.

94. *Vicious dead vivisecting.* This is the methodical, scientific 'dissection of living things.' In this case, it is a paradox, since these creatures are already dead. Perhaps the line should read, *vicious live dissecting.*

97-99. *That poetic-like grace . . . harrowing through motion.* Slow-motion *poetic* death sequences seen in popular movies are used to convey the meaning of this passage. *Harrowing* is to "pillage, plunder and torment," lending a further direness to the death scene.

102. *Supreme abstract of the impressionistic master. Impressionism* was a style or movement in painting and literature in France in the 1860s characterized by a concern with depicting visual impressions. It sought to capture a feeling or experience rather than to achieve an accurate depiction. Apparently Angel is so good at his blade that he 'paints' in this style, not so much concerned with fine detail or pin-point accuracy as Kari does, as with creating a mood leaving his vibe mark of shock, fear and awe, his *aura*; his essence symbolized through a spiritual uproar or *auroar* (poem line # 30 above) upon his enemy's.

TWENTY: DUST AND FOLLY

Harsh land, she tempered a man, taught him to endure,
Spirits shaped by godless wastes, *their* bestial lot confirmed.
Gravemounds of those nameless, none to remember at all,
Once fine friends and enemies, called by death's autumned fall.

Beyond the hidden coiling 'scarp The Mean lay hunkered down,   5
Peered he over the outcrop, a campsite he had found.
The stomachurning phantoms there numbered half-score and one,
Sat they around their *pining* fire to warm hands that were none.

Stripped to the waist, The Mean's heart-tympani drum *p-pp*ound*p*ed,
Ancient instincts boiled within, his pulsings resounded.   10
Those ghost men drank their wine cups, an inebriated lost lot,
A 'wretched' outcast served them, to fill their bony pots.

As The Mean moved, so he would motivate and move *them*,
The fate of a generation, he knew, was on him to confer or condemn.
He in his mind had already taken, conquered them one and all,   15
To find the answers he sought for, and the plans they irrationalled.

(He knew enough of sword film work–or so he thought that he could get by——
Not that many would escape, but that many would die).
After all his vanity supposed, didn't he work with Hollywood's best?
Like Error and Basil, *he* would out-hero them to death   20
(And starred in many epic sword movies wasting many to rest).
Poor dumb bastard soul—if he only knew—,
The wretched pain that twɨʒt the consciənce killing even a damnéd few.
But he felt quite ready in his blackening heart of hearts,
It seems he felt he was born for this—destined right from the very start.   25

Skulked around the camp and picked off unwary sentry shades,
He had seen this in the movies; plots now came to his aid.
When ready, he rushed the camp quite satisfied,
Felt surprise his ally, and knew he could not yet die.

An awkward gangly festivity of spitting bloodlust ensued,   30
Sloshed spirits *tripiping* each other, The Mean falling *assertively* too.
A drunken orgy of *clunsyclumky* swordid blood slick revelry,
The Mean becoming medium-efficient in death's choppy agency.

Sounds and cries solidead the air,
Curses slungeing at the devil-may-care,   35
Amidst the wood and metal thrown at him,
The Mean wrenched hard, slashing dim.
Yet confusion wrought his wonderful work,
The Mean unaccustomed to battles' jerks,
Am*ateu*'red in the rudiments of his trade,   40
Rank broken rhythms lucked his way.

He bent over their bodies for information to check,
A sword lifted forward, reaching his sweating neck.
The Mean stiffened and cast discriminating eye,
Onto the ground where those alleged bodies lied.   45

"Hooray," the 'wretched' false corpse did say,
Angel stood, and brushed the dust away.
"Hard to lie dead like that for any length of time."
The swordpacker noticed his confusion. "An old trick of mine."

He smirked, acknowledging The Mean's affront,   50
"Like someone said, 'Cowards die many times before their deaths;
The valiant never taste of death but once.'"

Angel moved around the heaving, beady-eyed man
(An animal on the run—or to take his stand).
The Mean studied Angel, to draw, hard up and down,   55
Angel shook his head slow, with an icening frown.

"She's not with them," Angel nodded leisurely to the man distraught,
"I could have spared you the trouble, if you had *um*, looked me up as you
ought."
"I killed innocent *shades?*⟶"
"Nothing's innocent here. We're all from the grave."   60

"¡Where is she!?" the maturing spirit-killer vimmed,
Angel glanced over his shoulder, thinking to behead him.

"North. To her ancestral land.
Wants you to come, to be with her or deadmanned.
In *'the mean'*time," Angel stacked the bodies,   65
"You've earned it," he mentioned–
"They'll bring you in some power-soul money."

"You're not taking me in—"
Angel nodded slow; a catted grin.

Chapter Twenty Valley Footnotes

Mark Theman, 'the man,' now 'The Mean,' launches his first offensive career action in the Mortuus Deadlands slaying a bunch of decrepit evil spirits. This action presents a 'step forward' for him (perhaps backward, depending on how you look at it) in that he is learning the ways of the Nether, albeit in a clumsy fashion. Angel amuses himself by playing along.

7. *Half-score and one.* A *score* is twenty items. There are around eleven individuals here.

8. *Their pining fire.* Everything in the Nether seems to have a mind of its own. Not only is the burning wood pine, it also 'pines' for them, 'longing' to consume these spirits, having a dullish yearning of its own.

9. *The Mean's heart-tympani drum p-ppoundped.* Theman is so scared his heart pounds like a symphonic drum and wants to run away real bad as seen in fragmentary remnant word *ped*, Latin for "foot." Apparently, Theman is experiencing the classic 'fight or flight' syndrome just about everybody goes through before an encounter of any kind. In short, Theman wants to take to his heels and get outta there, but is compulsed to duke it out *comp-p-ppounding* the issue.

12. *A 'wretched' outcast.* This is Angel in disguise.

14. *Of a generation.* Theman is intensely aware that his actions in the Deadzone will affect multitudes of his fans on Earth. Their *lives*, *via* his, would be affected forever. As said, "For want of a nail the kingdom was lost."

15. *He in his mind had already taken, conquered.* Sun Tzu says that superior warriors win first then go out and kick booty, while the losers go to war first and then seek to win (Ch. 4 on *Disposition*). Seems like Theman is learning.

20. *Like Errol and Basil.* Superstars Errol Flynn and Basil Rathbone of the 1930s-1960s Hollywood. They made classic epic film adventures together such as *Robin Hood*

(*Warner Brothers*, 1938) and *Captain Blood* (*Warner Brothers*, 1935). Rathbone was noted for his unrivaled sword choreography skills. *See* also his more than brilliant work in *The Mark of Zorro* starring Tyrone Power (*20th Century Fox*, 1940). Also, for an excellent display of 'broken rhythms' in combat, such as Bruce Lee espoused in his *Tao of Jeet Kune Do, see* Rathbone's work in the musical comedy, *The Court Jester* starring Danny Kaye (*Paramount Pictures*, 1956). The film is also noted for its tremendous witty lyrics by Sylvia Fine. Theman is trying to imitate these men but fails miserably.

32. *Clunsyclumky swordid blood.* The completely harebrained but desperate, awkward affair sounds like a stack of kitchen tins and pots crashing to the floor—a cacophonic *clinkcylankcylenkcylonkcylunky* and *clynky* concerto of Thematic solo cinereal steel and chicanery. Sword + sordid. A very base and lowly display of remnant virtues for rotted spirit fighters now turned criminal.

38. *Confusion wrought his wonderful work.* This translation is borrowed from *Macbeth* (II. iii.), "Confusion now hath made his masterpiece!" where Macduff discovers the murdered good King Duncan. Mark Theman's poor askewed combatmanship is such a low form of confusion that it fortunately carries the day for him. It is just dumb luck that Theman survives his fragmented actions are off-setting.

41. *Rank broken rhythms.* In all fighting arts, beginners have off-kilter rhythms, well known among the experts for being even able to throw off their own superb timing. But *rank* denotes Theman's technique is also stinky.

45-49. *Alleged bodies lied* . . . "*Hard to lie dead* . . . *An old trick of mine.*" One body, Angel's, was not 'laying' dead, it was 'lying' to Theman, deceiving him. *Hard dead.* This is not to say Theman 'killed' or even wounded Angel, but Angel's skills are such that he can allow a razor sharp Nethblade to miss him by a fraction, and thus fake his own death. This calls for complete mastery of timing and distance, and of course, melodramatics. *An old trick of mine.* Like an opossum pretending to be dead or laying low, Angel is very good at 'playing possum,' faking his death. One may wonder if he learned to grin as he does from them and so stare his opponents down (Ch. 33 note # 362).

51. *Cowards die many times.* Angel quotes from *Julius Caesar*. Right before Caesar is assassinated, he utters these lines to his wife Calpurnia (II. ii.). According to fragmentary accounts of Angel found in the thirteenth century *Kel's Yellow Book*, he apparently had 'died' heroically before and once was enough for him. Anyway, at least, this is what he would have Theman believe. As for how Angel knew this line from the Midgard play, apparently he is well read.

53-54. *Beady-eyed man (An animal on the run—).* *Beady-eyed* is an American *cliché* for a person who looks sneaky, like a weasel with dishonest characteristics. The phrase "being born beady-eyed" is a common expression. The look is said to be associated with the criminal type. *On the run* is the 'flight or fight' tendency of all animals displayed here. Theman is becoming more animal-like. *See* Eli Wallach's excellent portrayal as a Tuco "the rat" with a rat's movement qualities in the Western classic, *The Good, the Bad and the Ugly* by Sergio Leone (1966). These qualities perhaps describe Theman well. The movie's brilliant haunting musical score has influenced American and other cultures to this day, as can be heard in musical arrangements on television shows, commercials, radio and other movies.

TWENTY-ONE: RIGHT BUYS MIGHT

Heat-waving mead Hall danced with blazing hellkites,
Spektraled figures milled about in grinding dedlight.
Denizens of the depraved in their sleazy depths,
Seeking corrosive barren pleasures—
Of what none they had left.   5

Windows fliquoreding light scintillating ground,
Garish empty effigies dancjigging around.
Helish images elongating on floor,
Showed their essence all the no more.

Dusking eve brought about the cooling chill,   10
And those to revelry fresh from their cold-cuts kills.
Windswept village amid the wastes,
Gathered the dead for this evening's wake.

A gang of killers drank and stood,
With Burning Prairie of Dark Storm's hood.   15
Menaced she with slat demeaning eye,
Those she loathed surely died.

Many in all were in her band,
Yet from Storm only she took her commands.
Vicious agent of fleeted destruction,   20
Dark's right hand for death's compunction.

Some baited bears with their dogs,
Some threw axes at great hogs,
Some danced o'er swords that cut,
Some diced others who had no luck.   25

DOUGLAS M. LAURENT

Within this noisy thronging stinking smelly place,
St. Kari of Bladedom moved without a trace.
"What do you want?!" bellowed some, "You little pest,
Get outta here, find somewhere else to beset!"

Up to the scar'red table of Burning went she,   30
Watched the games then threw gold for all to see.
Curious looks went to her face,
Kari stared at Burning with tolerant grace.
Burning looked about, then quietly said,
"It's enough to ask a question—   35
But—not enough if you want someone dead."

Kari smiled and plopped another bag of sould,
Burning Prairie smirled, eyes ♪cha-ch$nnnged♫!! with *hard cold*.
"YOU?!? You want someone to kill for You!?"
(*cookoo—♪cookoo*)—*Whaddya* nuts!? w—*Who* let you out——   40
Do ya have some new loose screws?!"

And who—?" the shocked spirit then said with meticulous form.
"Your boss, that dissolute Dark Storm."

Eyes at table flowed, scarcely did their heads,
Kari threw more gold down, to each phantasm and said,   45
"A simple thing for such as some of you:
Your master to kill, power to gain—
And 'the man,' to *me*, subdued."

Burning paused, then weighed the bag's contents,
Smirked she in accord, then laugh-greed of a traitorous rat.   50
"Sure, why not, hear that y'all? Let's kill for this "c'harming" Saint!
I abhor her. I'll take her myself with my bowed strangulhate,
Huh, never figured that, I thought one of us you ain't."

"One thing more," Kari said, to add some finer weight,
"There's another, that 'disparate' Angel, the one whom I hate."   55

"*Hmmmm.* Oh yes. I do see your point.
Well, there *are* some here who would *love* to pull his blade fingers out of joint.
Don't worry 'bout him," laughed Burning, "we'll take care of him too."
Kari nodded coolly and backed away, laying odds on who was going to lose.

DOUGLAS M. LAURENT

Chapter Twenty-One Valley Footnotes

This unusual scene finds St. Kari 'buying' some muscle, hiring killers to bump off Dark Storm and Angel. She hires Burning Prairie and her underlings, Storm's first lieutenant and lesser gang members. Her ethics should not be questioned here. In the Dead, the key to victory is efficiency any way one can get it. Midgard k-fu master Bruce Lee said, referring to his *jkd*, that "In this art, efficiency is anything that scores" (*Tao*, p. 24). However, Kari's seeming underhandedness is not what she is all about. As an able tactician, she is merely moving rotten elements about to gain the advantage.

1. *Heat-waving mead Hall . . . blazing hellkites.* The mead Hall is seen in the heat, having a ghostly waving affect, and no wonder. Mead is an alcoholic beverage made of fermented honey and water. *Hellkites* are vicious, evil, wicked and disgusting persons.

2. *Moved in grinding dedlight.* Dead + de-light. Everything is caustic, wearing a spirit down in the Deadlands, taking away (*de-*) what little 'light' they have.

6. *Windows fliquoreding scintillating light.* Windows are motifs of the dead. They also allow us mortals to 'voyeur' into the world of the spiritually dead. In terms of Kari and Dark Storm, glass motifs also show their 'dis-fractions.' Through the *scintillating* glass, 'brilliant' flickering red-orange light is seen in the drinking hall. *Scintillate* means "brilliant, exciting, stimulating, sparkling, shining, gleaming, shimmering, exhilarating," *etc.* In other words, the flickering liquored lighting is stimulating the blood-drunken mead tavern patrons into a killful lust.

7. *Garish empty effigies dancjigging.* Effigies are 'likenesses,' dummies such as a lynch mob would take out and hang or burn, reflect these spirits personalities—riotous, screaming, hellish and empty. Carefully orchestrated effigy-abusing rabble-rousing scenes are a great tool used by the "Powers that be." They like to use props such as effigies mixed with sly or emotional speeches to channel and raise aggression to *Hi-Fi* levels of hostility where blind mayhem or perhaps self-righteous vigilantism breaks out among the thick clayish throngs. Alternatively, abusive proletariat riffraff can be worked over to let off steam and angst through mob venting and so extinguish,

"break apart" and "disassemble" them—the very strategic essence of using sports for 'crowd control' (good *bunkai* on the "Powers" part—*see* Intro.). "Hi-Fi" is short for the 1950s term *hi-fidelity*, referring to high quality as opposed to poor-quality sound reproduction. In either case, this *attack by the draw*, designed, Sun Tzu would agree (because he supposedly said it), is to slot people into what they expect, to make them discern and confirm their own pointy little views. This has the grand effect of railroading them into their own 'educated' choice of observable routines. Like a boa, this hoopla has the constrictive tendency to throttle and occupy their little pea-brains with fluff, with irrelevancies—with busyness. As the masquerade ball parties far on into the night, all the while the unseen killer-controllers sit back and bide their time waiting for the crucial moment to pull the rug out, undercut and strike—unto that subtle, yet crippling point which the plebes cannot even hope to anticipate, so blind they be. What an art! (They say Americans are the only people who will pay more to get less. The scribbler wonders why. *U*h-oh! Better look at Gibbon's book, *The Decline and Fall of the Roman Empire*.) In the end all this cheering chaotic uproar and misguided spent energy, like a stifling passing breeze on a muggy August day, amounts to zip, 0ero and *zilch-o* on the receiver's end. This calculated attack leaves its victims exhausted and impotent on their spiritual, mental and physical levels—just the right response and result the "Powers" desire and require for overall control and *man*ipulation of the earthy local-yokels. Edwin L. Haislet (1908-1992), former Head boxing coach to the University of Minnesota and inspiration to Bruce Lee observes in his book *Boxing*, that:

> Attack by deception is the attack of the master. The master boxer has at his command techniques to bewilder and confuse the opponent, thereby creating many openings. He feints his opponent into 'knots.' He combines hitting with feinting in such a manner that both appear to be the same. He draws his opponent to him forcing whatever leads he desires. Through defensive hitting and judicious movement, he keeps his opponent off balance. The master boxer has the ability to get in close and understands the value of infighting. He has so perfected the 'shift' that it is used for attack as well as defense. Finally, he is the master of counter fighting for he knows when to attack and when to allow attack (p. 65).

8. *Helish images elongating.* From the flickering shadights of the wanton tentacling fire, like shadows, these overall images are in-flux, eshortgating and elongating ('long-eat-ing'). The wispy, fire-licking, hellixing, strandy, coloring movements are grotesquing caricatures of these dead spirits that through the fire's nether-heat and light, continu-ally slow burn and consume them. That is why the stronger and smarter spirits among them stay at a safe distance in the lighdows.

11-13. *To revelry fresh . . . this evening's wake.* Classical mythology has recorded that the dead in Valhalla come to life after each day's battle. From there, they enter the feast Hall at Valhalla to tell of the events of the day. That is the story for the righ-teous warriors. Overall, though, cites Mythologist Etta Jörgens, there are many gathering houses in the region of the Deadlands in which Valhalla is a small part of that performs this feasting function. Some are good and some are wicked and seedy. In this scene, we are in a lowly 'dive.' What is not generally known, however, is that the more one is killed in the Nether, the longer it takes to come back to life from the 'dead-dead.' Indeed, in the Nether some quarters are known, like the cities of refuge on Earth, as neutral areas where no 'killing' is allowed ('killing' being the relative term here as all are dead anyway). These locales are where spirits may meet only to discuss and plan There are also 'no-man's' (or spirit's) lands that only the hardiest of spirits, good or bad, will enter. This is because ferocious landscapes, vicious predatory animals, weird spiritual entrapments and 'die-mentions' and spir-its of such wickedness inhabit those areas themselves, that those who enter therein might suffer terrible consequences.

15. *With Burning Prairie.* This is Dark Storm's lead hench-spirit from Chapter 1 with her hoodlums.

37-38. *Bag of sould . . . eyes* ♪cha-ch$nnnged♫*!!* *with hard cold.* Soul + gold. *Hard cold* refers to not only a hardened stare by Prairie but to *hard* or *cold* cash, meaning cash that is available at the register *right now*—♪cha-ch$nnng♫*!!* (This is a standard old-time cash register pop-cultural sound effect usually made when somebody realizes there is quick money to be made as seen in cartoons and comedy's. Often the char-acters eyes turn to dollar signs.)

52. *My bowed strangulhate.* Burning Prairie despises being under Storm's dark thumb. As an expert in the garrote and the bow, a compound weapon she uses, she plans to strangle Dark Storm with it and take over her gang and territory.

55. *That 'disparate' Angel.* Latin *disparātus* means "a thing that, unto itself, is so unlike anything else that there is absolutely no basis for comparison." No authority as of yet has been able to track this phrase to its source. However, linguist Mycroft suggests that the word may imply 'desperate.' The point of scholarly contention is if Kari is complimenting the *packin'* cold swordclipper or insulting him and his disgusting scavenging, snooping jackally ways always dogging her heels. Anyway, Kari cuts a deal with Burning to kill the Valzone's top swordduster Angel. (To *clip* someone in mafia lingo is to kill them. To *dust* someone means beating or winning over someone, even unto the point of making he or she "bite the dust".)

TWENTY-TWO: MARRIAGE AND STEEL

In sacred groves they spent the winding lasting night,
Orangered flames dancing on stone etched gods to light.
Fire pushed back the dread and **star**rish smothering black,
The swordslinger and The Mean; back-to-back.

In remoted distance they heard mute battle cries,   5
And far-off fires reddening purged the nighted sky.
Vanir and Aesir; armies in the same mechanic conflict,
Slither in black asp-ness; in battle do they pitch.

Sacrifices hanged on yonder oaks,
Animals and victims priests had choked.   10
Owl's periloused the nighted far starry sky,
While shadows bright eyes desired them to die.

"Hey," whispered The Mean to say,
"Just what is your secret, anyway?"
Angel smirked shifted and strained about,   15
His eyes moved to and fro, planning it out.

"Long story, see.
Don't know if you'll *um*, get it, or even agree."

"Try me," The Mean in half-earnest said,
Sounding him out, to learn the killer's stead.   20
Information he knew now had its double edge,
Could use it to learn——or to murder his new 'friend.'

"Yeah," said Angel, pondering deep,
A little 'bedtime' story to tell before they went to sleep.
He honeyed his sword with oil, rock and solitude,   25
Fondled its edge as lovingly as a snake would its brood.

Rolled his tongue slow about in his cheek,
Cooked up an answer The Mean could keep.
"Like a fine spirited woman, it's the same,
Like a man to be joined, on a day in late May.   30
The secret of weapons is in the mind,
An extension of soul and body; practiced and defined."
Angel eyed his blade's sheened deadly ringing 'drenalin,
"The trick is it doesn't come from here, but from within."

The man eyed him long in curious disbelief,   35
Angel watched the dark—night insects ceased.
Ravens hoarsed loud then in sudden quieted down,
Resumed he his thoughts with an impending frown.

"A man or spirit falls in love for many a reason,
Perhaps to fill the void of their vacuous needful persons.   40
The right woman comes along and he sees deep in her eye,
That the spirit is right and so the knot they tie.

In that wondrous mystical hallowed union,
Flesh becomes one in her springed season.
Man and woman together forever more,   45
To walk through life and all her doors.

The soul, she is a distant mystery for me,
Two becoming one throughout all eternity.
Love for love growing ever closer together,
Sacrifice above self–love's great engender.   50

When a man and a woman soundly entwine,
Their thoughts, emotions and bodies 'Divine.'
Like becoming like to bear each other's burdens,
Union of hearts for all love's exertions.

In the intimacies of impassioned nights,   55
Bodies moving in darkness and fleshed delights.
Sweet secrets pass from loving heart to mind,
Enters the souls of *those* lovers—a most potent wine.

Ahh, memories may fade, but there are a few,
Like embers from the fire, burning to shew,   60
That wherever lovers go, they always carry away,
A warming mellow glow, for *that* cold winter's day.

(Memories of lost love they do enpain,
Fleeting images of what once was never again to gain.
Hold tight those memories that slip through the mind,   65
To walk in those fields again with her—a dream divined.
Oh to be with that lost Valkyrie forevermore again,
To hold her hand delicate until the last world's end.
To be at peace once amore in deep loving soul,
Husband to wife in embracing hold.   70
How he loved her so, but she was now gone,
Leaf to the wind, heart tossed and tumbled torn.
Memories like arrows stick deep—ohhh so deep,
Shafts of pain and joy assail the soul's lonely keep).

A heart that is right ne'er grows old,   75
Never feels its age or death's coming blows,
Forever young in love's sweet eternal flame,
Where spirits sojourn unto those heavenly plains."

The Mean *puzzed* at the shade for a long moment,
Trying to figure out this—his angel of torment.   80
Shrugged at his comrade, then incredulously laughed,
"I don't see what that has to do with the killing act."

Angel's hands moved over arched longbow,
Pulled the catgut taut, its strength to foreknow.
Felt he sturdy the sharp arrow barbs,   85
Plucked at the feathers, and listened afar.

"If it were left solely to the lost soul and mind of man,
The essence of weaponry would lie in his grievous hand."
He eyed the arrowy shank in the glimmered light,
"She is your security, your very life.   90

What fools many is the instrument, she, herself,
Either blade, or shaft or bow or staff.
Motion undefiled is the pure and living key,
Stark motion alone makes weapons mere foolery."

"Go on," The Mean said, trying to ascertain,   95
The Angel-killer's secret—the technique of *insta*-pain.
Angel shook his head, smiled, had heard it all before
(Too bad 'The Mean' didn't know his competitor).

"Like someone once exquisitely said:
'Fine weapons are Heaven's ill omens'—enough to turn you into lead.   100
Like women, they should not condemn but make content,
To enjoy their hidden art, peace, is to be solitarily their embodiment.

So, the truer power of a weapon lies,
In she revealing secrets—don't listen to her overt lies.
Both lover and beloved need one and the other,   105

DOUGLAS M. LAURENT

A union to be whole, each not existing without their partner.
As for the weapon herself, she will disappear,
Losing herself like a brush, beyond the motion-painting so clear.
Vanishing, she won't exist as the eye sees the greater artist,
Like a woman's love, this truth shall always persist.   110

As it is, knowledge like you have abides in lowly estate,
Hacked and splintered apart, here there is no debate.
A weapon's true existence is in the motion she creates,
To see it other than that is to be the victim of *discriminrape*.

Notwith', the weapon in her high estate creates a beautiful way,   115
Breathing life into the soul union of a man and his blade.
In that swirl of consciousness, the self, he disappears,
As the true feel of motion cuts free what was held onto in fear.

In this motion what's all left is a marked fluency,
Removing the self from true mind then conjoined in two bodies.   120
Not just I, who wields the blade to sing, but *Angelinga'bladening*,
Or *bladeninga'Angeling*—this is 'we.'

The deception is finally ours," Angel curtly addressed,
"For what is a weapon in terms of petty static-ness?
For words and actions, like lovers are in unison displayed,   125
Yet descriptions deny actions, when it comes to weapons play.

The arc of circle, the thrust of line,
All things account for weapons of the spirit to mind.
Mars and Venus are like lines and curves,
Where they meet, rapturous insertions occur.   130
But would that Venus be to Mars *a'lovin'*,
Curves and lines would always meet in eternal thrusting!
It is true, then, that as a motion higher sings,
The soul of a spirit loosens her wings.

Designs taught in ignorance deceive,   135
Yet to go beyond is never conceived.
'With all to strike true when *nothing* is there,
Is to have the vision of the 'martialed' where'.

For as high as motion and marriage can go,
So is the mind in its desires that loves it so.   140
To consider all things through the highest of motions,
Is to be in love as with a woman in her loving devotions.

The more sublime the motion, the higher the thought,
Yet words imprison and bring many marriages to naught.
For words band the mind with iron steeling it roundabout,   145
Thus true motion and love is never seen, for it is chained throughout.

Such was your fate, my hungry young friend,
To be the victim of a whore's blasted deceiving ends,
Fettered you she, and to a motion-fashioned,
That limited your eyes—and fueled your ambitious damnation.   150

When one chooses a weapon in first fit of lust,
He feels her murderous glee, and there is no trust.
But that instrument has a gentler side as well,
To keep the peace—by sending someone to Hel.

So, a spirit's lone soul is one that has been reaped,   155
By the flesh that has sown its own weedish, deceptive seed.
Corrupted spirits are from the flesh begot,
They all derive from a weapon's dark natured lot.

Yet motion free is a beauty unparalleled,
Deliver you from danger of the fires of Hel.   160
A woman who cleaves to the soul of her man,
Is a lover who loves until the end."

The Mean grunted, *pffft* in dim resignation,
Unable to contend with this spirritant's convictions.
Lost himself in thought of things world's away,   165
Moved himself about as the crickets in quiet lay.

"Were you then→?" The man began to ask,
Angel nodded, keeping him to his back.
"A long time ago," Angel quietly squint and said,
"Rest easy, friend, I'll *uh*, take the first stand."   170

The man pondered these things then fell asleep,
Leaning over, snoring near the fiery, ashing heap.
Angel, he looked up to the dreamy stars that shone,
It was night and he went out; The Mean was left alone.

Fire crackled low with the last wane of night,   175
The Mean shivered with weapon moving slight.
SHRIEKING WAR-HOOPS he J⌒oLT↗ iNG upright¡ ! ¡
Ambushing spirits in murderous treacherous flight! ¡ !

Barely from h-his thr-roat The Mean spu-sput-gut and yelled,
And two were cut down with lit arrowings that felled.   180
The last *screeeeching*, reaching him raising her axe,
Bolt sped through forehead fhelling her onto the fire aback.
The man *frumplumplelingjumpumbleling* up about,
Seized his weapon and frothing at his mouth,
"w-*Who*'s there!" he shrieked, waiting for response,   185
"Relax," said Angel, from the shadows he announced.

Came he to the fire and kicked a leg around,
Smiled at the man and put his bow down.
The Mean, stared hard at this, his killer 'friend,'
Threw a right and punched him in the head.   190

VALLEY OF THE DAMNED

"You rotten good for nothing *sunnuvabitch*" said the stricken man,
Angel on ground dusted himself, rubbed his jaw with his hand.
"Well now, that makes two of us," he shrugged as he stood,
"You're worth a lot more now that you shed *bloode*."

The Mean backed off, clamored to his skelspechorse,   195
Jumped to the saddle and rode off with galps of force.
"You haven't seen the last of me, *my friend*," Mean rend.
Angel smirked and nodded, "such ingratitude to spend."

DOUGLAS M. LAURENT

Chapter Twenty-Two Valley Footnotes

This scene finds Angel and Theman, 'The Mean,' sharing camp. This is the second major speech in the story, given by Angel. Theman tries to dig information out of the spirit, Angel tells a magnificent tale of love, women and weapons—to his advantage, of course. He uses Theman as bait by the fire to lure in and kill three mercenary killers.

1. *In sacred groves.* In the Deadlands, there are sacred groves such as oak and elm where Druid-like priests perform ritual sacrifices, hanging people, animals and power objects, talismans, in trees, on rocks, and elsewhere.

2-3. *Orangered flames dancing . . . starrish smothering black.* "Or anger red." Even though the text does not explicitly state it, someone or something around Angel and Theman is very angry. Perhaps it is the living warm colored flames, existing only to heat up and consume, that want to devour them. *Starrish.* This is a paradoxical foreshadow portending future trouble. It begs the question how can it be pitch black out there in the dark and yet be starry, or *starrish.* Do the stars reflect on the 'tarrish black sky, or does this allude to Theman, the black (hearted) star? Time will tell.

24-25. *A little 'bedtime' story to tell . . . He honeyed his sword with oil.* That is, 'bed + tie + me.' Angel is going to spin a tale to 'settle' 'the man' down for the evening so that he does what Angel wants him to do—allay his worries so he does not stir. *Honeyed.* 'Honed + eyed + honey.' Angel hones his blade, eyeing it with sweetness.

29. *A fine spirited woman.* Angel compares love and women to the ways of the sword.

30. *On a day in late May.* May is the 'fertility' month, when spring blossoms forth.

34. *"The trick is . . . but from within."* Hawkesford suggests that Angel is being facetious by using a biblical phrase from *Jeremiah* 17.9, "The heart is deceitful above all *things*, and desperately wicked: who can know it?" This indicates that Angel is

stretching the truth a bit when it comes to his domestic little 'bedtimes' story for 'the man.'

37. *Ravens hoarsed loud.* A portent from *Macbeth* (I. v.), in which Lady Macbeth, upon hearing that King Duncan is coming and witches have prophesied that Macbeth would be King, utters, "The raven himself is hoarse that croaks the fatal entrance of Duncan under my battlements." In context, the raven signifies coming trouble (Macbeth murders Duncan to get the throne).

44. *Flesh becomes one.* This refers to the mystery of marriage. *See Matthew* 19.6.

93. *Motion undefiled is the pure.* As a marriage undefiled, motion, in its pure, unfallen state, is the cleanest and most efficient of cutting truths. A popular line, "He is a man of his word, he does what he says he's going to do," is an apt description of this.

94. *Stark motion alone.* According to Hawkesford, this phrase is akin to 'stark naked,' or ashamed, as Adam and Eve were after they failed a test of basic obedience (eating the forbidden fruit). This primer-level test would have simply brought the couple from a point of unconfirmed innocence to a relationship of deep, intimate abiding trust in and with their Creator. Christ gives all in love eternal, but the choice of returning love to Him must come of one's own free will. Hence, naked motion without love, without morals, is shameful and wasted. Love and mercy must temper the blade.

100. *'Fine weapons are Heaven's ill omens.'* This is a borrowing from the *Tao Te Ching*, Chapter 31. The idea is that weapons are believed to be repugnant to Heaven and peace but are used as a last resort by Heaven when all else fails. The way of Heaven is life, not death, Heaven herself must defend life, and thus there is weapons play. Swordmaster Yagyu Munenori (1571-1646) clarifies for us the concept of Heaven's view of weapons (Cleary, *Japanese*, p. 69):

> It is bias to think that the art of war is just for killing people. It is not to kill people, it is to kill evil. It is a stratagem to give life to many people by killing the evil of one person. There is an old saying, 'Weapons are instruments of ill

omen, despised by the Way of Heaven. To use them only when unavoidable is the Way of Heaven.' The reason weapons are instruments of ill omen is that the Way of Heaven is the Way that gives life to beings, so something used for killing is truly an instrument of ill omen. So it means that what contradicts the Way of Heaven is despised. Nevertheless, it also says that to use arms when unavoidable is also the Way of Heaven. What does this mean? Although flowers blossom and greenery increases in the spring breeze, when the autumn frost comes leaves always drop and trees wither. This is the judgment of nature. This is because there is logic in striking down something when it is completed. People may take advantage of events to do evil, but when that evil is complete, it is attacked. That is why it is said that using weapons to kill people when unavoidable is also the Way of Heaven. It may happen that myriad people suffer because of the evil of one man. In such a case, myriad people are saved by killing one man. Would this not be a true example of (the Zen saying) 'The sword that kills is the sword that gives life'?

107. *She will disappear.* The seventeenth century *Book Haiku* and other writings speak of reaching the 'artless art,' an art that springs from the intuitive soul, this decisive moment surpassing all rational learning. Just as a brush loses importance in the master's hand because the vision of the portrait is so clear stemming from the artist's soul, so does the weapon disappear in the hands of a motion master. As a result, the eye of the artist begins to *ontologically* see the greater artist, the Divine, the 'hidden' Artist behind all creation and nature, who draws all men and women to Himself with gentle voice and hand found in all that they love and cherish. Gk. *Ontology* is the philosophy and science that deals with the nature of being, becoming, existence and reality.

114. *Victim of discriminrape.* Discriminate + rape. This is the same.

118. *True feel of motion . . . in fear.* According to kung-fu historian and adept Peter Hsu, true motion, that is, at the 'moment of truth' action, transcends all petty life-attachments to which a self-centered soul clings to in order to protect itself (in fear) from harm whether legitimate or false. Here the 'I' of the person, that which

is associated with self and selfish preservation, disappears and only the 'doing' is occurring. This passage also shows the way beyond crippling materialism and the like, *i.e.*, what a soul 'thinks' it needs for protection. Cutting to the quick, the mind becomes 'free' of ego-interference, crippling emotions such as fear, and divisive, conflict-ridden reasoning—the bane of Western man—a liberating effect experienced by many masters who practice the blade and other martial arts.

121-122. *Angelinga'bladening, Or bladeninga'Angeling—this is 'we.'* Angel's point here is where the spirit, through thought and action, are one inseparable unit of existence. In the *Water* Chapter of Musashi's *Five Rings*, translator Victor Harris footnotes the sword master's *No Design, No Conception* cut: "'Munen Muso'—this means the ability to act calmly and naturally even in the face of danger. It is the highest accord with existence, when a man's word and his actions are spontaneously the same" (p. 60).

As can be observed in the stanza, there are no known word structures in the English language to capture the reality of this action/being. That is why '*ing*' endings are used in the translation of the *Valley* documents. Mostly, '*ing*' endings show up in action sequences. They are used for displaying compounds of thought and action, both being considered a unit. Of further added interest however are the '*ing*' endings themselves. They are Anglo-Saxon in origin. This type of ending was a literary device used by scribes and was known as a *scribal doublet*. The purpose of the doublet was to lock key information into a manuscript in order to avoid spelling and other errors that occurred during translations. This method was used extensively for royal genealogies, each name being written out twice, *e.g.*, Seaxreding-Seaxred, the '*ing*' ending at the end of somebody's name meaning "the son of," the doublet making it fairly impossible to erroneously repeat or edit a name out. This not only made legal documents safe from error, but oral transmissions were made easier and more dependable by the poetic rhythms set up by the repeating of the names.

According to the historian Atterbury however, on the surface Angel is speaking of the union of mind and body in swordplay, but his words run deeper. Atterbury cites that coupled with the above information there is yet another literary device within the stance known as a *chiasmus* (*chiázō*), Greek for the letter 'X' meaning to "crossover" as noted in the reversal of the *'Angelinga'bladening, Or bladeninga'Angeling'* phrase. This phrase, Jonathan Mycroft would agree, perhaps implies yet another hidden meaning to the line here referring to Angel loving a woman named Angeline (Angelina, Angela), further compounding the idea intimate idea of love and family. In all, it appears that behind the staccatoing description of bladework, Angel may be reminiscing about a possible wife and children.

126. *Descriptions deny actions.* Words can only point to a reality that can only be experienced *via* action; *e.g.*, one must drink the water in order to experience, no words can adequately describe it. Yet, in so many arts, superficial, pop-ish wordy descriptions of actions are the norm. These, cites Peter Hsu, degenerate what should be true learning experiences *via* action, inhibiting the student's greater potential. Negative, descriptive wordy activity binds student's capacities for a more accurate perspective of the arts, the study and understanding of one's self in the light of raw motion, and this in an ever-increasing efficient *ontological* (head to the source) and experiential way.

Because stupid idle talk and trite rational wording is substituted for direct experience, people who have great potential are in actuality kept in ignorance and never grow. This is a matter of keen perception in the arts. This fallacy can be mastered through awareness of flawed teaching methodologies oral, written and physical (*e.g.*, kata *gestalts*), and how these cloud the pure view of self and motion unhindered. Indeed, according to the brilliant Donn F. Draeger (1922-1982), swordsmen, upon beginning to teach their disciples the inner secrets of their arts were known to have said, "Let me demonstrate what I mean; for my lips have lied" (*Classical*, p. 48). This means that the proof is in the pudding, that truth can only be found in action, in *the doing*, as there are really no available 'static' words out there that can adequately describe or capture highly intuitional 'flow-state' motion, a language unto itself far beyond mere verbalism—it is the very stuff of poetry! *Sanjuro* proverb: "Stupid friends are sometimes worse than the enemy."

It is a truism in the martial arts or any discipline for that matter, that set techniques *via* wordy descriptions automatically eliminate other thoughts of possibilities, or different forms of thought-structures and thus movement, from the artist's mind. This is the essence of martial art systems, which can only package increments of selected motions for its students, in the end educating them in a particular way of thought and action—but also blinding them.

This so-called 'educational process' is called *stultification*. It means to be "made st*oo*pit step by step systematically." A zillion times over, even the best students are not alert to the prospect that they are self-encircled, trapped and shrink wrapped, being 'carefully' handled and 'placed' by '*the others*' within an enclosed 'crate box perspective' of their own making. They are not able to 'see' outside their respective circle because the sophomores *are not even aware of it*, or the fact that they are ready to be packed off and delivered overnight by the midnight special express to oblivion. Some schools use traditionalism and social status to accomplish this deliberately dusking yet shining black alluring *oxymoronyx* (sharp-dull) act. Strategically speaking, readers must answer just why this is so themselves (now, who would stultify us Midgarders into being a bunch of *oxymorons*?).

Many arts today, being educational systems that promote their own programs must, due to limitations, either add or remove info from their agenda. Because of the theoretical environment they are in such as rules for school safety—or is it more the safety of a school, this allows their program to 'in-breed,' becoming very set in their purposes. This breeding program produces all sorts of marts, including ones that work great in the sterile confines of their martial labs (*e.g.*, sparring the same type of stylists), but do not work in the real world, as they should if indeed effective self-defense is the main goal.

Beyond doubt, some systems/schools are so xenophobic (Gk. *xénophóbos* "foreign, strange, fear") they have entropically turned so far inward hooked like a junkie on her-ointrospection that they clam-up, isolate and in-breed themselves right into extinction. Within this collapsing process, the original vision of the arts' creator-designer withers and the art becomes a *krispie* 'snap, crackle and pop' punchy leftover. These relic arts wax into intellectual curiosities or physical exercises set apart from the realities of daily life struggles. This is what happens when verbalism and conjecture takes over and the 'doing' of the motion with its initial combative intent is lost. False fronts and a whole lotta shuck and jive sweet talk, that's what it is—all part and parcel of the scheming unseen aspects of the war against humanity (nobody ever said war was pretty). Sifu Lee (*Tao*, p. 14) spells it out his combat view extends into the realm of everyday life:

> Instead of facing combat in its suchness, then, most systems of martial art accu-
> mulate a 'fancy mess' that distorts and cramps their practitioners and distracts

them from the actual reality of combat, which is simple and direct. . . . Worse still, super mental power and spiritual this and spiritual that are desperately incorporated until these practitioners drift further and further into mystery and abstraction.

Even the master sleuth *shéntàn lit.*, "miraculous detective" sifu Holmes with his phenomenal "detection" *zhēnchà-fu* skills says in *The Adventure of the Sussex Vampire*, that, "It is simpler to deal direct." Great minds think alike it seems. Further, scope out what else master Draeger has to say about all this mass produced illusion stuff in the m-arts. Writing of Indonesian *silat*:

All systems of *pentjak-silat* are based on the use of weapons. They are positively not considered empty-hand combative measures in the purest sense of that expression. No *pentjak-silat* system is combatively idealistic, so foolish, or so naïve as to require the exclusive use of empty-hand tactics for solving all combative situations. . . . No such martial snobbery exists for any classical *pentjak-silat* form. This consideration is true of all genuine combative measures. Modern-day emphasis on the empty-hand aspects or sporting outlets for Chinese, Korean, or Japanese fighting forms has particularly clouded the issue. Japanese *karate-dō* or other quasicombatives influenced by that form display the fact that they are not classical combative measures, by their refusal to permit the operator the use of weapons. Japanese *karate-dō*, a twentieth-century development, completely untested in actual combat, is especially guilty of this combative unreality (*Indonesia*, pp. 33-34).

This is the kind of premeditated edited mental sludge Theman, the all too willing bearer of false scabby images, arises and intentionally wraps himself in. The relentlessly rotten movie star is a trimmed sucker-branch way out on the limb by-product of such overgrown wedging events. As an act of war, the 'karate' film industry he is enmeshed in *de facto* with its distorted larger-than-life legendary heroes, heroines and flashing combustionable *eidōlon* images is a deliberately designed "confusing, reflecting" glittering lure with a sharp barbed hook at the end. The obsidian-hearted "Powers that be," vampiric creatures such as Storm and her kind, continually pour into the unwitting heads of the sweltering, overheated, easily excitable masses of bleary-eyed, dust-congested mobs, lying visuals and vocab made to keep the local troglodytes in check. At the same time, the poor ignorant plebes and their feeding frenzied cravings are brought up to blood-lust pitch, always screaming for more—just right for harvesting the heaving swarms of these dead, blood-glutted ego-ized souls. Karate these days is a global sport and now, as in Rome, old-time sporting events were used by those in power to direct, like a water sluice gate, the erratic passions of the maddened feverish throngs in order to channel their micro-minds off of the real issues of life, like who was in real power and pulling the strings. This was so that the bumpkins would not be so much of a threat or in the mood to revolt against those who ruled—*just like today*. Inevitably this can only lead but one way—down the screwing spiral staircases, which in life there are myriads, into the long-suffering Valhallan wastes, that with thrown open arms, awaits our grimmest pleasures and our most unspeakable short-circuited electro-mares—and far, far beyond.

In fairness though, reiterates Hsu, the idea of system, in its useful sense, is to provide students with outlines of motion from which, if they are sharp enough, are expected to build upon, much like a Da Vinci taking his first drawing lessons. Certainly, the idea of conforming to basics found within a system is the key to success, as these basics—stances, kicks, punches, *etc.*—were derived from actual combat realities. In a final sense, the problem that arises is found in the 'disconnectedness' of how these basics actually function apart from the battlefield and their becoming a broken, repressive sub-standard training methodology that is substituted for the initial combat result and not the means to it if one could say that. Here the journey is definitely *not* the destination. The result should be highly cultivated individuals who are not suppressed by the means in which they become cultivated, but rather liberated, having the awareness enough to oversee and look beyond their own educational systems. Donn F. Draeger's book, *Classical Budo: The Martial Arts and Ways of Japan Volume Two* offers excellent insight into *kata* training to this end. A fine piece of scholarship, Draeger describes the three levels of *kata* practice, which is a sweat-popping monastic-ascetic training regime students undergo striving to achieve mastery of their selves and craft, a most difficult task indeed.

In the Deadlands, all the warped ink-black "Powers that be" and their underling all-adoring suck up obsequious fauning sycophants (Lat., *sȳcophanta*, "flatterer, informer, slanderer"), the wasted masters of dead-fu and croaked-dō, suffer none of the above watery illusions. Even though having made or participated in said events for personal power tripping, they all are, nonetheless, self-deceived and self-made victims of their own shrieking, fiery *illusory* ('ill-used') devices, these having buried them, they now having learned to 'love the lie' because that's all they possess. Learn well as they yearn to feed on unwaries. Often "the obvious things are the ones most hidden" (—the poet; unknown. *Cf.* 2Thess. 2.11).

127-134. *The arc of circle . . . her wings.* On a deeper level, this erotic section speaks of lovemaking, but on the surface, also mirrors the age-old argument as to which is better in the martial arts—circular or linear methods of attack and defense, as whole systems and controversies have sprung up around this argument from ancient Europe and Asia to the present time. This passage, points out Peter Hsu, also reflects the 'deeper energies' that drive earthy *genetic*-based worldly martial arts that are based on fear, competition, rivalry and envy. The deep quest for life presses the arts on, not their popular commercialized mass-marketed 'karate-ized' surface forms. Angel is also saying the greater the motion, its intensity, the greater the love and single-minded devotion to a cause (which transcends the flesh and enters into the spiritual). Attacks, characteristically speaking, are linear/angular, of high-impact and percussiony in nature, more destructive as in Western fencing, Filipino kali and Okinawan/Japanese karate, whilst defensive and counter-offensive measures take on a more circular, softer orientation, diffusing attack through re-direction as in Japanese aikido or judo, indicating an art's origin, philosophical base and the minds of its operators. Literally, one can 'read' a soul through its body's motion.

135-136. *Designs taught . . . never conceived.* Either this line refers to systematic teachings taught in ignorance or deliberately as part of a propaganda 'spin' package both usually making one *stultified*, or gradually and sophomoronically "stupid bit-by-bit." Most, if not all evil, by any stretch of the definition is "stupid and unimaginative," meaning the designers of such systems and everyone or thing on down from it is PhD material for a case study in low-wattage, dully ill-umined stupidity, like a dim, faintly glowing corner street light on a very dark, slushy snowy wintery night. Within this sphere, students of an art are taught *not* to think their way out of an art's limitations, perceptual, spiritual or physical, but rather, perpetuate and maintain fixed ideals or standards as part of one's chosen discipline or tradition to keep the tradition rolling. The subtle problem here is that many arts are of extraordinary caliber, potentially speaking, but the way they are taught—the bridge student's are supposed to cross over with for enlightenment may be very poor, crippling them in the long run. Training methods may be likened to cheap *Yugos* or powerful *Corvettes*, and students should learn to build their own engines. Both are cars, but one is a chugger and the other is a fireball. A martial art system, no matter how noble or lofty, is only a limited curriculum of training, a method of progression that sooner or later must bottom out as it is no better or worse than its inventor or the one who currently teaches it. A bad captain means a bad ship.

137-138. '*With all to strike true when nothing is there* . . . '*martialed*' *where*'. Topically, this acrostic-like reversal '*With all . . . where*' (*i.e.*, 'wherewithal') speaks of the 'martial-led realm,' being 'in the know' about the inner workings of the arts, the 'wherewithal' of its Zen-potency and giving ones all. Additionally, according to Hsu, there is an old adage in kung-fu wing-chun boxing that says, 'If he comes, go join him, if he leaves, go with him, and if there is *nothing*, hit.' This statement, observes Hsu, has to do with the tactics of sticking to an opponent's arms and striking him when a hole is created in his defenses when he drops his hands. This is in line with the Chapter 6 *Emptiness and Fullness* philosophy of Sun Tzu who, like his comrade general Du Mu, is keen on avoiding the full and in great favor of whacking the empty (p. 100).

In light of this, the concept of *striking true* implies 'seeing' holes and exploiting them, or more so, truth hits on the 'empty,' or 'void,' the 'blind spot,'—an obscure reference to a Zen-like perception of movement-reality. In terms of training one's perception, the problem of 'not seeing holes' is the fundamental result of early training. Early in the student's training regime, observes Hsu, they are initially taught patterns of movement soon becoming 'fixated' on these 'positive space solid motions,' exclusively focusing on them. As a result, they fail to see 'negative-space' openings—where nothing is there and their arts lack a fuller intensity. After all, the bulk of a technique is mostly empty space. As mastery in the arts is a question of perception, cites he, a balanced approach to teaching them is to see and strike on both the 'solid motion' and the 'empty' or 'negative space' surrounding the motion— those gaps and transitions where nothing is occurring. Later if students mature, they will break these patterns and just move accordingly, striking when and where they will. *See suki-point* in the *Introduction*.

144. *Yet words imprison.* Limited thinking and speech patterns, as mentally entrenched systems of faulted perception, undoubtedly imprison a person's mind, spirit, body and soul. Words can free or bind (Laurent, *Laws*).

155. *A spirit's lone soul is one . . . reaped.* Reap + raped. Reaping, as in a harvest, and rape.

164. *This spirritant's.* Spirit + irritant. Angel is bugging 'the man' with his idealistic talk.

174. *It was night and he went out.* A translation from *John* 13.30, said of Judas the night he went out to betray Christ. It appears that Angel is sneaking about up to no good, using his companion, 'The Mean,' as soul bait—for his own ends.

183. The man *frumplumplelingjumpumbleling*. If we have trouble pronouncing this tongue-twistering onomatopoeia, this is a good thing in unterms of non-describ-ing Theman's hijinks, our fumbly unpronouncements imperfectly uncaptures the inessence of the sceene-saw's *kakóhoraocháos* ("ill-gaze at a supernatural spectacle of pandemonium").

TWENTY-THREE: APOLLYON DESCENDING

On hard ground The Mean did fly,
To carry his revenge past horizon's confines.
Looked he over his left shoulder thrice,
Felt the presence of that spirit of ice.

Past the graves of rock-laid long-ships,   5
Past those outposts of heaped megaliths,
The Mean rode firm his bestial bay,
Windstorms *whirrrled* ahead, coming his way.

Down through fields a bleached army of bones did lie,
Weeds pressing through ribs of those who were pois'ed to die.   10
Off in the distance war troopers stone-dead marched,
Eternal ghosted armies of those spirits dry parched.

On gutted land, over rise wind showed he down,
Mean looked upon; saw; an empty, tombish town.
The haunt of the unclean and all their host,   15
A strange mixture of dwellings and their ghosts.

Scrut he over the dank little town,
A collection of pine boxes readied for the shrouds.
Lone dogs prowled dust stung streets,
Wind moaning, portending *the* grim reap.   20

Cold dunes had entered the near-buried burgh,
From these stray slopes his horse did he urge.
(The sands were composed of granulated bone,

Telling of catastrophes—forgotten and known).
This callous arena told much of hidden strife—   25
Spirits and men-shades here plundered of their lives.

A lone slingsworder whittled he totem wood,
Eyes reflecting The Mean's entry and prelude.
Drank he some mead to kill the time,
Everything else he would soon find.   30

VALLEY OF THE DAMNED

Chapter Twenty-Three Valley Footnotes

Mark Theman, 'The Mean,' in his travels to find Dark Storm, descends upon a nearly sand dune-buried sparsely populated 'ghost' town. It is the perfect killing ground to sharpen one's skills—or lose one's life as many have. He is a brazen cuss to be sure.

0. *Apollyon descending.* Gk. *Apollyon, lit.,* "Destruction." The name is taken from the great abyss King, *Revelation* 9.11, where mighty demonic powers are locked up waiting to be released at *Armageddon.*

3. *Left shoulder thrice.* This is a portent of trouble, like the throwing of salt over one's left shoulder when spilled to ward off evil. This 'superstition' came about because folks once believed that the Devil stood behind them waiting for them to make a mistake or influence them into 'making' a mistake. The tossing shoulder salt thing means one was throwing it into the Devi's eyes, thus blinding him to their mistakes.

5-6. *Rock-laid long-ships . . . heaped megaliths.* As in the Deadlands, graves in northern Europe were often in the shape of Viking long-ships—symbols of travel to Valhalla. *Megaliths* are huge rocks buried in the ground to form parts of temples, graves, astronomical observatories and whatnot. Megaliths, as in the Mortuuslands, are all over the north of Europe. *Stonehenge* in England is the most famous example of a megalith grouping.

10. *Those who were pois'ed to die.* Poised + poisoned. As in fate, or *kismet*, these warriors were poised, ready and set for battle only to die metaphorically horrible 'poisonous' deaths at the hands of their vanquishers and they 'knew' it. There is nothing worse than seeing disaster on the horizon and being powerless to change its course for the good getting sucked right into its screw. The solution that the mortlanders came up with to deal with such a sand-blasting Underworld reality was to 'live' and 'ride out the moment,' exploiting the energy and attributes of the situation to adapt and strengthen themselves. Yah, it takes a good person to prevent a disaster; it takes an even greater person to make use of one. In other words, if one is handed some lemons from the fates in life they should make lemonade. Philosopher Friedrich

Nietzsche (1844-1900) would like this, saying, that which does not kill us makes us stronger.

12-13. *Spirits dry parched . . . wind showed he down.* Also, 'de-part.' This phrase, rendered by Jonathan Mycroft from the tenth century *Irish Monastic Script*, refers to wicked long-dead atrophying *de-parted* (chunked up) war-like spirits that find themselves eternally trapped and ultimately victimized in spiritually dry-rotting and truly dead places, where nobody with brains would ever want to hang out or haunt. *Showed he down* literally means "Show down."

14. *Empty, tombish town.* This is a dusty, windblown ghost town as in the old American West.

19. *Lone dogs prowled.* This is a borrowing from the movie *Yojimbo* (1964), by Kurosawa. In the opening scene, a lone dog with a human hand in its mouth reflects the spirit of the alienated warrior (Toshiro Mifune) coming into town—a mongrel killer, looking for an opportunity.

23-24. *The sands . . . forgotten and known.* 'Yet known.' The phrase *forgotten and known* refers to how historical events eventually turn into old yellow newspaper bits and myths that are commonly known but paid little attention to. Is this a case of willing ignorance? Things of this nature have been recorded in the Midgard and as a rule of thumb; here is that to *forget means eventually to repeat.* These greedy, always-sifting devouring 'sand dunes' are composed of the granulated 'bones' of multitudes of spirits and animals left decaying there for eons. This phenomenon is also known on Earth. In Siberia, there are small islands glistening with the remains of extinct *Mammoth* bone and ivory, telling that some sort of tremendous *kataklysmos* occurred in Earth's past. In fact, frozen Mammoths have been found with buttercups and grasses still in their mouths and stomachs indicating a massive quick-freeze occurred of around one hundred and fifty degrees below zero. It takes three to five days to freeze a modern elephant (its parts), but whatever froze the Mammoths took place in a matter of hours (Whitcomb, pp. 76-82).

27. *Whittled he totem wood.* Angel is an excellent sculptor of fine woods that he often works on as a prelude to action.

TWENTY-FOUR: ENEMIES TRUST

Quietly Storm stood at the end of the village.
Lead-dead air impended the insinerating pillage.
Looked she around for those of her tribe.
None to be found—*but* many to die.

Patient glare as she efficient scanned.   5
Empty streets, save en*graving* dust and sand.
Drew her sickle from her sash.
Flicked it open at its shaft.

In back alleyway she hearing the noise,
Feet *grav*eling hard, the sounds!—*the* cries!¡   10
Echoings, battle, stinging steels,
One killing hard in meticulousing zeal.
A curse. Thenn—shouts!! Then <u>*that*</u> cuttᴠ*tting* sound!!!
Metals chińnnking; spirits going down.
Listening for a moment—then—moving on—   15
A time to kill, once upon.

Pawed Storm down that empty-hutted street,
Eyed for her predators, the ones she did keep.
A great roar and a spear from behind,
Dark sw*ivel*ing, ripping the spike off-line.   20

Instant raging fanatic held her at bay,
Menaced her with longsword to cut and to flay.
Thrust he in despirit for himself to bfr'ee,
Dark Storm sweeping, hamstringing his Achilles.

Around the back walks Angel did tranquilly greet,   25
Killing Dark's people as he did them meet.
Three repulsives opposed him with fiercest wresisted onsets—
Discontwist *A*rtions his body though bloodings and bladelets.
(He liked the spray on the wall–the chromatic offset).

Strolled she down rough-hewn street.   30
Doors flinging open, spirits rushing to defeat.
Cutting them down she one by falling one,
The mercenary cordially sending them oblivion.

Two arrows let loose from hidden shaft,
Covered the lanceman in his attack.   35
Dark Storm feigning indifferent step,
Passing the blade and cutting his neck.
A spear missing his head from thatched roof,
Angel piercing his blade through the evil's foot.
Fell he to the ground cursed, spit and screamed,   40
Another leaping, Angel cutting both brawlessly clean.

Three ex-partners blocking her way,
Attacking at once, to the side she sways.
Bladeings cutting arcing hard and down,
Slivering light 'splaying fresh rubying crowns.   45

Projecting she now to the village square.
Casting her eyes for those who dared.
Air chilling with dreadingly thought,
Storm felt *that* time of the coming wroth.

Calmly now reached she and pulled a like-sickle,   50
Fastening its twin to a shaft in the middle.

Two fangs now that bit so terribly deep,
Unmercied weapons of deaths bequeath.

One shade rogue grimmed toothless at him,
Squared with the 'slinger, weapon pointed to chin.   55
Angel attacking then stutt'ring back,
The shade over-parred, the Death Angel—*flassssht*!

Slowly they came from all four sides,
Surrounding her in the middle: the quicker to die.
A she-bear *a'maulin'* vile bloodhounds,   60
In heat and battle, ravenous stares found.

This 'Mistress of Carnage' now setting the distance,
Laid her defenses out for this beautiful instance.
Come they one or all in their accord,
Sickles (didn't care); they would hew through flesh and sword.   65

Longing tension, posing *that* final question,
As shade upon shade pressed for position.
Held they armaments 'tween they and Storm,
Knew her ways, and her battle plans formed.

Weapons, limbs, hands, feet,   70
Maneuvered deftly for death's swift feat.
Wills fighting will of one wicked ambition,
To consume *that* spirit of Eviled precision.

In contemplation Angel eyed the sculpting,
Admired its woodwork and her carvings.   75
Blade *chunnnkeked* into wood as he dropped beneath,
He opening from below, a belly to meat.

Prolonged shadows casting on ground.
Stage was set without a sound.

Blinding motioning bursting,   80
Shades slicingancollapsing,
Clisppets of motion blurringly seen,
Steel shaftings catching in death's exacting machine,
Whirrrling, wicked swirrrling motion,
Dark Storm havocking, wreaking commotion.   85

Shades attacking in anglings fine,
Hacking at Storm crossing centerlines,
Stormy raging turning blacked,
Seizing; tearing weaknessings of their lack.

Upheld swordings with her ebony shaft dripping,   90
One cresc-blade hooking, the other sickling–*unpitying.*
Meeting and countering simultaneously,
Passing backside, ripping carnivorously.

Following in a razor's echo from one who deftly swung,
Storm inserted low and jerked from beneath; classic 'malestromed.'   95

Reeling colors dusting blending,
Screamingcursingreckoning those dying,
Axingswordingspearings bolding,
She-creature moving as Darkest⌂ Storming.

In the eye ☙ 🐛 she knew the rottenest secreting,   100
Of training her underlings in lies of her false weakening.
Knew the day was coming when they would rebel,
Trained them from the start with mistakes to *heh,* deceive *them* to Hel!

Exploding fury of red bodies rounding,
Bodies' ellipseing, hurling with groundings,   105
Limbs departing with weapons from grippings,
Fanging weapon departing hands from limbings.

Dusting uproar under cold, cruelling sun,
Spirits shocked into false martyrdoms.
Horenching bodies' s l oo   wvw plummet through air,   110
Weapons and limbs dashing in despair.

A classic piece in metallic tones,
'The Death of the Dead,' she played and composed.
Technical grace of killing achieved,
Through the master *maestra* of combat perceived.   115

Balleting death of those so many,
Damned lives end in direing agony.
A slowing medley of wasting, downing travesty,
Motioning death by the mistress so befittingly.

A smattering of motions of line and curve,   120
Lacing of bodies, their victory desured.
Bodies cease, collapse-stopping on ground,
Silent wind ensues, no one around.

Storm looking over her spirit-frieze,
A festival of positions, in seeming peace.   125
Spread across the satur*ate* tabling ground,
Bound them together in patterns quite profound.

A steeled portrait by an Aesir so long ago,
The bygone craft that no one knows
(Unknown to all save those who read *this* tale,   130
Of the forgotten mistress of insidious martial end trails).

———*Yet*, 'lessers' slain to her elicited a loathsome disgusting,
Skills unequalled———a prodigious N♂THING.
Contemplated for a moment the technique she waste,
Too progressive an abstract, her critics; unappreciate.   135

"Quite so," a voice soft spoke and Storm looked slow up,
Angel stood tall, stretching from the front.

Walked she deliberate among her 'collection' of fine art,
To discuss with Angel business they had from the very start.
Admired he her work as she saunt from her wor cathedral,   140
And kicked he to the side to clear for her bodies steepled in evil.
"—Seems our transaction needs to be made complete."
Angel unlatched he his blade, her head to keep.

Two pairs of dead eyes long stalked the other.
Kindred ♂ sharks of the highest killing order.   145

Chapter Twenty-Four Valley Footnotes

Having sold out their boss, Dark Storm's wicked ex-hench spirits seek to 'do her in.' Burning Prairie, Storm's chief goon, is markedly absent, although it is more than probable she sent these bunch of misfits in to spy out and take care of her chief. Later, Dark meets up with Angel for a little *tête-à-tête* on the art of swordplay. Angel Jackal, as will be noted in the play, just so 'happens' to always be around at the right time and place, saving Storm a lot of trouble. As to why this is so, we shall soon see.

2. *Lead-dead air.* The concept of negative 'airs' runs throughout the story and we may draw some parallels here to Earth history. According to Dr. Peter Hsu, in old Japan, samurai were said to be so sensitive to impending attack seemingly because the air was bristling, negatively charged like a battery or as before a thunderstorm before action occurred. This is not ESP, but apparently the fruits of high-level training. Derived from the concept of Japanese *haragei*, roughly translated as the "art of the belly," this awareness is the product of concentrating one's mind, thoughts and 'energies' (Japanese *ki*) 'into the belly,' or *hara*. According to Japanese belief, the *hara*, located slightly below the navel is the inner center of gravity and source of breath-energy, and is where profound and vital forces (*ki*) reside, where all physical and psychic forces emanate. Training in *haragei* makes one supersensitive to the attitudes and feelings of others, giving warriors the ability to read (*yomi*) the very thoughts of potential attackers, thus they are able to detect attack before it physically develops. Through the study of *haragei*, it is further possible, Hsu relates, to tap into, 'be at one' and 'communicate' with universal energy, to feel in harmony with others, and is indispensible for achieving perfect control over the self (Ratti and Westbrook, p. 375, *et al.* Further, our Ch. 27 note # 14).

6. *Engraving dust and sand.* This is an energy-motif for Angel. The wind, with a predatorial mind of its own, is blowing so bad that the sands are etching everything down, eroding things to their 'grave' so to speak, including the weaker spirits who are hiding out not only from the gusts, but who are waiting to jump Storm.

9. *In back alleyway.* This is the only battle-piece in the poem fully described in terms *of sound.* Dark Storm is so sharp, she can 'see' the struggle in her mind by listening

intently. It is a kakódaímōnic cacophonic ill-fated masterpiece. That is to say, yes, there are a bunch of chaotic, noisy smashed together sounds going on around there, but evil genius kakóStormónic is as such that she can select choice noises out of the resounding sound slop pile and set them to composition making sense just for her. Hence, the text relates that the askewed noisounds are master-pieced in her mind, rather than being spent out in the street and wasted upon lessers who have no ear (literally), or mind for music. Her kakó-compositions are so refined she can tell which performing 'musicians' are going to be the ill-fated losers. Although there are some discrepancies, a true hard core *kakódaímōn* is an ill-starred, ill-fated evil genius who in the end is tormented and miserable. Storm transcends this def.

16. *A time to kill, once upon.* This stanza tells of the surreal dream-like mythic 'fairy-tale' quality of the battle, but also refers to 'destined' killing, or the concept of one's time 'being up' as a divine appointment, "Once upon a time" in the Deadlands (Eccl. 3.3) (Eccl. 3.3).

23. *Despirit for himself to bfr'ee.* De + the. This particular fiend is so fallen, ugly and debauched of soul, mind and body that he does not even look like a 'regular' spirit, but is a 'de-spirit.' *Bfr'ee.* To be free + fee. This spirit-ghoul wants payment for killing Storm and be free of her. For the poem, the term *ghoul* is used in a loose sense. The original term, *ghūl*, is Arabic and from Muslim folklore. It literally means "demon of the desert." It is also associated with the word *ghāla*, "to seize." A ghoul is an evil spirit who robs graves and eats the flesh of the dead. Nowadays it is meant for basic grave robbers or those who get pleasure from sick acts or things. Sum: ghouls are very evil, sick, distwists—spirits, human or otherwise.

29. *Wall—the chromatic offset.* Angel critiques the bright singular monochromatic color of the red blood artistically sprayed at various angles due to his professional cutting, a known phenomenon in samurai times. Great samurai in the heat of mass battles or in duels were known to cut so artistically that the blood spray would gush in a certain direction, let us say into a crowd to psychologically control them, all the while the samurai being free of any blood stains at all due to his expertise in cutting. Such cuts are par for the course for Angel, Storm and Kari, all being well-schooled in the high art of angular bloodsmanship. Angel can also

hear snippets of the other battles going on so the word *chromatic* also carries a sound effect to it. He concludes upon the artwork both in sight and in sound with a slight nod and smirk.

45. *'Splaying fresh rubying crowns.* Display + splay (cut) open. The text is unclear whether Storm has beheaded these people or merely scalped them.

46. *Projecting she now.* Storm puts forward a strong spiritual attitude.

50. *Pulled a like-sickle.* In this instance, Storm has made a three-sectional sickle-staff consisting of two sickles attached at their bases to a stick in between them. The fifth century mythology of *Lu* suggests that Dark Storm learned this secret art from Hachiman, Japanese god of war. As we continue, we will find why it was so necessary for Dark Storm to learn this art and elevate it to such a high degree.

55. *Weapon pointed to chin.* Peter Hsu cites the translation as more toward *the eyes* because the angle of the weapon is coming up from below the usual horizontal-oriented vision from a forty-five degree diagonal angle, thus looking like its pointing at the *chin*. This eye-posture effectively 'splits' the vision of potential attackers, as it forces them to focus on two points—the tip of the blade and the person behind it.

61. *Ravenous stares.* Raven + ravenous. This death motif is very hungry.

62-63. *Setting the distance . . . beautiful instance.* Storm is a great master and as such strives to control distance, space and timing in combat—what the Japanese call *maai*—this requiring a very high order of ability. Timing in martial arts calls for a keen perception of events and from a master's interior point of view, she (in Storm's circumstance), can actually 'slow down' the actions of an opponent. This, according to Peter Hsu is a question of what he terms *perceptual physics*. If one trains with small, fast weapons such as a dagger, actions are naturally faster than if practiced with, for instance, longer and thus slower weapons such as the power-oriented six-foot staff. Storm knows this secret and has trained with small and fast weapons so that when confronted by those with larger weapons, they appeared naturally slower. More to the fact, since Storm's perceptions are attuned to small and fast motions, the larger objects in reality, through her mind's faster trained eye were in actuality not going very fast relative to her at all. *Beautiful instance* refers to the excellent opportunity Storm has to work her art at a high level—a level, however, at which she will later be disappointed.

68. *Held they armaments.* Again, the Japanese martial term *maai* describes this phrase well. It is the concept of *distance, space* and *timing* that lies between two opponents. To manipulate all three components means a good chance of victory. Fighters all, these *evil–vile–live* spirits of the *veil* keep their weapons directly before them as shields and use the spatial distance between their enemies to cover themselves as well. In this case, Storm, or they, would have to come around their own weapons to get at each other (*see* note # 86-87 below for centerline). .

72. *Wills fighting will of one wicked ambition.* Alternate subtexts render this line "Wills fighting will of won wicked whambition." Simply this means Storm's gang, composed of a conglomerate of evil wills, are attacking her, but she, in her own will to the extremage, has already won, the wicked one intending to hit them hard, biting them (wham-bit) with her zeal, drive and personal ambition.

74. *Angel eyed the sculpting.* Angel's calm qualities are exhibited in the battle. He utilizes a lull in the fight to admire some local artwork.

86-87. *Anglings fine . . . centerlines.* Weapons can only be used at certain angles of attack for full effectiveness. *Centerlines.* The *centerline* is a defensive line that runs down the front and middle of the body. It is used in many arts as a defensive plane. Whoever's weapon is on the guarding centerline forces an opponent to 'circle' around the weapon to get at them. This takes more time and exposes the attacker to linear counter-thrusts, affording the defender greater opportunity for control, as linear attacks are shorter than circular ones. Western fencing, chess and wing-chun kung-fu are world famous for their centerline theories and structures. Generally, whoever 'occupies' *centerline* usually wins. In chess, there are two useful terms to delineate the above concept further, *space* and *scope.* Space is the amount of the territory of squares that are controlled by a piece, either occupying it or attacking it. If there are opposing attacking pieces that want the same square, the more powerful piece controls. Occupying center allows for greater board control, more power, spatial and positional advantage, mobility and opportunities to attack and defend. Scope is the theoretical range that can be covered by a piece. The knight in the center can hit its choice of eight target squares. Overall, there is more power in the center.

92-93. *Meeting and countering . . . passing.* In weapon's play, one can 'pass' a weapon (usually against an angular attack) with a blade, 'meet' it, or do a combination of both, all requiring a cool mind and great skill to pull off.

94-95. *Following in a razor's echo . . . classic 'malestromed.'* 'Following the *echo*,' is a useful archaic description for this passage. It is borrowed from a technique found in old Japanese swordplay. Peter Hsu cites that the technique utilizes an opponent's strike to get behind the weapon's flight path, thus 'entering' (*irimi*) its echo, or shadow, for a safety zone. This is used many times for multiple attacks. Attackers themselves provide the way of escape, as defenders, after cutting their attackers down, step into the spaces once occupied by their opponents. This is very tactful as it forces the other attackers to constantly realign themselves. *Classic 'malestromed'* (the sixth century *Upsalan* translation uses "malestrummed") is a version of *maelstrom*, indicating a stormy, chaotic, and 'whirlpooling'-type activity. In context, Dark 'Strom,' in her unleashed stormy combative whirling fury, has just calmly 'strummed' her weapon like a musical instrument, castrating one of her 'male' opponents, making him 'sing like a canary.' Apparently, Kursch Cherval of Chapter 16 isn't the only one who knows how to compose music with her blade.

100-103. *In the eye ☙ ☙ she knew . . . deceive them.* As in the eye of a hurricane, Storm is very calm in battle, wreaking terrible destruction along her perimeters. In fact, she is so wily, sneaky and pre-emptive she 'trained' her followers for millennia to believe she had certain holes in her play that they could then eagerly 'exploit' in order kill her off. At the same time, she also taught them to 'have' their own 'mistakes' as well, so she could easily defeat them when the time came she having done this many times over. Sad dummies—fooled by all that lustful eye-glitter. This is called a *trap-door* concept, where deliberate faults are built into a system to require periodic repairs giving the graphic designer of such subtle, heinous *lambasting* "stick-a-knife-into" one's eye programs an excuse to return and keep them in business. She really knows how to prepare, using the pronged dual-edged attack! Do you? Looks as if this disciple of *diabolique* likes to play *Twister* with the Deceiver in that she enjoys plotortions using bent-angled *antinomies*—paradoxical contradictions between two beliefs/conclusions that in themselves appear reasonable but approach a subject from opposite ends—very obliquitious of her. It is a move that fools everybody—even us poor, deluded Midgarders. Seems that Theman does the *trap-door* trick a lot too, perhaps in part accounting for Storm's appreciation and lust to get a hold of the creep, '*it*' being a kindred dead-endtity unto itself (Ch. 2 note # 49).

109. *False martyrdoms.* These spirits were shocked into dying for wrong and false reasons, as if by mistake and conveniently so. They underestimated Storm's ability and wiles.

110. *Horenching bodies.'* Horrid + wrenching. A very ugly, horrible, brutal twisting of mind, body and, in this case, deed, as exemplified through how the thugs' bodies are tumble-twisting about due to their folly. The bigger they are the harder they fall, *i.e.*, their body's death-motions are pure ironic poetry, so archaic and jumbled are they, reflecting their innerly kinked evil souls.

121. *Their victory desured.* The bad spirit's planned victory was not ensured but *desured*, meaning that they were meant to lose. Storm's foresight and plotting made sure of that.

124. *Her spirit-frieze.* A *frieze* is a sculptured or richly ornamented band decorating the side a building. Contextually, the dead bodies are an artwork of three dimensions, much like a relief frieze sculpture one would see on classical buildings.

133. *—A prodigious NOTHING.* The fools Storm fought were beneath her dignity and ability hence she did not derive any *real* artistic pleasure or satisfaction from offing them. She is experiencing *diminishing returns*. This reveals a subtlety found in

the Deadlands, the difference between doing what is necessary, as in this particular chaotic 'shooting gallery' scenario as opposed to performing high dueling artistry, as one would find in the 'arena' scenarios that all top fighting artists and mercenaries seem to enjoy and aspire to.

135. *Too progressive an abstract.* In the case of any great artist, they are ahead of their time and peers and so are little understood, their art going unappreciated by the critics. As time tells all, it usually takes the thick critical folk years for them to play catch up. In this *mêlée* though, Angel has a keen eye for great art, appreciating Storm's handiwork for the moment or rather movement, or as they say in the Nether, the *mootion* (movement + motion). As Sherlock Holmes (*Norwood*) would imply, "it was a masterpiece of villainy" carried out by a master. *La Espada de la defunción* also knows this premise about Storm. Like Holmes, and telling by her deliberately finished sickliwork, Angel well realizes she has the supreme gift of every great artist—"the knowledge of when to stop." That if she wished to 'improve' upon that which was already perfect by her own hand, she would have ruined her art—and killed herself. A most deadly enemy, he nonetheless thinks she is quite a gal (after all, he does kick a corpse out of the way for her, this showing *some* respect).

140-141. *Wor cathedral . . . bodies steepled in evil.* To 'Angelic' eyes, it looks as though Storm had been religioning in her own house of 'warship.' Steeple + steeped. In the old days, a *steeple* was part of a fortification, part of a tower, a battlement that eventually transformed into the iconic church steeple. *Steeped* is to saturate food or tea in a liquid to soften it or extract its flavor. In this case, these dead ectospirits are steeped, soaked in their nether-blood and are going cold bluer.

TWENTY-FIVE: BURNT PRAIRIE

Under blue overgloom slowly she looked from drinking cup,
"The future is now," smiled Storm and bade him come s'up.
The Mean poked in and cast around,
An empty mead Hall save one evil bound.

Cautious, The Mean came slow to the rigid table,   5
Sat he down sword poised, feeling so—*so* enabled.
Had seen those dead, catted in brawl,
Had her mark, they written in her scrawl.

Dark Storm poured mead, cautious, from horned flask.
Studied his eyes, knowing 'the man' behind his mean mask.   10

"Your message," The Mean at once curt to her,
—Lone silence ensued—   —he swore at the cur.
"No rush," she said, as she walked to the cask.
The Mean clasped sword, she eyed his advance.

Sat the Mean back down into hardead seat,   15
Dark tossed back her honey-eyed drink.
"You're soul," at length she spoke on,
"How strong it is, how far it's gone."

Outside the Hall rot boards padded with faintest steps,
Four phantoms shadowed past windows with malicious intent.   20
Dark Storm at stand spied her glassing cup,
Curving images moving; portent of destruct.

"If you, *ehh*, value your life don't move at all,
If you hear a metallic click, drop to the floor."
"*Wháa*——?" The man gushed, starting from his seat,   25
Saw shades outside, ready to impel bereave.

Slowly opened they the heavy sunken door,
Dark Storm set cup, removing an item from her store.
Quietly strapped it to her flexing right hand,
Readied her sickle in sheath–its fierceness to brand.   30
Walked in the four with echoing steps,
Dark Storm calm for actions commence.

Eyes met eyes in silent recognition,
Of four killers sizing one of a greater perdition.
"Well now, chief," Burning Prairie smiled in retort,   35
"'Pears you have that Alive Yet Dead of some import?"
Storm *grhmmm*aced slow, brushed lazy back her hair,
A spider luring its prey into its webb'ed lair.
"You've done your job," she said, "but it's no business of yours.
Ask him yourself–if you *uh*, got the nerve."   40

Long pause and hard eyes told of coming business.
Weapons glistened in their hilt, telling of their quickness.
Faces lean spoke a thousand taut horrors.
Hands intching forth to fill the gripes of their employers.

The killer shade smirked, looked Dark up and down,   45
Far too feminine a war spirit (despite her helish renown).
The three arched up aside Burning in subtle show of force,
The killer's thoughts moved to The Mean: a confession to coerce.

Pitching tension. Burning drawing on the man,
Dark Storm sickleing into her with sickening slam,   50

305

Snapped retracting chain onto blooding sickled shaft,
Pirouetting~~, flailing her blade in long arcing attack,
Spiritsscreaming out, half-drawn killer blades,
Being cut through by sickle's voraciousing range,
Cutting over, the chaincoiling back inside,   55
Sickle slith'ring home to the leathered grip to ride
(Crumpled down they went and neatly so,
Ringed around poesy, in mate's death row).

Dripping, in desperation's lust Burning quickly cast her bow,
Tried to throttle Storm's neck from behind so blood would not flow.   60
Dark orbing about, that old hold now reversing,
Redressed the tining toothing wire with her sick' perversing.

"*Hmmmm*, come now——" Storm *paráclēte* the heaving Prairie,
"——Here to sow some wild oats?
And with that gently herped her bow about her throat. . . .   65
(The master *garrotter* now strung by her own chosen dischord,
*Ahhh*stringent end for this double-crossing vipe-o'-war).

Kari listened long to the wind in its sighing,
Smiled coyly like a raptor on the hunt high flying.
"Every blade to me seems to re*hearse* its own poetic song,   70
And it's over this one for quite some time I've longed."
She eased her horse down the drifting steep,
No one to meet her, no one to compete.

The man stunned at the flamboyant killing display,
Jumped to his feet panicked to do or say.   75
Heart *p–p–pa—poundped* long for this beating man of fate,
Storm held cruel finger to her lips, looking in lax haste.
Whipped she around unclasping her blade,
Sidearming her sickle impaling lone berserk's face.

VALLEY OF THE DAMNED

Screaming crazied *pinnedcrassshing* through door,   80
Last card to be dealth to the s′player on the floor.

G-g-asped in slowing sound; gurgling underscore,
Dark Storm pulling her instrument, wiping off the gore.

The Mean, feeling enrageous now looked into her beamed eye,
"An animal deranged," she mused, "just right for my ply."   85
"What do you want?" The in*grate* snarled to the snake,
She mixed blood with mead; raised her horn to his fate.

Quaffed she did her fervent fomenting cup,
Knew in *the* twinkling his time was up.

Chapter Twenty-Five Valley Footnotes

In this sequence, Dark Storm purges her gang of undesirables, killing off the last of the traitors, particularly finky Burning Prairie. Moreover, she meets with Mark Theman, 'The Mean' to offer him a cut-rate business deal.

2. *Him come s'up.* 'What is up?' As Storm drinks and eats, she wants Theman to come to her and exchange information, perhaps have a drink and dine with her and/or on him.

6. *Feeling so—so enabled.* There are three perspectives going on here, Theman, now 'The Mean' is feeling very tough and *so enabled*, but Storm thinks he is a mediocre *so-so* hack. *So—so* also reflects the notion that the poem itself is at a loss for words to describe how Theman feels about himself. The line thus fumbles about, searching for an appropriate term finally settling on this revealing phrase of mediocrity.

7. *Had seen those dead.* Theman had seen Storm's devastating handiwork at killing all those spirits from the previous scene.

8. *Had her mark.* Theman by now recognizes the exemplary high killing 'artistry' of certain spirits, such as Storm.

10. *Studied his eyes . . . his mean mask.* Storm 'sees though' Theman, knowing what type of rotten person he beyond doubt is. The word *mean* implies 'lowly,' 'paltry,' 'wretched,' 'downcast' 'squalid' and so forth. The idea here is Storm further laser's through Theman's pathetic ways and pompously hollow acts.

13. *She walked to the cask.* This speaks of a 'barrel' of mead, but the phrase portents danger, death, a 'casket.'

21-22. *Her glassing cup, Curving images.* This is a *convex* 'curved outward,' or literally 'against-vexation' motif for the warpedness of Storm, danger and the weird reality of the Deadlands in general. The image further means that her underlings are getting on her nerves. Storm does not like the idea of getting vexed, frustrated, annoyed, nettled, irritated or irked by anyone in the Dead as she is getting now, having to sidetrack her plans to deal with a lot of useless filthy traitors, especially her infuriating number one hench-goon Burning Prairie. Being well read, she recalls the line of the illustrious warrior The Dawg, "Intelligence does not threaten me, stupidity does." Taking her cue all will be solved soon enough to her satisfaction.

34. *Of a greater perdition.* This refers to utter destruction, ruination and eternal damnation.

38. *Its webb'ed.* Web + dead. Storm surrounds her opponents with a web of deadly intrigue.

44. *Intching forth.* Inching + itching. An 'itchy trigger finger,' is the used Wild West American idiom for those who are ancy, keyed up, who just are 'itching' to fight, like plenty of action, to out-shoot others, *etc.* In this case, these spirits are 'dying' to kill Storm, literally. If they do, they become the top dogs on the mercenary food chain, becoming, with prices on their souls targets themselves, lesser spirit's always trying to sword them down.

47. *The three arched up aside Burning in subtle show of force.* If the spirit's had just meant to talk, they would have just lined up behind Burning Prairie in a non-threatening way, but since they lined up along side of her, it meant they were spoiling for a fight, Storm reading their signals very well.

58. *Ringed around poesy, in mate's death row. Poesy* is an older term for 'poetry.' The children's rhyme, *Ring around the Rosy* describes the effects of the Black Plague of the Middle-Ages: "Ring around the rosy, a pocket full of posies, ashes, ashes—we all fall down!" Characterized by black, ashy, rose-shaped splotchy marks, flowering posies being thought to cure it, these diseased spirit-mates, or comrades, were standing in a semi-circle, or 'ring' when they were sliced through by Storm's steely 'poetic cuts,' they all falling down dead in a curved, bunched-up semi-circle *row.* These were not 'inmates' in a criminal sense, but rather the phrase describes a kind of a certain foredoom overhanging them, they being thrown together as mates in a cause (death) and were of the 'in' crowd, as if they were all to be killed

that day. *Death row* also equals 'death throes,' pretty much implying the same—their death throes were agonizing.

61-62. *Dark orbing about, that old hold . . . Redressed.* Storm uses a circular, orbiting motion to get behind Prairie as she desperately attempts to strangle Storm. Storm is used to Prairie's technique, it being an *old hold* she is familiar with and knows how to counter. *Redressed*, *lit.*, "red-dressed." The whole scene is a bloody, gruesome mess. By 'redressing' it, Storm sets it aright.

63. *Storm paráclēte.* Greek *paráklētos*. A 'paraclete' is someone who 'consoles, comforts, encourages or uplifts,' interceding for one's behalf, as an advocate in court does. The text is citing Storm as being sarcastic, as she 'with joy and weeping' (yeah, right) comes along Prairie's side to 'console and comfort' her one-time 'friend'–her now traitorous lieutenant at the hour of Prairie's 'more' death.

65-67. *Herped her bow . . . Ahhhstringent end.* A *herpe* (Gk., *herpeton*, "creeping animal") is another term for 'snake.' In this instance, the '*H*' replaces the '*S*' so instead of *serped her bow* like a snake, Storm 'herpes' it. This is a play on the word 'harps,' where she 'strings' Prairie's' final *dischord*. *Ahhhstringent*. *lit.*, "a stringed end." In a s(h)erpentine fashion, Storm coils the twisted bow 'string' around Prairie's neck. Prairie dies like all notable movie villains do—in an ironic fashion, in this case death by her own perverse weapon. A *stringent* is something that is 'strict, exacting and precise,' while an *astringent* is something 'sharp, penetrating and severe.' Both terms are useful here for describing the fitting 'strung-out' end of this evil spirit. *Ahhh* was the defreshing sound BP made when she was going to relieve her *intentsions* in Ch. 1 by stringing along with Storm and then using her bowstring to string her up as it were. *Ahhh* is an abridged sound effect of her death gurgle and sputumy *ahhhrrrghhh—!*

84. *Feeling enrageous now.* Enraged + outrageous. The events are so incomprehensible to Theman's pop-*mentality* that he is beside himself and outraged and as a result, violently angry.

87. *She mixed blood with mead.* The Valkyries of old were notorious for drinking blood after battle. Apparently, Storm had an acquired exotic taste for this too.

89. *Knew in the twinkling.* This refers to 'in the *twinkling* of an eye.' Some say the eye twinkling business is about 1/6,000,000 of a second. Pretty fast, but others give faster figures. The idea is that Storm instantly and intuitively nano-knew that Theman's time and fate were up, showing how fast she is to grasp hold of things.

TWENTY-SIX: ELEMENTS AND AESIR

As 'Lady Dread' harangued and talked,
The Mean became stupefied as one child lost.
Storm Rising weaving a conspired tale—
The spider looming her final veil.

"→ From the chaos, the foreboding Ginnungagap,   5
Allfather conceived that one time only cosmic act.
Stretched forth his spirit his plan to contain,
To deceive the void with foundations to lay.

The Ginnungagap, *that* cháos, she then proceed,
To fill her children's visions with form's leads.   10
The gods of emergence to be one with the tale,
Deemed themselves sprung from nature's travail.

From out of god Allfather five elements he did fashion,
No, wait, six he thought fit that were of contrary dimensions.
Formed he and threw them over the spans of the Heaven,   15
With the vault of Midgard, like a Hall to dwell therein.

Of water, Earth liquid born of ethereal-like substance,
That gives life to all, denying none her sustenance.
Pure from the deep springs of Midgard and sky,
Those who drink of her pristine shall never die.   20

Now wood, that glorious timbred sacred being,
Is the living testimony that makes Midgard ring.
A creator herself of instruments for they who delight and labor,
She is magnificent to those whose hands caringly shape her.

Of fire, hot and heated with austere blowing out rage,   25
From Helish bowels of Midgard her strength is contained.
Therein she tempers elements of all persuasions,
Purges or burns those under Yggdrasill—Tree of Creation.

Of sweet Midgard with her climes and pleasantries,
Giver of life unto those deserts of death and destinies.   30
Honeyed smelling savor, hearth home of man,
Halfway, 'tween Asgard and the land of Niflheim.

Too, unto metal born of Midgard, so called 'secret of the gods,'
Elements for divine call sojourned, the enigma to be shod.
The *riddle of steel* is known to all barbarian men,   35
Which shapes their hearts and holds the coveted land.
As for wind—a great mystery goes where she wills,
One cannot contain her, and by her the empty hand is filled.
Blows *a'plenty* upon the Midgard and fine metals alike,
The Master born to shape both is the one who gives the life.   40

From thus this multi-god did handily made,
Asgard for a home and stars for evening shade.
Nine worlds in all were fashioned by his hand,
This Ruler of Weather, Spear-shaker—
This, this Lord of the Dead."   45

Kari in the back room listened to this so 'endaring' a story,
Smirked she once at Dark Storm, in all her lying glory.
The Mean, engrossed, nonplussed and so taken aback,
Ohh, the incredible subterfuge of *that* seducing maniac!

Spun she her net around this man victim so,   50
Promised *it* power—if he would only let go.

DOUGLAS M. LAURENT

"From those great fiery pits the gods, we smite,
We Aesir lending blades their imperishable life.
Giving them fashion with strokes in twilight dark,
Making them god-like within our noble mark.   55

We churn the winds to billow and to blow,
Then to set fine blades, the wind would bellow and glow.
Asundering them in the thunder of many *a'beating* hammer,
Forging stubborn metal after her own spark-flying manner.

Fire joined sister water immersed in hot bed of forge,   60
Lays the blade in watery boudoir, a union of firewater formed.
In merge of opposite elements there to be genitor of life,
By their cleaved adjoining, arises *that* child—ironed strife.

Hands dashing down the hammer on bed of hardened anvil,
Fire bath percussioning the metal's will indomitable.   65
Beyond that rhythm when the heated blade was struck,
Came orange blood's fevered pitch in those passions of amok.

The smith of us gods, Weland his name,
Smiled did he upon these raw and lusty blades.
In womb of fire as the babe to be born,   70
Weaned on battle's infant color, redly adorned.

From the great master smith he laid the steel bare,
To acknowledge no fate save self-will, and unto us to declare,
Our blades embody the precious eternal and present ideal,
That movement is our law; to us she is freedom to wield.   75

Unchronicled now, but on high thousands of years ago,
We were once mighty, unto *that* Odin we would go.
Numbered our power beyond the stars themselves,
Ripped from our lighted womb, *pfff*, when Asgard was rent!"

The man leaned forward, listening to her glitzy promo sales pitch,   80
Fully captive now to these scheming wiles of her 'itch.
The promise of greatness loomed before him and told,
Of ambitions achieved—if he would only say so!

"Set we our kingdom on Earth and the firmament above,
Set the land to conquer, our dominion in self-estate and self-love.   85
We are those powers, those heroes those mighty gods of old,
Etched in stone and the minds of men, who bow to us alone!

The unseen king of Tyre, *he* showed us the way,
How we heroes *heh*, use clay masks down through the Age.
This mirror of man is before his face,   90
Yet we are those images that usurp his place!"

Kari, resigned, *had* to listen to Storm's droning *spiel*,
Pulled a file and started on her nails with a consecrated zeal.
Listened to Storm yap down to that human imbecile,
"So many times," she thought looking o'er her cute ill kills.   95

"Then came that purge, a day long ago,
Of gods loving women, to take unto their own.
'Odin' in his majestic fierceness did he command,
That those gods who loved women wer*rrr* to be condemned!

With war in Asgard, 'the gods' in anger did hurl,   100
Lightning bolts against 'the giants,' their eternal churl.
Asgard's secrets by way fell unto lowly Midgard,
Therein metal was found by *that* creature so marred.

From beyond Bifrost Bridge the sibling gods were spent,
Thrown to the Midgard by a rainbow's curving bend.   105
The Aesir, they use that bridge to this very day,
But claim it a token of past war, and of judgment's pay.

To have been a god, and now it's sluggardly remains,
Means corruption unto elemental parts, fixed in permanent stain!
(*And pain and pain and pain . . .*)   110
No longer whole, but a vapid shadow of what one once had been,
Fire with neither light nor heat—*an ashed pile of depraved sin.*

Insult to injury was now added more,
A creature of dust blowing to the fore!
We mighty gods to attend this creature meddlesomed?!   115
Celestial spirits, *pffft!* Made to serve *that* mortal speck and crumb!

From the great four winds the gods of eternity breathed,
And fashioned the breath giving life to both man and sword to please.
From this wind the gods derived a noble creature anew,
And at his side *the* symbol of hope, a ray of godly dew.   120

The *Runes* did prophesy an ancient tale in disguise,
That the men of old would smote a million times, orange sparks to fly.
Until there was peace in his mind (about the instruments of war),
And a blade not made by us gods, but by clayish man in perfect accord.

Now the man of dirt had a warped and wandered mind,   125
To exalt himself above us gods, himself being *hummph*, in part divine!
(Can you believe that? To us this is not where it is at).
Yet the secret of the gods lay in his own blistered hands,
The knowledge of metal given over was his to command.

Now in *that* tiny spark and strike,   130
Man's genius took off in vainglorious flight.
O'er powering the wondr'us gods of old,
We were put aside as a new day arose!

Men of puny countenance grappling for the Earth,
Our home in the stars did they then compel to convert.   135

To destroy our land in all her godded majesty,
The Midgard of the gods, not men, and all our vanities!

Some blades to hone and some driven to despair,
Cursed forever from the foundries of insane master's lairs.
Yet the wicked know what the noble sword eschews,   140
In their heart her metal condemns them always ringing true.

To turn aside from battle with an innocent man born,
To finish the wicked off, a timely thing shorned.
They bestowed them names, many spring from their master's sheath,
Exalted to defend the right and avenge the blood of the meek.   145

All this given into man's lowly, sweaty paltry grip,
To shape the great elements in his palms were slipped,
The craft of hammer and anvil given by that fool *Woe-dim*,
To debase the mystery of nature in their pawish grimps!

Yet unto herself the sword is our worst enemy for man,   150
For with that love we deny, she sears the flesh and shortens his span.
To wield the blade thusly for us means their untimely death—
For by the sword's naked edge they are their own match; granite
kismet set!

Now the soul of a war-like man always goeth forth,
He does not see the flowers or their excellent worth.   155
Tramples the delicate that breathes the dust of his feet,
Choking the air that to him should be always so sweet.

Soon *the* final battle will ensue, bloody Ragnarök,
'Destruction of the Powers' is the term we use (we need all the luck).
The end of world when monsters slay those rotten gods!   160
Midgard and Asgard destroyed—I've, *uh*, calculated the odds."

("*C'mon* windbag," picked Kari, "your delusions talk *way* too much—
Get to the sticking point, you psycho-phantasmic nut.").

"For even now *a'coming* is the bitter cold winter,
That will fill the Midgard, Tree, and those lands of the hinter.   165
That bitter time, Fimbulvetr, thriced shall tell the deed of day,
Then the sun winds down to judgment—
And will call those to be slain.

A time of great fear shall hover o'er the land,
Like carrion vultures, hate and strife shall stalk every man.   170
Crimes committed in secret, that no one should speak,
Of murder, ravishings and defilement, kinships deplete, *ha-ha*!

Many will be the portents of *that* dark and horrid time,
Ushered in by the Angel of Death and all his concubines.
The Dísir and Alaisiagae will walk alone in the weeping land,   175
Chanting, '*Lay of the Spear*' before that great war's firebrand.

Mountains will crash and Midgard she will shake,
Wolf Fenrir devours sun in his gaping rabenous chase.
The moon consumed too and stars fall from black sky,
World Tree quivers under burden, and monsters let fly!   180

World Serpent emerges from the sea and engulfs the land,
Blows its poison upon all, to kill both Asgard and man.
On that torrent, ship Naglfar is launched (made of dead men's nails),
Carrying giants of destruction, with Loki lashing the sails.

From Muspell's fiery realm, Surt and his followers ride out,   185
Against their eternal enemies, to meet the gods at 'Narök.
With shining swords they strike forth, determined of their fate,
Then the bridge Bifrost is shattered with their spiteful weight.

Surt's tribe joins the frost giants on that Vigrid plain,
The last conflict to be fought, destiny to be gained!   190
Place of final battle, against those Northern gods,
Contention of the Age is fixed, these mighty hosts do trod.

That accursed Heimdall, then his Gjallarhorn will sound,
Blaring out warning, summoning the Aesir to the battleground.
Odin, that slime, rides to the spring beneath the World Tree,   195
Secrets with Mimir and to the battle with champions goes he.

Clamor begins when *that* Odin in full battle array,
Aligns the field with heroes of his Hall and his way.
In battle mood hurls spear Gungnir o'er his enemies' heads,
Thus the consummation begins—   200
Meadows of corpses in the end
(Or more like it, corpses to the meadows to send).

There they clash the gods of Asgard's vaunted way,
'Gainst the giants, those shining ones who continually rage.
To meet with their enemies, that last supreme time for all,   205
To encounter the wolf and serpent-beast, and all his base hordes.

Tsk, tsk, pity, the gods in the end are all miserably destroyed,
And yet in the conflict the giants too, fall to the ploy.
Survivors? *Yesss*, but Surt seeks his dark revenge,
Throws fire o'er the Earth—   210
Destroying the last of that race called 'men.'

But *all* is not lost for those fools whose hearts do bleed!
Midgard she shall a'born again from far fertilher green seeds.
Purified from all past suffering and so pretentious an up swell,
Sons of gods will reign with Balder, who has returned from Hel.   215

They will then rule a new universe regenerated *a' fresh*,
While two from the World Tree will come from this ash.
Guarded from destruction, they will again entwine,
And reconcile Mid and Asgard with inhabitants divined.

A new sun will sojourn the Heavens, greater than the old,   220
Pouring out her warmth onto her fair Midgard orb below.
The land, she will find favor from all those gods above,
As they love Midgard, the jewel, as one greatly beloved."

Dark Storm *heh*, sneered at her 'quaint' little tale of revenge,
Licked her lips like a laughing hyena, as one who would scavenge.   225
"As that poet said, 'Some say the world will end in fire,
Some say in ice,' Elements contrared—no matter—
To me a new universe to exploit—now *that* is really nice."

Kari *sheeshed* and nocked an arrow to her bow,   230
A hard rubber head would lead its thu*dd*ding flow.
Readied her aim at the man's stupid little head,
Cursed him for being so dense to the very end.

'The man,' benumbed at this all too br'illaint a speech,
Forgot the revolting fact that Storm *was* a Valkyrian leech.   235
"Why tell me all this?" asked he—the big sounding man,
"To offer you headship, *of course*," said she rolling her eyes—
"If you'll follow my plan."

This she did always with her pawnish little men,
Seeking to control them, their wills inevitably to bend.   240
"By the way, what is your name that I may know?"
The man benumbled his parched lips—

St. Kari with arrow ¡THOooo→→→→*WOP!!*—let *go!!!*

A man unconscious is a truly disgusting thing,
Especially on the floor between two fe-spirits valkyrie'eening.   245
"*Wow.* Nice shot," Dark Storm calmly said,
"I almost had him y'know, yet I'd hate to see him dead."

"Would you?" Kari entered she with sword,
Dark Storm finished her drink, smiling, quite bored.
Kari waited for Storm a response to decide,   250
Glanced at Burning's body in its state of spiricide.

"As you can see, Dark scoffed, I've been *pfff,* busy today.
Take your prize and go, I'll get mine out of the way."
Storm shrugged aside and with a hand and a leer,
Rendered Kari a malicious smile, moving to the clear.   255

Eyes told eyes a story known and untold,
Kari frowned and led 'the man' out, dragging him in choking hold.
—Let the she-beast play her trumping bloody hand,
—Let Kari alone–to unfold her deeper brooding plans.

Once out on the street a blade pressed Kari's throat,   260
A score or more monsters railing about her in delicious gloat.
Dropped the man down as they stripped her of blade,
Dark Storm waved, "*ehhh,* these you did not enough pay."

"Soon I'll have *that* name from either of your lips,
I'll have his soul yet and all the power it befits."   265
Dark tossed her sword, "take them, and see that they are secure,
She's nothing without her *toy* blade, *hmmm,* about that–I am quite sure."

DOUGLAS M. LAURENT

Chapter Twenty-Six Valley Footnotes

Dark Storm gives the third major speech of the play. It is a testimony to her views on politics past and present in the Nethers, also why Theman should join her. Norse myths are used as mirrors to behind-the-scenes history. It is obvious that early Christianity, particularly that of the *Revelation* fused with the ancient tales. The ancient-modern-future Deadlands/Midgard poem is a faithful rendition of those historical mixings, except where Dark Storm adds her own opinions on the Great Flood and the fall of the angels. The text, however, does not make it clear whether or not she is using this information to lie or just for dramatic effect.

0. *Elements and Aesir.* The chapter's title speaks of the gods of Asgard. Apparently, the *Aesir* were Asians that migrated to the Northern countries of Europe, along with other tribes such as the *Vanir*, whom they continually fought with, creating certain hazy legends.

3. *A conspired tale.* Inspired + conspiracy. Storm uses an inspiring tale designed to seduce The Mean to come into agreement with her. She loves to embellish by putting a lot of frosting on her 'devil's food' cake. For Theman he will soon find out he can't have her cake and eat it too, although she makes it tantalizing and lip-smacking for him at the same time.

5. *Foreboding Ginnungagap.* This is the 'space preceding the creation,' from which all things were made. Other terms are 'chaos,' the 'great void,' *etc.* The Greek 'god' Chaos is a hacked up term for the name 'Cush,' the grandson of biblical Noah, *Genesis* 10.6. The name was acquired during the Tower of Babel rebellion. In Greece Cush/Chaos was known as the 'god of gods.' This 'father-god' from whom all other gods came into being (like evil King Nimrod) was also known at this time as the 'god of confusion'—just another name for Cush. The 'confusion' that is implied here is Cush's role in confounding the people at Babel. In his interpretive role as the messenger god *Hermes*, a synonym that means "Son of Ham," Cush, along with his son Nimrod, deliberately caused political anarchy and disorder, chaos, to cover up their schemes of dominion. They then conveniently interpreted, or 'divided' the sayings of the 'gods' in their own way, *i.e.*, the way of the rebels, confusing and duping the gullible people into building the Tower as a self-righteous act

of worship. The post-Flood world of Noah, Nimrod and Cush was mayhem, very chaotic, turbulent and frenzied, there being a free-for-all to gain world control.

6. *Allfather conceived.* This is one of Odin's many names, or better, 'aliases.' Accordingly, there is some discrepancy as to whether Odin fits the bill to this god at all, who may be another person altogether. It was only later when Odin was popularized in a mythical sense that he was tagged with this title to square with this other god and/or the God of Heaven. However, using the tool of *Euhemerism*, if we look at the derived genealogy below from *Genesis* Ten, his titles make sense. In understanding the 'Table of Nations' (aforesaid *Genesis*), from where we get our information, we find that this chart on early origins is not designed to trace direct lineages of ancestry but to show political, geographical, and ethnic affiliations among the early tribes for various reasons, one most notably being holy war. Further, we find that the term 'sons' in the family listings imply three things—descendants, successors or nations, so that when the chart speaks of the 'sons' of Noah—Shem, Ham or Japheth, it is referring to these three generalized things. The whole list 'floats' historically accurate information ideals and concepts down through time. We find in the Table that Noah's sixth-listed grandsons, Peleg/Joktan, had a falling out, and this is of interest in studying Odin's royal genealogy, *Genesis* 10.21:

1. Noah
2. Shem
3. Arphaxad
4. Shelah
5. Eber
6. Peleg/Joktan
7. Joktan's prince-god titles handed down in time = Germanic 'Woden,' Icelandic 'Oth,' 'Óthin' or 'Óðin.' According to ancient hist/myths, Joktan at one time was an ally of Nimrod, who apparently 'absorbed' some of these god persona-motifs, which then passed through history with his imprint on them.

The name *Peleg* means "Division," and the term *divided* implies things divided 'in a splattering, forceful way.' Apparently in a bloody *coup d'état* known as the Erech-Aratta war of 2308-02 B.C. (Pilkey, p. 126 *et al.*), a war that took place 49 years after the Tower of Babel incident, *Genesis* Eleven, Joktan, led by King Nimrod and others attempted to usurp the royal messianic line from Noah, Shem and Peleg which Christ was ultimately to come. From this world-event, Nimrod/Joktan passed along prince-god titles in the form of and to Odin's *Allfather* label that then is somewhat valid. Nimrod's propaganda machine attempted to make Joktan look credible as if Odin was on the God of Heaven's side and so we have the more modern Odin's many 'god' titles of which *Allfather* is one. From the *Genesis* list we run into the original Woden or Odin in the person of Joktan, he being sixth in line, but later we find that this original root name re-surfaces in six Anglo-Saxon royal genealogies (East-Anglia, Kent, Lindsey, Mercia, Northumbria, and Wessex.) as the 18th listed name Woden (Cooper, p. 84):

1. Noah
2. Sceaf (Japheth)
3. Bedwig
4. Hwala
5. Hrathra
6. Itermon
7. Heremod
8. Scealdwea
9. Beaw
10. Taetwa
11. Geat
12. Godwulf
13. Fin
14. Frithuwulf
15. Freawine
16. Frealaf
17. Frithuwald
18. Woden

There are many centuries between the two historical names and personages. How are the discrepancies of Joktan's name showing up in Anglo-Saxon genealogies to be explained? Furthermore, how is the myth to be explained concerning this historical person as being a Northern god?

While this cannot be the same person there being thousands of years between the two, are we asked to believe a person's personal propaganda about him is to last for centuries? The answer to this is strange and not so strange. If we take *Genesis* as a literal history and consider the fact that people both before the Flood and immediately after it were living hundreds of years as cited in the *Genesis* Hebrew genealogies, then the problem and answer makes sense.

Longevity at that time was due to the vapor canopy that once covered the Earth, making it a tropical hothouse (as observed in dinosaur fossils and footprints found in the Arctic and Antarctic regions). The vapor canopy, shielded the Earth from the harmful effects of the sun's radiation, which is now known to age things. After the Flood the vapor canopy was gone and people and animals began living shorter lives (the source of gigantism in pre- and post-Flood animals was in part due to the vapor canopy, *e.g.*, reptiles do not stop growing hence their enormous 'dinosaur' size before the Flood (Whitcomb).

In addition, nations are known to fight each other for thousands of years, their emotions and mythic propaganda passing down. *E.g.*, the Israeli-Palestinian conflict is at least three thousand years old, as the modern name Palestine is derived from ancient Philistia, from where the Philistines came from and with whom Samson once fought against (Judges, Chapters 13-16).

With the idea of longevity and supreme regal power, both Peleg of the royal line fought with his princely brother puppet Joktan under Nimrod's manipulation and that their war is still imprinted on the pages of ancient history, they both living to be of a very, very old age. In fact, Nimrod took over Joktan's persona and office, so we might say Odin is also a caricature-stamp of Nimrod's personality and office. What happened then was that Joktan's name and power, his office and propaganda, his hype, his story, attitude, angst and demeanor were *euhemeristically* all carried down *via* Nimrod's manipulative propaganda imprint through history and settled upon this person Woden/Odin and melded into the line of Japheth, the 'Great one; Chief of Race' for political purposes. As an aside, Japheth, or 'Jupiter,' *J(I)u-pater* in Roman times also meant 'Father of gods,' 'Father Jove,' from PIE *Dyeu-pater via* Gk. *Zeus-pater* (Nimrod), hence the phrases "by Jove" or "by Jupiter." *Iuppiter* is connected to being the god of sky and thunder, quite apropos to Japheth and Noah. Roundabouts Rome however, wicked King Nimrod's swiping of Jasper's titles meshed into the Jupiter (the young) theme from Japheth and he along with his father Cush, god *Cháos* (Gk. *Hermes*), were known as the integrated 'two-faced' Roman god *Janus*, both of which according to legend ruled Rome even before the city was built, it having many earlier Jupiter place names.

On a deeper, perhaps more chilling level is the Underworld view of the situation. As Joktan took power away from Peleg, this may be a chief demon's attempt to replace the royal messianic line with its own, a thing not unheard of. In this case the royal genealogy that passed through time to Anglo-Saxon England and Northern Europe as embodied in the person of Odin may very well account for its 'owner-possessor-demon' keeping his interests, his 'business and office' affairs running throughout time *via* royal families and their genealogical lines, considered his 'property.'

Was the historical Odin-Woden in an unknowing sense the recipient of an actual demon's program, it carrying on its own propagandistic religion after the manner of his earlier attempts with Joktan through Nimrod? Nimrod was pretty much a good pal of Satan, so why not? Or were both Joktan and Odin 'demonized,' the demon being the same fallen angel hidden behind the *façade* of the two men, working his stuff out, his record of accomplishment being caught in snippets of biographical history? This is a thought to consider, it opening up many possibilities. In *Beryl Coronet*, Sherlock Holmes, explaining his peculiar methods of investigation to his colleague Dr. Watson, once remarked, "It is an old axiom of mine that when you have excluded the impossible, whatever remains, however improbable, must be truth." Historians Hawkesford and Atterbury might agree with Holmes, saying this is all a Deadlands political ploy on the part of the adversaries to make their side look good and continue their work in our Midgard world today (Ch. 28 note # 28).

10. *With form's leads.* Jonathan Mycroft cites that a more accurate translation of this phrase is "forms *mis*lead." The idea is that everything in the universe is energy, part of the whole, not able to be created or destroyed, and that this energy takes on myriads of forms, deceiving, giving illusions to those who would observe this energy in a broken, fragmented state of mind, they buying into these broken images for the real thing. These are called *eidōlons*, which can be reflected images that confuse the mind or they can be

phantoms, which also cause mind-muddling. We get our word *idol* from this. In the Deadlands, Nature herself schemes and deceives. She feeds on those that return to her womb *via* the tomb. She fools those who think she is the 'end result,' a supreme God or living force or being of sorts, and not the means to that end—which is that 'despicable' Creator God of *Genesis* One—according to some malcontent Mortuuslands citizens. The land takes care of her own ambitions, visited upon those who trod her—whether they are good or bad. The oddity for us mortals is that if the land sets out to fool people, it shows she has some level of intelligence, her schemes of which to us ordinary folk would completely deceive us, catching us by surprise. Perhaps that is why, says Job (*Job* 12.7-8), we should learn to "speak to the earth, and it will teach you." The translation though, is unclear whether our poem stanza is an actual metaphor.

11-12. *The gods of emergence . . . nature's travail.* This is a reference to angels (Rev. 12.4). Lucifer sweet-talked a third of them into believing they somehow sprang from the watery realms and that they were not created by that mosquitoey 'Creator God' fellow. He espoused to them in so many words that the Annoyer got there just a little bit ahead of them in terms of evolution. In the Netherworld as in our own, there are only two 'religions' to speak of, *evolutionism* or *creationism*. The fallen ones favor evolutionism as it offers them a convenient 'out' in terms of having no need to give an account of themselves and is the jagged gouging pig iron base for anti-Creator philosophy they promote that is so prevalent in the Dead and in our parallel world today, both of which they, by Divine fiat, temporarily rule.

14. *No, wait,* six he thought. Writer Hector Kyle believes that Storm is making fun of Odin's alleged dimwittedness in this passage. As such, the author lists seven ingredients that many ancient cosmologies have, more or less—wood, fire, water, wind, earth, metal and ether, or void.

16. *Vault of Midgard. Vault* in ancient Hebrew (Isaiah 40.21-22) is *khug*, and means "circle, zenith or sphericity," allowing for the idea that the Earth is a sphere or ball suspended in space. This same term is translated as "circuit" and "compass" in *Proverbs* 8.27. Hence, scholars *knew* that the Earth was round seven hundred years before the birth of Christ! This info is the cat's pajamas! Zeitgeist spirit of Stultification—you

are here! Talk about scientists being slower than tortoise races in January. Why do we pay the eggheads to teach us? According to greedy soul-slurping Nether *zeit-stult* logic, they are trained and paid to be thick for much darker purposes than the "Powers that be" wish to let on—for now.

20. *Drink of her pristine.* Water gives life to all. In a larger sense, this refers the Spirit of Eternal Life.

28. *Yggdrasill—Tree of Creation.* This is an ancient reference to the 'Horse of Yggr,' or Odin's horse, meaning "*gallows*." Drasill means 'horse and Ygg(r) is one of Odin's names. Odin 'sacrificed' himself, allegedly (he was so sneaky) by hanging himself, making the Ygg-tree 'the *gallows* Odin." This *eternal green* ash (*askr*) tree is also the 'World Tree.' This forms the 'epicenter' of the worlds of men, gods and giants. Kind of sounds like something Nimrod in his role as Odin at his downtown Babel complex would cook up. Since ancient times ash was the preferred wood used for poles and spear shafts due to its tough resilient pliancy. From Proto-Indo-European (PIE) roots we see that the word **sper–* implies a spear or a pole and that **os–* means "ash tree," *to wit* comes Proto-Germanic **askaz/kiz* to ON *askr*, Old Saxon *ask* and in OE *æsc* or "ash tree" that ofttimes meant 'spear made of ash wood' or a 'unit armed with spears.' In Old Norse, it is *spjör*.

In biblical lands Hebrew *'ōren* meant strength as in the ash tree, noted for its bold versatility. Compare the Hebrew word *'ēṣ* which equals `astah, a tree (from its firmness). Therefore it means wood, pole, piece of wood, sticks, carpenter, *gallows*, staff, *etc*. *'Ēṣ* describes the tree of life and the tree of the knowledge of good and evil (Gen. 2.9; 17; Rev. 2.7; 22.2). Within this word-scrabble game, we find other terms such as *xylon*, which is any wooden article or something made of wood, *i.e.*, timber for material or fuel, sticks, clubs, staffs and stocks with the overall meaning of 'tree' and 'wood.' *Galatians* 3.13 speaks of those accursed as being any unfortunate chap who is 'hung on a tree,' whilst *xulon*, a parallel wood word, tells of wooden objects like clubs, crosses and stocks. Hence, in *Luke* 23.31 we find, the '*eternal green* tree' Christ, noted for His strong resilient pliancy, and the *stauros*, a special upright stake, pale or cross the Romans used, for example, as in crucifixions. One of murderous Cain's evil monikers is *Qayin*. In the original, it means 'fixity; striking fast, said of a lance or spear.' It was an evil ashen pale such as this that the heavy-handed Roman blackguard guard thrust into Christ's side to check out if He was really dead, the wound producing 'water' and so, symbolically, Christ became the *green tree of eternal life*, water gushing out from this fountain of life just like in Eden. Good scores once again (*Strong's Talking Greek & Hebrew Dictionary*).

32. *Land of Niflheim.* This place is the abode of darkness and freezing mist, underneath the World Tree. It is said that within this realm pass those who die of disease and old age.

34-36. *Elements for divine . . . coveted land.* This stanza reflects the 'mystery of steel' said to be given to the men by the gods. *Riddle . . . barbarian men.* This is also a loose reference to *Conan the Barbarian*, a film by John Milius, 1982, where "the riddle of steel" is central to the plot. In it, Conan (Arnold Schwarzenegger) cries out, "Crom is strong! If I die, I have to go before him, and he will ask me, 'What is the riddle of steel?' If I don't know it, he will cast me out of Valhalla and laugh at me."

37. *As for* wind. This is a referral to life. The Greeks felt that the *pneúma* or 'spirit' was like the *wind*. This passage also reflects Christ's discourse on the wind-like propensity of the Spirit of God, *John 3.8*. A *pneúma akathartós* is an unclean evil spirit.

40. The *Master born.* This is a referral to the Creator God.

43. *Nine worlds in all.* Allfather Odin, it is said, created the nine worlds. They make up the whole of creation. They are, as far as documentation can make out: *Muspell, Hel, Niflheim*—at the bottom, *Jotunheim*, the land of giants, *Midgard*, the place of mortals, *Nidavellir*, land of dwarfs, *Svartalfaheim*, land of dark elves, *Alfheim*, land of light elves, *Vanaheim*, land of the Vanir in the middle, and at the high point, *Asgard*, home of the gods. It is interesting to note that modern science, based on mathematical computations, has plotted the possibility that nine dimensions exist. Whose ancient perspective is this we may ask?

44-45. *Ruler of Weather . . . Lord of the Dead.* These are some of Odin's many names.

52. *The gods, we smite.* Dark Storm openly identifies herself as a goddess, one of the families of Aesir, or Asian gods. She places herself above the measly Valkyries.

55. *Making them god-like.* In some societies, weapons are thought to be deities.

60. *Fire joined sister water.* Not intended as incest, but this joining does produce off-spring as the union is likened to elements giving birth.

63. *Child; ironed strife.* This speaks of potential strife, but partial manuscripts from the eleventh century *Heliaspur Saga* read "Child of ironed strife." This is a weapon, a sword.

67. *Came orange blood's . . . amok.* This refers to *libido*, that is, sexual 'energy' in the home and let loose in war. Stated in *Prologue* note # 25, that war was ultimately feminine in its space and scope, Consider for a moment what the current martial genetic mentality at the end of the day ultimately means in Midgard (Eccl. 4.4), as it demands that a person who is stronger or more skilled rules over the many who are not. According to Lord Mars' hard-line extremist genetic martial doctrine (1Tim. 4.1; 2Tim. 4.4)

weaker or less skilled individuals are of no importance, except of course, to serve the 'master' and 'the system.' This view by the way, can easily lead to very grue-some things as cited in George Orwell's nightmarish novel, *1984*:

> The ideal set up by the Party was something very huge, terrible, and glitter-ing—a world of steel and concrete of monstrous machines and terrifying weap-ons—a nation of warriors and fanatics, marching forward in perfect unity, all thinking the same thoughts and shouting the same slogans, perpetually work-ing, fighting, triumphing, persecuting—three hundred million people all with the same face (p. 74).

And:

> Unlike Winston, she had grasped the inner meaning of the Party's sexual puritanism. It was not merely that the sex instinct created a world of its own which was outside the Party's control and which therefore had to be destroyed if possible. What was more important was that sexual privation

induce hysteria, which was desirable because it could be transformed into war fever and leader worship. They way she put it was: 'When you make love you're using up energy; and afterwards you feel happy and don't give a damn for anything. They can't bear you to feel like that. They want you to be bursting with energy all the time. All this marching up and down and cheering and waving flags is simply sex gone sour. If you're happy inside yourself, why should you get excited about Big Brother and the Three-Year Plans and the Two Minutes Hate and all the rest of their bloody rot?' That was very true, he thought. There was a direct, intimate connection between chastity and political orthodoxy. For how could the fear, the hatred, and the lunatic credulity which the Party needed in its members be kept at the right pitch except by bottling down some powerful instinct and using it as a driving force? The sex impulse was dangerous to the Party, and the Party had turned it to account (p. 134).

Finally, in the genetic view's final and most demoniacal phase:

Any society which evaluates its members by their worth to itself is not attaching value to the individual person at all, but only to his functions. When these functions no longer serve a useful purpose, the man ceases to have any value. This was Nietzsche's philosophy—and Hitler's. (Custance, *Sons*, p. 64).

Submitted for your approval: Storm's ways are, shall we say highly polished culturobarbaric, void of any heart whatsoever, at least that is what she implies as she spins her little history lesson—a bleak mirror into our own past, present—and future.

68. *Weland his name.* This is the famed legendary Anglo-Saxon/Germanic smith to the men/gods, who created swords of exceptional quality.

74. *Eternal and present ideal.* 'To move' is to shape, and 'to be,' reality. In the Nether, motion appears to be the basis of the law. An interesting analogy might be a traffic accident that instead of the auto having the right of way based on prior 'static' thought-out rational law it would have the right of way based on the logic/intuition of flowing momentum.

75. *Freedom to wield.* The following passage from Sir Richard Burton's work, *The Book of the Sword, xiii,* exemplifies the meaning of the stanza:

> In knightly hands the Sword acknowledged no Fate but that of freedom and free-will; and it bred the very spirit of chivalry, a keen personal sentiment of self respect, of dignity, and of loyalty, with the noble desire to protect weakness against the abuse of strength. The knightly Sword was ever the representative idea, the present and eternal symbol of all that man most prized—courage and freedom.

The sword brings even mercenaries like Storm self-respect. It is symbolic of the code of high ethics spirits in Valhalla adhere to or fall away from; it is their ticket to change the world.

78. *Beyond the stars themselves.* These are angels, celestial spirits, *Job* 38.1-7. Storm is citing that 'the god's' former power was beyond the count of all angels.

79. *Lighted womb, pfff, when Asgard was rent!* The *lighted womb* is Heaven or Asgard. *Rent* refers to the remote pre-historic angelic rebellion led by Lucifer that ripped Heaven apart.

85. *We are those powers . . . gods of old.* Storm reiterates many of her 'roles' from the past.

85-88. *Self-estate and self-love . . . The unseen king of Tyre.* Jonathan Mycroft suggests that there is a phonetic '*H*' in the term *estate,* making it 'esthate,' indicative of Storm's and the other spirits' feelings over the matter of fallenness. *Tyre.* Also 'tear.' This too reflects the above sad, hidden sentiment. In *Ezekiel* 28.11, the King of Tyre is used as a political front, or 'mask' to convey Lucifer's rebellion. Thus, we are given a rare glimpse of how the wicked spirit-powers work in Midgard and Valhalla—they hide behind people and demo-fabricated cultures, using them as fronts, masks and dupes, history and *zeitgeist*—the moods, trends, tastes and fashions of a particular era, being designed and carried on by the immortals. A penetrating example to this is found in the 1956 *MGM* movie, *Moby Dick* starring Gregory Peck. Peck, as fanatical Captain Ahab delivers an excelsior, deep-sinking line to his first mate, the good Starbuck who, listening intently, stands transfixed (as Ahab would soon transpierce Moby Dick with the same sticking-fast "cold iron shaft of eloquence"). He tells why he, like a rabid dog pursues the white behemoth, allowing us some insight into the "Powers that be" behind 'the masks' (*see* Ch. 1 note # 24 for Zeitgeist):

> Look ye, Starbuck, all visible objects are but as pasteboard masks. Some inscrutable yet reasoning thing puts forth the molding of their features. The white whale tasks me; he heaps me. Yet he is but a mask. 'Tis the thing behind the mask I chiefly hate; the malignant thing that has plagued mankind since time began; the thing that maws and mutilates our race, not killing us outright but letting us live on, with half a heart and half a lung.

99. *Those gods who loved women.* This is a reference to the 'sons of God' in *Genesis* Six, who cohabitated with women and through direct possession and genetic cross-breeding allegedly produced 'giants,' or *Nephilim*, hideous, crossbreed offspring. Storm is very vindictive, as one of Odin's many habits was to run around in disguise and impregnate women, making him, in her eyes, a *sick-o* hypocrite.

100-101. *'The gods'* . . . *'the giants'.* Storm is using general phrases to describe elect and fallen angels.

104. *Bifrost Bridge.* The rainbow used by the gods to go from Asgard to Midgard, the Earth.

108-109. *To have been a god . . . fixed in permanent stain!* An angel. The text shows that Dark Storm is reminiscing, but, as the Mythologist Jörgens points out, it does not make out that this is about her past, and that it is not clear whether she is being dramatic just to lie to Theman. *Fixed stain* or 'imbrued stain.' *Imbrue* is a stain upon one's sword or hands, a bad thing. Here it is double-worded to show how intense this realization is to Storm, allegedly. Seems that she is recalling the permanently insulting, forever dishonorable staining after-effect fallout of the great rebellion wherein a third of the angels fell, all being caught ectohanded (*see* Ch. 32 note # 47 for imbrued).

112. *An ashed pile of depraved sin.* In C.S. Lewis' *The Problem of Pain*, he presents the idea that the *remains* of a log set on fire—gas, light, heat and ash—are much like an inciner-ated soul that rejects the grace of God through the substitutionary death of Christ. In that rejection of mercy, the only other alternative the soul has is to be judged by the perfect law, and thus the fragmented imperfect soul, not God, by default *commits its own self* to Hell! As a result of denying mercy, whatever is in Hell, Lewis says, is not angelic or human any longer, but their broken down warped *remains*, growing ever sour and debauched by the moment, as a soul can only find its true life and fulfill-ment in the light and union with the eternal Spirit, Who is eternal Love.

117. *Gods of eternity breathed.* This is the Creator God(s) of Heaven, the Trinity.

118. *Fashioned the breath.* Just as God breathed life into man to become a living soul, so God also 'breathes' life into metal, making the sword have a soul and life of its own.

120. *Symbol of hope.* This refers to swords and the sword of the Spirit.

121. *The Runes did.* *Runes* are ancient obscure 'writings' of the old North peoples said in part to foretell events. A Rune can also be any poem, verse or song, especially one that is mystical or obscure.

123-124. *A Million times . . . peace . . . instruments of war).* *Million* refers to the number of times master sword smiths of Japan beat and folded the metals that go into the producing of superb blades where the insides were soft and pliable while the outer edge was more harder and sharper. This allowed the blades to 'breathe' as it were, by being able to bend. In context, sarcastic Storm implies that smiths literally "beat to death" war instruments until their own consciences are appeased and so at peace due to their making such lethal weapons. In fact, Japanese sword smiths usually invite the local martial-deity or sword-god to strike the blade through their hammer at the crucial moment in order to create the perfect blade.

130. *That tiny spark.* This is the gift of divine life, humankind being made in the image of God. A little lower than the angels, humankind is endowed with great gifts. No dog, ape or pig ever laid out a city plan, wrote a novel, composed a symphony, scripted a play or did Euclidean geometry!

134. *Grappling for the Earth.* God gave humankind initial dominion over the Earth, not fallen celestial spirits (Psalm 8 and Genesis Chapters 1-3).

136. *Destroy our land.* Storm tends to think that Midgard is a hunting ground for spirits of her ilk, not the property of us dumb Earth-dwellers. Biblical records bear this out, *2Corinthians* 4.4.

139. *Insane master's lairs.* According to Peter Hsu, in old Japan some master sword makers were known to border on lunacy. As such, it was thought their blades 'carried bad vibes' and were to be avoided. This was because the smiths' katana-deliriums and personality derangements, often very strong, were thought to be beat 'senseless' into the blades while they were fashioning them, the finished razor 'emanating out' their maker's dark soulish madness just dying to be used. One such 'insane' master smith was Senzo Muramasa (*ca.* 1341). His blades were believed to lust for blood, forcing their owners to commit suicide or murder as proven on several occasions (Ratti and Westbrook, p. 263).

141. *Her metal condemns.* The old adage, "the wrong man with the right tools" is the idea here. Even a good sword used for bad purposes cuts well, but every ring of the blade is another nail in the coffin of the evildoer, as the good blade acts as a witness, indicting a spirit's conscience. As on Earth, 'what goes around comes around' is also a forceful reality in the Nether.

148. *That fool Woe-dim.* Old German *Woden* (*Odin*), *lit.*, "rage and frenzy." The term was initially used to describe phantom warriors riding on turbulent, stormy nights. This was known as the 'raging army' and the 'furious hunt,' from which the term 'Woden,' or 'rage' derived. Storm is again being sarcastic, calling him *woe*ful and *dim*, a 'miserable nincompoop!'

150-153. *Yet unto herself . . . untimely death—. . . own match; granite kismet set!* A weapon stripped of its spiritual value is nothing more than just a tool used for killing. Turkish *kismet* "fate," "destiny." This term implies that it is man's *granite* fate to be his own match or demise. Also, kismet + kiss + met. In other words, the 'kiss of death,' *i.e.*, fate/destiny tells mankind to *kiss off* (a "rude dismissal") leaving it to its own self-generated fate by its own hand.

154-157. *Now the soul of a war-like man . . . so sweet.* Storm alludes to the very sad state of mediocre, non-challenging martial proficiency in the Deadlands and in Midgard today, which advocates the glorification of bulk generic violence and loud macho attitudes as a cover up for the lack of exacting ability. Once Storm was questioned by the top-notch mercenary Noctifer, the "night-bringing evening star," as to why he should hire out to her to which she responded, "Well for years I've been surrounded by morons. It's refreshing to see someone of your caliber." Does not this say it all? A parallel to all this may be found in modern rock bands where third-rate bands play loud to drown out their incompetence and hide their lack of ability as they try to get the audience screaming for more and more and more.

163. *Get to the sticking point.* Impatient Kari knows Storm is working herself up into a feeding-frenzy sales pitch to get Theman's name, just waiting to stick the right words into his gullet at the right moment with her *suki-pointed* word-sword, she maneuvering him into accepting a deal with her through careful phrasing. However some texts believe Kari is alluding to a line in *Macbeth* (I. vii.) where Lady Macbeth chides her husband because he is chickening out of killing good King Duncan trying to bolster his courage saying, "But screw your courage to the sticking place and we'll not fail." The image that comes off her line is that of tightening up a crossbow bolt to its highest load-point, ready to trigger. What Kari is saying is that in either case Storm is getting her bravado up to make the final sales blitz that will decidedly skewer Theman; she wants his name that bad. She's so into it that she's into it.

167-168. *Sun winds down . . . to be slain.* Dark Storm speaks of the sun itself as being Valkyrie-ish, 'choosing the slain.' This passage also mirrors the Son of God luring his opponents, of their own self-imposed volition, to their deaths at *Armageddon*, *Ezekiel* 38-39 and *Rev.* 19, *et al.*

175. *Dísir and Alaisiagae.* Both groups are female war spirits. *Dísir* were spirits attached to families. They brought nature's bounty to man. In addition, like good health care workers, they visited the homes of the new born for good luck. The *Alaisiagae* were known as goddesses, their title being found on Hadrian's Wall during the Roman period. Two notable leaders of the Alaisiagae were *Baudihillie* and *Firagabi*. Their names literally mean "Ruler of Battle" and "Giver of Freedom."

178. *Wolf Fenrir.* The son of Loki, the evil trickster-god. *Fenrir* took the form of a wolf and grew more threatening to the gods. *Rabenous chase.* Ravenous + rabies. A hideous, frothing creature. It is said that *Fenrisúlf* ('Fenris wolf') breaks free at Ragnarök and chows down Odin, a good thing.

181. *World Serpent emerges.* This Serpent is 'Jormungand,' child of Loki. This creature at *Ragnarök* will arise from the sea causing great destruction, as its power propels the ships of the giants. This beast kills Thor (an early named *Euhemerism* for Shem, son of Noah, the 'god of the thunder storm,' or 'storm god.'). The sea in biblical literature is often identified as peoples, tribes and nations. In light of this, the Anti-Christ (energized by 'the Dragon,' Satan) will arise out of the nations (the European Union perhaps), to wreak havoc on the Earth, his special vengeance being upon Israel, a 'S(h)emitic' nation.

185. *Muspell's fiery realm, Surt.* A Southern or bottomland, said to be a great realm of fire and ice, believed to have taken part in the creation. At *Ragnarök*, the final conflict, the sons of Muspell ride out with their great fire giant leader *Surt* to fight with other giants against the gods. At the end battle, to gain revenge, he destroys the world of men with fire.

189. *Vigrid plain.* The area in which the last great battle, *Ragnarök*, is fought. This is akin to the Valley of Megiddo in modern Israel, better known to us as where *Armageddon* will take place.

191. *Those Northern gods, contention of the Age.* *Northern* implies the Triune Heaven God. This is the showdown of the Ages between good and evil, God and Satan (Ch. 19 note # 61).

193-196. *Accursed Heimdall . . . with Mimir.* *Heimdall* is a god of Asgard and the guardian of the great bridge Bifrost. *Mimir* is the wise person associated with the World Tree put to death by the Vanir, the despised enemies of the Aesir. Odin conveniently toted this person's head around to consult with it from time to time (and was it a big hit at parties!). Big-mouth prophetic jabbering heads like Odin's moldy green *Chia Head* were a big thing back then, a great source of mediumistic information in the old North.

199. *Hurls spear Gungnir.* Odin's great magical war spear, said never to have missed its mark. In the old North, a huge spear was thrown over the heads of the enemies. This signified for the Norsemen the beginning of pitched battle.

200. *The consummation.* This is the end of the Age, or *aion.* Biblically speaking, the world, according to *dispensationalism,* is divided into seven epochs or Ages. These seven eras, covering roughly seven thousand years of Earth history are the Ages of Innocence, Conscience, Government, the Law (OT), the Church Age (the Age of Grace, New Testament times), the Great Tribulation and the Millennial Kingdom. We earthlings are now at the far end of the fifth, or Church Age.

213. *Midgard she shall a'born again.* According to fragmented accounts of Norse mythology, after the destruction of the world, a new Earth and Sun will be reformed to begin life anew. From the World Tree, two people who survive the disaster will repopulate the world, and with Balder, son of Odin, who has spent time in Hel, they will begin a new race of gods to dwell on the Earth.

226. *As that poet said.* This is an allusion to Robert Frost's (1874-1963) poem, *Fire and Ice* (*Harper's Magazine* Dec. 1920). Spirits are often educated in Earth literature and the arts, as theirs is but a *veiled* step away in mind and spirit. Interestingly, both Hawkesford and Etta Jörgens hold to the idea that many 'masters' of letters, arts and sciences are actually fallen angels, *i.e.,* demons that go from one human host to

the next (a form of *Nephilimism*) through the years. They shape their and our (fallen) world culture and history. This perhaps explains why dumb things so often repeat themselves in history, mythic story lines and cliché archetypes remain standard fare, lineages and traditions are of so much importance, and there's nothing but dribble on TV at night. A general axiom by philosopher-poet George Santayana (1863-1952) to consider is, "Those who cannot remember the past are condemned to repeat it." Is this 'cannot remember' stuff a trained behavior by the over-gloomed malignant "Powers that be?" Cud on that for a while, gang.

The evidence the scholars cite is hidden in the collective unity, conscious and vocabulary of specific groups over periods. *E.g.*, there is an elite *esprit de corps* or 'group spirit' of pride, honor, belonging, *etc.*, shared by those in the same group as they experience events over time, as seen in nations, tribes, and small groups. *E.g.*, in military matters, young recruits might join a famous regiment because that regiment is responsible for 'such and such' an operation, and that on certain dates in history the regiment did 'this or that.' Upon joining, the young recruits, now part of "the Borg" collective, begin to say, 'we did this' or 'we did that,' referring to events the regiment did scores of years before they were ever born as if they were there a long time ago.

If, according to scholars 3,000 or more demons can be sardine-packed into one man as cited earlier (Ch. 7 note # 4, Legion), could not one or several dominate a regiment down through the years figuring they 'owned' it? Obviously, the regiment would empower them, giving them mobility, a sense of identity and pride, not to mention using it as an interface to manipulate people and shape events. Like a good car, it gets them where they want to go. After all, there is hearsay that speaks of group members becoming 'possessed with' or 'caught up' in the 'spirit' of the group. A metaphor perhaps; but never underestimate the nether-phantoms. As for recruits, are these unseen spirits now in-dwelling them, *they* being the one's talking as to *who initially helped create* the tradition from long ago as seen in the term 'we,' or are the recruits just basic folk who merely wish *to be identified with* a particular tradition? This, according to the theory of how spirits netherform our world to suit their needs, gives us a behind the scenes look at what may be going on in the hidden spiritual realm, the counterpart to this Midgard, which is a front for many spiritual activities good, bad and *nil*.

245. *Fe-spirits valkyrie'eening.* Jonathan Mycroft uses this terminology to describe two feminine war spirits squabbling, on the brink of fighting as they argue about their loot.

251. *Its state of spiricide.* This is when a spirit is 'killed.' In context, it is a sarcastic comment toward Burning Prairie's stupidity and arrogance. An oft-quoted proverb in the Deadlands runs, "Stupidity attacks; intelligence does not" (The Dawg).

257. *Led 'the man' out.* Kari is so used to controlling things she leads Theman out not so much with sympathy, but like a jackass, only it's a 'big jackass' in this instance, she using a jūdō-style choke hold to keep him in line.

258-259. *—Let the she-beast . . . brooding plans.* This lends insight into the deeper workings of Kari and Storm.

267. *She's nothing without her toy blade.* Like a samurai dispossessed of his sword, Storm sarcastically feels that Kari is a child, nothing, powerless without her 'soul,' her tool of self-expression and justification. A slice of this can be seen in the Kurosawa movie, *Yojimbo* (1961), starring Toshiro Mifune.

TWENTY-SEVEN: FLESH, SPIRIT AND CANVAS

In cross-thatched hut wherein a king of old might sit and reign,
Storm painted quiet as her familiar elementals played her game.
They beat the *saint*; they beat the *ain't*,
They struck them together, blinded in hate.

"The ♪ Na͡mme→♪" Storm malodied as she scumbled a stroke.   5
They held The Mean down and with rope they him choked.

Hummed she quiet to gain the detailed realist perspective,
They iron *⋛ ¡*SMACKED*!¡ ⋛* backhand St. Kari for incentive.

Laughed they at their fistic orgy,
Depraved spirits hacking the glory.   10
Punched the man deep with blows to the g'race,
Beat him to each other to his dis-face.

Yet both Kari and the man struck and fought,
More survival instinct than enlightening thought.
Made the knaves laugh all the more,   15
Striking the two harder as they curswore.

Far back among *that* score of fresh sliced bodies,
Amid their bluing eerie descending folly,
Lone sigh, Angel's eyes opened to twilight,
Glanced he about, sat, grimacing at the sight.   20

DOUGLAS M. LAURENT

Heard the sound of laughter chortling in the distance,
Wafting through the cool air with the grossest of indifference.
Grasped he his weapon from the stacked redonyx heap,
Moved toward *those* lights, feeling the dirt's 'neath.

Dark Storm concentrated, stroked away the time,   25
Painting surrealed by many a curious de-sign.
"Now then ♪ ♫ ♪ tell♯ mee♪♪ —" she lullabyed, removing a smear,
"Or my *Van*dals will *go* cut you, taking *both your ears*."

Took she now her pallet knife,
Looked at her work, then through it she sliced.   30
Held blade to St. Kari of   ,
"An appropriate end, don't you agree?"

"*Ohhh*, I've been dying to kill you for such a real long time,
Want to know why—?"
I'll soon have your power, that is, when you *really* die—   35
(*Tsk, tsk*. Such a still life you will make; a *nutucopia*,
—When I put pennies on your eyes").

"⸘Recognize me? No, I don't believe so,"
Kari eyed her, trying hard to know.
"I'll snip you a little yarn, annoyance, then you'll guess.   40
I am a person from your past, your long lost mess—."

Kari watched Storm's mind in slow ferment,
A hidden darkness that would not relent.

VALLEY OF THE DAMNED

Chapter Twenty-Seven Valley Footnotes

Now that Storm has captured St. Kari and Theman, we see Storm's troubled *kaleido-kakódaimōnic* ultimately 'ill-fated evil genius' being meticulously worked out. Hers is a spirit of such fixated mania and intensity that she can calmly paint while mayhem ensues around her. The painting of course, and her subsequent actions with it, is merely symptomatic of what is really going on inside her aberrant mind.

2-3. As her familiar elementals played her game . . . they beat the ain't. A *familiar* is a demon that attends a witch or some other classic baddie, often said to assume the form of an animal, such as a cat. They are also consummate *manipulators* and *liars*. The author himself on more than one occasion has observed in his own home, snippets of a 'holographic,' hazy, see-through, swirling 3-D gray cat running about that looks as if it had been painted in the *Cubism* art style (early twentieth century, *cf.* Pablo Picasso 1881-1973), attesting to the fact such shape-shifting creature-beings *existiolà. Elementals.* That is, 'mental men.' Storm's hench 'men' are in actuality *elementals*, a lower form of wicked spirit. And she is calling them 'mental' cases, to boot. Inwardly she knows they are a bunch of whacked-out wacko *sintering* psychopathic spirits, which annoys and disgusts her. 'Sintering' is a metallurgy term. When metals are super-heated, small glops of metal fuse together and become bigger glops. They are then easier to handle. Sintering often causes partial meltdown of the material due to surface tension and the whole process is actually caused by 'roasting' the metal—a very apropos descript and fate for these guys.

Ultimately, Storm is saying her people are a bunch of loony's—strong when together weaker when apart and easier to handle overall because it is they who suffer meltdown when their passions tense and begin to run high. This is what happens in the Deadlands economy. Blob-like lesser spirits band together to become stronger, in order to take on greater spirits so they can absorb them into their own "Borg collective" becoming powerful, solid and more functional not to mention having a higher status. In our world, there are also *group elementals*. When enough spirits or powers join together it or they become one conscious entity that goes about seeking power, sustenance, opportunity, conquest, *etc.* for the benefit of the group—just like corrupt, ruthless corporations do! It is not a good thing. What is Storm's solution to all this meaning? She just merely takes advantage of them. Even though they are incorporeal, they nonetheless are still ele*mentally* 'thick.' *They beat the ain't.* Kari is '*the saint*,' Theman is '*the ain't*,' nothing, less than zero which is what these disgusting spirits really think of him and feel for humankind in general. (For a *real-time* snotty demonic view of humans, *see* Job 4.12-21.)

5. *She scumbled a stroke.* 'Scumbling' is an acrylic brush painting technique. Whereby light opaque is put over dark colors to give it a broken rhythm effect. It also makes it look softer and duller. In short, Storm's technique is capturing the action scene around her that may include inflicting some 'strokes' of her own as well. As the scene is a jumble, so is Storm's similar *Cubist* art technique. *Cubism* as an art form was characterized by subjects being drawn as cubes or other geometric shapes in abstract, broken arrangements rather than by starched representations of reality. This is paradoxical to her painting from a Realism art (*ca.* 1840-late nineteenth century) viewpoint at the same time. Apparently, she can compose both forms of art, and mixes and matches them at she desires. *See* also poem line # 1 for *cross-thatched.* A 'cross-hatching' painting technique takes the brush and crisscrosses the strokes, giving the impression of depth, like a bird's nest.

8. *They iron . . . backhand St. Kari for incentive.* This line is delivered in the present tense, indicating that it is an on-going action taking place right now.

10. *Hacking the glory.* That is, beating on St. Kari.

11-12. *With blows to the g'race . . . his dis-face.* According to Mycroft, these seemingly mixed enigmatic lines can only mean one thing. The evil spirits are punching the man 'below the belt,' as forwarded in the term '*g'race*,' *i.e.*, 'race,' as in 'race of men,' his 'loins,' *dis*respecting him, causing him deep embarrassment and "loss of face," or *katanashi* as the Japanese might say, as in de- or '*dis-face*.' The term *dis* is also suggestive of the level of these spirit's depravity as well, as *Dis* in some classic texts such as Dante's *Inferno*, is the capitol of Hell proper.

14. *More survival instinct.* Lower forms of fighting come out as survival instincts. This is both an expenditure of energy and a change in tactics for Kari, *allegedly.* Mythologist

Etta Jörgens likes to think that Kari allowed herself to be intentionally captured and beat up to advance her overall plans, as cited in other fragmentary accounts of her exploits, most notably from the eighth century Anglo-Saxon *Ferhthgenithla*, the *Flying Reptile Saga*, and *Kel's Yellow Book* from the thirteenth century. She and others affirm that Kari is willing to 'ride out the storm,' as it were, as part of her overall amazing ability to plan things out, although in this particular instance we cannot know for sure, the text not readily lending itself toward this idea. On a deeper tangent, according to psychiatrist Greta Hastings, these lines may be intended to reflect the idea of showing her psychological limitations without a weapon to do her bidding. As with the 'soul' of the samurai, their swords, not only was the weapon an extension of their living wills and souls, but also a symbol of their virility. To be stripped of the weapon meant loss of social stature and with that, its accompanying (psychological) power and ultimately their manhood. Here we may be seeing a rare glimpse of this in terms of the intricate links between powers, social and psychological cohesions in the Deadzone. Perhaps Kari deeply identifies her bottomless ingrained sainted personality with her blade and through it, her phenomenal work, it conceivably being her black 'Dumbo feather' (*Disney*, 1941). In the story, the baby elephant did not believe he could fly without his 'security feather' until it was proven otherwise.

Coaches are known to 'exhaust' their players with the intense physical practice of their sports so that the more constrictive 'left-brained' rationalistic, conscious controls over their motions are 'let go,' the players 'loosening up,' they getting their 'second wind.' At this point, greater right-brained intuitional fluency and freer 'artistic' natural ability over their skills comes out, allowing for maximum performance as found in the maxim, "pushed to the hilt." This metaphorically and in actuality may be Kari's case, she perhaps 'harnessing' her enemies evil activities to help hype and integrate her spiritual, psychological and physical make-up, her energies, her *ch'i* into a powerful magnifying focus 'mask,' coordinating her whole being (Laurent, *Faces*). Sherlock Holmes (*Baskervilles*) might agree, saying, "There is nothing more stimulating than a case where everything goes against you."

Does this pain intake business make Kari some sort of *highfalutin'* drama-queen masochist that needs to 'feel' pain in order to 'come alive'? Is this how she preps herself for her dramatic life performances? Maybe. This would be an interesting insight into this curiously troubled one after all, she is the poet-extraordinaire of the Mortuus. Nonetheless, this is a very martial-arty thing to do with the coordinated energy bit, the result of such concentration produced in this lengthy *progressive indirect attack* generating great psychic force of personality, character and determination, and at the *nowing* of release, instantaneous physical power (Ch. 24 note # 2).

Also, this left and right-brained business may also reveal Kari's more formidable, mental orientation and her reliance thereof, she knowing how to exploit her own well-studied potentials for the greatest output, honing her inner tools not over the years or centuries, but over millennia. Her plans may take ages to unfold, making the spouty vampire Dracula (Stoker, 1897 novel) sound like a snot-nosed kid when he said, "My revenge is just begun! I spread it over centuries, and time is on my side."

18. *Amid their bluing eerie descending folly.* *Lit.,* "iridescent folly." These hacked spirits from the previous battle in the burgh with Storm and Angel are in a state of rotting, or *descent*, giving off an uncanny, eerie 'iridescent' glow, a common thing in the Nether.

24. *Feeling the dirt's 'neath.* *Lit.,* "beneath." Angel wants to metaphorically 'bury' these mangy dirty cruds beneath the ground, that is, kill them all outright.

28. *"Or my Vandals will go cut you, taking both your ears."* Vincent van Gogh (1853-1890) was a Dutch, post-Impressionist painter, whose works are noted for their rough beauty, emotional honesty and bold color. He had a great influence on twentieth century art. As the story goes, mentally ill and in a fit of rage against fellow artist Paul Gauguin, he cut off his left ear. Storm here is word playing and being sarcastic, threatening *via* exaggeration.

31. *Held blade to St. Kari of, "An appropriate end, don't you agree?"* This stanza in the past had caused controversy. For year's scholars thought that the original fragmented line was garbled or lost. However, Jörgens in her analysis of the sixth century *Upsalan* translations now believes that the author of Storm is physically enacting a 'rhetorical' question using a Gk. style *aposiopesis*, a literary device that means, "becoming silent." *Apo's* are figures of speech wherein a line is deliberately left unfinished or

broken off, used by characters to express an inability or unwillingness to carry on. Here, the dramatic rendering is not spoken but acted out. Thus, we are expected to 'fill in the visual blank' and '*live*' the scene. Others concur. They of the story (and we) are expected to get the hidden visual poetry of her dramatic action of holding a blade to St. Kari of '*the*' Blade's throat. Northern literature, remember, was recited by wandering actor-poets, providing live interactive entertainment to audiences as they told stories of love and romance, of great deeds and daring, allowing listeners to participate in the tales.

35-36. *Your power, that is, when you <u>really</u> die . . . nutucopia . . . pennies on your eyes*"). Storm is vehement over the prospect of gaining Kari's eternal power when she finally bumps her off. *Still life* and '*cornucopias*' go hand in hand, the cornucopia often showing the fruits of the Autumn harvest, only in this case it is a *nutucopia*, (*alt.*, 'nut you cope with') meaning sarcastic Storm will reap the crazy, 'nutty' corn-ball Kari's fruitful psycho-basket of goodies for her own harvest of power. *Pennies on your eyes* refer to the old-time practice of placing coins on dead people's eyes so they would not open. This has mythological Greek roots, as the dead could not cross the river Styx to the land of the dead lest Charon the ferryman had a fee to pay for his row-boating expenditures. Coins were often placed on dead people's mouths as well to prevent their souls from returning from the dead.

40-41. "*I'll snip you a little yarn . . . long lost mess——.*" Storm is being facetious. She is referring to the old legend of the Norns both spinning and cutting a warrior's yarn of life as they loom that life on their life-giving spinning wheel (Ch. 28 note # 54).

TWENTY-EIGHT: ODIN'S SHOWERS/MAY DEFLOWERS.

"—Seems that one fine day in a lazy May,
Fields flowered and breezes made sway.
Gentle zephyrs flowed o'er that land,
She worked those fields with her man.

Family and friends and lovers so,   5
My mother a maiden engaged; betrothed.
Then came Odin over hill on slow charger,
Jumping forward in passion's vile ardor.

On his 'quest' to gain the Mead of Poetry,
The 'mighty god' really out performing mere thievery,   10
Stole something far more precious than *that* poetry-mead,
Deep in his lust he desired to satiate his greed!

As they trimmed the grain with dulled knived scythes,
Odin spied my mother, enthralled by her sight.
Lecherous pig! Wanted her in the cool of the eve,   15
But could not have her because her man in the sheaves.

Drawing his whetstone from his belt,
He offered to grind *their* scythes to help.
And when they found their blades now sharp,
They desired of Odin to buy that shard.   20

The stone they knew would make one rich,
A harvest of gold at one's mere fingertip!
Odin played with his whetstone *all so well*→
An evil seed sown straight from living Hel!

Odin, diseased god that he truly is,   25
Suggested a 'fair' price to all's chagrin.
Throwing the whetstone in the air,
Eight fell upon it like bears from their lairs.

'Cept one, my mother, who knew the stark truth,
Of Odin's contemptible ways from his deceitful youth!   30
The friends and family, they hacked each other,
Using those very scythes on their lovers and brothers.

Of Odin? He laughed his grim, heinous laugh,
And with his wicked spear he finished off the last!
Then *took* he my mother in/to that greening field,   35
I was conceived a child of lust, on his great-war shield!
A magnificent work of *evil* am I,
Not that I care—, I am just *Í* !¡
Live I now in this 'Land of the Dead,'
My business you see is what all do dread.   40

Now you, dear ♂ sister, are Odin's kin,
Blood of my blood, skin of *his* sin!
I've killed many siblings in this ensnaring way,
I'll inherit Asgard's fortunes in time someday!

Heh, so now in part you know the trap,   45
Of this little he man and his trite mishap.
Deception upon deception is my solid deal—
A predator supreme, of the stealing field!

Now, without further delay," Storm becked,
Held the instrument to Kari's lovely neck.   50

Kari held her eyes wide tight shut,
The man gasped, out of breath and out of luck.
"*Awwwright*," he slobbered, and in pain informed,
Whispered his name to her ear (that damned witching Norn).

Smiled content, shew on Dark's dark face,   55
A shrewd mixture of triumph and calculhating-hate.
"*Ha*! Tie '*em* up," she sneered to her rancid ghouls,
"Don't let them escape, or I'll kill you all as the rule!"

Later Dark mounted with many a troop,
Left a gang to guard the saint and the stupe.   60
"Leave her to me," she said to her men,
"As for *that* human, for yourselves turn *it* in."

The battle of wills *it* came down to just this—
✓Termination✓ of a righteous ⫽ sister by one in helish bliss.
One little pink-slip would be all it would take   65
To end the agony, the torment, the hellacious angst!

Dark Storm turned and rode to the North,
With all her co-minions of ghastly distort.
Night, and there came with her many oozy shadows,
Some wicked and one, *as the crow flies*, that was *apropos*.

VALLEY OF THE DAMNED

Chapter Twenty-Eight Valley Footnotes

Here is an intimate if not twisted glance into Storm's deep, dark past and probable early childhood, if a bragging, lying spirit and alleged Valkyrie can have one. This passage may or may not prove to be yet another one of her 'possessive' lies to tip things in her favor. What is more, within this script we find a curious fragment from Norse mythology that no one seems to know where it goes. It concerns Odin setting up a fight between sickle men quarreling over a whetstone he presented to them to sharpen their blades with. However, part of this puzzling poser may be answered in the footnotes below. The author uses this fragment to weave a tale of passion and woe. This scene presupposes that Odin was on his way to steal, through seduction, the *Mead of Poetry*, a great power from the giantess Gunnlod. This 'poetry-mead' booze, once bestowed on a person and that is 'guzzled,' enabled that charmingly sloshed individual to speak in rhymes as fast as he or she could talk (or perhaps in this case walk), they feeling no pain. This it is said is how Odin himself often spoke. In the ancient Northern European societies, poets could win as much honor as a warrior could and travel in the best circles because of their great wit, poets being held in very high esteem, and if a poet knew how to teach swordplay, untold opportunities would arise. Also in this scene we can see why Storm 'allegedly' hates Odin so, he being her alleged '*ill*egitimate' father.

13. *With dulled scythes.* Huge, two-handed, reaping shears for grain, such as the Grim Reaper would use.

16. *Man in the sheaves.* This speaks of the particular maiden's lover, her man.

17. *Drawing his whetstone.* A whetstone is a very smooth rock used to sharpen blades. In North mythology, the whetstone was thought to be the symbol of a King's power and authority as it was his duty to provide warriors with weapons that were sharp and in good working order. In the poem, apparently Odin used his 'power' to cause a small war among farmers as a scam-cover up to ravage Storm's mother. The whetstone was also associated with the sky god (Zeus, Jupiter, Nimrod—who took over Japheth's Jup title) because when it met metal, lightning-like sparks flew from it. It was further

linked to Thor, the thunder/'storm' god. He was said to have a piece of whetstone in his forehead. This is very interesting as we see here connections to the sons of Noah, Japheth (Jupiter) and Shem (Thor), both being 'sons' of the 'sky god,' that is, the 'god of the storm,' Noah, who was the Flood-Storm God's main representative.

28. *Eight fell upon it like bears.* Why the number eight? Apparently it is a highly mystical number in Norse/Scandinavian numerology and in Eastern martial arts as many of these are based on the number eight, as in 'snake crane eight-step' (*shé hè bā bù*) kung-fu, 'eight postures' in t'ai-ch'i, *etc.* The great metaphysical Book, the *I-Ching* is also based on eight. It is said Odin (Nimrod, Hislop, p. 312) possesses magic powers or mental forces to influence, which predetermines his authority coinciding with the number. He also has the gift of prophecy that corresponds to the number eight in numerology and to the Greek god Apollo (Nimrod). From *Genesis* the numbers 'six' and 'seven' speak of man's incompleteness and God's completeness, whilst the number 'eight,' being over and beyond completeness, tells of a new beginning, of regeneration, resurrection, new life, as seen here with Odin and the woman and on Noah's Ark with just eight people. Apparently, this is a true fragmentary garbled leftover from ancient times. This myth of Odin seems to be highly regenerative (Ch. 26 note # 6, also Ch. 7 note # 109 for Jackie).

42. *Skin of his sin!* Storm reveals the notion that Kari allegedly is one of Odin's daughters, a goddess, and that Storm herself is a 'bastard' daughter—a demigod, half-human, half-goddess. Odin is well known for traveling in disguise and getting pretty women pregnant. Although official records do not reveal the fact, Kari is considered Odin's daughter but, having forsaken the luxuries of Asgard, is out in the lower Deadlands performing knight-errantry. Apparently, being a Valkyrie is both a spiritual essence and something of a career choice, which fits in with the personal belief-realities found in the ever-shifting mind Nether-zone. As *Euhemerism* runs rampant throughout the work, we find both Storm and Kari in a number of roles: Valkyries, heroes, goddesses, mercenaries and humans. All are 'literary' representations—devices and mirrors—to capture the essence of the incredible reality of mental and spiritual juxtapositions found in the Deadlands (of our minds, perceptions and realities) as these spirits play powerful roles to achieve their ends.

44. *I'll inherit Asgard's.* Dark Storm is plotting the overthrow of Asgard by killing off the royal family of Odin. This is interesting in light of *Euhemerism.*

48. *Of the stealing field!* Apparently Storm likes to steal souls off the killing fields.

54. *(That damned witching Norn).* This is an insult to Dark Storm, in terms of dictating fate. In Norse mythology, the *Norns,* powerful maiden 'giantesses' (*Jotuns*), ruled the destinies of gods and men. They were three in number—*Fate, Being* and *Necessity.* Their literal names were *Urdr,* "the past," (*Fate*—"that which became or happened"), *Verdandi* "the present" (*Being*—"that which is happening"), and *Skuld* the youngest—a Valkyrie, no less—"the future" (*Necessity*—"that which should become," or "that needs to occur").

Mythologically, *Norn* "to twine," refers to twining the thread of life and fate, and when a person's time was up, the girls simply 'snipped' the yarn of their *lives.* Collectively, all three *nornirs* (plural) represent destiny as it is entwined with the spinning wheel of time. The historic, earlier etymology of the word *Norn* is uncertain but may relate to the Swedish verb *norna, lit.,* "to communicate secretly." It refers to the perception that the Norns were shadowy backdrop figures who only chose to reveal their fateful secrets to men as their fates loomed upon them.

There were many other mythological/historical/metaphorical lesser Norns, both good and bad, being portrayed as either goddess's protective of life or the perpetrators/overseers of malevolent tragic events. In *Skaldic* poetry, the courtly poetry of Iceland and Scandinavia during Viking times, they were negative beings associated with transitional situations such as violent battle, emotional turmoil and death and hung out with the Valkyries, who 'chose' or helped 'fate out' the warriors to be killed on the field.

As a more positive aspect of their line of work, they were known to visit newborns, allotting and appointing life to the sons of men, determining the strength, intelligence and luck that would be given to every kid. Consequently, the triad forged the destiny of every person, clan and nation. Although records do not show it, perhaps this reference to Storm being a Norn is a bit of information Theman picked up about her. It might indicate an 'activity' Storm was once involved with. Not only Valkyries, Norns are also linked to the *Dísir,* who are ghosts, spirits or deities coupled with fate, and can be both benevolent or antagonist towards we Midgarders.

They may act as protective spirits of Norse clans. Their veneration may derive from worshipping the spirits of the dead (Ch. 27 note # 40-41).

56. *Triumph and calculhating-hate. Lit.*, "hating-hate." This is a double word here. Storm admires Kari in many ways but she loathes and detests all that she stands for, thus gaining her the acidic 'hating-hate' title. In fact, like the 1978 *Life Cereal* breakfast commercial of "Mikey," the obstinate cereal-snubbing little boy who disliked trying anything new ("he hates everything"), Storm is the same way. She hates a lot of things, especially Kari and apparently Odin. Perhaps being 'illegitimate,' Odin cut off or suckered Storm out of her inheritance and rightful place as a 'Slay-Chooser.'

63. *The battle of wills.* Nothing is superficial in the Zone. Everything has a deep meaning and undercurrent that affects all.

65. *One little pink-slip would . . . To end the . . . angst!* A *pink-slip* is a dismissal letter from one's employer or teacher as in high school signifying penalties to come. Metaphorically, here the phrase cites Storm's desire to cut Kari's fragile neck so Storm could heal and end her inner torment and angst about this creature-girl.

66. *All her co-minions.* Companions + minions. This tells of Storm's dead-brained dupes and underlings for companions.

68. *And one, as the crow flies, that was apropos.* Angel, like a scavenging crow, snoops about, citing Storm's path. The early Scottish phrase, *"As the crow flies,"* is an allusion to the bird flying directly from points A and B, without encumbrances of roads and landscapes that restrict man. "Crow roads" there were made without many curves in them. The phrase is also used in the land of the Scots as referring to death, which lines up well with our phantom-killing Angel. He is adept at tracking, with no wasteful movements and unimpeded by any obstacle, a testimony to his abilities. Smelling ectoblood, he knows where Storm is going, but right now has some business to attend to with Kari and 'the man.'

TWENTY-NINE: THE DEPRAVED
AND THE DESPERATE

Tied they at posts at each end of room,
Long distance between them in the crow howling gloom.
Some spirits were abusive some spirits were drunk,
Rising temperatures of screwballing were vomiting up.

An ugly corpse now leering at the girl-saint,   5
He stroked his gash, "*eh*, you don't like my face?"
Drew he his knife slowly,
"Say hello to my *lil'* friend; hell take care of that in your case,
Soon you'll be pretty like us—only lower in disgrace."

He laughed and on the bottle he glut,   10
Draining booze glugged from his shot-hollowed guts.
Smashed he that bottle on post above,
Showering Kari in his token of 'forthcoming' love.

Then they sat at table and ate,
Disgusting creatures bloated on hate.   15
Six to the left, six to the right,
One in the middle, a profaned sight.

(Food oozled through their coarse rotted ribs,
Plopping to the floor in unmeticulous dribs).

Laughed *they* hysterically at the pitiful saint girl,   20
Cast insults at the nuisance, their lust beginning to uncurl.

She cast swollen eyes for a way of escape,
Looked at the man who had been beat too great.

A riotous company going insane,
Oblivious to all except that girl's frame.   25
Too wit coolly scanned the windows did she,
Did a *bbl-blink* when Kari spotted *he.*

Angel smiled at her and then he winked,
Kari nodded her head, a pleasant *oui.*
Braced she herself for what *must* happen,   30
She sought the ghoul, the one misshapen.

"Hey you," she grunt with utter disdain,
"If you had guts, I'd hate *'em* just the same."
The skelfiend turned round, wiping his gone mouth,
Began to leer, and his friends began to shout.   35

"I like your spirit," he no-breathed 'urped on her,
His putrid bo' odor made her eyes *w*ince burn.
I think we'll borrow you for our amusements,
The boss won't mind → just more inducements!

He laughed and reached hard toward her,   40
She recoiled back as far as she could squirm.

"A sad commentary, it truly is," Angel querled,
"Spirits picking on that, *ha!* 'Helpless' girl."

Stood he now tall, leaning in door frame,
The sotted spirits realizing now his terrible, terrible game.   45
Rushing weapons fumbled for, harried and *a'grabbin',*
Drunken wrecklessing spirits to him now *a'blastin'*!

Angel cutting bladening down,
Angelin'swordenening through maddening crowd,
Shrilling ingedgings pro-test in *clissszíng* sounds,   50
Grossing shades *crumpl'ump'ling* down.

Kari, cheering, gaped at Angel's candid *heal-thy-fray*,
(The swordpacker had given them their iron 'ills for the day).

Amid the 'bath the Angel let showing,
Excelling art, bonds severing for their going,   55
Kari inspired; amazing swordsmanship,
Whilst The Mean in the annihilation, away he ≈ slipped.

Then spurt the saint, in divine ecstatic,
Words of wisdom from the motion-ecclesiastic:

"Heaven knows the ways of souls,   60
Whither they are cut, whither they go.
Thus motion is what makes one great,
Spirals of steel seal one's fate.
Hell knows not this soulish way—
Recipient only of Heaven's downing rains."   65

Scrapingsslippingcchiselinghhits,
Angel winding rebutting *slilsilvering* spirits,
Sluicening bloodennings straightlightlying blade,
Angel katananing—the classic asymmetrical way,
Voices choking in steeled wañññging fierying wails,   70
Squealies unshrieking in brimstoneing's bloodying hail.

The air still rang with visual memory; quite mnemonic,
Of dimensioned art in all its patterning stingingly harmonic.

Seven strokes in all most impressively befell,
Direct from *the* hand of the swordketeering Angel.   75
One cut for two each, and lives were dievest,
After the seventh cut, he sighed and rest.

Upon this mighty work St. Kari in awe stood,
Having witnessed this creative ⇆ destructive act
She pronounced it—*"very* good."   80

Knew in her heart judgment had come fast,
She chuckled darkglee; had supped they their last.

"Bravo," Kari, pained, smiled nonchalant,
Admired the technique of the killer gallant.
The spirit from Thule gave her a glance,   85
Smiled he sardonic at the teenage lass.

Rip-roarin' bronc pounded off in the night,
Kari looked past the stomach-churning sight.
"Theman—" she mouthed in wisped faint,
"Let him go," Angel said, "He has *that* date."   90

Angel then looked her up and down,
Gave her a blanket, sighed then spoke with a frown,
"And as for you—
I see *umm*, we have a little work to do."

Another pair of eyes bugged agog, watched the man leave town.   95
Revenge tore at the sorely vexed Turk, when he 'the man' had found.

Off in the prairie deep hearing the moans,
Dark Storm listened, browed, then pushed on alone.

VALLEY OF THE DAMNED

Chapter Twenty-Nine Valley Footnotes

This action scene allows us to see two sides—the base and the sublime—of Deadlands reality, of how the arts (in this case Angel's high sword art) and spirits there can either ascend or descend into their own Heaven or Hell. Attitudes portrayed show the spectrum of what we may find buried in the Netherworld of (our own) over-looked, forgotten souls.

4. *Of screwballing.* 'Screwball' is a phrase used for 'crazy' or 'absurd.' However, this has more than one meaning here. Like loading a spring, the crazies are working, balling themselves up to no good.

16-17. *Six to the left . . . profaned sight.* Conveniently, much like Da Vinci's *Last Supper.*

42. *Angel querled.* Querulous + incredulous. Angel is complaining and finding fault with the sickies. He cannot believe what he is seeing.

50. *In clisssźíng sounds.* Click + hiss. This is the hissing sound of a blade during a high-velocity stroke, then meeting metal (the clicking sound), and continuing on.

52. *Kari, cheering, gaped at the candid heal-thy-fray.* Candid + Candy. Watching Angel work his sword, Kari's mouth gapes open in amazement. She is in the middle of Angel's all-cleansing 'healthy-fray.' Like a toy 'PEZ' candy dispenser, a noted American icon, he is meting out to the fiends their 'iron (p)'ills' for the day, setting things right, energizing or 'healing' the situation. It is all gorgeous eye-candy to Kari, a real piece of poetic just and icey wrought ironic art work.

54. *Amid the 'bath.* Blood bath.

59. *Motion-ecclesiastic.* An 'Ecclesiastic' (Gk. *ekklēsia*) today is a priest, minister or churchman. A *motion-ecclesiastic* is person whose beliefs are based on (the cutting [edge of] truth of) motion (*i.e.*, "actions speak louder than words"). In context, Kari is a *holy* person, more so, an *ekklēsia*, one "who is set apart," or "called out from the

world and to God," a 'saint,' given over to the study of motion and its flowing intu-ition/logic. In fact, going all the way, she is *the* supreme *ekklēsniac* (a set way, *way* over to the side "called-out maniac") of the Mortuuslands. One might even say martial motion is her holy order she has taken her vows in. She is a 'motion-nun' as it were.

63. *Spirals of steel.* Elegant motions that will always drive right to the point.

67. *Slilsilvering spirits.* Silver + sliver. The glint of the silver blade at a high speed appears to be a thin sliver of light. Its cutting trajectory, due to its exacting nature, enters its target like a fine, unseen sliver that is only later felt.

69. *Angel katananing the asymmetrical way.* Angel uses a blend of straight sword and Japanese samurai curved sword *katana* technique for his artwork. He employs a broken rhythm, *asymmetrical* style of artistic swordplay as well as the formal *classi-cal* Japanese method. In his travels he must have studied extensively and like Storm painting in the Cubism style earlier, is able to produce masterpieces of mayhem in his chosen field of expertise, that of being a swordslinger. In both their cases, they paint or sling in both the abstract broken rhythm and formal design Realism methods.

71. *In brimstoneing's.* What fell upon the Egyptians during one of the plagues of Moses—hail and brimstone. In this stanza blood spatters and falls, reminiscent of Moses turning the Nile into blood, *Exodus* 9.18, 7.17. Angel, in short, is a bloody plague unto these spirits and regards his person as an act of judgment upon them.

74. *Seven strokes in all.* From *Genesis*. It took God six days to create the world and on the seventh day, He rested. Kari makes the connection to Angel's action and clasp-ing her hands, is delighted overall.

82. *She chuckled darkglee.* Dark + glee. Here Kari wryly chuckles, appreciating the fact that the baddies got their *just desserts.*

96. *The sorely vexed Turk.* The warrior from the Valhallan Hall, Theman, or 'the man's' enemy, makes his reappearance.

THIRTY: HOLLOWED GROUND

"All megaliths and monuments on a dark,
Wind shrouded plain—
Nothing remains of you save the nameless grave."

Angel led Kari to three sacred knolls,
Where kings were buried and Celt crosses leaned old.   5

Kari cold in blanket, thunder, lightning, rain,
Watched Angel break in where the ancients were lain.
Lit he lights and she from the mists sojourned in,
A lone burial vault of *those* who long ago were forgotten.

Horses pawed in patience yet in cold 'spiration endured,   10
The secret of the grave and what their treasure succored.
Angel with sword butt stuck a painted wall,
The gods cracked opened, revealing their all.

"I've been here before, a long, long time ago—
Try this out; it's *umm*, my old fighting sword   15
(From which I sent many b'low").

Kari grasped it, flourishing long blade fluently about,
A magnificent piece, Bloodhawk etched, she feeling devout.
Came to the entrance Kari's impatient horse,
His spirit emboldened, for its future vehement course.   20

Then in tomb she began her great dervishing war-dance,
The sensuousing ritual from her vanished Indo-tribal past.

Motioning of war, motioning of dance,
Perfections achieved; the mind to enhance.

And in her mind as she *swhirrrlyfeverred* around,   25
Blu*rrr*ing days of war and peace blend and abound.
For causes lost but found in the soul,
For lies cast asunder, and the truth to hold.

Ancient tribes, those sons of Ham,
And from Shem's sons where it all began,   30
And how her tribes of Japheth long far away,
Withstood those giants who lied in their way.

All motions sublimed with totals intent,
No motions passived for an enemy to let.
Feeling her way through obscure sacred dance,   35
Soul stirring forward, death having no penetrance
(*b-bl*inked she dimblot memories of a once vivid life,
The corners of her mind—unremembered; cobwebbed plight).

Then movement absolute on point concentrated,
Prepared her spirit for sole flight's consecration.   40
The spirit, the motion were one in the same,
It was she who lived—St. Kari of the Blade;
Her mind set on things best spoken of as errantry,
To send her enemies off well → to *that* cold steel eternity.

A smile came to her face and her grateful eyes shone,   45
"There's some work I have to do—" then her eyes turned cold stone.
"*You pig!*" she spat, "*Huh*, use me to reduce the odds?!
It doesn't matter. I'll finish this alone, this path I do trod."

Riding off, Angel, tongue in cheek, shook his head,
Knew the girl was right, to decrease his chance of being *true dead*. 50

Yet Angel at distance, admired Kari's hair flowing in wind,
He smiled dryly——knowing of her kin.

Kari strode hard, appreciated Angel's double ⇄ edged game,
Riding freely, being life, she smiled all the same.
Music crescendoed in her head to the horse's beat,   55
The Ride of the Valkyrie——*the conflict to be.*

DOUGLAS M. LAURENT

Chapter Thirty Valley Footnotes

The Deadnether is loaded with ancient graves. In this particular instance, Angel has made a hiding place out of one. He gives Kari some 'help' so that she may exact her revenge. She figures out that he used her for his own little game plan and rides away with a miffed smile, yet appreciating his wiles.

1. *"All megaliths and monuments . . . nameless grave."* Megaliths are huge stones. According to Dr. Jörgens, this line is an insert from the fragmentary remains of a *very* lost poem, *Dark Sword Midnight* (Laurent).

6. *Thunder, lightning, rain.* This is a very dark portent borrowing from *Macbeth* (I. i.), where the three witches prophesy concerning their meeting of doom with Macbeth.

10. *In cold 'spiration endured . . . what their treasure succored. Lit.*, "spiration." The term tells us the horses had been worked hard covering many miles on a drizzly grey day and so they were 'steamed up,' giving off a glowing mist. *Succored.* Succor + red. 'Succor' is to give aid, help, comfort, assistance and relief. The color *red* speaks of such 'humble' actions as being bloody business in the 'Lands that are Bad.' Contextually, this particular burial chamber houses many secrets and treasures hidden, but only Angel and the horses know of such things, as it is one of many of his hideouts.

14. *Long, long time ago——.* This alludes to Angel's past. On a deeper level, this concept unites the universality of stories in our ever-shifting minds all the way from fairy tales, "Once upon a time," to *Star Wars* "A long time ago in a galaxy far, far away."

18. *Bloodhawk etched.* The sword has a carving of a mythical bird on it, and tells of its fine character. Many ancient swords, like those of the samurai, were decorated with animals, such as dragons, stingrays, crabs and cranes. They tell of the swords' spiritual attitudes believed found therein. Both decorative and symbolic, they were meant for inspiration, beauty and of course killing, although it is said that the best blades were always kept in their sheaths as prized implements.

19. *Kari's impatient horse.* The horse is a well-known symbol of virility. In the wastes, 'whole' animals take on their greater animal nature intelligence, sensitivity, *etc.* Even animal 'remnants' such as the horse, the pole-cat, the wolverine, the wolf, the stag, *etc.* that are depleted, half-visible, skeletal and so forth are all still powerful, mighty alert critters.

22. *Her vanished Indo-tribal past.* According to the historian Von Hauser, Kari's most ancient roots extend back to the Japhetic Indo-Europeans, who came to Europe from west-central Asia roughly five thousand years ago, revealing her alleged 'age.' However, as she is a spirit, she is probably much older than that. The Indo-Europeans, then, are her earliest known 'associated' tribes. *Vanished.* Kari has long 'out-*lived*' the many tribes she worked though in time that 'are no more,' making her gloomy and homesick on occasion as she bears witness that many nations come and go, she clapping an eye on the passage of millennia on a daily basis and what this ultimately means.

23-25. *Motioning of war . . . to enhance . . . she whirrrlyfeverred around.* In many ancient and modern societies here and in the Nether, dancing was and is an integral part of the training of a warrior, as the practice gives warriors a sense of rhythm and movement. The Spartans (*ca.* 600 B.C.) used dance to supplement martial training, and Plutarch (*Plóutarkhos*, A.D. 46-120?), noted Greek biographer and essayist wrote, "The military dance was an indefinable stimulus, which inflamed courage and gave strength to persevere in the paths of honor and valor." Greek laws actually prescribed dancing for training warriors, and individuals or groups of warriors performed what was called *pyrrhic* dances. The term means to be "dressed in red," as in a combative, bloody, theatrical mode. Furthermore there were 18 *géranos* 'crane-dance' forms, close cousins to the crane kung-fu styles of Tibet and southern China, showing a common ancestral bond (18 is a very big and mystical number in the eastern martial arts). The Greek youths, naked except for sword and shield, moved rhythmically about, miming hand-to-hand battle tactics, and this was all to the tune of flute music. Plato (*Plátōn, ca.* 428-347 B.C.) describes the dances as having great zeal, with much footwork, side-stepping, springing and attacking motions, and included other weapons as well. For combative dancing, precursor of the Japanese *kata*, Socrates' (*Sōkrátēs*, 470-399 B.C.) famous dictum stands tall. He said, "The best warrior is also the best dancer." *Katas* are pre-arranged sequences of physical offensive and defensive techniques, housed within a particular physical 'form,' which carries its own stylistics such as the use of a particular weapon, or unique body techniques, such as short-range punching. Katas also store the philosophies of a fighting art, guiding the practitioner in the fighting style's principles—spiritual, mental and physical. The strategies found within these classical exercises have existed for ages and are metaphorically applicable to anything in life, even in today's world. In Kari's situation, she is a master of her very ancient dance-fighting kata forms. And even though she for the moment is running a temp, is delirious and dances *whirrrlyfeverred* about, her spiritset is nevertheless feverishly red, bent on what she is now gearing up to do.

34. *No motions passived.* According to Peter Hsu, faulty martial art training leaves unprotected 'holes' in one's motions (and mind)—signifying lapses in concentration. In Japanese martial arts, this gap is known as *suki*, literally, the "space between two objects." The *suki-gap* or mental drift is a hole in which something (spiritual, mental, physical), such as a thought, word, technique, emotion, *etc.*, can literally enter in, destroy or kill. For example, if A and C are bold actions and B is the transitional movement between the two, it is easy for the mind to 'bypass' the necessary offensive or defensive concentration-preparations for B. This is because the mind is already thinking in terms of C, the conclusion. Martial training is an unremitting *now* and to go from A to C indicates trying to get to a future event/action that does not even exist, which may end up getting one killed. Timing, as always, is critical. One must be in conjunction with the speed of the opposition's action neither being too fast or too slow so one may 'fit in' one's technique with the action as a whole. Combat motion is always in flux, never set to a pattern. These *suki-gaps* of mental concentration, mirrored in motion, are easily exploitable by experts. Samurai were especially adept at penetrating *suki-points*.

36. *Death having no penetrance.* This translated line essentially is borrowing from Taoism. For insight, here we can use Lao Tzu's *Tao Te Ching*, Ch. 50:

> He who knows how to live can walk abroad without fear of rhinoceros or tiger. He will not be wounded in battle. For in him rhinoceroses can find no place to thrust their horn, tigers no place to use their claws, and weapons no place to pierce. Why is this so? Because he has no place for death to enter.

37-38. (*Blinked she dim memories . . .—unremembered; cobwebbed plight.*) From the musty *corners* of her mind, Kari is having trouble remembering her way distant past from being beaten so. In fact she is so disoriented she cannot remember her sacred war-dance, rather it is a feverish, blind, confused jumbled sort of thing, like a cobweb that goes off in all directions reflecting the workings of her troubled mind. *Unremembered* is *not* remembering. It seems as though there are holes in Kari's memory she blanks out. If so, this is a defense-mechanism to keep her from remembering past pains and memories. From former trauma, she 'blinks' a lot when troubled, as if to ward off memories. This is a well-known phenomenon. Distraught Angel looks on shaking his head pitifully. The sad visual commentary sickens him to see the premier Deadlands Valkyrie feebly stumbling about, most definitely "*outta her mind*" and quite besides herself. But then, Kari begins to grow stronger.

39-40. *On point concentrated . . . for sole flight's consecration.* Kari's mind is beginning to focus on specific matters to the *point* of jumping up and taking care of business. *Point* also refers to the blade type she will use; a sharp pointed straight-edged beauty. As for *flight's*, she is not running away, she going to run towards an up-coming battle where the baddies will get their b*less*ed comeuppance. It is her 'sole' sacred duty to make them 'lesser' or so she feels.

43. *Spoken of as errantry.* That is, 'error.' Jonathan Mycroft cites that this has a double meaning. Chivalrous activity is not exactly on Kari's mind. Her vastly troubled self has slipped toward dark-minded revenge, a reoccurring motif in the Deadlands. Revenge is not a word or thought used much by the educated of the Underlands. Classier warriors 'respond' to situations, in a 'business-like' fashion. They do not exact 'revenge,' as this would interfere with the clarity of the (Zen) intuitional-flowing mind being an emotional 'rock' in the stream of consciousness, which the flowing mind, being encumbered by, must then move around. This really tells us that Kari at this point is very bugged. As 'vengeance is the Lord's,' Kari, deep down inside knows she may be violating a holy standard, but having studied the Scriptures, she more than likely has rationalized her actions away, having read for example, *Psalm* 149, getting a head start.

50. *Being true dead.* The dead in the Netherfields can die and go to deeper levels of pain and physical-spirit bodied grotesqueness. To be a 'true dead' in the Nether

means to be really dead—one that is written off, so far beneath others. It is to be more degraded, hacked, extremely weak, nearly nonfunctional, a spirit with no real spirit-solidity or redeeming qualities whatsoever. It means to be deader, at the bottom of the heap, a scum-sucking bottom feeder.

56. *The Ride of the Valkyrie—the conflict to be.* Our association with understanding the poem through art forms, in this case, music, is important here. The scribbler has rendered this phrase to refer to composer Richard Wagner's (1813-1883) masterpiece, *Die Walkure* (The Valkyries) written in 1856. *The conflict.* Not that Kari is going to *a* conflict; *she is the conflict.*

THIRTY-ONE: THE TAR
AND THE TURK

The man rode past deserted 'scapes,
A land of cold fire and heated ice wastes.
Stretched forth terrain, he looked a'fair,
Totems and skulls stacked; called him to a'ware.

Avoided he the Vanirian armies; spearits in long rows,   5
Despised of the Aesir, in battle capes they flowed.
Pieces of shadows marching in silented broken disgrace,
These conscripted entities; helmeted slaves with no face.

Scarce had he passed sulphrus bubbly pits,
Oozing out their tars and charbroiling pitch,   10
Than the stench of death wafted up,
Sight unseen; a pleasant 'front.

A patchwork of tar and quiet abscessed grass,
Displayed dark ends and lingering forgotten pasts.
Night rains turned pools into lovely ebon water,   15
A pleasing sheen luring the unwitting to slaughter.

Surveying intently, a warrior on beast took account,
The Turk from Valhalla saw the man flushed out.
Yea, a grim purpose gorged his hate-silled mind,
To revenge himself, and kill slowly the man in kind!!   20

Now The Mean, half dead from his unearthly mort,
Was near asleep and fell hard from his ghostly horse.

Sprang alert now as he heard the yowling *scree-cshout*,
Of the Turk on high ground ➡⟲➡ with lance thrust out!

"I've been seeking you for many months now!" wretched he,   25
"I've come to avenge my arm, for it you will now ¡bleed!"
Reared he his horse with his back to the sun,
Then sped his charger down on its murderous run.

Spun The Mean his horse on solid ground,
Turned to *those* pits and their clutchy bounds.   30
Raced past meadows and leapt from steed,
Rallied his *bolas* in the wind to be freed
(A trick he learned in a Bolivian movie).

Twirrrled them *r-r-r-rraround* and released their flight,
Whuuwhuuwhuuling, circing airtight,   35
Ent*whinny*ing warhorse's legs in their winding might.
Charger buckled and Turk hurling headlong over,
Fell to his face—**splaaaat*! On the tar-laden water.

(∞∞∞∞∞∞ He dashed against him now, *this* cinefied karate man,
Against The Turk, one-armed and scimitar in hand.   40

Battled they near a tarish jet-ink onyx pit,
Scimitar to claymore–the dead and the quick.
Three strokes of blade and their bodies clashed,
The Dead Yet Alive advantaged [he had more mass].

Brought his deadly claymore 'bout 'round,   45
Flinging the scimitar into deep tarring down.
A real-mental struggle now, not a screen battle won,
Either he or Turk—there would be only one.

Then flaunted he *this* Turk his long sharp *J*-dagger,
But The Mean in time stripped the knife wielder.   50
Faced he now the 'oathing Turk unarmed,
Who blooded at mouth, cursed, breathing hard.

The Mean, exalted, poised the stroke high,
To kill this Turk, ecstatic for him to die!
A thread of light then penetrate Mean's brain,   55
He smiled at the Turk and tossed his sword away.

"*C'mon!*" he yell-motioned to the swarthing Ottoman,
To test his 'karate chops' against the one-armed ghoul-man.
Felt *this dis⌒mal* Turk a 'safe' test of skill——
The hardened warrior against one with many film kills.   60

Mimicked he a cat that had long been dead,
That forgotten Saber of most infamous dread.
Struck he a poise in catlike stance,
Reflexes sharp on tar and gas stygian rance.

Lowered his hips and kicked forward *z̄oofast*,   65
Propelled himself *fró�* with *¡Ki–aaai!!* and *fl⌒aash!*
Fought like the beast, that was his film fame,
The 'lost' tiger style, his solid gold claim.
Launched he attack with the fore of his leg,
Seized the tiger pose of karate movie way.   70
Neko ashi-dachi with blocks and shifts to safely conform,
Hard fighting fists (he looked good) by them he performed.

But as he fought the more and more,
Ragged motion hacked its truer nature to the fore.
The 'Tooth' The Mean now was; and this Turk, he deplored,   75
Slashed at him with thrusty claws, the *ole'-ing* catador.

Wrenched the Turk a series of deadly throws,
Sprung from those ancient fighting holds,
The Mean's blood craving surged from his core,
He devouring the real karate behind his phony store!   80

Plastic philosophies now could not contain,
All the bloodlust he felt to give this Turk more pain.
Drowned he now in the primordial heated beat,
Throat whelling thick–his enemy to defeat.

Fist of Furying against Turk shade-man,   85
Losing teeth as hits were incisively slammed.
All that false veneer had been ripped away,
The Mean now instinctual, falsekarate shamed.

The Turk then snatched leg out of air,
Racked The Mean's leg with a grab'bled dare.   90
Drew *that* cord, The Mean clung to him,
Stark reality at silk's edge so thin.

As they fought their feet sank,
Buckled beneath them——
The Mean's went quicker 'cuz of more weight ∞∞∞∞∞∞).   95

In the distance the great night beasts roared and bayed,
Gathering to judgment around this–their tarry domain.
Mal eyes watched in voracious mirrored delight,
Moanastic fur-cloaked figures savoring *this* sight.

(∞∞∞∞∞∞ Twisted The Mean and he threw the shade Turk,   100
With leg over head into tar pit he lurched.
Recovered he and grabbed scimitar out of the muck,
Which pulled him in deeper to The Mean's good luck ∞∞∞∞∞∞∞).

Then this was over, this twinkling *batterfang* of mind,
Battle was not struck like this, just fantasies–   105
To find the man inside——

Now with scimitar the Turk ran sloggingly across,
Feet becoming victims of that blackening slick gloss.
Cursed he The Mean from sticking, asphalt pit,
The Mean snapped: 110
"!–!-!-You should have just speared me and had done with-!-!–!"

Yet puffed he up for killing this hostile spirit-man,
A *hol'low* sense of victory though——for his first 'hand-to-hand.'
Realized the lies that he had been told,
But he enjoyed himself immensely ⇒   115
The wilding fit was upon him, making him bold.

Now the netherwolves and the lions, down they came,
To tear blue spirit-flesh from its Turkish spektral frame.
Soon too, those were caught in abundance's disloyal calm,
Carrion birds were also thick-coated with feathers embalmed.   120

In the end a slimy, dark morass,
A ball of melding tar, sinking slowly fast.
Evening out, the attractive rain pools once again
(Baiting one's *mindtrap* that never ends).

In all, another quiet occurrence in the wastes of Valhal,   125
A screech overhead; time of the night hunting owl.
The man felt a bridge had been crossed, it st'ealed his fate,
A minor incident today; yet he felt strangely out of place.

Scarcely a moment, then the man snorted his lip,
"If only to be more real, that is the trick.   130

DOUGLAS M. LAURENT

The animals," rationalized the man as he laughed,
"The ancients were right; knowledge, unsurpassed."

The Mean, he grunt as he rode away,
"A dead spirit out to get me—
Yet left for extinct beasts of prey."   135

VALLEY OF THE DAMNED

Chapter Thirty-One Valley Footnotes

This scene invites us to read it on three distinct levels. The first and most simple, is a 'rite-of-passage' type of reality for Mark Theman, in which for the first time he would have a 'real-*live* karate' fight. However, this rite of passage into real 'manhood' takes place mostly in his mind (signified by the insertion of *infinity* signs, *i.e.*, ∞∞∞), the confabulation-fantasy of which is a definite problem for him. Second, the 'real action,' not the stuff that takes place in Theman's mind is meant to depict the fragile, Zen-like qualities of cutting to the chase and the 'doing' of forthright actions found in the Deadlands. As established in earlier notes, we are using cinema for translations. This 'real action' is reminiscent of that excellent 'Zen' scene in Sergio Leone's film, *The Good, The Bad and The Ugly* (1966), in which the bandit Tuco (Eli Wallach), while taking a bubble bath is confronted by a killer he maimed some months before. After the killer brags about how he is going to take his sweet time killing him, Tuco guns the man down with a pistol hidden beneath the soap bubbles, after which he sardonically adds (accompanied by haunting twiscrewing ironic now iconic music), "When you have to shoot, shoot, don't talk." This section is a strong statement to both Zen and the lore of the Western gunfighter, in which the 'showdown,' the 'moment of truth' and 'doing' is paramount. It is the standard by which the parallel world of the spirit-dead *live* by. For this scene, the real action with the Turk takes place in a matter of seconds while a completely 'super cool' movie-battle takes place within Theman's 'heroic movie' mind. All three insights—the rite of passage, the real and fantasy action, are found in the two action sequences, showing 'surface reality,' and the 'illusory fantasy interior' of Theman's self-absorbed, self-loving 'narcissistic' drain-bamaged daydream world. The moral is that we must decide which 'reality' suits Theman (and us) better for his growth—the real or the fantastic, which to his mind, is just as legitimate. Both worlds, in short, are affecting his future, and by the way, ours as well, we being kindred in soul and so in choice.

2-4. *A land of cold fire . . . he looked a' fair . . . called him to a'ware.* This is a *terrify-ing*, *rainy* glaciated thermal area with geysers, mud pots, *etc.* A' fair. Afar + affair + air. As Theman looks the hard landscape over, it has a negative air, foreboding trouble, conflict, an *affair* or ordeal he must contend with. *A'ware*. The landscape not only told Theman to be aware, but it called him to war.

5. *Vanirian armies; spearits.* The *Vanir* is another ancient tribe of gods, the deadly enemies of the Asian tribe called Aesir, the gods of Asgard. *Spearits*. Spear + spirits. This term depicts many spirits in a tight-knit spear-bristling marching phalanx. Additionally, these *'its'* not only having no faces, had *no face*, or honor as well, making this massive group a particularly despicable lot. Pilkey, p. 181 lines the Vanir/Aesir with biblical Peleg ("divide/cleave") and Joktan ("made little/not worthy/disgust") in the great political conflict of *Genesis* 10.25.

12. *A pleasant 'front.* Lit., "affront." Theman is now keen to confront and get into action.

19. *His hate-silled.* Filled + silt. Like water run-off choked with dirt.

21. *Half dead from his unearthly mort.* 'Mortality.' Theman feels half dead; the result of his human constrictions of mortality in the wastes, besides the fact of being beaten nearly to a pulp earlier on, taking 'unearthly' mortal blows.

32. *Bolas in the wind to be freed.* The South American *bola* (Sp. *boleadoras*, 'ball,' Inca *ayllo*) is a *gaucho* ('cowboy') lassoing tool and has been found in China and used by the Eskimos. They are a set of cords or thongs with heavy balls set at the end for throwing at cattle and entangling their feet. Apparently, Theman learned a lot from foreign movies!

39. *This cinefied karate man.* Cinema + sissified. Only in the movies is Theman 'tough.'

42. *The dead and the quick.* The term *quick* refers to 'the living,' as Theman certainly still is (*cf.* 2Tim. 4.1-4 *et al. kjv*).

43. *Three strokes of blade.* In an actual life-or-death battle, cites Peter Hsu, real fights rarely go beyond two to three strokes although this is disputed by other combat

authorities such as boxing-detective Jim Mellen. Likewise, we see some of Theman's technical martial training background in the very triangular Filipino stick art of kali, popular in America today (especially in the movie industry). In this fighting art, striking patterns are executed in oval actions of 'three' either 'slash-thrust-slash' or 'thrust-slash-thrust.' Due to Spanish Catholicism, this effective three-in-one action activity is haloed with religious terms used to honor the Triune God. Actually, however, the moves carry a rather formidable and secret combative tri-technique hidden deep within. Three motions, explains Hsu, are all about one can do before one starts to run out of air on the battlefield and go into oxygen deprivation. As such, three primary techniques *más o menos* can be done very fast without drawing a breath. In the cinema, this is one reason why kung-fu and karate experts appear to be seen screaming, chopping and slashing about so fast, as they wade into the opposition. This scream-chopping designed pattern action usually starts out of distance from the opposition and covers the empty space between the hero and villain. There is however a method to this madness. It is devised to pick up any in-coming strikes so they can be deftly countered by the advancing 'windmilling' about hero.

47. *A real-mental struggle.* Psychiatrist Greta Hastings cites that this is an all-out fight in which Theman uses his skills to the utmost, but his 'heroic' confabulated 'Walter Mitty'-like fantasy takes place, allegedly, all in his head. *Confabulation* is a psychological term. The person who has this condition sees fantasies so intensely that they are real to him or her. *The Secret Life of Walter Mitty* is a short story by James Thurber (*The New Yorker*, 3/18/39). Mitty, a very meek and mild man is given to immense flights of the imagination such as being a war-time ace pilot, emergency-room surgeon who fixes a squeaking, broken pump ("*pocketa-queep-pocketa-queep*") with a pen, a devil-may-care assassin and so forth. His name has come to mean in American slang as "an ineffectual dreamer who indulges in fantasies of great personal triumphs." Although a funny story, there are darker overtones to it. Even in the midst of his heroisms, sometimes Mitty fails, his daydreams interrupted by reality—events and strangers inadvertently robbing him of what little remains of his personal dignity. In Theman's case, mild Mitty is an alter ego good twin mirrory posi-archetype to his celluloid, plastic *live/evil* anti-persona, who lives off the 'vapors,' not the 'solidity' of dreams—he is that far gone. Can this be said of us as well? (*See* Ch. 17 note # 22 for glosses, vapors and remnants.)

49. *His long sharp J-dagger.* A *Jambia/Janbiya* is in mind here. It is the famous *J*-shaped dagger of the Middle East.

50. *In time stripped. Stripped* is a term meaning to take away someone's weapons.

54. *Ecstatic for him to die!* The phrase implies Theman is '*de-light*ed' totally without the light of mercy in his dark desire to kill the Turk.

57. *The swarthing Ottoman.* This is another name for the Turk. The rise and fall of the Ottoman Empire (modern Turkey) is usually dated from around 1299-1827, the Ottomans taking over Constantinople in 1453. These rough dates hint at the age of this spirit, or rather, where he can be traced.

62. *That forgotten Saber.* This is the great *Smilodon* Saber-Toothed Tiger of yore.

64. *Reflexes sharp on tar and stygian rance. Stygian* is a term that means "dark, foreboding, gloomy and hellish." It is related to the River *Styx* ("Hate/Detestation") of Greek mythology—the river of unbreakable oaths used of gods and warriors. Located in the Underworld, it was a barrier between the living and the dead, and drained into a great stinking Okefenokee-like muskeg swampy quagmire with four other great rivers—the *Acheron* "Woe," the *Cocytus* "Lamentation," the *Phlegethon* "Fire" and the *Lethe* "Forgetfulness" (Hamilton, p. 43). *Rance* is 'rancid,' so the place, full of rotting matter and foot-sucking muck, smells terrible. Like the petite yet alert green-eyed carnivorous electro-Venus Flytrap, the vigilant slough just 'yearns' to shock-suck them down to victimize and bloat on Theman and the Turk.

66. *With ¡Ki—aaai!! and fl⌐aash! Ki-ai* "the meeting together of energy" is a Japanese term and is a "martial spiritual shout" coming from the abdomen and is designed to consolidate courage and initiate powerful action. Moreover, it is used to frighten or momentarily paralyze an enemy's mind or action. *Ki* embodies 'vital breath and energy,' and *ai*, 'life, union, harmony.' The screaming *kiai* then is the joining of these forces together for a tremendous, concentrated effort. Some Japanese masters were known to knock people out or down through the extraordinary use of their *kiai*. The art was known as *kiai-jutsu*.

68. *The 'lost' tiger style.* Apparently, this is one of Theman's learned martial arts styles, perhaps 'Black Tiger' (*fu-jow pài*) kung-fu meaning "tiger claw" technique or "sect." It is a method supposedly derived from the Shaolin monastery in southern China but it goes much farther back. The tiger is one of the five classical animals of kung-fu, the others being the crane, dragon, leopard and snake. The tiger system is powerful, working the bones and muscle with ripping motions designed for one-blow kills.

71. *Neko ashi-dachi.* This is a Japanese karate term for "cat-stance." In this posture, seventy percent of the weight is on the back leg, and thirty percent on the lead leg that is slightly bent, resting on the ball of the foot. Looking somewhat cat-like, it is used for quick kicking and agility.

74. *Ragged motion hacked its truer nature to the fore.* Theman becomes exhausted, losing his karate 'film' form, relying more on bestial and natural motions.

75. *The 'Tooth' The Mean now was.* Theman's only chance of survival, because he is not fighting the real battle but rather the mentally-gapped *suki*-absurd one in his mind, is to act out being a *saber-tooth* tiger, using the animal as a 'mask' or 'prop' to magnintensify his kung-fu catfight abilities in his cat-scratching struggle with the ever-doggish Turk. So unrealistic is he in need of using the false feline inflammatory image-prop to fight the real fracas instead of his own human mind, we must surely come to see clearly that Themanimal is truly an animantasy.

78. *Ancient fighting holds.* Western Asia is famous for many ancient wrestling arts.

80. *Real karate behind his phony store.* Jonathan Mycroft's analysis of this phrase reveals that true combative motion lies locked up, impotent, behind Theman's showy forms. This stanza also reflects just what bad shape he really is in. First, Theman is allegedly fantasizing all this, so it is not 'real' karate by any stretch of the imagination. Second, we should also see that he is thinking through 'canned' forms and images of what he has learned, and so cannot even begin to conceive of the real art, let alone get to it. A perfect example of this is to watch kids 'play' karate. The first thing they do is to strike up outrageous 'ninja-turtle' or 'karate-kid' stereotypical fighting poses—the result of watching too many movies and TV!

81. *Plastic philosophies.* These are the pop-philosophies and the entire '*ism's*' that surround modern American martial arts—a strange mixture of ancient Oriental ideals and Americanized mass-marketed consumerism. In Theman's predicament, the thought of really killing the Turk is so ghastly and overwhelming and incomprehensible, that the childish 'philosophies' that he has *lived* by through the alleged 'martial arts code of the movies' all his cheap life is on the level of trying to use a bottle cork to keep the Titanic from sinking.

85. *Fist of Furying.* In 1971, Bruce Lee broke box office records with a film entitled *Fists of Fury*, which catapulted him to international fame. Here, the text is unclear whether Theman is seeing himself fighting through filmic images in a like-heroic role, but more likely at this point the '*ing*' ending has become very important. It tells us that he is beginning, at least in his mind, to fight like his new acquaintances, Kari, Storm and Angel, motion and thought becoming an in-motion a '*one'ening.*'

87. *All that false veneer had been stripped away.* *False veneers* are the lies, illusions, glitters, trends, views, hypes, facades, fashions, paraphernalia and tinsels—the Orwellian *"doublethink" *zeitgeistisms* that orbit and swirl about the "ornately decorated" pop-martial arts *cosmos*. However, author Hector Kyle says that this interpretation of the line makes no sense because this titanic battle is taking place in Theman's mind (allegedly) *i.e.*, Theman is deluding himself. The real fight with the Turk is actually very short. In other words, because of Theman's interior delusions, nothing unreal or false in his fantasy-mindworld has been realistically removed but more so perhaps 'put on hold' for a while, as time will tell. *"Doublethink," according to the novel *1984*, is essentially the ability to hang onto two contradictory beliefs at the same time and accepting them both as a unit. This is a Western form of frictional, fretting scratchy dualism, not the well-honed, in-tandem, interlocked, firmly gentle/gently firm *Teflon* no-stick *yīnyáng* ☯☯☯ *gnàynīy*.

88. *Instinctual, falsekarate shamed.* Instincts, and the attributes thereof, make intellectually bogus, non-combative karate look 'silly.' *Shamed.* Shameful + sham. Theman's pop-karate is a sham and is put to shame by the real thing.

91. *Drew that cord.* This refers to a *garrote*, or silk scarf used for strangulation, much as the Hindu goddess Kali *thugee's* of old would use for their religious strangling of people. We derive the term *thug* from this.

99. *Moanastic fur-cloaked figures.* The text is unclear whether this is strictly speaking of the sounds (*moan*) the animals are making, or more than likely, the animals are acting as metaphors to the animal-like brooding inhabitants of the tar pit regions. According to Dr. Etta Jörgens, in the Dead there are many religious orders (monastic) that hold territories. Since this is an unusually dismal and deadly place, she surmises that this particular troop, which 'preys' upon the miseries of the ghostly animals that are sucked into the tars and haunt this area, are a particularly nasty Neanderthal-like group, a few of these lowly elementals observing the fight.

101. *Leg over head.* Most likely, a judo *tomo-nage*, or "circle throw," where defenders fall onto their backs, insert one of their feet into the groin of the opponent, and flip him over. This is very popular in the movies.

104. *This twinkling batterfang of mind. Batterfang* is an old American frontier term used in Davy Crockett's (1786-1836) time. It means a "total, vicious all-out assault." The line can also be read as "This twinkling contention of mind," meaning that the assault upon Theman took place in an instance and was more in his mind than anywhere else, although he did have to physically deal with the Turk.

105-106. *Just fantasies—To find the man inside——.* Theman has dreamt of this macho pea-brained greatness all his meager hollow life. Perhaps it is because he wants desperately to escape his incredibly insipid watered-down diluted self and prove himself 'a man.' He is tired of consuming himself (*in-sip*) by gulping down the poisonous wines of his own grossly turned inward soul, which offers him nothing more than a groping, bestial, totally sensual "*I want it now*" in-sip-id hellish low-life gutter reality. At least he does not want to die dieluded. Perhaps there are other reasons as to why anybody would seek escape from their own selves *via Band-Aid* fantasies when they have deep serrated open psychic wounds.

113. *A hol' low sense of victory . . . 'hand-to-hand.'* *How low* does Theman feel? Apparently, he feels pretty dim on the inside, experiencing *dim-in*ishing returns, feeling low, cheated and empty, the real actions depriving him of a chance at true martial greatness like his imaginary actions did.

116. *The wilding fit was upon him.* According to Mycroft, this is the *fit* of bloodlust. In the instance of the real action, Theman nonetheless liked his growing prowess and strength. It gives him a 'pathological thrill.' *Wilding* is where groups of animals such as sharks or chimps, even humans, go collectively 'nuts,' the groups losing all semblance of orderly coherence over an object, such as a shark feeding frenzy or a riot.

117. *The netherwolves and the lions.* Many ghostly creatures in the Deadlands have their earthly counterparts, so within the Under-realm there are many extinct (and fantastical) beasts such as the netherwolves, netherlions and werepigs.

119-120. *Were caught in abundance's disloyal calm . . . thick-coated with feathers embalmed.* The watery tar pits are deceiving, giving the unwary Nether creatures a 'calmness' to dine leisurely off their abundant scavenging. Little do they know they are soon entrapped themselves, being hauled down into the tarry mire. As we all know, looks can be deceiving.

125-127. *In all . . . occurrence . . . owl . . . bridge . . . st'ealed.* Jonathan Mycroft translates this stanza using like-words from Ambrose Bierce's (1842-1914?) short story, *An Occurrence at Owl Creek Bridge* to reflect the above sequence of fantasy action similarly mirrored in Bierce's work. In the short story, a man about to be hung fantasizes his escape and goes through tremendous difficulties to get home—only to be "jerked to Jesus" as they said back then and into grim reality by the end of the rope. *St'ealed.* Stolen + sealed. Theman's fate, once the bridge was crossed, both steals and seals his fate. Finally, Theman envisions his greatness. Only in the end does he 'feel out of place' because he knows in his heart it was just a dream, allegedly, a 'fact' he did not want to admit. This stanza also portends his coming fate.

129. *Scarcely a moment . . . his lip.* *Scarcely* shows a hidden fear that Theman covers up with a violent rubbing of his face.

132. *The ancients were right.* *The ancients* refer to the Shaolin Temple martial masters of the animal styles of Chinese kung-fu. However, at this point Theman is irrational. Panicked, he became an animal in his mind (Lat., *Smilodon*, the "Saber-Tooth Tiger") and in reality, but the masters never taught that literally to 'become' an animal in kung-fu meant giving up the dignity of the human spirit. Rather, animals should be observed for the lessons they teach as humbling examples as to the fragility, beauty—and tenacity of life.

135. *Extinct beasts of prey.* The tar pits of Los Angeles, CA. inspire here, as they have trapped thousands of animals. Theman is smug for having escaped the Turk and the danger of the mental and physical tar pits but nonetheless, the pits are a dark foreshadow of his future. In spite of this, the tar pits as a metaphor stretch way beyond Theman's thin linear-brained earth-bound logic. They exemplify what is in many minds, including his own—that we ourselves are tar pits of our own making *to wit* we cannot escape. We dig our own tar-pit graves as it were, and are ensnared by them. Or worse, we are forced, sucked into living out another's dreams and power play-pits at our own expense that become our nightmares and these types of soul-vacuuming 'energy vampires' are all over the place! These energypire *macrophages* ("big eaters, consumers of specific things") want our time, resources, money, talents, presence, powers and abilities and space—just name it, *etc.* In sum, the human energy-slurping Nosferatuians are voracious, unclean, spirit-sucking, odious ghouls—all-consuming dev*ou*rers even unto our very own souls! They want to suck everything out of us just to maintain their holds on their power and interests. Happy bubble thoughts from another person may imprison us into doing things we desire not to do; their dreams come at our expense—just so they can maintain their 'happy thoughts.' Subsequently the question is, why live in somebody else's dreams. Are we forced to be in 'orbit' around another person and their lifestyle, or do we make our own orbits? Freedom versus forced conformity is a battle that has been going on for thousands of years. The Midgard is the final field to this momentous personal decision and the last stepping off point before eternity. Choose, because if you do not, the sinispidery Nether-agents or their deceived automatons and there are tons of them around these parts nowadays and who come in all sizes, shapes, colors and walks of life will do the choosing for you, sealing your eternal fate—and we all know what that means. *Yea, verily, yea,* "But evil men and seducers shall wax worse and worse, deceiving, and being deceived (2Tim. 3.13 *kjv*).

THIRTY-TWO: REVENGE
OF THE VALKYRIE

On far high bank they spied *that* soul-dreading figure,
St. Kari of the Blade—on steamy, rearing charger she spur.
A great sword slung over her armored shoulder,
Battlehelmed and bear-red steel told of the she-berserkr.

Direct attack, with a line so fine,   5
Kari determined best to upbraid her time.
Compel them she would their blades to missmatch,
And intercept them on her arcs and *brassh*!

So unto Holmganga, the place of duel pursued she,
To repair the honor of her—the raving, wanton Valkyrie.   10
Dark Storm riding hard to the long beyond secret pass,
Had ordered her tribe to see if they could out*lass*t the lass!

Met them on rock and snow slushed tundra'd ground,
With broad sluggish stream coldly cutting her bounds.
Up to the steeped riverbank went ValKari,   15
St. of the Blade in *that* righteous dark fury.

The mercenaries, they on the other side,
Drew up to formation in a small battle line.
Shrill of the shrike breaking the damp greying air,
As eyes devoured eyes in cast-iron black plutonian glares.   20

They sat and stared as statues for the longest time,
Some swallowed hard, facing *that thing–that—that* scourge divined!
The land of duel was a *terror-firma* 'voided and deplored,
A playground of death–which settled many a score.

Warhorses pawed the ground and snort,   25
Thirteen debauched beaded on the abhorred.
They remembered last night's lewd ribald tirade,
Now regretting time spent with *that* maniacal sword maid.

Corpses fingered nervously battle-scare-red weapons,
Empty hearts *p-p-pphounded*, confirming their intentions.   30
"If that devil's-whelp gets us, be *'not~her* thousand years,
We'll become far worse, Nox, slaves to more fear."

"*Awwright*," spat Nox, drawing his greazy war hammer,
"Kill her right away, better for us to damn her."

Water gurgd through the brown shallows of lonely plain,   35
Silently foretelling of that vast approaching girl pain.
Predators watched the Valkyrie of gold,
To destroy *this* she-devil, her strength to hold.

Greed overcoming their fear of her blade,
Cursed her to Hel and launched their raid.   40
Unsheathed war lance from her whell-kept pack,
Pushed her beast into the melt for attack.

Thirteen depraved shades hauling out their choice weapons,
Screeeching across the spit intercepting *that* 'choosy' braven.
Gushing into ice water *sllooowwww* rising splashings,   45
Horses *a'churnin'* their master's quick dashings.

Broodm*ares* packing pale riders loosing,
Valkyrie-*bansheeing* in all ther looning,
Shattering together on sanding bar,
Perturbid spirits bash and mar,   50
Clepting horse's feeta' footin',
Clashing bars of metala'toolin',
Thrashing bodies in saddles wheeling,
Sting'ed cháocophony of cgrimsinging greetings.

Screamingscursingsdowningbodieshorsesblurringsurging.   55

Kari battle furying cutting lefting righting,
Drawing great sword after lancing's bloody purging,
Shearing through limbs, taking mort'ling blows,
Fury unfurled for the *Wælcyge* bloodfoamed.

In the o'erpowering wrath of St. Kari of the Blade,   60
She chanting her insaning song, remembered to this day:

"Lever and wedge on hellish plane,
Cuts the opposition, who's to blame?
In thy force of momentum prayerfully driven,
To but cut———'tis Heaven's decision."   65

Amidst the meshing, metal *whining pingeling* out,
Clackings of spearings, swordings, axings in redoubt,
Baseing spirits caughted in trappings dire,
Hackings pitifuled against sublime spirals a' f'ire.

Carnaging motion into *slurrrring* mass nightmared,   70
Tapestry of pristining motion from the teen *swordinaire,*
Bodies water horses in death throes falling all a'discrewistortioning,
To acquit her righteous bladeings in its trajectory of dísirings.

386

Echoing steel, *swirrrling* spirits and men,
Quick vision of horses ravaging in watery end,   75
Silenting terror blanketing spilting odious land,
Kari's great hatreding quenched, no longer flame fanned.

Blade star showers from *the* graphic *artiste* so prime
(Her etched masterpiece exists only in motion and time).

Silence eulogized floating, distancing seeping stiffs,   80
Scar-let water carrying slow *mean-daring* trophies adrift.
Revenge of the Valkyrie, her raising she sword,
Hawk eyes now discovering movements in discord.

One skull freak, fleeing battle, terror stricken of the flay,
Kari stabbing sword in ground pulls hand bolt from her array.   85
Walks to sand's edge, the distance to allygn,
Extending hand, *aim-m-m-ming* through bloodletting eyes—.

Dark Storm on ascending 'clined mountain ground,
Hearing crying battle echoes craned her neck around.
Sees fleeing crazy galloping fast away,   90
Cut from the saddle as Kari's bolt finds its way.

Then in distance saw Storm that annoying, lone coming figure,
Knew it was the Val-kid of last night's all too brief a massacre.
Goad Storm her horse up steepening slopes,
Watched wolves move to the river in their frenzying lopes.   95

Chapter Thirty-Two Valley Footnotes

Kari is not only settling accounts, she is responding to a tight situation, the rescue of Theman's soul from the hands of the diabolical Dark Storm. In an epic manner, we see the classic Valkyrie Kari going out into the wilderness to do battle single-handedly against all odds. Not really, though, as she knows who and what she is. She also certainly knows what her opposition is, and that Storm's underlings just do not stand a chance against her. Such is her confidence.

7-8. *Missmatch . . . intercept them on her arcs and brassh!* Not only is Kari going to make them miss her with their blows, but she is their 'Miss Match,' meaning they cannot deal with her expertise. *Intercept.* The shortest distance between two points, in this case, is a spiral that goes on a line while others are swinging wildly. *Brassh.* It looks as if Kari is full of gumption and is going to 'dash' them to pieces.

9. *So unto Holmganga.* Old Icelandic *lit.*, "to go to the island." According to Mycroft, this is a mistranslation. This term refers to official honorable dueling procedures where contestants fought at a sanctioned dueling place before judges, even though these duels were also known as 'revenge' duels. At the city of *Thingvellir*, Iceland, the dueling zone was a small island next to the village assembly. Mycroft cites that, more in context to our passage however, this personal return *raquette* by Kari leans more toward the term *einvigi*, or unsanctioned "personal revenge" that was outlawed across Iceland. The vague passage seems to be trying to say that even though the idea of revenge is involved, Kari nonetheless sees it as an honorable thing.

12. *To see if they could outlasst the lass.* Storm tells her underlings to outwit and outlast 'the lass,' and kill Kari off. She doesn't have high hopes.

22-23. *Facing that thing—that—that scourge divined . . . was a terror-firma 'voided.* In some circles, Kari's reputation was such that she was known as 'the scourge,' or 'hammer' of God. *Terror-firma* refers to the Latin *Terra-firma*, the 'dry land' or 'earth.' This particular dueling zone is so evil and corrupt that it is a terror to enter into and is to be 'avoided,' as many of the best met their untimely ends here. *Thing—that—that.* The poem 'stammers' here as if shaking its finger at something as it tries to describe to us how these creatures attempt to express their feelings and views toward Kari. The poem and they are at a loss for words.

31-32. *"If that devil's-whelp . . . be 'not~her thousand years, We'll become far worse, Nox."* Nox is one of Dark Storm's chief male hench-spirits. Nothing more is known about him. *'Not~her*, or 'another.' The spirits are afraid that if Kari gets a hold of them it will take at least another thousand years for them to regain a semblance of what they are now. Too, they are truly worried about her coming on strong, having apparently dealt or heard of her before. In this case the phrase runs something like, 'Oh no, *not her* again!' *Whelp* implies impudence as well as a young offspring of an animal such as a dog or wolf. They really do not like Kari at all.

44. *Intercepting that 'choosy' braven. Choosy* implies Kari's title as a Valkyrie, a 'Chooser of the Slain.' Here the fiends disdain her, making it sound like she is way too picky or snooty for her job. *Braven.* 'Brave one.'

47. *Pale riders loosing.* This is a referral to the Death rider's pale horse of *Revelation* 6.8, one of the Four Horsemen of the *Apocalypse*. He is the only horseman named— Señor Thanatos Muerte with his lil' friend Hell tagging along after him. *Pale* in the original Greek translates as *khlōrós*, a sickly 'greenish-yellow' color indicative of pestilence and disease. What this stanza seems to saying is that these spirits unleash 'Death and Hell' against Kari, yet she *loosens* them from their saddles, cutting all the grim(y) reapers down. The poor horse is definitely having a bout with the *chlorosis*, the 'green sickness,' well, hell, they all are at this point, Kari included, she doing her 'spring cleaning' with *Clorox*, she "tackling even the toughest of *stains*" or 'imbrues.' Imbrue + brutes. *Imbrue* means 'to stain,' especially with blood on one's hands or sword. In other words, she is cleaning house, ridding herself of the dishonorable spiritual stains on her hands and sword, mostly a black gloppy feeling she has from the night before from dealing with these ogres.

48. *Valkyrie-bansheeing in all ther looning.* A *Banshee*, or 'woman of the fairy mounds,' is a female spirit in Irish mythology, usually seen as an omen of death

and messenger from the Underworld. They are noted for their wailings when someone is about to die. In Kari's case, it appears she is a raving, battle-spirit— screaming her head off amidst all ther (the + her) crazy, lunatic (*looning*) carnage, portending the spirits' deaths.

50. *Perturbid spirits bash and mar.* Perturbed + rabid. A 'perturbed' spirit is one who is greatly distressed. A *perturbid* spirit is one who is so distressed he or she is frothing at the mouth, churning in great agitation. The phrase, "Rest, rest, perturbed spirit!" comes from *Hamlet* (I. v.). Hamlet is telling his father's ghost to rest, swearing that no one will tell of his visit and that, from Hamlet, revenge will be taken for his murder. In light of the poem, the rotten spirits are so *perturbid* they will only find rest at the edge of Kari's sword. *Mar* ('ruin, tarnish, mark up') or 'Mars' indicates they are restless war spirits engaging in battle and are getting beat raw and royally—Kari leaving her characteristic signature scrawl.

56. *Kari battle furying cutting lefting righting.* In her great anger, the long sword she borrowed from Angel hampers Kari as the sword and dagger is her usual method. However, in the end, the long blade does not deter her. It is perfect from the viewpoint of fighting on a horse. *Cutting lefting* is a Musashi-ism. Musashi felt that the use of two swords in mass combat was more the thing and that one must crowd their opponents, chasing them right and left to pile them together. Here, Kari is performing the same battle deeds with one sword. She is a consummate artist of universal battle principles (Ch. 19 note # 91-92).

59. *The Wælcyge bloodfoamed.* Eight century Old English for 'Valkyrie.' Kari is literally foaming at the mouth.

62. "*Lever and wedge on hellish plane.* Of the six simple tools that shaped world and Deadlands history–the lever, wedge, inclined plane, pulley, screw, the wheel and axle–the lever and wedge are the most murderous. Wedges form blades and the arm is the lever. This combination has produced swords, axes, spears and their related arts. It also initiated the development of armor. *Hellish plane* refers to the trajectories the weapons take or create on their way to doing destruction. This affords us a

glimpse into how Kari sees motion, in its most simple, component states (both static and in fluent action), enabling her to be a great master.

68. *Caughted in trappings.* Caught + cauterized. Jonathan Mycroft suggests that this phrase leans more towards a feeling. Not just caught, but jammingly stopped in mid-motion with a rude, sickening jar. Then, it is that secondary, burning panicky sensation one gets when trapped and in trying to get out realizes for the first time, how hopeless the situation is. Kari understands this horrid, panicky feeling all too well, and uses it in a masterful fashion to further confuse her opponents.

69. *Hackings pitifuled against sublime spirals a' fire.* The word describes the opposition's level of expertise compared to St. Kari's. Wild undisciplined hacks are no comparison whatsoever to the cool, almost indiscernible, *spirangling* motion of a well-trained sword master, displaying a state of mind more than anything does. Although in fairness, it can be said that the best swordslinger in the land would not fear the second best, but the worst, because his or her timing and manner of technical execution would be all broken in their rhythms. Bruce Lee realized this and capitalized on this principle in his seriously 'bad' combative art *jeet kune do*, or "the way of the intercepting fist." The spiral it is said is the 'perfect form,' tightening and transcending upward or downward becoming more intense and fast toward its end completion, it carrying a lot of spring-loaded power. *Spirangles* are geometric patterns such as a square or triangle that has conforming lines within its lines going ever out into the larger geo pattern. Kari's *acute* techniques are so refined between "iron and silk," the metaphor for yin-yang, that she circles, lines, spirals and spirangles her sword *mootions* (motions + movement) eloquently. Her techniques are so simple, bewildering and complex they have been curiously described as, "Like not trying to unfit a triangle scalene out a hole square in a round peg." If this line does not make sense don't worry about it. Kari doesn't. Her alter ego gave up trying to explaining herself and ways to the thick ones millennia ago.

73. *To acquit her righteous bladeings.* Like trying to get away from a swarm of bees, the shades want nothing to do with the terrifying teenage Kari or her infamous, erratically flowing intuitional poetic-inspired bladework. Borrowed from Angel,

her sword is a 'good' blade that spreads alarm among the baddies. *Its trajectory of disirings.* Desire + Dísir. Kari is a supernatural female spirit, either Odin's daughter or the offspring of mortal kings, maidens whose privilege it was to remain immortal/invulnerable as long as they obeyed Odin or remained virgins. However, many a times she played the role of a *Dísir*, a female guardian spirit of good things who sets things straight. Not only that, her blade it seems is 'alive,' openly desiring, stalking its opposition.

78-79. *Blade star showers . . . motion and time. Lit.* "sparks." In the heat of battle, Kari's blade moves so fast that it sparks against her opponent's steel. As suggested from *Kel's Yellow Book* (thirteenth century) wherein the *Gestalt*-like phraseology forces readers or listeners to make their own mental connections to the descriptive actions, here, because all of this is 'unrecorded' history, Kari's high artistry is a lost one. It is forgotten and no one 'knows' about it, except of course when we, in our own minds, imagine it and piece it together connecting•⌢•the•◡•dots. However, some artists like Kari, Angel and Storm leave carefully cut-positioned dead bodies to mark their artwork, their signature swordgraphs, footprints in the sand, *etc.* Sherlock Holmes (*Scarlet*) cites that, "There is no branch of detective science which is so important and so much neglected as the art of tracing footsteps." This is a diverse observational-oriented metaphorical axiom that can be applied across the Midgard for the tracking of such spirits. Such things, Holmes would chide, are right under our very noses—if we had but the eyes to see, we failing however to reason from what observe we being too timid in drawing our references. As he says in *Identity*, "There is nothing so unnatural as the commonplace." Get a clue.

Kari is a mass-battle artist, her artwork being preserved through historically described battles. The concept of Japanese kata or martial exercises she utilizes as well. *Kata* means, "That shape which cuts the ground," she etching her epic life story into the ground *via* sword-pray and HSS *high-speed steel* cutting ability. All of these killer-phantoms have other hobbies too, dance and poetry—Scriptures Kari, painting and music for Storm and woodcarving and music for Angel, so all is not lost. Like Japanese sword duelist Musashi, he is better known today for his artworks of ink and brush, calligraphy, sculptures and masterful literature rather than his swordplay, although he did establish a school of swordsmanship (*Ni Ten Ichi Ryu*) which exists to this day. In samurai times, like setting up the cue ball to line up shots on a pool table so you could sink one ball after the other, in the chaotic heat of mass battle, cool-headed warriors were so adept at cutting their enemies at particular angles, they could directionally 'direct' the blood-spray away from them. They sprayed other opponent's with their comrade's blood, disorienting them to kill them easier. This left the cool ones clean to go home at night.

81. *Scar-let water carrying slow mean-daring trophies adrift.* The bloody water is scarlet in color. It is also scar*red*, or scar-*let* from the heinous battle. *Mean-daring*, or 'mean-dering.' The spirits were men, mean, and daring. Now they just meander by, the cur-*rent* (in this instance, Kari the wild dog having ripped them apart) carrying them downstream.

85. *Pulls hand bolt . . . allygn . . . bloodletting.* The *hand bolt* alludes to a crossbow type pistol. A*llygn*. Align + ally. Kari uses the ground to help line up her trembling hands for *aim-m-m-ming* this last shot. *Bloodletting.* Kari is bleeding and shaking horribly from the battle. She is literally "seeing red," a known phenomenon where the eyes turn red due to anger or stress.

THIRTY-THREE: LOW MIDNIGHT

Auroras impassioned in the arctic night,
Elements grappling into colden light.
Eternal fires to eternal wisting winds,
Loveless arcs and wastelands dune in.

Cosmic powers rifting, ion-shearing overhead,   5
Mute testimony o'er the land of *those* frozen dead.
Somber lights pale shadow's darker forms,
Enter the malificent, darkening deep Storm.

Past Helgrind to finish her little double-cross,
Gate 'tween living and the dead blacketed in hoarfrost.   10
Mountains hung tall in *that* cold, hard wheezing air,
Smothering clouds covered; oppressive peaks in despair.

Lone she stood on iced plateau,
A ruthless land that no mortal can know.
Watched the man from greatened distance,   15
Amid reddish icestands of ghosted existence.

Lavaandred horizons and marooning sun,
Ice floes *a'bluing* where day is never done.
Unto this land of faceless graves,
The man had come up souly for his name.   20

Black coald eyes glittering icily stonily back,
NethArctic deadness and her lacking—a most powerful attack.
Storm shimmering in dark reflect*shun*,
Easily, a frigid morgue of no one's redemption.

Watched she now as he cut crossed wastes,   25
Cragged tombstones of ice told of soul's gone fates.
A land upheavaled by eternal scald freeze,
The man g'raving vengeance; his short lot to seize.

Amid he now the jutted bluiced blocks,
Black figure moving silhouetted in shock.   30
Ices grotesquing, shifting shapes,
Sculpting forever passions of fhate.

The man coming upon now o'er frozen hill,
Horror-stricken at the sight, his body chilled—
A vast living cemetery as far as the ice flowed,   35
Miles deep, as far as *es caps go*.
Here were *those* remnants of men and spirits shamed,
Confined for millennia or more in lost icelinked chains.
And here Dark Storm walked refrigerate amidst,
Among freezer-burned souls and their vaporous mists.   40

Thissztling rime winds had seared their meaningless fates,
Tearing souls to nothing, laying them blasted in waste.
A mountain of packed ice took its grim, ripping toll,
Remains of the once living now heaps of freeze-d'ied souls.

Frozen alive in bluewhite death,   45
A Valhallan judgment (a just recompense).
Exacting land for irredeemable criminals,
Locked in a 'no-men's land eve*red* abominable.

Now for reasons only she could cordially explain,
Admired Storm the bodies in their white blocked frames.   50
Ice-frieze solid with writhing souls,
A reliefed masterpiece—in *tsk* damning cold.

It was here *this* she-creature had placed her dryiced well,
Sunk it in hoarfrost, pittedly closer to bottomless Hel.
Had lowered the box containing the spirit of *that* man,   55
Another trap set (*heheheh*)——to be sprung by his own hands.

The eyes of Kari studied the walls of frozen souls,
Shivers swept through her to be near her old home.
Spirits of martial adequacy even are in ice met,
Permanence of ability: their thawless quest.   60

Yet watched she too in morbid fascination,
As 'frozens' contended in slowest animation.
Took a century and then some to move a yard circumvolved,
Numbing scorching agony strengthening their hoarrid resolve.

Listening, Kari heard the massive ice slow-*th-th-tiching*,   65
From bodies straining within ᙡᙡᙡ
——And the cemetery imperceptibly shifting
(Mountains dissolve over eons of time,
Drop by drop by the hand of the Divine).

Dark Storm sneered at their adversity,   70
Never was bound here to her paralyzing misery.
This was her land (there was *nothing* to fear ᙡ *she told herself*),
——BUT——the sounds were right, *ahhh*, music to her ear!

Now she waited for her thick human prey,
To find *itself* under this eternal midnighted day.   75
Watched him move from shard to shard,
Searched about these ruins of death's discard.

Kari, too, measured the coldish man,
Spotted Dark Storm and knew her oft-used plan.

Knew the ways of she and her iced-desert land,   80
Could ≥ *sniiifff* ≤ smhell her evil in the colden damnped.

Promptly the moment of truth had arise,
All who played 'fore and sought the prize.
The man finding what appeared to be a door,
Slid he it back from the iced troughed floor.   85

There he pulled with a rope hardback,
With all his strength⌣he did not slack.
He sloely heaved from the shaft a boxonyx black,
A heavy locked chest, with a skelectokey that lacked.

With ripped hands fumbled he in coldish wind,   90
Striving for the secret: to be finally let in.
A shade man playing for its own soul decrepit,
Identity to be gained–there was no more to stop it.

Thought he of his miserable scratchy life,
Of his current situation, a god-awfuled sight.   95
Cursed the day when he was into *that* world *a*'born,
Felt that blade at his side, breathed, and felt reformed.

Kari eyed the swine and with disgusted tongue wrung—
"What wondrous things there be in a weapon,
Needs be the knowledge that comes from Heaven,   100
A natural way that draws all men—
To master her path means divined mind and hand
—To make them kings or *wretches* in the end."

Now the man pawed on knees at ground,
Beat on the box with his pommel sound.   105
A pallid, invisi'bled shadow cast over he,
Dark Storm's foot on box, *heh*, leaning—with the key.

"Try this," she said, leering at the thief,
A snake to the sparrow, wolf to *that* black sheep.
The man dry-eyed her in his high suspicion,   110
"That easy?" he said, and loathed her elicitation.
Tossed she the key on the ice beside,
"Take it up, if you really want to v'ie."
The man gazed at her cruel, slender hip,
Buttressed in leather and sickle blood-dipped.   115

Cold eyes registered no reply,
Only an excuse to kill him (he gulped-complied).
Slowly he took the lock and insert the key,
Turned it hard, and heard it snap free.

Uncoupled now the froze steel bar,   120
Opened the latch, wiped his face hard.
Great war spear now splitting, pinning crate,
St. Kari of the Blade—always on hand to *altar*cate.

Sealed she the box with her own brand of key,
"Destinies change, possibly, even toward me."   125

Dark Storm smirked in malicious glee,
Salivaed frozen dripping from her teeth.

"Bane, you seem to have a propensity for interfearing too much.
But I welcome you 'evermore, dreary sister, if you take it as such.
How did my friends treat you?—I see I must make amends,   130
For not inviting you to 'its'—hmmm—*this* puny mortal's end."

Then she turned with unsettling grace,
Placed the man in front, by moving back a pace.
"Do what we agreed to do, its business," said she,
"Kill the Valkyrie now, and I will help you from her go free."   135

The man now stood, cold sweat flowed,
"I told him lots more, before you showed.
He's with me now, this important little mort'al man,
I'll make him a master, in this, my spirit hunting land."

"Kill her," she snarled at the former movie star,   140
Valkyricide, to see if, for her, he would go that far.
Sharp pause in winding, bluing dipping cool,
Two Choosers of the Slain glaring at *that* mortal fool.

Frozen in time and eternity together,
Pictaresque scene that no one remembers.   145
Dank thoughts shrouded the man's trited mind,
The Mean overwhelmed, he wanted to abie.

The Mean looked at Kari's dainty sword hand,
A bloodied item supernaturaled, fresh from the killing lands.
Her cold steel eyes reckoned hard love determined,   150
To strike down if necessary, *that* ungracioused vermin.

Wolves' rubied eyes reflect at solitary distance,
Scent of bloodshed was nighing and immanent.
Gnawed they now upon joints jut from ice,
Thirsted for the fresh—none else would suffice.   155

Talked the man back to the Dark Storm,
"I-i*i-i* can't't—" and turning, mhorre words he tr-i *i*-ed to form.

Slashing sick'ling from loosening tight grip,
Arc cutting through the saint's gold hair to hip.

Spun she around snow helix sword flying,   160
Red line up the body drippling darking,

399

Twhissstling to the ground in crumpling moan,
St. Kari receiving her final deathblow.

Dark Storm laughed at her underhanded trick,
Worked many times before (many times since).   165
"Sorry, dear sister," as she secured her blade,
"It was me or you, on this—your judgment day."

"Don't look *too* hurt," Storm did contend,
"You meant this for me, anyway, in the end.
No matter now, you're out of my way.   170
The man here helped me, Asgard I'll gain."

Crawled Kari onto her knee and keeled right over,
Tried to reach her blade for the darklithe comer.
Leaned herself up on a nearby rock,
Breathing her last, her violets on *that* box.   175

"⸮No words today? *Hmmmm*, that's too, too bad—
(Should have signed off on your own epithet in that chicken scratch
of yours)
—Those who read it would be *heh, soooo* sad."

The Mean's dry mouth fell open wide a'gape,
Shocked at Kari's death by the fiendish reprobate.   180
Siblings in life struggling none any or the more,
The sister of hate devilering the pure to death's door.

Pushed beyond the edge by this final action,
The Mean metámorphed into a killing antagon'.

"Finish her," Dark whispered to the 'fused man,   185
"Kill her now," she urged, "take her power to stand."

Dark picked up and twirled the Bloodhawk-etched blade——. . .
. . .——Admired its handiwork, and gave it to the man
——To make more pain.

The sword-saint's blood-blade thrust into hand,   190
Rend his spirit, giving him semblance of a deranged man.
The Mean now insaning from all those killings gone by,
Knew in his heart what his mind had denied.

Had become so like Storm in mind and according,
Scorned his humanity, his putrid existence deploring.   195
A ravening animal, unchained, finally free,
Bestial unrestraint: to 'dulge all his monstrosities.

Relished he the thought of this ghastly life,
Living forever, killing to survive 'rife.
Rolled his eyes, and tongue frothed ecstatic about,   200
A disciple of death, becoming demoniacally devout!

Archaic surges 'roiled in his blood,
Primordial instinct stirred ancient rudd.
A base animal now on lone instinct,
Carnalities supreme: a predator; succinct.   205

Dark mewed, "use it and finish the girl,"
Nodded at the Bloodhawk in his hand and deferred.
Sluing he the blade he in evil unfeeling air,
Looked into Kari's eyes and felt dim pangs of care.

(A horrid spectacle to see a man grapple with soul,   210
Down in the hellish deapths, clay to the iron condoned.
The terrible choice he now began to make,
Shred between himself and his soul tearing great).

Aside from his greater nature he in-turned himself,
—A deliberate denial of his divined part self.   215

In warped t'reason impassioned he murcie's swift flight,
To crush the thing he love-hated out of his sickening shortsight.
At full length, all the strength he summoned, he in blackout rage beget,
Strike like the clarity of a ⚡make!—At least 'twere done quickly and set!

Struck her once ↗ *thenn*—*nTw′iced MHORR* ↗ ↗ ↗   220
The savage [with\in him] ⇌ *it*—*a′* distant star was now *a′* Ƃ★rn*!!*
Yet mercy staid Kari's relentless hand,
To give him choice to where he would stand.
Hung blade over her head; the shrilling Visigoth,
A diabolique unmercied, im'personal twisted wroth.   225

Still the Valkyrie shown through her clear eyes,
A Teutonic cut'ie whose love lovingly decried.
Reaching out beyond past those "Powers that be,"
Beyond carnality's trappings and vile barbarities.

Shot he through with thoughts of her green reedy love,   230
Hated himself for holding that horrid metal above.
His dark love for her grew strong instead,
Knew he was becoming as one with these dead.

"Now!" Storm screamed, "Before it's too late!"
But the blood was in him, to kill *this* fiend of hate.   235
"Fool!" foamed Storm, opening her blade,
"Get back, squirt, you're in my way!"

"I'm going to kill you, fill your hand!"
"I know," Storm smiled coyly, *hmmph*—"I had it all planned."

The man screerushed her, chop'd with blade,   240
Sheshearing him, cutting him nearly to his grave.

Swore at her from his blood gushed wound,
Steam fisszing in cold air, told of his dying soon.
Grabbed she him and throttled his neck,
"I have a worse fate for you, *Ha*: I'll send you back4!!//   245

Back to your own dull useless little liefe," she ratled he,
"Filled with your own nothings and selfish vanities,
Back to where you think you are self-made and big,
Back to where we use you for your own graves to dig,
Back to where you use your own dupes to make yourselves pigs.   250

And here," she teared momentarily then pounded fist she,
("If you fools only knew what you could in eternity be—
Ahhh—but from *that* First and Last I must keep from thee").

Dark storm sneered then cursed the fallen man,
Then after a moment's thought, calmed herself again.   255
"It doesn't matter," said she, as she mused in depth,
"I'll have you all when I meet you in *that* final death."

"What do *you* mean?" the man sput-t uttered and spaat.
"To that land of Midgard, where you mortal's habitat.
There you will collect power all the excruciating more—   260
When you die, 💣 your vast corruption will be my glhorr'."

Dark Storm despised the fetid, little slave,
Knew him a fool, that *it* was *its* own grave.
"So now 'dear friend' with your name and soul,
My power's assured; millions you will bring to *my* fold."   265

"¡¡Damn you*!!*" he screamed and started to fade.
Kari watched in distance, her eyes to the grey.
"You won't be able to help yourself〰〰by the way〰〰,
There's enough of me in you now, to ensure your 'in-fame.'"

Kari moaned and Dark Storm grew annoyed,   270
"One more task, I think, her very sword I will employ."
"¡No!!" screamed the man, "don't do Ii–tt*t! —!!*"
"*Oh yeah?* Turn aside runt, and watch *this*—➤ "

"Not so fast," a smooth drawling voice now soft-spoke the sooth,
The Angel of spirit stood 'tween Storm and *that* damnseled youth.   275
Dark shaken visibly, now taken aback,
Recovered quickly, gripping her shaft.

"You're back," she slur*r*ed, "—I see you're healed."
Unlatched he his blade. "no . . . *this* time, let's try it *for real*."

Her smile dropped from her blanching face,   280
Solutions in motion, she s l o w e d   h e r   p a c e.
"You're here for its clay spirit, I do see.
You can't have *it*; I'll have it all for me."

Brushed she then her hair from her cheek,
As if to incite all to mourn and to peek.   285
"Besides, I owe you for this—"
"Oh. You mean, *um*, that little scar '*s.*teeled' *w.*ith *a. k.*iss?"

Stood they now less than two ◊ feet apart,
Angel and Storm, kindred spirits with no hearts.
Total efficiency was their killing trade,   290
A hair's breadth difference〰〰
The end? In blinding pain.

Kari watched the duel in winter's dark light,
Appreciating the drama of the low midnight.
Probed they the deapths of each other's souls,   295
Mirrors to each other, no weaknesses to show.
Eyes without movement studied their grips—
Gauging *that* distance from hands to hilts.

Hands slowly to position's power,
Man on the ground heaving dour.   300
Wind's rhythm *abrazzzing* the land,
Two lone warriors; one must stand.

Feet gripping icy floor.
Bluish ice spattered from past gore.
Tempered hands to tempered blades   305
(Weak movement's make ones grave)—

Eyes, hands, feet, hilts,
Furyexpl•deninginicedeathinggriiipźz
Blindendingspeeatingsteeylizingfauxpass,
Stood they both——to feel the gash.   310

Twin statues in curved arctic time,
Standing alone fade from memories prime.
Motion actioned once long ago,
Seeks the end, and reminds one no.

Blood slowly dripped fresh on virgin snow,   315
From one realizing statue, life ebbing slow.
Dark Storm she spat, then falling to ground,
Fell on her face and rolled around.

Began she now to cast her sickle,
Angel swipening her up the middle.   320

Slid she down through troughed iced floor,
Sealed he the shaft, a fatal-led, volumous door.

A cryptic tomb, one so fine,
Upon her pains she would dine.
Closing darkness overhead shone,   325
Rumbles shut and slams he the stone.

The Mean, now turning pale and thin,
Picked up a blade to hack at him.
Angel moving to dying St. Kari,
Without looking, 'the thin,' he parried.   330

The Desperate now bre-heaved, "*G*-Give me that Box!
My soul is it—y-*you* must-can't—it unlock!!"

"Think I'll keep it," said Angel, calmly spitting on the ground,
"If you want it that bad, you'll *uh*, just have to come back down."
"Rotten bastard!!" screamed the man, "it belongs to *me*!"   335
Angel shook his head, sighing, "What a great pity."
Cinched he the box to his pack,
"Look me up some time—
—That is, if you ever get back."

"I'll be back!" frothed the ranting Mean.   340
Angel winked at him and rode from the scene.
Mean screamed and cursed as Heart lessed from sight,
"Poor pilgrim," Angel shook, riding into darkening light.

The last thing The Mean saw was Angel in the night,
And before he disappeared—   345
Cursed him to high Hell as he misted from his sight.
Ghostly Dire Wolf growl slathered jaws, chomping the man of sin,
Felt the *severest s-z-sh-zhaking*, Wolf chasing his tail~s~p~i~nnnn~~ ↶!

Way off in distance Angel reared his steed,
Rhythmed back the creature the stage once more to see. 350
The personal history in which he played and took part,
His mind to contemplate before remembrances depart.

Walked he around the stage of frigid slaughter,
Grimaced about, picked up his Bloodhawker.
Sweet dreaming Kari, gone Saint of the Blade, 355
She lied in state, Medievaled statue on mar-bled grave.

Bent he over Kari with blanket to cover her,
A blade slid to his neck, as he soon discovered.
A moment's pause then his sardonic nod,
"Bravo" he spoke, realizing Kari's *façade*. 360

"Hard to lie dead like that for any length of time."
She noted his cynicism "——A new trick of mine."

Opening both eyes, she smiled at him.
"Not too bad for a spirit many times done in.
But I was expecting to get the drop on she→" 365

"——*A*nd would *you* mind ·⸫· telling *me*——"

"Not at all. My sister idiot thinks I'm dead,
Her reentrance into this world, *ha*, a fire underfed."
Helped her he up and handed her the Bloodhawk,
"Look after her for a while; will ya, help you with 'your talks.'" 370

"As for the man, 'twas better he struck at me,
Diverted his attention; his colors shone free.
As for his finality, that decision must be,
A vision he alone shall have to stand and see."

Angel smiled cat-like, appreciated her acumen,   375
Mounted their horses, pointing them to the barrens.

"You're too honorable," he said at the last,
"If you're not careful, get yourself killed *reeeal* fast."

Kari thought, pondered Angel's soul-box game,
The killer hid his good streak; it could be used just the same.   380

"As for ones like Storm better let me,
Take care of her kind, being the finest in elegant cutlery."

"You are?" Kari condescended, "I'll remember that,
When I meet you later, Thulander, on other quests."

"You're great with that sword and good in flashfights,   385
But you have to learn to outwit others; she's beyond your type"
("Oh yes," she acquiesced, she being such a neophyte).

Looked Kari down as she sheathed exquisite blade,
Not a nick within, to impede its determined way.
"Reduce the odds?" she cut a smile as they rode far,   390
On flung horizon's thin line their ways did they part.

Both to the South—nowhere else to go,
Back to the hinterlands and those Valhallan holds.
Dark Storm now interred a thousand degrees down,
Longed for the sun, her tenacious emergence icebound   395
(A fiery percolhate was she, would boil herself free).

Winds moved free and horses bold,
Swayed to the music of the story told.
Strong spirits in an even stronger land,
A mercenaried tale of manipulation grand.   400

Kari singing in the wind,
Sang she her song, her soul akin:

"*Freebairn forever in eternity,*
A spirit in time ne'er shall I be,
A soul immortal is what I am,   405
'Pon Heaven's Love I'll always stand."

She rode well into dark declining sun,
Shard frozen images prism'd her a new fated run.
Past those fragments of icened yellow and blue,
Shaped her spirit's impression in distant broken hues.   410

As the two rode off long after the twilighted instance,
The land they were on cracked deep down within it.
With Dark storm entombed, an iceberg now dissented to sea,
A Northern spirit, only now a tiny *pseudo*viking funeral had she
(And yea, she cursed, "even soon I will be free").   415

DOUGLAS M. LAURENT

Chapter Thirty-Three Valley Footnotes

This scene is the climax, the final battle between the four main characters, Kari, Angel, Storm and Theman. Taking place in a frozen waste, they contend for the prize, which may or may not be Theman's soul, depending on how one looks at it. To some deadlanders, the game, the pursuit, is sometimes the better end of the bargain than the prize itself. The Midgard phrase, "The journey *is* the destination" thinly and insipidly parallels this Underworld richness.

0. *Low Midnight.* The title of this chapter is most apropos for a duel in the northern Deadlands, much like a Western's 'high noon,' the classic time of the 'show down' where gunfighters step out into the street to settle their differences by the gunslinger's code of who is the 'fastest on the draw.' Here, the midnight sun dominates the sky.

8. *Enter the malificent.* Maleficent + magnificent. This phrase describes a magnificent capacity to do harm and evil as Dark Storm certainly has.

9. *Past Helgrind to finish.* This is the Norse gate between the living and the dead. In this case, it is one of the many boundary gates found in the Deadwastes. Formal Valhalla, the area of the Deadlands controlled by the righteous is (metaphorically) separate from the Valley of the Damned and other areas controlled by powerful kingdoms or regions, many having their own boundary markers.

10. *Gate 'tween living and the dead blacketed in hoarfrost.* *Hoarfrost* is frozen dew that forms a white coating on a surface. Here the color is symbolic as white, or purity, but it is switched to black, or rather the text renders the subject 'blanketed' in black hoarfrost, an evil, dark connotation and foreshadow.

16. *Amid reddish icestands of ghosted existence.* The land of 'Low Midnight,' Storm's stronghold, is yet another bloodstained warzone where she fought many a battle. Many ghosts of the slain are said to abide there, their phantom-esque bodies grotesquely frozen in ice.

17. *Lavaandred horizons and marooning sun.* Lava + lavender + red. This is a land of fire and ice, of flowing lava glowing red, and while the sun sets, the dusk sky turns lavender color. The 'red' implies 'dread.' *Marooning.* The dark reddish-purple setting midnight sun has a tendency to 'maroon' or strand spirits in these wastes, unfortunately, for a very, very long time.

21. *Black coald eyes.* Coal + cold. Storm has the blackest, coldest of eyes that pour 'the heat.'

22-23. *NethArctic deadness and her lacking.* The high dead NetherArctic does not 'lack.' In actuality, it does not have to do anything to kill a person. Its 'power' lies in just sitting and waiting, *a most powerful attack* by the draw indeed as it 'ice-ol(h)ates' and slowly sucks the life out of one. *In dark reflectshun.* All things considered, when Storm thinks about this place and *reflects* upon it, she wants to *shun* it, it being almost too morbid even to her liking.

28. *The man g'raving vengeance; his short lot to seize.* As in the simple game of chance, depending on how one defines it, drawing the short straw or *lot* means one is out of luck. In this case, unbeknownst to him, Theman, trying *to seize* the moment for victory inadvertently and metaphorically draws the short straw, meaning his chances of success are virtually *nil*.

32. *Sculpting forever passions.* The land herself carves destinies.

35-36. *A vast living cemetery . . . as es caps go.* Some of the most evil spirits of the Deadlands are incarcerated here. More than a cemetery, it is a soul ice-prison, one of the many 'prison houses of pain' to be found in the Deadwastes. *Es caps.* Earlier translations read "ice-caps," however; later textual translations by Jonathan Mycroft read 'escapes.' In either instance, it is a treacherous place to try to get out of.

39-41. *Dark Storm walked refrigerate amidst.* Storm walks calmly amongst the many victims interred in this icy graveyard. She definitely is cool-headed but also a 'frigid' one. *Thisstling rime winds. Rime* is a frost formed on cold objects by the rapid freezing of extremely cold water vapor in clouds or fog. This coating of ice as on grass or trees forms almost instantly on cold surfaces. Metaphorically, the wording is also a 'dark rhyme' or riddle we must muse and be wary of, it attuned to the *Thisstling* winds of the area that have *freezer-burned* and ice-*seared* the interred's ('in terror red') *meaningless fates*. To inter someone is to place their corpse in a grave or tomb usually with honors, but there is nothing of the sort here. Besides, these 'corpses' horribly so, are still 'alive' somehow with a ponderously slow and frozen consciousness about them, making them think and move like molasses on Pluto. These 'iced' spirits placed in this godless waste are to get rid of, and torment them. For these multitudes, this is tasteless, pitiful frozen *just desserts*, something that is 'deserved and merited.' To Storm, the fresh-frozen ectobone-garden is a macabre but impressive sight.

47-48. *Exacting land . . . 'no-men's land evered abominable.* This verse has several meanings. The term *'no-men's,* Jonathan Mycroft believes, is an allusion to a type of 'no-man's land,' as on a battlefield, but is also a shortened version of 'snowmen,' or, possibly 'omen.' Coupled with that, the scholar Von Hauser believes this is a parallel reference to 'abominable snowmen,' further supported by the term *evered,* a supposed reference to Mt. Everest, the area that is said to be the alleged home of the giant snowmen. The hazy text seems to be saying that not only is this a vast cemetery of frozen 'soul' beings, but also an area of the legendary creatures that possibly feed on them 'ever-red,' making this an extremely dangerous, 'no-man's' land for anyone.

51-52. *Ice-frieze solid . . . A reliefed masterpiece—in *tsk damning cold.* Relief + fed. A 'relief' sculpture is where the sculpted material has been raised above the background plane by cutting away the backdrop giving it an elevated appearance. '*Fed.*' This wasteland is continually gorging itself on the living-dead spirits. A *frieze* is a sculptured or richly ornamented band decorating the side a building. Hence, here is a frozen relief sculpture with bodies frozen inside and sometimes partially or almost jutting out of the walls and floors of ice. Since these are evil, pure spirits and humans from all times, it is a rather colorful setting, as their garb reveals the dimensions and eras in which they lived, reflecting many 'northern light' colors, translucent and opaque. *In *tsk.* Storm shakes her head as if in pity, making the **tsk, tsk* sound as she does, almost as if she is thinking, "damn, what a waste." But in reality, she is not overly concerned; she just cannot believe that such a place exists, so she makes the metaphoric non-word onomatopoeia.

56. *Another trap set (heheheh)—to be sprung by his own hands.* Dark Storm has successfully used this ruse many times before and chuckles about it. She delights at Theman's stupidity and the prospect that his soul shall soon be hers. It is a good day for her all things considered.

57-58. *The eyes of Kari . . . Shivers swept through her.* This phrase indicates that this may be or like one of Kari's former prisons, giving her swooning chills. Apparently, she relates or connects in some deep way to the cold and grisly frozen *licburg* (OE. "graveyard"), to a time perhaps when she was 'put on ice' suffering a frost-biting, fiery quick-frozen freeze-drying living death, those prison disciplines making one feel as though they were gnawing on frozen hamburger for sheer survival—a graphic depiction of the soul-consumption atrocities that occur within these austere towering screamingly silent *inpeniterable* high-walled unspeakable necro-penitentiaries.

As a matter of telling insight, the whole works gives her 'the creeps' and rightly so, because there is a tremendous unseen evil force laboring silently here, namely the frozen corpses itselves. In Materials Science, *creep* or *cold flow*, means the ornery disposition of a solid material to move about slowly and thus deform permanently under long term exposure to stress. At the start of 'primary' or 'initial creep,' the strain is very high but grows less over time. However, the material grows tougher as it slows and hardens. This is called 'strain' or 'work hardening,' and 'cold working,' aptly named because of the dislocation of the movements and the crystalline structures within the solid. Well, this is a very good description of what is going on here with these berserkly benumbed ice-dried overly wicked spirits and their slowly twisshapening ectobodies. No wonder the kid has 'the creeps' and no further wonder they hate freeze-dried instant coffee.

60. *Permanence of ability: their thawless quest.* That is, 'perfection of ability.' Even the ice prison and the pains thereof do not stop determined or permanently fixated martial spirits from perfecting their essence and art forms. And because they are froze in ice, they move slower than t'ai-ch'i forms (*tàolù*) in Siberia, which are *realllly* slow to begin with, the spirits using the ice as a kind of 'resistance training' to re-build their nearly perma-frozen wispy ethereal bodies and re-discipline their chilled ice-cubed chunked brittle minds and souls.

In Japanese, martial forms are *kata. Mandala*-like these 'shapes that cut ground' serve as temporal blue prints to help focus the soul as it strives for balance within the universe and in its own three-tiered essence—*spirit, mind* and *body*. But, this is an *entropic* energy depriving temporal treadmill.

Notwithstanding, Katas are motion-books or portraits, recordings of a past masters' fighting essence but they go way beyond this. As a masterpiece painting carries with it the unmistakable identifiable personality resonance of its creator impressed into it, such as an easily recognized Pablo Picasso or a Grant Wood, katas too are psyche-imprints. They bear the indelible trademark of their designer's person—their spiritual panache, vitalities, attributes, integrities, ways of thinking, perceiving, motion preferences, accrued knowledge, wisdom, demeanor, strengths, *etc.* Nonetheless, masters of any media, even martial, see as though through a glass darkly. Their unrealized shortcomings and limitations are inevitably found tucked away in the far cobweb-ridden hidden recesses of their psyche's kata-schematic portraits where a whole lot of people never go. One wrong turn here and these one-dimensional followers are inevitably jerked into oblivion at the end of a rope and left swinging in the wind, a pretty sight, as there are many *obliquitious* trap doors to this cunningly wrought Midgard outlet. In any form of literature, including kata, blurry, vague or confusing statements are deliberately made shadowy and *obscure* for effect, for results. Kata is slamjamcrammed with obscure enigmas. In systems engineering, *obliquity* is a view that says the best way to reach a goal when working with complex arrangements is to take the *indirect approach* rather than a straightforward one for overall greater efficiency. The point is on all levels there are many booby-traps in the study of kata.

Then again, katas do have some temporal merit, having developmental tools, ideas and concepts. As a loaded perception toolbox, they are used to view many things that go past physical limitations and other boundaries. As our views of reality are defined and so limited, katas serve as spyglasses, reflection devices to our nature, invoking scrutiny as we analyze and challenge our limits as barriers that needs be broken applying kata-paradigm tools.

A journey in self-discovery, kata is sort of a 'self unraveling form of moving meditation' and can be metaphorically anything in *thought, word or deed*, as it is the three-fold package of *spiritual, mental and physical* endeavor of which peoplekind is singularly made of. As there are many intriguing *fascia* of wisdom, shrewdness, acumen, intelligence, discernment, foresight and knowledge, *etc.* that are to be had from kata, one can learn much from the life-perceptions, values and strategies these moving *kōans* (riddles) hold.

Each 'kata' experience is highly personal, trunking down to the deepest roots of the person's own being. A person's essence, attitude and actions displayed during kata sessions and from them lessons applied in daily life is the 'soul' of kata. Kata metaphor can aid in untangling and revealing many mysteries about one's person and their balancing with others, nature and the Almighty. Self-illumination is the hinge-pin of all kata and what this means in relation others and to the Grand *O-Sensei* of us all with whom we have to do. For these frozen martial spirits, in a macabre tortwist-distuous sort of way, their 'kata practice' is all that they have and is both a punishment and a pleasure since forms are what they 'love' to do or rather made to love to do, just like in our world today. How can something think, let alone move, such as these 'its' do when they are froze? But don't we do the same when we allow our spirits/minds to be encircled and iced off like cold margaritas by the subtle depraved coal-black "Powers that be" and their *stultifying* designs? Unseen designs teach us to deceive ourselves we in the end 'loving' to blast freeze ourselves to death, and this by our own 'trained hands.' How kind of them.

Their thawless quest. Thaw + flawless. What this implies is that these spirits are set in perma-ice, they cannot exactly be 'thawed out' so to speak, and so, realizing this they nonetheless use their environment to sharpen themselves, as if on a spiritual/physical quest to achieve 'flawless' perfection.

81. *In the colden damnped.* Cold and + damned + damp.

83. *All who played 'fore.* All who played this game 'before,' not just this time, but in many times and in many situations.

88. *A boxonyx black.* Theman's spirit-*box* is described here for the first time as being very *black.*

91. *Striving for the secret.* Theman seeks to understand himself, to get to the bottom of his soul.

97. *And felt reformed.* The sword at Theman's side gives him a feeling of security.

98. *Eyed the swine.* Kari sees through Theman into his truer nature.

106. *A pallid, invisi'bled shadow.* This is an ashen pale, nearly invisible, bloody shadow—Storm's. Storm's shadow not only reminds us of the intercontinental trend-setting Death Rider, but his Apocapale "pony pal Pokey, too." If shadows can teach us anything, now is the time. Whereas healthy dead spirits usually have your ordinary black or animated unto itself shadow, her shadow is essentially a see-through pukey green-yellow color splotched with red, allowing us to 'see into the soul' of this truly sick, diseased and violently bloody dead spirit. Is it any wonder why she does not like light? (Ch. 32 note # 47).

109. *Wolf to that black sheep.* Theman is by no means an innocent lamb.

111. *Loathed her elicitation.* Theman hates the idea of Storm selling ideas to him and drawing him out.

128. *Bane, you seem . . . interfearing too much.* Storm's line "*Bane*" refers to the saying, "the bane of my existence," in other words Kari is a class-A pest, a royal pain in the neck. *Interfearing.* Mycroft suggests that the word implies butting in, causing concern—and perhaps fear or worry on Storm's part.

138-139. *Little mort'al man, I'll make him a master.* The term *mort'al* or 'mort all,' is Storm's sly way of saying 'mortified,' which to her means humiliating and injuring Theman's ego and pride and any shred of self respect he has. She is out to shame the useless disgustoid human, ultimately killing and destroying his spirit preparing 'it' for an eternity with her. Theman will be one of her many 'mortiffs' (dead mortal motifs, also *mort*, the triumph note sounded on a horn when a quarry-deer is killed) as she controls and banquets upon his blighted soul for eternity. *Him a master.* This is the left-handed, underhanded deal Dark Storm is cutting with Theman to get the upper hand that is, to get him wholly on her side.

141-143. *Valkyricide . . . glaring at that mortal fool.* This is the murderous killing of a Valkyrie. Storm has long put up with Kari's antics and so she is truly relishing the moment reveling in the scrumptious fact that idiot Theman is actually going to be the trained monkey to do her killing for her, sort of like the killing of two birds with one stone thing. Theman murders Kari and sucks up her energy, Storm then kills Theman *via* soulpirism and Storm gets two for the price of one. Oh, how Storm cannot wait for her dupe to waste Kari the Val-kid. She has long suffered at the hands of the teenage prodigy's ways, the sword-poemketeer always and inevitably being a stumbling-block to her loss on more than one lucrative occasion.

145. *Pictaresque scene.* Picturesque + picaresque. 'Picaresque' is a type of fiction, Spanish in origin that deals with rogues, heroes, vagabonds and the like. As here, it is a highly charged, dashingly dramatic epic scene, Storm getting into the romanticism of it. Romanticism in literature (*ca.* 1700s) was a movement characterized by greater interest in nature and a person's imagination and emotional expressions. It was an intellectual and artistic rebellion, the turning away of classicism and social mores. Apparently being caught up in the moment, Storm's imagination and emotions are idling quite high.

147. *Wanted to abie.* Abide + die. The petty, vain, egotistic Theman wanted to do formidable things, but, being engulfed in dark thoughts, wanted to die at the same time. In psychology, this is known as an 'approach-avoidance' conflict, ripping him.

157. *Mhorre words to form.* More + horror.

158. *Slashing sick'ling.* Storm is a sick psychopath with a slicingly slick sickle.

165. *Worked many times before (many times since).* Many have argued that this phrase is an insertion put in later from the original cycle-texts, since at the end of the story

DOUGLAS M. LAURENT

Storm is placed in jail for an indeterminate amount of time. However, both Von Hauser and Hector Kyle agree that since this is a constantly shifting Netherworld of spiritual realities, and our own souls and minds we are studying this line may refer to our minds making solutions up before events actually occur. *I.e.*, some readers may think or perhaps more so desire Storm as already being free again to continue on her merry way. Is she free or isn't she at the end of the story? That is for us to decide. This is apropos for us on Midgard as well as for those in the Deadlands, revealing the connectedness of the soul and mind to past, present and future events as a right-at-the-*now*. This of course would reflect the idea that, as Hawkesford cites, once made, spirits, human or angelic, live on forever, and those who have a mature mind, see eternal ramifications in a nano-second of time and vice-versa. The remembrance of the past and the perceiving of present and future actions as a collective whole affect one's present behavior. Perhaps this can be best understood in Lady Macbeth's famous *future-instant* line. Upon learning of her husband's future rule as King at the poor, 'unfortunate demise' of good King Duncan, she says, "Thy letters have transported me beyond this ignorant present, and I feel now the future in the instant" (I. v.). Curiously, as a matter of choosing how to help hubby Mac 'pump metal' into the old coot and knocking him off, she methodically uses the *historical method of analysis* to take care of her 'little problem.'

By the study, cataloguing and assessment of the past, she sees where she is, and charts where she is going based on the principles of *prediction, redundancy, preparation* and *repetition*. She uses *prediction and redundancy* as well as *preparation* to line out her future actions and uses *repetition* to gnaw continually at Macbeth to do the job right and to keep cool and a straight face afterward. *Prediction* is to say in advance what one believes will happen or to foretell a future event, which she well known for. *Redundancy* implies excess, more than what is needed. Here, she is a real champ nagging her old man on knowing exactly what buttons to push. *Preparation*, well she does a lot of the masterminding, Macbeth being "too full *o'* the milk of human kindness" (I. v.) and is 'not insane' enough *via* ambition to do the trick. *Repetition* repeats acts, doing or saying something constantly. Habits of hers are based on past and present patterns that are predictable and reoccurring. At the end in Act V. i., when she goes totally bonkers, she numbingly falls into the repetition mode once again, always rubbing her once blood-stained hand, screaming "Out, damned spot! Out, I say!" She would be good working in detergent commercials.

171. *Asgard I'll gain.* Mycroft translates this as 'ill-gain.' Storm here refers to her future takeover of Asgard, as in her 'ill-begotten gains,' she nearly drooling at the prospect.

173-175. *The darklithe comer . . . her violets on that box.* Storm not only is dark and lithe, she is a 'darklight' as well. Also, there is a death motif running here. Kari's eyes are the color and temperature of cold steel-blue violet, she casting her sorrowful, dying, longing eyes on Theman's soul-box. Her last thought is that she wants to help him (allegedly). The color *violet* is metaphorical for flowers put on his coffin.

179. *Wide a'gape.* In the Greek language, *agápē* love is the highest form of love, it being self-sacrificial. At this point, Theman loses all semblance or aspiration to this so-called 'lofty' type of high and pure reality and turns into a regular 'aces and eights,' the very darkest of poker hands. This metaphor refers to the poker hand Wild Bill Hickok held when he was shot dead in Deadwood Dakota Territory on August 2, 1876 by the unlucky gambler Jack McCall who was promptly hanged. Sketchy tradition says Bill was playing five-card draw, his cards consisting of aces and eights of both black suits—ace of diamonds with a heel mark on it and ace of clubs plus two black eights of clubs and spades. This hand usually shows a player is likely 'dead' in the poker game. In short, Theman is *outta* luck. The letter 'A' in Greek is also a negation, and so 'no love' is meant here, plus the fact Theman's jaw gapes down wide open.

184. *The Mean metámorphed into a killing antagon'.* The Greek term *metámorphosis* is a "change of form." Essentially, Theman zagtwisflexzigs here, losing his humanity, giving in to his deeper primordial urges and gut animal (survival) instincts. He has despised people before, but now has realized the true meaning and nature of visceral soul-exploding hate. He loathes Kari as a person and as an icon for all she stands for. He can't stand her light. The term indicates quite a change in his spiritual dimension. In reverse fashion, it is like a Monarch butterfly turning back into a grubby little caterpillar. *Antagon'* is 'antagonist.' Theman has become Kari's *big* enemy.

188. *Admired its handiwork.* Even in the midst of lawlessness, Dark Storm admires the artistic beauty of Kari's sword.

DOUGLAS M. LAURENT

191. *Rend his spirit.* To hold Kari's weapon was too much for Theman. In a flash of insight, the symbolic implications of its use for good were too overpowering for him, tearing him up. As a general observance of humankind, ➤ what people do not understand they inevitably *must* destroy.

193. *Knew in his heart.* Theman's conscious self kept suppressing the fact of what he knew deep down inside–that he liked being evil and violent. Consequently, his spirit began to shred, slam-jamming him to the *left.* As a set of guidelines, the old school *readerought* concept suggests that readers ought to 'perform an autopsy' on the term *left* and on the *tao,* or "the *way* of the left-hand path" as it affects them deeply. In ancient Greece, 'the left' *aristerá* was a term used factitiously with *left-handed*–for poets who were supposed to be a little 'mad'—a gift from the gods. 'Left' also meant mischievous, insincere, awkward, unlucky, silly, clumsy, slow and 'stoopidest.' Later on it absorbed dark meanings such as *kerastēs* 'asp horned-serpent,' *skoloiplanēs*, 'darting aslant; crooked of serpents,' *kakódaimōn,* 'bad, having, tormented by evil genius,' Sanskrit *jihmá* 'oblique,' malicious, dubious, lying. Word studies go way back on leftism. Gk. *skaios* and Pie **skeh-i-uo,* 'shady' and 'shadowy' imply 'left,' on the 'left-hand/ left-side' and 'devil touched.' *Skaios* and **skeh-i-uo* also mean Latin *sinistra,* from where we get *sinister.* In all, **skeh-i-uo, skaios, sinistra* equals underhanded, shady, dubious 'left-handed' enterprises. Many 'left' wordings and phrases describe much in many cultures (*e.g.,* "out in left field"), and the personality traits of lefties are markedly different from the *dexterous* right-handed, from birth trouble to mental illness and genius. *Dexterous* implies being on the right side of anything, clever quick mental wit, crafty, moral cleanliness and being sharp with the hands among other things. "The way of the left-handed path," upon which Storm is launching Theman up without a paddle is not the *dexterous* right path *'way,'* she fully knowing and reveling in this. What a crumbnik.

198-199. *This ghastly life . . . Living forever, killing to survive 'rife.* Or 'strife.' Theman relishes the idea of living this hellish Mortuus Deadlands afterlife, he enjoying tapping into his baser instincts to kill in the 'zone,' which is *rife,* rampant, endemic with evildoers. Although he has only been there for a 'short while' (perhaps in a coma-induced dream instigated from the thunderbolt at the beginning of the story), maybe he thinks he can truly be a real hero now, feeling good about overcoming evil and strife. Little does he know the Deadlands wear one down over the eons of 'time' into their true essence, that is why in part our top sword-packing friends look the way they do and strive to keep it that way. Their exteriors only reveal their inner natures made manifest. Whether they look good to us or not we must decide. But knowing who, what and where they are, we all must eventually look into the (soul) mirror and evaluate what we have been taught to value and to what end (Ch. 2 note #'s 48; 112-113).

202-203. *'Roiled in his blood.* Theman is highly disturbed and agitated, in chaotic b'*roiling* disorder. *Rudd.* A reddish color of skin or hair. In Theman, an ancient string was being plucked. He is turning ghastly blood red from his blood-lusting actions over the prospect of killing Kari.

205. *Carnalities supreme.* Theman is drunk with the passions of his animal-flesh nature. He loves the power-tripping surges that he is feeling for the first time in *al extremo.* In old Greek, the term for 'carnality' or flesh indulgences is *sarx.* This term describes all the sensual indulgences one can imagine with the volume turned up to maximum. Victims of *sarx* attacks are given over to their bodily appetites and in the end are usually consumed by them in a spirit, mind and body feeding frenzy.

208. *Sluing he the blade.* Slew + swinging. Even swinging his weapon about in a dry run, Theman feels an intense evil aura dripping off of it, or rather, as Dr. Hastings contends, off his 'male' mind, she citing the masculine '*he*' twice in the line. In short, Theman is projecting his fried ego onto the blade s'killet, it becoming his twiskinked icon for his own blinding evil, enlarging his stunted maleness.

211. *Hellish deapths, clay to the iron condoned.* Depths + dead. This is being in the depths of spiritual deadness. *Condoned.* That is, 'okayed' or 'sanctioned.' Theman's baser 'clayish' nature, fused to the murderous iron, takes over, getting the 'go ahead' from his fevered brain.

214. *Aside from his greater nature he in-turned himself.* From the Greek word *entropy* we get 'in-turning,' or 'self-collapse' from within. The *second law of thermodynamics* says that everything in our universe is in a state of decay as available energy within

closed systems burn out (balls deflate, houses constantly need repair, we die, *etc.*). So now, we find Theman in a state of *entropy*, or 'self-collapse,' he 'in-turning' in on himself. The wording, *in-turned* also connotes the idea of him 'interring' or burying himself. Like us, he is his own *just desserts*. A *dessert* is the leftover plural of the older term *desert*, which means "that which one deserves." In its negative vein, it tells of 'comeuppance,' 'ironic/poetic justice,' or 'what goes around comes around.'

216. *In warped t'reason impassioned he murcie's swift flight.* Treason + reason. Theman betrays Kari with torqutwisting reasoning. *Murcie's.* Murder + mercy. This is *not* a true mercy killing. Theman is insane. In his blistered mind, he knows he is murdering teenage Kari, but he has somehow warpedly *rationalized* it out *as* an act of mercy *justifying* it. Rationalizing and justifying are two extremely common *defense mechanisms* that guard lop-sided egos every day lest they deflate and feel pain. These mechanisms are *deflections* or parries against intrusions into the psyche that are distasteful and not to a person's liking or demeanor. Parries are much sharper than blocking, as deflective parries allow punch-intrusions to slip by to set up counters. Blocks just attempt to bulk-stop inflow of whatever nature. And to block something means one is already a move down as they are forced to be in a position they did not want to be in the first place and now have to come back out of the hole their clumsy block made, all to the advantage of the opponent (*cf.* chess *zugzwang*). Block's are poor man boxing and karate. The lesson: the sharper the spirit, the sharper their defense mechanism skills of spirit, mind and body and there are a lot of them out there, that is, both sharp spirits with their machinating mechanisms.

219. ᘒnake!—*At least 'twere done quickly and set!* This garbled fragmented line is a leftover from *Macbeth* (I. vii.), "If it were done when 'tis done, then 'twere well it were done quickly." Here Mr. Mac is freaking over the idea of killing the good King Duncan, and apparently, this line from the play strained through Theman's brain as *it* is on its way to kill Kari. Perhaps the ego-maniacal pitch-dark star is relating to Macbeth somehow, groping for a feeling or a behavior pattern or some sort of justification or excuse to murder, like Duncan the Valkyrie who he now believes, thanks to Storm, stands in his way. Maybe he is so psychowarped that he identifies

with the throne-hungry Macbeth, reveling in the murderous Thane's predicament, feelings and ultimate solution to achieve greatness—and then he slips like Macbeth into madness taking on Mac's aura and power as a 'mask' to carry out his ruthless de-sires.

220-221. *Struck her once ⚡ thenn——nTw′iced MHORR⚡ ⚡ ⚡ The savage [with\in him] ≒ it—a′ distant star was now a′* ♭★rn*!!* This is an extremely difficult '*Hallan* passage to translate. J. Mycroft suggests this line is transcendent of the written words/symbols that are but sallow attempts to convey deeper occurring realities. Rather, he suggests the obviously hurried, intensely heated eyewitness scribbling points to an unspeakable act, and that a clearer understanding of the passage must occur in one's mind, not from the writing itself. He goes on to say that the intense iconic passage, although *chronologically* presented, in reality represents a '*Hallan* phenomenon which requires a shift of perception to understand. *I.e.*, the writing, no less, is actually *parenthetical*, overlapping, stacked like a bunch of pancakes describing a pressurized, jumbled collage of *simultaneous* visual and audio stimuli occurring on the *now*, that is, back then, and *now*, occurring in the mind of the reader. Hence, reader-witnesses to this act must decipher the passage for themselves, their own interior horrific interpretation of the atrocity being the echoey resonate 'correct one.' As is, the *vile* act is still very much '*alive*' and still reaching out, all its *evil* angery transforming into the reader's personal views as it carries itself along like waves.

In all, this spirderous action by Theman perpetrated upon sweet Kari is so intense and graphic that it begs description and is beyond the ability of the poem's original versificator to describe it with ordinary human script. For this reason, many translators use the 'black lightning bolt' icon affect in a futile attempt to capture the heinous power of the scene. In an anti-religious sense, as is Dracula and the Anti-Christ, like a man savagely possessed (*with\in*), Theman is now *a′ dis* ('evil, bad or dark') t*ant* or anti-*star* or *aster*. That is, Theman has now become a living *disaster*, a rising ill-crossed black ★ star. The *a′* also implies 'no or nothing,' and so, Theman is not actually born alive, but '*no* born,' or truly spiritually dead and ultimately impotent, his being at this point utterly meaningless. Yes, this is his baptism into darkness by the blackness of the negatively charged red bloodiness of it all. All this is metaphor of course so we can understand what is going on, after all Kari is a spirit.

The mathematical symbol ≒ means "approximately equal to or the image of," which says it all for the debauched Theman.

225-233. *Im personal twisted wroth . . . as one with these dead.* This is a problematic passage to translators as the line reads three ways. Mycroft cites that either the phrase-word *im personal* is a misspelling and can be read "in personal," meaning Theman is getting deeply involved 'in person.' Or it can be read, 'I'm personal, twisted wroth,' the line giving Theman a symbolic name (this is known as a *kenning*—an Old English/ Norse compound metaphorical expression, *e.g.*, *sword* = 'icicle of blood'), making him out to be a spiritual entity as in, 'I am personal wrath,' just like his Deadlands counterparts. Spirits are known to give themselves descriptive names of their interests and activities. If on the other hand the line is read 'impersonal,' it may also mean Theman is doing this action with no feeling whatsoever. Whatever the original writing was, overall, *personal wroth* appears to be a compound act. Theman knows he is doing the action and is very personally and angrily involved in it. At the same time however, he has rationalized and is *detached* from this violent act, yet another *defense mechanism* of his mind that shields him from the horror he is committing. By killing, he knows he is becoming like the other inmates of the Deadnether.

245. *I'll send you back↯!!!* Theman is such a waffle. After he kills Kari he instantly 'loves' her and attacks Storm because she is so rancid and had set him up. Storm is now going to lay waste to Theman by sending him back to dull ol' Midgard and his pointless, ineffective, cliché, bland, corny, zestless, spicelessly useless life with its meaninglessly chronic damning routines—in her eyes a fate for him worse than death! Does she know the score about people and the way things are around here or what?

252-253. *"What you could in eternity be . . . but from that First and Last I must keep from thee."* Storm doesn't want to spill the beans that there is a God, the First and Last of all truths of Truths. Why, idiot Theman just might turn himself over to The Enemy if she did that, thereby cheating her out of his eternal soul! She tears up, realizing a little bit of her lostness, future glory only to be 'wasted' on the annoying highly irksome stupid humans. To her they are like a constantly irritating stickher in her sock. One could scratch at them but couldn't never really ever get to them in the course of a day. Besides, nobody ever asked her if she wanted to tend specks of watered-down conscious atoms for eternity. Is she just being dramatic or is this the way it is?

275. *And that damnseled youth.* Damn + damsel + led. Kari is not exactly a 'damsel' or 'young woman.' She's a 'kid.' Not only that, she is one of the 'damned,' and is 'led' about by such inclinations. At least, this is what Angel in part thinks about her as.

278. *"You're back . . . I see you're healed."* It appears that Angel and Storm already had a duel and apparently, he faked a wound or his death, a standard technique of his, he letting her think she won (Ch. 24 note # 138-142).

281. *Solutions in motion . . . pace.* Storm tries to regain the rhythm of the situation to control it.

284-287. *Hair from her cheek . . . that little scar 's.teeled' w.ith a. k.iss?"* S.w.a.k. or "sealed with a kiss" is a popular term for an affectionate 'sweet nothing' kind word as when one signs a love letter. It seems that Angel and Storm have been in scraps before and he is the one who 'swhacked' Storm giving her the scar on her *cheek* with a sword cut above, or rather before 'the rest'—a 'term of *endearment*' of course. Full of brass, He is well-steeled and is being 'ironic,' metaphorically for now, making a word play on the popular expression, but soon, he will be real 'ironic' with her in more ways than one. She gets the point.

288. *Less than two feet apart.* The art of 'fast drawing' blades to kill in old Japan was known as *iai-jutsu*. During this era, whole schools were dedicated to this science. For an astounding cinematic example of this, *see* the end sequence of the movie *Sanjuro* (1962), by Kurosawa. The art of iai-dō, the spiritual path of sword-drawing, is still practiced in Japan today.

292. *The end? In blinding pain.* As Storm and Angel posture to duel, this question is rhetorical, a figure of speech that is asked to make a point, not to be necessarily answered. Rather it is to encourage readers to consider the message or

viewpoint. Whether Storm or Angel wins the fast-draw to see who is the fast-est blade in the Netherwest doesn't really matter, the outcome of the contest is obvious—*mega-pain*.

306. *Weak movement's make ones grave.* This phrase does not just refer to the basic hole in the ground, but making a *grave mistake* that makes one grave, solemn and somber, not to mention making these unsmiling grim types end up in the basic hole in the ground.

309. *Blindendingspeeatingsteeylizingfauxpass.* When it comes down to nanoseconds and millimeters, in their duel, Storm made two slight miscalculations. Apparently, one of her errors was in misjudging Angel's ability to control the *maai*, the "interval" or "engagement distance," the timing, space, distance, rhythm and angle between oppositions, which allows an exact spot to strike from. A matter of physics, in swordplay, the slower opposition's *maai* is closer than the faster opposition, which is farther. Here it seems that the *thēlyspneuma* was a tad slow. Controlling the *maai* allows one to preempt the opposition's move, which Peter Hsu and the scribbler think Angel did. Underrating Angel's phenomenal ability to 'maai-*shadow*' distance by being as close to the cutting line as possible, was the one major "false step," or *faux pas* Storm made. This term is used nowadays by us Midgarders for embarrass-ing social blunders. However, there are usually two sides of a story. In terms of *timing maai*, this phrase refers to mental lapses or gaps of conscious awareness or alertness (*suki-point*). TM also makes use of the *kyo-jitsu* "you caught me off guard" concept of the *emptiness-fullness* compound of *ki*, or *ch'i*. Mental gaps or drifting minds plus *kyo-jitsu* combine to form *kokoro-no-maai*, the "mental interval." This means that even though the physical distance between oppositions may be advanta-geously equal, the person who possesses a non-rambling mind-interval as opposed to the mental meanderer will have the decisive advantage. This was Dark's second biggy. For whatever reason, and no text known clarifies this, the *virago* hesitated, flinched, wavered, costing her the duel. Angel simply detected this resonance vibe within her, overrode her blazing technique and cut to the chase. The end.

311. *In curved arctic time.* In the Arctic, with the *aurora borealis* (ON *norðrljós*) "northern lights" surging lively around, one can see the curved shape of the upper atmosphere.

Coming off as billowing sheets of reds, blues, violets, oranges, yellows, magentas and greens, the Vikings and their associates thought of them as mighty Valkyries galloping into battle with their glistening armaments, a subtle portent and fitting to the point symbol for this arena 'duel of the champions sequence' where only one will rise to the occasion. For stoic Storm and Angel, after they draw, fleeting micro-seconds tick by, but it seems forever, they waiting to see if one or the other has been cut. For timeless creatures, it is a 'time of no time,' an eternal all-encompassing *now* with no past or future. The Midgard Arctic, in all its eternal unchanging timeless coldness is a metaphor to this.

322. *A fatal-led, volumous door.* Literally a 'fate-led' or 'fataled' door. In either case, Angel leading the way, slams shut this extremely heavy leaden door on Storm effec-tually sealing her fate by burying her, she now being a genuine *Alive Yet Dead* (if we can say that of these creatures) inmate of the much slower and lower vast frozen *cryo-nethergenic* regions of the Mortuus. There she will find many dieverse curiosities in which to occupy her mind and time. Like a dead hockey player, Storm has essentially and paradoxically been taken off the ice and put on ice in the Dead Games penalty box. For all intents, Theman is much better off than poor Storm is, as he still is a *Dead Yet Alive* 'living human soul' with enormous potential for power enhancement. Gk. *Cryogenic* "cold production, low temperature performance."

347-348. *Ghostly Dire Wolf . . . Wolf chasing his tail~s~p~i~nnnn~~ ↷!* A Dire Wolf (*Canis dirus*, "fearful, awful dog") is an extinct species of wolf much larger than the one today. Storm sends Theman back to the boring world of man by sicking the ferocious beast on him, causing him to literally "pass out" of Valhalla and enter into our own plane. The last thing Theman sees is the wolf chasing 'his tail,' he spinning into unconsciousness.

351. *The personal history.* .According to Dr. Jörgens, it is important to many in the Deadzone to keep a personal history, a journal of sorts of what they do. It gives these spirits a form of identity and reveals a hidden code of ethics. Those in the Nether are conscious of their actions in an eternal sense, and they are aware of making history personal *on the now* of action, bearing the full responsibilities of that action, as 'doing' is their main mode of identity and existence. Many hardened spirits however, do not

take responsibility for their actions. This however is double-edged. It is 'no-responsi-bility of responsibility'; all actions catch up with everybody, anywhere in a 'reap-sow/reaction-action' [negativ ∓ positiv] effect. By keeping a log and learning from the past, the smarter ones grow in knowledge and power as it is the curse of all in the Nether to grow ever-sharper in mind while at the same time fade and so forget.

356. *She lied in state, Medievaled statue on mar-bled grave.* Like those tombs from the Middle Ages that were ornately carved in marble showing the likeness of the person in one, Kari's corpse lies statue-like on the battle mar(s)-bled ground, ready for the grave.

362. *"A new trick of mine."* Kari imitates one of Angel's tricks, honoring him (Ch. 20 note # 48-49).

377. *"You're too honorable."* Angel decries Kari's high ethics, saying she is both too nice and *naïve*.

389. *Not a nick within.* Since swords in the Nether have the consistency of mind, the lack of nicks on Kari's blade reflects her brilliantly polished 'un-nicked' albeit greatly troubled paradoxical 'nicked' mind.

395-396. *Tenacious emergence icebound . . . a fiery percolhate.* Storm has been in prison before, but not necessarily this icy one. Temporarily stuck, she is so filled with anger and hate toward Kari and Angel that she percolates and boils, her sizzling inner strength already beginning to melt the hyper-nether-ice. Absolute zero (−459.67 degrees Fahrenheit) in our world seems like a lemonade *sippin'* lazy hot, humid August day compared to the cold here.

400. *A mercenaried tale of manipulation grand. Valley Damned* is a poem, but it is also an allegory, a metaphorical looking-glass study into our souls, of personal and spiritual relationships. As it is designed to be open-ended, it has many intertwining dimen-sions of meaning to be explored and realized, limited only by our own perceptions, insights, imaginations and values that the poem demands of its readers to expand. However, whether that expansion is positive or negative, well unlike Virgil, the

Poem, she no tells us. That is up for us to decide. Even so, study D. T. Suzuki's writings on *kufū* and how to get out of a blind alley, a real ass-saver. In its panoramic sense, the poemish tome is the observance of soulish conflict as the soul clashes with itself, other souls and the oft-questionable, very dubious, gnarled "Powers that be." In consummation, it is how we Midguardians—of the High Noon Redemption—confront such *excelsiōrēs* of life and work our problematic abstracts out.

403-406. "*Freebairn forever . . . Heaven's love I'll always stand.*" 'Freeborn.' After Kari outwits Storm and mops the floor with her, she is now once again free to do as she please, acknowledges the eternal solidity of Heaven's love and the fate it has written her that she can only grasp at since she is insubstantial and incorporeal, a shadow. Nonetheless, upon realizing this, it still is a good day for her and she cheerfully goes on to her next adventure.

408-410. *Prism'd her a new fated run . . . broken hues.* These images again reflect Kari's disturbed broken rhythm off-kilter askewed skewered nature and past records.

413. *Dissented to sea.* Dissent + descended. A metaphor; the great block of ice cracked off from the graveyard with its packed souls argues, objects, *dis*sents about going into the sea (deeper into Hell, or *Dis*), tenacious to hang on to the land before it melts into nothingness. This is a ponderously great and slow movement of further dissolving dissipation.

414. *Tiny pseudoviking funeral.* A real Viking funeral may consist of being burned on a funeral bon(e)-pyre, buried, or put adrift in a ship set afire with a dead dog at one's feet with precious items and iron weapons for the next world. Storm gets none of this. Her 'funeral' is chintzy, *tiny*, false and cold. It is poetic come around/ goes around ironic justice. A dark vortex of an all-consummate actress, she either absorbed others or destroyed them. She never gave true love or respect to anyone other than her own misshapen warpwisted narcisōriumistic self—except to play them for fools and plyiar those to get what she wanted—hence never was true love returned upon her, although some did try, but those are other stories. What do you expect? Don't be that way.

THIRTY-FOUR: SOUL TO KEEP

Mark, Theman awoke to florescent dullgloom,
On his king-size satin bed in a plush Bel Air room.
His Agent, dressed sharp, past the worry shook his arm,
His property would not lose value; would do him no harm.

"What happened?" asked the man.   5
"Lightning zapped you, as you ran."
"Don't remember anything, I didn't see."
"That's okay, Mark, it was tremendous publicity."

The Agent then picked his nails, told him to rest assured,
There was business to be had, engagements to be procured.   10
He would be stupendous now, colossal, bigger than ever before,
Billed as "The man who returned from the grave to give his fans his all."

"Jack," the man voiced, wringing his Agent's wrist,
"A dream I had, it was tremendous—blhiss."
"'Bout what?" Jack irked, as he unpealed the grip,   15
He humored his charge, and pressed a finger to his lip.

"Something, about a valley, and a lot of fear.
Seemed like a million miles away, but, somehow, very near."

"Interesting. Okay. Right now, we need a lotta bucks, though.
A standard contract, you play a killer. We'll make lotsa dough." 20

"Fear, you know? And emptiness, it gives me the shakes⌇⤳"
". . . Great story, you're perfect for it, we call it *My Soul to Take*."

"—⌇*What!* ***?!*** ⌇" reMarked Theman.

430

"Another action flick—*you know* the type—
(You play a French ballet-karate master   25
Who to the tune of "The Nutcracker,"
Avenges himself against midget cowboy
Ninjas with Ginsu® knives)—all hype for taking your lover's life.
But don't worry. We'll talk later," Jack soothingly said,
"When things are better, you know, in your head?   30
Right now, though, there's *this* contract to renew,
Sorry to be pushy, but it's me, against them, and you."

"I don't know, Jack,
The dream, *the snow*—"
"*Riggghhht*, but first, sign *thiss*."   35
"Sign what? My memory has slipped."
"The contract, you'll be an idol to millions by far."
The Agent frowned at him, a dark urge behind the sharp.
"—What did you say?"

"This contract, c'mon. It's getting late. Your fans are around the block.   40
Time is money you know, our lives governed by the clock."

Mark looked slow at his Agent's old face,
A friend not there, rather, tints of impatient malignant grace.
Felt his spirit pressed by negative coiling rising air,
Jack put his hand on the man's shoulder—   45
To give some comfort and pat, "there, there."

"If I sign this, my greatness will be assured?"
The words stung in his mouth, but they addictedly allured.
"Guaranteed," the Agent smiled, "it will make you a god,
The fools will pack to see you, if you do a killing job."   50

The man thought it over for a minute or two or less,
Sloughed his worries off, saying, *ehh*, "a dream at best."

Greed now kindled in his heart, made him *egoed* once more,
Grasping tyrant of a man suppressed all his dark whorror.

"Sorry, Jack, for a moment there I was worried I have to confess,   55
'Tis the eye of childhood that fears a painted devil,'" and
(**Cough*) had the laugh less.

The Agent chuckled, *knew* his star's temperament,
The shock had tolled him, but pressed the detriment.
Very quickly opened he *the* contract which he sought,   60
For the man to sign it—more prestige to be bought.

The man looked it over, ran it up and down,
Liked the details, made him more so a man of renown.
The man then glanced over, "what's all that stuff?"
"Belongings from your office, I had them brought up."   65
Jack unfolded a chair with the man's name plastered thereon,
A deep-seated gleam in the man's eye told of something going on.

His name on *that* chair, the man stared for longest time,
The Agent noticed and smiled, looking at the print so fine.
"Like I said, I had some of your personal stuff sent over,   70
Give you get up and go, therapy, to help you recover."

The man in bed then heard his heart beat,
A damned rhythm that made his heart leap.
His impulse maddened with *that* 'namned chair,
Bar glasses reflected it, his memory, layed bared.   75

"You have no choice, you gotta sign,
Your career's at stake, if you lose it now you'll never shine."

The man's eyes met with the Agent's hard stare,
("If you don't want to sign, there are others to take your share")

The Mean welled up, his Agent to later, take care. 80
Eyes once more tell of a deeper contract yet set,
The Mean and Agent, contenders in the immortal quest.

"What's the matter?" asked the Agent man with cool,
"Nothing. I have a little work to do—
A friend to see before I fix my scheduel." 85

"Yeah? A *lotta* work. You'll fly Northwest."
"Perhaps," said Theman, "and I'll see you there at the last."

Jack then smiled slow and in deliberate, airing care,
Took out *that* pen, and handed it to Mark with stylized flair.
The man long stared at his fateful, authoritative grip, 90
Eternal action compounded at the small of a fingertip.

"You'll be finished, you know, if you don't down your name,
I won't represent you," he grin-winked, "you'll never play the game."
The Mean now trapped deep within his underlying fit,
Knew his greed had snared him, unto *that* bottomless pit. 95

Length en⇀ end pause, greed coursing through veins,
Overcame himself, his greater nature defamed.
Power was his to control, and his alone to command,
A prince of this world; his loving millions demand.

The man, quiet twhyisterical, fidget and willed to consign, 100
That delirious recipe to be human dead: *a'One* immortalized.
Freedom beckoned, he realized enemies were all about,
Yet he himself had sprung the trap ~~~~
And *that* bastard Angel had shown him a way of getting out.

"*Kari——*" 105
"What??"

Then sneered the man at *that* tiny, insignificant chair,
Thought of himself in this world of deadly noncare.
Stalled he once to harden and to look at inky ebony pen—
But fear and reality met, in his haunted, shaking hand.   110
Cried to sign and not to sign, his Agent *cooing* on,
Gently put his pen to the paper, the writing thus begun.
Wretching, grasping, twistorting heart, greed murdering fear,
The compulsed one had set his standard, his soul becoming sheared.

—And so—by his own hand—by his *own* relentless hand—   115
There was nothing left for him—except *the Valley of the Damned*.

Chapter Thirty-Four Valley Footnotes

Having been chastised by Valhalla, Theman, 'the man,' is quick to forget his raging fever-driven lessons and begins to lose himself to his old, worldly nature and dull, 'no need to inquire' thought routines. However, the effects of the Deadlands have impressed themselves so much upon him that he is or rather wants to be 'insane,' so that he might have the 'right tools' to re-participate in the vibrant Nethereal he has just left. In fact, he finds that 'dead' reality, based on ancient warrior ethics, which places great emphasis on the concept that any action may be one's last full and final action, is much more conducive to his tastes. It puts a lively step into every action of his, he never having felt this way before. He realizes now even the slightest of actions, or non-actions, when added up can eventually spell doom. As the old child's rhyme runs, "For want of a nail the kingdom was lost," everything coming crashing down. Fans of Sherlock Holmes will appreciate what he says as it ties into this. In *A Study in Scarlet* he remarks, "To a great mind, nothing is little" and in *A Case of Identity*, he pipes, "The little things are infinitely the most important." These are truisms of life. Like an inverted triangle or a spinning toy top, their larger parts precariously balance and whirl above their smallest points that support them.

This view of rendering decisive action allows its adherents not to waste precious resources and time, but to live daily life fully (albeit here in a dead state) every waking moment. As in Earth-Zen and many other beliefs, to 'be dead' to the world is to be free from its elusive illusory attachments that magnetically draw rusted away souls to them. The 'dead' Deadlands mindset, paradoxically speaking, is much more 'alive' and attractive than Theman's generically modern, routine-ridden, dull-minded present one. As he is involved in filmmaking, perhaps Theman is reminded of what Dracula (Bela Lugosi), said in the 1931 *Universal* film, "To die, to be really dead, that must be glorious!"

1. *Mark, Theman.* This is 'the man's' full, real name. For the disturbed, sloe, sooty, knurly serpentine "Powers that be" though, his name literally means, "mark the man" out, 'The Mean' being a big now and forevermore target for their *de-mand*-ing lusts and their *nth*-degree burning *de-mented* 'throttle-icing' true heart 'loves.' *Throttle icing* is a description for ice that forms in an engine due to the cooling effect of expansion in a carburetor. Here it is a metaphoric depict of wackos in wanderlust,

they 'love' the idea of putting ego-rat Theman 'on ice' by sucking and shriveling his soul dry by throttling him—"just because," and just because that is all they have left. They want his shrunken head and soul as their personal prize they can put on their mantles or barter with for maybe something better on a rainy day.

13. *"Jack," the man.* This is Theman's red-haired Agent. *Jack* is slang for the 'Devil,' or 'Red Jack,' implying a 'Jack the Ripper'-like attitude. Theman's Agent is relentless and corrupt.

17. *"Valley, and a lot of fear."* This line is a fragment taken from verse four of *Psalm* 23, "Yea, though I walk through the valley of the shadow of death, I will fear no evil: for thou *art* with me; thy rod and thy staff they comfort me." The implication is that Theman has not exactly tasted real death but has only skirt its shadow in the Mortuuslands. This means he does not really know what in hell he is talking about, although the entire shadow skirting near death experience has scared the *bejesus* out of him. The event has ingrained itself so deep into his warped-torqued-fretted psyche that he is both fearful and desirous to return to the dead. At the same time, he has learned to 'love' (just like the frozen spirits do), to participate in what he hates, fears and attracts him the most—the deepest kinktwistering malformed hell-bent blackness that is his own debauched eternal soul. Yes, his putrefied soul—the much worn, tooth grinding Hell-Mouth soul carrion chawing entrance to the hellish Land of the Dead, which in the final analysis, is his own horrible self! There he will abide forever just as the other terminal inmates do—trapped within an chewy eternity of their own dead selves. Waffly Theman 'wants very badly,' *somewhat*, to enter into Hell-Mouth's soul-smacking chops although he is afraid to—even whilst he has one foot in the grave already and the other on the proverbial banana peel, although he doesn't know it. *Bejesus.* This is a mild Irish oath displaying anger, fear, dismay, *etc.* It originates from the early 1900s, and is a weathered version of the phrase, "oath by Jesus." (*See* Ch. 16 note # 44 for more Hell-Mouth mania.)

23. "—⌇*What!* ?!⌇" *reMarked Theman.* Theman's old greedy nature is arousing again. However, it is now open season on Theman as he is once again on Midgard a

'marked man' with a price and a great big bull's-eye on his head for any wannabe, Johnny-come-lately or low-life spirit to scope and take him out.

24. *"Another action flick—you know the type—"* This translation borrows from and parodies the pop-American martial art film genre with all its brainless fluff and the mindset of continually feeding the movie 'machine' as it churns out grade 'B' garbage. Theman's Agent wants him to 'star' in another cheesy 'kung fu killer karate' cliché-ridden Saturday matinee low budget movie to make dough. If readers look at translated kung-fu and karate movie titles on line, they will get a laugh at the translations, *e.g.*, 'The eighteen bronze toes of terror,' and other similar amusing nonsense.

32. *"It's me, against them, and you."* At first, it sounds like the Agent is with Theman all the way down the wire, but if we read the passage carefully we find that the Agent is out for himself.

38. *A dark urge behind the sharp.* Theman is beginning to suspect that there is something going on with his Agent, more than meets the eye. Something is up as his Agent's demeanor and body language are sending out the wrong signals and vibes he is now starting to see. Theman feels as though there is some *veiled* hidden agenda, his cryptic Agent having ulterior motives. Theman's guts tell him so.

41. *Governed by the clock.* *See* Chapter 2, in which little motions, like that of a ticking atomic clock, build upon each other and set a person's eternity and larger destiny in motion. The Agent is sending cross signals. Theman is definitely noticing that there is upstanding wrongness going on here.

51. *Minute or two or less, Sloughed his worries off.* In light of the notes above, it does not take long for Theman to blow off his valid suspicions and re-greed his mental shop, "slip sliding away," back to his old weasely ways. What was he thinking, he wonders. *Sloughed his worries off.* Like a snake that sheds its dead skin, Theman is 'sloughing off' his worries. To *slough* is to "shed or drop off dead tissue from living flesh." In a reverse sort of fashion, Theman is dropping off his living flesh replacing it with 'dead' tissue, so he can go back to the Mortuuslands. Here's a winner for you.

53-54. *Egoed once more . . . man suppressed.* Modernism with modern words and perceptions begin to clog and appeal to Theman's worldly selfish 'Me'—centered *id* part of his *egoo-ey* allegedly 'sophisticated' mind, showing how easy brainwashing is. His thoughts have been subtly worked over in the corner and he is now controllable by labelism. Unwittingly, he has been quietly but brutally made 'thought punch-drunk' through subliminal, relentless repetitious staccato-like conditioning that has pounded sensory overload into his skull—just like those cheap eleven o'clock at night commercials *as seen on TV* do! What this means is that he *auto-responds* to labels and icons in ways as accorded to the whims of his unseen overlords, and *auto-elims* ('automatic elimination'), dismisses anything or anyone that keeps him from choosing to act in accordance to their premeditated designed labels or icons. Like found in a can of tuna, labeling things makes for superficial, easily manipulated, separable 'chunked-apart canned thought' and greased up 'mental spam,' the products of mass consumerism and propaganda; a main bane of modern existence.

56. "*'Tis the eye.*" From *Macbeth* (II. ii.). After evilly murdering good King Duncan with some daggers, Mac is afraid to go and put back the dagger's by the King's doped up bodyguards because his psycho wife and he intend to pin the crime on them so they take the fall. Seeing her hubby hesitate, Lady Macbeth reprimands him with the famous line, "The sleeping and the dead are but as pictures. 'Tis the eye of childhood that fears a painted devil." In context, this passage tells us that Theman is thinking his fears and dreams are just childish baloney—supposedly. *See* the Orson Welles version of *Macbeth.* The stylized sets are way out there as is the camera work and choreography and the acting is excellent. Welles, a definite genius, had his own ground breaking innovative stylistic vision he brought to the screen, and it shows in this masterpiece (*Republic Pictures*, 1948).

57. *And (*Cough) had the laugh less.* Not that Theman had 'the last laugh' as in a final sense. Rather, Theman is blowing off his worldly fears and those concerning his 'pal' the Agent as well as reflecting on his more than *bizarre-o* experience in the Deadlands. But his timely dramatic cough shows he still wonders and worries about them in a sobering fashion. In actuality he is thus 'laughing less,' that is, he's really not laughing about anything at all. Seeing Theman relax his Agent chuckles 'darkglee' about the matter because he knows Theman is a greedy, parasitical wretch, but his chortle is suggestive of hidden undertones to his actions, as if Theman deep down inside was in the final analysis, a tried and true-blue sucker *sophista-hick*. Agent Jack knows Theman is a *springle*. Instead of spiraling upward and onward to greater heights, *springles*, similar in kind to spirals, are wound up pieces of wiry steel that expand outward from an up-tight center point, as they grow larger, like Theman's ego. *Springle* also means a person who thinks they are overwhelmingly self-important but in actuality, they are a complete and utter low life. If that were not enough, springles are traps to catch small animals, using a spring door. Obviously, AJ knows his quarry all too well and enjoys Theman's little 'predicament' of self-entrapment, his own weasely, piggish, rat-like, snake-ish, worm-ridden bloated lopsided ego springing his own self-made trap.

59. *The shock had tolled.* Toll + told. The dark Valhallan vision, the Agent knows, has rung a warning bell with Theman, and the Agent knows Theman knows the truth, revealing the Agent's darker truer nature. Theman however, is still hard-boiled and greedy, his wretched ways overdrives all his survival instincts.

66. *Jack unfolded a chair.* This is a director's chair with Theman's name on it. Seeing it begins to stir many things in Theman's mind and the Agent seeing a certain look in his eye, is now a little bit more than concerned, and continues to soften and deflect Theman's growing awareness.

71. *"Therapy, to help you recover."* Jonathan Mycroft suggests that the subliminal micro-phrase 'the rape-ee' is the best translation here for the term *therapy* and implies one who is *ravished* ('seized, snatched, violated, molested, abducted') emotionally and spiritually by the cold, unfeeling spiritually sterile soul-ghoul practitioners of the psychiatric trade. Theman has been 'raped' as it were, by the callous, searing movie industry leaving only a partial leftover greedy shell of a shallow man. Agent Jack knows Theman's condition all too well and exploits it for his own gain. As a side bar, because of his trained hard biz background, his inner rotten core and the fact that everybody has used and twist-tied him like a baggy, sealing in his ill-fated *vile* juices, Theman just might qualify as the poster child for

the seven classical deadly sins. It was from these negative virtues, that the spoiled preemie movie star was force-fed to 'nurture' upon, the bitter and *soulicide* caustic murderous mother's milk being filtered through the dead besmirched souls of others to him. This malignant freshly squeezed rancorous gall deprived, shriveled and at the last, *star*ved his spirit out. The seven deadly classical sins in the West were envy, gluttony, greed, lust, pride, sloth and wrath. Like a black and evil *springle-slinky* all wound up, each of these terms would require a word study to know and understand the true sprung out nature of Theman, the *micro-diabolus in pseudomārtiālis ars* ("small devil in false *martial arts").

> ✌ *Latin, Mārtiālis: "of or belonging to Mars." ➤ Questions for the martial ori-
> ented and life-strategy readers: are you *of* or do you *belong* to god Mars as a
> devotee practitioner of his ways, or are serving him as a public servant or in a
> priestly capacity or as though you belong to his legions? Do you feed his eternally
> famished saber-rattling unsleeping war machine, or does it snack on you at high
> midnight? Like Cicero, you should well know that "endless money forms the sin-
> ews of war." Muse upon these, for the potentate of negative war is still quite alive
> and active on this planet, he being a grand prince among the legions of Satan. His
> arts, enshrouded in a beautifully dark, seductive, 'ornate and orderly arrange-
> ment,' a *cosmos*, advocate and promise 'freedom of soul and spirit'—but do they?
> Or is this mere propaganda spin-off from his war office enveloped in pleasant
> sounding and inspiring philosophies and colorful myths upon which to *draw* us in
> as He and his cohorts take a bead on us? (Ch. 18 note # 166 on the Five Ways of
> Attack by Bruce Lee. Also, *cf.* 1Tim. 4.1; 2Tim. 4.1-4 for demons and myths.)

74. *That 'namned chair.* Damn + name. The chair is really piquing Theman. It reminds him of his pre-destined chair at the great Valhallan Hall the night of the 'great raid' battle by the evil baddies and ultimate fate in the very treachernetherous Deadlands (Ch. 7 note # 108).

75. *Bar glasses reflected it.* Now Theman remembers Dark Storm at the end of the mead bar where she saw reflected in her convex glassy cup her gang coming in to try to kill her and him. It was then that she decimated her worthless crew in order

to protect him from these wrongdoing evil spirits and make a deal with him (Ch. 25 note # 21-22). She could have killed him right then and there too, and collected his 'soul reward,' but she had other far-ranging plans for the runted movie star he realizes, boiled down into the saying, "being fattened up for the kill."

81. *A deeper contract yet set.* A contest of wills now is going on over a much deeper matter than a mere movie contract. The Agent, like himself Theman suspects, is a contender for power in the Deadzone and in Midgard, Earth; the plane *die men*sion where he now is (Agent wants to kill Theman, the pathetic mortal). As such, Theman now *knows* that his Agent is a wicked spirit, trying to get him to sign an eternal contract. However, Theman is double-minded. He cross-*s*words Agent but does not really fight him, having crossed purposes within his own wedging fried ego psyche, he rather fighting himself more so to make the eternal choice as we all must eventually do, this weakening him. A momentous approach-avoidance struggle ensues, and waffly Theman inwardly screams at Agent Jack to "Leggo My Eggo," something that the feeding ancient spirit will never do, knowing just what gears to grind, terrifying the young nether neophyte and paralyzing his good side, that is, what little he has in him, preventing the triple-crossed star from acting. Records from the historical fragmentary eleventh century *Valhallan* cycles and the sixth century *Upsalan* translations bear out that The Agent's identity is revealed in his name, which is a shortened version of 'Aged Entity.'

85. *"A friend to see before I fix my scheduel."* Theman is speaking about swordslinger Angel, who had both saved his life and had used him. He has mixed feelings about him as Theman realizes Angel provided 'a way out' of his soulish swan diving enterprise in the Dead by allegedly 'ripping off' his spirit. But to Theman '*a*-way out' does not necessarily mean a way of escape. He interprets Angel's efforts as part of a long-range scheming plan with many bizarre wacko twistorteds to it. He leans more toward the bitter than the sweet about the slingsworder, and is irked at the sly entity and craves like a heroin junkie to wipe the smirk-eating grin that he always had off his face. Thus, Theman wants to get back at him and '*exact* a revenging' *duel of wits* with him for his soul, one that is 'planned, methodical, scrupulous, demanding and severe.' It is either that or be at the mercy of the cool manipulative *bladerado* for a very long time. (*See* Ch. 19 note # 80 as to what Theman might be grasping a bit.)

86-87. *"You'll fly Northwest."* On the surface, this passage seems to be speaking of *Northwest* Airlines, but more so, speaks of the North, a reference to the land of the spirits and the West, the Land of the Dead as a lot of myths say. 87. *"I'll see you there at the last."* Seems that Theman is beginning to think he might have a run-in with the Entity Agent one day and have to kill him. All the stops are being pulled now.

90-91. *Stared at his fateful, authorative grip . . . of a fingertip.* Once again, the motif of the small leading to the big comes up. Combined accumulated small actions begin to bear weight and momentum leading to very big dramatic occurrences. A very large action when examined is composed of thousands of tiny actions. Consider football. Each team makes dozens of mistakes on the field some of which are caught by the referees, but underneath, there are thousands of movements—twists of feet, breathing, eye visuals, proper technical execution, *etc.*, that go into the making of a play. Despite all the errors made, one team wins—the team that made the least errors.

100-101. *The man, quiet twhyisterical, fidget . . . That delirious recipe.* Outwardly quiet, on the inside Theman is 'hysterical and twist bending' bad. Terrified over yet irresistibly, irrevocably and inexorably drawn to his overwhelmingly lusty screaming wants, like a hapless steely marble to the formidable and imposing *Magnetar* (magnetic neutron star Soft Gamma Repeater 1806-20, the most powerful known magnetic object in the universe), Theman is in a 'delicious delirium.' He is wild over the prospect of being a forever hunting dead (yet alive) human immortal fulfilling what he calls his truer *Apocalypse Now* "Colonel Kurtz" nature. *Fidget*, literally "id-get." Theman's mega "I want it now" cooks in one minute instant-oatmeal gratification part of his bloated gray-matter steamy hissing psyche is inwardly squealing to sign his soul away and pack it off to the Deadlands where it can run eternally and shamelessly free.

107. *Tiny, insignificant chair.* The chair reminds Theman of much and seems to focus his mind and intents expressed in his sneer, his sneer a sign that he is gathering himself up a bit. He despises our illusory fleeting world with all its fluff, nonsense and relatively comfortable, but powerless and according to him, purposeless, impotent

and inert life. He now realizes that the Deadlands is an exacting place to be to sharpen one's self. In that Nether-reality, he could be a 'real somebody,' a 'real' hero, not a shadow-slave to hollow film characters or mere celluloid images with 'lives' of their own. He grasps that his spirit-character on Earth would endlessly perform inane empty deeds trapped in a two dimensional reality forever, that is, living 'its' life out through his films, they being the final ugly remains of Theman himself—both on the screen and in real life. He has seen old movie clips of actors of long ago, these being grainy, ripped and splotchy and so forth. He concludes this is all he would end up being as well—an image of 'what once was,' a faded footnote on some backwater library's smudgy card catalogue, long having been consigned to the dust bin of history where he would be there 'now a no more' that never really 'was' in the first place. This riveting, dead-bolting thought sends chills down his spine—as it should everybody's.

110. *But fear and reality met.* Theman wants to go back to the Deadlands but is terrified over its eternal prospects, yet his base nature, greed and the remote possibility of regaining his soul, if only for the wrong reasons, overpowers him. He is quite willing, deep down inside to 'sign on the dotted line,' as they say and where his pal 'the Agent,' awaits him. Awash with *vileness*, to Theman, deciding to sign up for Hell is a killer desire both horrifying and alluring in its own overloaded imbalanced tumbled dry spinning state (much like a beat up old gym shoe whumping the inside of a dryer when it is being dried at night).

113. *Wretching, grasping.* This line is a borrowing from *A Christmas Carol*, Stave 1 in which Dickens describes Scrooge: "Oh! But he was a tight-fisted hand at the grindstone, Scrooge! a squeezing, wrenching, grasping, scraping, clutching, covetous, old sinner!" This is an apt illustration of Theman's true heart of darkness.

THIRTY-FIVE: THE RECKONING OF ANGEL

Wind howled, snow swhirrled and Angel sat on horse,
Seemed to eye the man and his deliberate wayward course.
Smirked he once, then wheeled high his spinning icy mount,
Would keep the prize, he thought, and the man's strength, to count.

(But that sweet Kari of the plain,   5
Ohh how she had outwitted them all at *the* most dangerous of games:
Had played before, arriving early to empty the mean-spirited box,
Had taken the man's soul; the swordpackin' slinger had it not).

Sang she the song to him from distant way,
Angel could not hear–though he heard his name.   10
Saw her raise she his sword to Heaven's high edge,
Rendering a judgment now for this rhyme's end.

He realized then that Kari foxedly had snatched *the* prize,
With her child's face she had deceived even his own hardened eyes!!
He started after, chuckled, then, *heh*, set back in place,   15
Admiring the offspring of that bloody Valkyrian race.

As she left the cold arena Angel had to laugh,
Beaten by that of a wisp girl and her subliming cunning craft.
—Jove lay silent in his orbit; brooding, deep, dreamless forweep,
And faithful dog Sirius rising tracked behind on dusk's purpling adeep.   20
Scratched he his chin; counted the cold and early evening stars,
He had miles to go that night, they being so very far.

444

VALLEY OF THE DAMNED

Only the music of the wint'ring span,
Vanished he away in the shimmering land. . . . . . .

Chapter Thirty-Five Valley Footnotes

As Angel 'stole' Theman's spirit, he knows that if the movie star had any guts at all, he would come back down and get it, giving him the 'option' of a Deadlands Valhallan redemption. As he peers through time and space, Angel realizes Theman's decision to come back to Valhalla will probably be for the worse, and relishes thoughts of upcoming events. Finally, Angel is shamed, in a charming way, by the fact that he was 'out done,' losing out to the plain wispy teenage St. Kari, whom he had earlier chided for being too *naïve*. To him, like Kari, the game of testing one's skill must go on continually. As he ponders events, Kari disappears into the snowy wastes. As for Dark Storm, she is but for a brief moment, in Mortuuslands time, literally "put on ice."

6-7. *The most dangerous of games . . . the mean-spirited box.* Whether in the Nether or on Midgard, stealing souls through whatever agency or method is for celestial, earth-bound or hellish spirits the most dangerous—and profitable of all games. Why? Plain and simple, vacuuming up souls is power acquisition in one form or another. *Mean-spirited.* 'The Mean' is Theman, but his soul-box, which carries his essence, is also *mean-spirited.* 'It' hums throbs and drips electro-negative electrons, just like a pitch-black, deepest dyed wet ebony raven upon the stroke of midnight in a cold autumn downpour. It emanhates cruel, spiteful, caustic, selfish, hurtful, unfeeling, slanderous, malicious, cold-base impulses, unto itself being a conscious lover of oth-er's failures, a killer of joys, a malcontent finder of faults, a sporter of spoils and last but not least, an all-around party-pooper. That is pretty damn dark folks. In sum, Theman, the *micropsychus cockalorum* is a "narrow-minded, petty, self-important little man" who is grossly top-heavy from believing himself to be of great importance. Delusion cries the loudest.

19-20. *Jove lay silent . . . dreamless forweep . . . faithful dog Sirius.* Jove (Lat., *Iovis*) or 'Jupiter' (*Iuppiter*) is the ancient Roman king of the gods and the god of the sky and thunder. It is also the obvious planet, while *Sirius* (Lat., *Sīrius*, Gk., *Seirios* "glow-ing," "scorcher") the "dog-star" (Gk., *astéri skylión*) is found in the constellation *Canis Major*, or 'Great Dog,' following the famous hunter Oríon in the evening sky.

VALLEY OF THE DAMNED

As Jupiter reflects the light of the sun and is farther out from us, and at the same time one can see the sun setting, one begins to appreciate the immensity of its silent heavy powerful brooding orbit. *Dreamless forweep. Forweep* is 'to weep much.' This word implies that those who observe such occurrences in nature might feel sad, or weep over the passage of time as seen in the slow and ponderous movements of the planets in the heavens above. These herald in different seasons, attitudes and whatnot, and perhaps through them one might feel they are getting older with each tick of the clock. Sometimes however, such realizations are very sense-evoking, poignant, comforting and restful, as when in our "deep and dreamless sleep the silent stars go by." Angel appreciates this quiet time of day, the constellations; the cosmic 'artwork' of it all and mulls on it. In the autumn/winter at twilight in the Midwestern USA, the sky-prism displays, the sun sets mellow-yellow, the firmament turns lavender then indigo, and the planets shine, and soon Oríon, the great hunter comes out followed by the *faithful dog Sirius.*

On dusk's purpling adeep. The meaning of the text is simple yet profound. It stands for *twilight*—the time-point fulcrum for the shifting balance between the differing arrangements of our two perceptions of what is night and what is day and all what these visual, mental and cultural percepts contain. The hazing purpleness or lavendering of the twilight opens doors for day and night animals to switch out and where things unnatural creep in and things creep out of their existent ordered planes as seen in *Disney's Night on Bald Mountain (Fantasia,* 1940). At this momentous block of time, which is but a transcendent poetic fleeting moment, the heaven above begins to reveal her awesome majesty, beauty and power. "'The twilight is the crack between the worlds,' don Juan said. 'It is the door to the unknown'" (p. 294). According to anthro-author Carlos Castaneda (1925-1998), "the crack between the worlds was more than a metaphor. It was rather the capacity to change levels of attention" (p. 279). Deeper, to shaman Yaqui-warrior Don Juan's way of thought, entering "the crack" meant the epic epiphanic realization of love. "Thus the mood of the warrior who enters into the unknown is not one of sadness; on the contrary, he's joyful because he feels humbled by his great fortune, confident that his spirit is impeccable, and above all, fully aware of his efficiency. A warrior's joyfulness comes from having accepted his fate, and from having truthfully assessed what lies before him" (p. 289). In context, the long dead *packin'* cold *swordolero* hitAngel is at peace with himself, his surroundings, recent events and his appointment in eternity, and in his own way, loves and cares for Kari.

21. *Scratched he his chin.* As in the movie *Sanjuro* (1962) by Kurosawa, the alienated samurai's use of this action acts as a genre 'snub' against the wearisome proprieties of samurai etiquettes, decorum and primping. Chin scratching is an action that suits Angel well.

22. *Miles to go.* This is a borrowing from the poem, *Stopping by Woods on a Snowy Evening* (1923) by Robert Frost (1874-1963). In the poem, the phrase, "And miles to go before I sleep," is a metaphor to dying. In Angel's circumstance, he is tired today and wishes to rest, if a spirit can really do that.

EPILOGUE

Now, dear reader, please embrace,
Those four elements within–and their place.
Of water, wood, fire and ground,
And yet *there* is a fifth portion that needs be found.
Thou be that 5ifth, *that* divined spirit~wind,   5
Who delivers sound rulings to all that is therein.
"Spirit cannot be killed, that's what the harbingers say—
Only filled or spilled, and that alone on your appointed day."
For those who hearken, one's mirror is the key,
To ensnare thine essence, or to make it go free.   10
(Yea, Kari, Storm and Angel–they're all awaiting thee—
For now we see through a glass, darkly—
But then as yet what we may be).

DOUGLAS M. LAURENT

Epilogue Valley Footnotes

According to ancient perceptions, the four elements of the play's cosmology—the four main characters of the poem—are missing one more element, and must have it in order for the poem to come to life. *We* are the final element—spirits, who make the poem work, according to our own interpretations. Two motifs serve here, the *tabula rasa* (Lat., "scraped tablet"), and the *rorrim*. The idea of the *tabula rasa* is very important. From the old ways, masters considered a student's mind to be a 'blank slate,' where there was a marked absence of preconceived determinations and goals. It was up to the masters to etch indelibly onto these precious mind-slates their teachings and life lessons that would make a deep impression upon them making for a lasting positive life-enhancing effect, passing brilliance on down the line. Thus by now, being the sensitive soul sifting searching tutor that she is, the poem has impressed and etched her profound teachings of the astonishing ways, mores and means, the spirit and soul of the netherpoem—of herself, deeply into our psyche-slates so that we may learn her lessons well and traverse the Field of Mars, of life, victoriously.

As for the poem *rorrim/mirror*, we are to peer into it passionately, profoundly, decidedly, gravely and with great fear and trembling, plumb it to its very soulish depths. In this, we *tabulae rasae* gather into our own souls those lessons, those reflected images, those etched impressions that we alone individually and inwardly must perceive, accept or reject, as any honorable poem is fashioned to allow us do, as the highest of Heavenly Courts await our final eternal decision. She has taught us well, our graspless *Snót kvæði* "Lady Poem" tutor, and as for the likes of Kari, Storm and Angel, they and their sort of ilk lie in wait in our quaking 3hree a.m. terrors for us too (that is when the demons come). As the text implies, 'hear ye well, o' ye denizens of the Earth.' This is all well and good, but maybe Poem Spirit, she who is of the other side, of the howling inferno-driven wastes called the Netherworld, well, maybe she has other plans———.

5. *Thou be that 5ifth.* There is a saying in martial arts, "I am karate." What this means is that the person, the living entity is what give an art form its 'life.' Karate does not exist 'out there' as it were, but on the inside of the artist's living soul. Hence, you, dear reader, *are* the poem. The poem she now asks whether you liked seeing yourself through her—her horrid little *obscurum speculum ab vester vanitiem?* ("Dark mirror of

your vanities"). For all that life throws at us, the one thing we all can do, is learn from our experiences, for one would not know the sweet, save for understanding the bitter.

7-8. *"Spirit cannot be killed . . . your appointed day."* This line is a fragmentary remnant from the poem, *Dark Sword Midnight* (Laurent).

12. *For now we see through a glass, darkly.* This comes from *1Corinthians* 13.12, "For now we see through a glass, darkly; but then face to face: now I know in part; but then shall I know even as also I am known." The idea here is that the characters, being eternal archetypes to our own innermost psyches and sanctums, are waiting to see what choices, good, bad or *nil* we will make. But are the characters truly our psyche and soulish representations? Because things are difficult to see, perhaps we are blindly buying into a *real-live* prime-time 'Valhallan' deception of sorts when it comes to getting us to see ourselves through *their* 'dark glass,' that is, *our* trained 'archetypes.' Possibly this info was 'fabricated' to train and deceive us to enslave our eternal souls, which wouldn't be a surprise, as it would be a typical Underworld underhanded stunt to prevent us from getting the upper hand.

VALKYRIAN REMEMBRANCES

For additional insight into the workings of the abstract prismatic mind of St. Kari of the Blade, Valkyrian writings entitled *Tales of the Valkyries* have re-surfaced in the obscure literary work collectively known as *Letters From Mars* and is presented here. This unique and extremely archaic Volume is made up of essays and personal letters to the warrior-disciple Prince Thomm by god Mars, thus lending further credence to the Thomm-Mars-Kari cycles. From these oblique sources and others, the vignettes below are all that remains of what appears to have been a once formidable corpus of writings that Prince Thomm was said to have written as part of his personal library.

Curiously, in Chapter 28 of *Mars*, we find the fragmentary remnants of what is entitled the *Kari Compilation*, an extraordinary ancient treatise on the study of in-motion intuitional logic flow. The entries in this particular set reveal that she in part acted as a tutor for the Prince although how long and when is not known. Editor's note: as number eight has been blotted from the main body of *Compilation*, scholars have for years searched for this missing portion of information, which may not have existed at all. According to all accounts, Kari was *októphobic*, and avoided the number eight. It is said that in her dealings with humankind she never used it ⇀ *stricken: erased from the mind of men* ↽. The following selections are from *Valkyries*. Some of the word-play is tight, reflecting nearly "Zen-like" yin-yang quality abstracts on warrior fullness and emptiness, solidity and things graspless, reason and intuition, in-state flowing intuition being the link here—all quite on par with the likes of Sun Tzu, Musashi, Zen Priest Takuan and even Sherlock Holmes.

1. Watching Thomm traverse the nations, Kari was seething at his approach. He had finally come to her far land.

"Why should I teach you anything, you young whelp," she said, admonishing him.

Thomm laughed. "I have not come to learn, but to unlearn. You can teach me nothing."

Kari started teaching Thomm the art of mind and sword.

—A Youth's Education, *Lessons of the Valkyries*

2. Thomm searched high and low for the perfect blade. Exhausted, he finally turned to Kari. "Search the interior ground," she said, drawing her blade. Then, with intent, she thrust toward Thomm's heart, trying to kill the wicked thing.

—A Youth's Education, *Lessons of the Valkyries*

3. Upon learning the use of the dagger, Prince Thomm was woefully cutting too hard, much to the consternation of Kari.

"Be gentle," she finally whispered. "It is a knife."

—A Youth's Education, *Lessons of the Valkyries*

4. No doubt about it, the object that the Prince was searching for was misplaced. Upon asking for Kari's help in the matter, she responded, "Where did you search for it?"

"All over," he responded. "I thought it was where I put it."

Then said she thoughtfully, "then look for it where you put it not."

—Dialogues, *Valkyrian Persuasions*

5. The other Valkyries were complaining about their young charges, chiding about their lack of using their family swords, which they had for generations guarded.

Kari smiled as she put on her festive evening gown. "Swords, the best of them, are kept in their sheaths."

—Dialogues, *Valkyries in Waiting*

6. While Kari was demonstrating a technique Thomm inadvertently flinched, raising his hands. "Don't move!" snapped Kari, calmly pushing the Prince back with the point of her blade.

"That is how people get killed with swords."

—A Youth's Education, *Lessons of the Valkyries*

7. "What was the one knot Lord Alexander could not untie?" Kari asked the young Prince, her words bounding toward him.

Thomm was dumbfounded and found himself tongue-tied. He could not unravel it.

—A Youth's Education, *Valkyrian Riddles*

8. With sword in hand, Thomm peacocked. He killed twenty that day. The movements, though, as he had learned them, were not the same as he had been taught. There was something different about them this time. There was blood on them.

Then Thomm remembered what Kari had told him about using his other edge. Hearing the lamentations of their women, he cried.

—Far Off Fields, *Valkyrian Remembrances*

9. "Kwei, as a maker and doer of words and deeds, I see you have constructed a new fortress," said young Thomm airily to the ancient teen Valkyrie Kari.

"Verily, indeed I have," she responded coolly, quite satisfied with her work.

"But say," continued the young valiant with hands on hips, "I did spot one thing wrong with your verses."

"Oh?" Kari said, turning toward him.

Thomm reckoned good about himself, he finally getting his tutor's attention in earnest and feeling that he at last had one over on her.

"Yes," the inflated green one replied. "I noticed that your 'Keep of Poems' as you call it has a serious weakness in its design, a hole in its defenses, a breach through which the enemy will eventually ferret out and attack."

Blinking, Kari smiled. "Yes."

—Far Off Fields, *Valkyrian Remembrances*

BIBLIOGRAPHY

I. *A NOTE ON PSEUDO AUTHORS, TEXTS, STANZAS, PHRASES AND WORDS*

Valley is laced with false books, false authors and ultimately false fronts. One reason for this is that as imaginative input, they reflect the poem's character. As *Valley* is based on insubstantiality and things of the spirit, a pseudo author, or text, like the poem, "is out there," in the vaporous intangible. On the edge of the mind where fact and fantasy meet, the books and authors, well, they exist and what wonderful things they are. They can say and do anything our minds want them to say and do. Such freedom may not exist for a true straight lined scholarly work, but *'Hallan* freedom is limited only by the *insight* and *imagination* of the reader. If we could only burst these two sun-baked viscous asphalt perception bubbles it would be a good thing. Here we need to be like little green Gumby and his pony pal Pokey too, and stretch out, skating in and out of many books. The effect of this would be epically *kaleidoscopic* in scope, brilliantly colorful, mind-catching realizations of past, present and future to be hand.

A true *'Hallan* book is any book that exists or not exists. It is the storehouse of what we have in our minds, the known and the unknown. When we understand a *'Hallan* principle and say "Now I get it," that glistening fractal point of realization *is* the *pseudo book*, *author*, *stanza*, *line* or *word*. The names of the books or the authors are not all that important, except to say they serve to stir the fires of imagination. As for stanzas, phrases, lines or words, they are nuclear, atom-packed and electron-orbiting, radiating and glowing with energizing, compact multiple meanings just waiting to provide *electrisoulicity*. They are infinite space "bounded in a nutshell" packing their own peculiar heavyweight ununseptium metal punches, and *Valley*, unlike Hamlet (II. ii.), likes her "bad dreams" and likes to foist them.

What is important is that these ungraspable books and people with their otherworldly thoughts and concerns, on the way out fringe of our minds, "exist" only when we come to understand, on a personal level, the intent of the poetry as we focus on it. An old Wisconsin martial master of the seminator, Yamashita Shōrin-ryū sensei Dan Schroeder once remarked, "If you can imagine it, it's out there." The conditor has a tendency to agree more often than not these days.

When we say or write, "I'll quote so and so," that book to be quoted is both inside of our heads and is "out there," at the library for instance, waiting to be used. The writer then goes on to complete his or her thoughts, knowing that they will have to go on line or to the library to get the information desired. Even then, the information is "out there," on the "fringe" of the mind waiting to be used. But it is not so with 'Hallan references. As the *Valley* of the shadow of poem we just walked through and all that therein lies, they are intended to be graspless, elusive and obscure, much like catching the fluttering glints of a red oak leaf in an autumn sunset. It is soothing and appreciated more in the mind than in the eye.

Through that tiny oak leaf's simple, beautiful image, perhaps many rustlings of the mind will come too. Memories what seem to be from another age and time, another person altogether. Memories from the past, old friends (how young they look), events, concerns, dreams now dim, passed on loved ones, realizations of time's passage, personal changes, seasons, victories and defeats, blessings and curses, a love from long ago who visits you in your slumbers and lucid recollections—still so very beautiful—, visions and hopes for the future. Yes, the painful fleeting images of love, like arrows, still yet stick very deep (Ch. 22 line # 63-78).

At the last, all a person really has is their memories, hopes and dreams—and God—and soul—and prayer—and a pet cat named Barney, the spoiled yellow-striped tabby, my future memory, to snooze with me and share the today, the "here, upon this bank and shoal of time" (*Macbeth*, I. ii.). Sherlock Holmes (the pons-structor loves to mix his metaphors) says in *A study in Scarlet* wise persons only store worthy tools in their mind-attic, that it is not elastic and that it is the mark of a dunce to continually stuff it with useless fluffs, foofles and frivolities (*cf. Philippians*, 4.8-9). It is strange how people, things and events pass in and out of one's life bringing to mind many things, and how one little jot can trigger a Niagara of memories. Focus in, love deep and make memories good and pack 'em in, as winter comes upon us all, for an eternity of regrets cannot make up for a single lifetime of lost opportunity. But here is a thought before you go:

But alas, the night grows wane and we are cold,
Curled to the blankets; fire grows old.
Embers red, sooth languid, dark eyes,
And touch our souls; memories that lie.

Winter storms swirl in gleeish intent,
Fire stirs past ages (we live in them yet).
A somber mood for a lonely night,
And while away the hours and loneliness' flight.

Huddle we do, against the chill,
Cold seeps in, nights dread does fill.
Hold we close each other to ourselves,
To ward the night and to its knell.

Hear now, you Muse, who guards our ways,
To tremble our souls as light seeps away.
A tale to tell in dark, rusting time,
And beckons to ourselves—what we have inside—
(Aye, a tale born from the womb of the mind,
That travails its essence—in rhythm and rhyme).

—*Prologue, Garden of the Dragon*, Volume III

"It is said giants grapple in the Earth so deep, To contend for souls that they might keep" (Ch. 1 line # 29-30). How we deal with life and its daily challenges with an eye on eternity is the Nether. The elusive, fleeting poetic beauty of the compositions is the strength of the phantom books from the 'Lands, and what unusual keys, like *Valley*, they make. Keys that can only be turned when illuminating self-realization occurs, unlocking what the poem is trying to share with our souls—now and unto eternity future.

"O for a Muse of fire, that would ascend the brightest heaven of invention: A kingdom for a stage, princes to act, And monarchs to behold the swelling scene" (*Prologue, Henry V*). Lost causes. Lost poems. Forgotten poems and poems most stolen. Poems that were, and are, and are yet meant to be—and one precious love from long, long ago—can the poet ask for anything more?

—And dreams die hard; the charm's wound up.

Douglas Laurent
February 19, 2016
Scottsbluff, NE.
Friday, 6:21 am

The "Real" Bibliography
- Bierce, Ambrose. *An Occurrence at Owl Creek Bridge*. Short story. 1890.

- Bullinger, E. W. *The Witness of the Stars*. Kregel Publications. Grand Rapids MI. 1979. Ancient proto-biblical interpretations of the constellations.

- Burton, Richard, Sir. *The Book of the Sword*. Dover Publications. Mineola, NY. 1987.

- Browning, Robert. *Andrea del* Sarto. Poem, 1855, line 98. Any publication.

- Castaneda, Carlos. *Tales of Power*. Washington Square Press, a division of Simon and Schuster. New York. 1992.

- Chervál, Kursch. *The Legend of Kursch Chervál*. Laurentbooks Publishing. Scottsbluff, NE. 2015.

- Cleary, Thomas. *The Japanese Art of War*. Shambhala Dragon Editions. Boston, London. 1991. *See Tzu, Sun* entry below.

- Comte, Fernand. *The Wordsworth Dictionary of Mythology*. Cumberland House, Crib Street, Ware, Hertfordshire, England SG12 9ET. 1994.

- Cooper, Bill. *After the Flood*. New Wine Press. West Sussex, England. 1995.

- Curtin, J. *Seneca Indian Myths*. Nabu Press, 18 Carolina Street, Apt. A. Charleston, SC. Var. dates.

- Custance, Arthur C. *Noah's Three Sons*. Zondervan Publishing House. Grand Rapids, MI. 1975.

- Dante, Alighieri. *Inferno (Hell), Purgatorio and Paradiso (The Divine Comedy)*. Translated by John Ciardi. New American Library, NY. 1954; 2003.

-Davidson, H.R. Ellis. *Gods and Myths of Northern Europe*. Penguin Books USA Inc., 375 Hudson Street, New York, NY. 1964.

- Dickason, C. Fred. *Angels Elect and Evil*. Moody Press. Chicago, IL. 1975.

- Donne, John. *No Man is an Island*. Poem, 1624, Meditation 17.

- Douglas, Thomas. *I Never Go Into A Place That I Don't Know How to Get Out Of*. Laurentbooks Publishing. Scottsbluff, NE. 2016.

- Doyle, Arthur C. *The Complete Sherlock Holmes*. Doubleday and Co. Garden City, New York. Any publication really.

- Draeger, Donn. F. *Classical Budo: The Martial Arts and Ways of Japan Volume II*. John Weatherhill, Inc. New York, Tokyo. 1973. This is the second volume of a three-volume set. The others are good too, but this one shows the development of the 'war' arts into 'way' arts, or *jutsu* into *dō*. This volume also has excellent insights into kata training.

- Draeger, Donn F. *The Weapons and Fighting Arts of Indonesia*. Charles E. Tuttle Co. Rutland, Vt. Tokyo, Japan. 1993.

- Draeger, Donn F, and Smith, Robert W. *Comprehensive Asian Fighting Arts*. Kodansha International Ltd. New York, Tokyo, San Francisco. 1983.

- Frazetta, Frank. *The Fantastic Art of Frank Frazetta*. Peacock Press/Bantam Books, NY. 1976.

- Frost, Robert. *Stopping by Woods on a Snowy Evening*. Poem, 1923.

- Funakoshi, Gichin. *Karate-Dō My Way Of Life*. Kodansha International. Tokyo, New York. 1975.

— *Karate Jutsu: The Original Teachings of Master Funakoshi*. Kodansha International. Tokyo, New York. 2001.

— *Karate-Dō Nyūmon: The Master Introductory Text*. Kodansha International. Tokyo, New York. 1988, 1994.

- Gibbon, Edward. *The History of the Decline and Fall of the Roman Empire*. Any edition.

- Gibran, Kahlil. *The Prophet*. Alfred A Knopf, Pub., New York. 1979.

- Grose, F. *A Classical Dictionary of the Vulgar Tongue*. 1796. All other information unknown.

- Haislet, Edwin L. *Boxing*. The Ronald Press Company, New York. 1940.

- Hamilton, Edith. *Mythology (Timeless Tales of Gods and Heroes)*. Little, Brown and Co., Boston, MA. 1942 (More recent dates available).

- Hislop, Alexander. The Two Babylons. Chick Publications, P.O. Box 3500 Ontario CA. 91761-1019. There are many publications of this book. This has a lot of great little-known mythology info.

- Laurent, Douglas. *Dark Sword Midnight* and *Letters From Mars*. Unpublished manuscripts, *ca*. 1992.

—— *Martial Genesis: Martial Arts from Noah to Today*. Unpublished manuscript 1991, revised 2003. In works.

—— "Laws of Change, or Seeing the Unseen in Martial Arts." *Journal of Asian Martial Arts*. Via Media Publishing Co. Erie, PA. Vol. 1, no. 4 (1992): 91. This article studies the unity between martial motion and language. *See* www.laurentbooks.com/ or you can look up article on the Internet.

—— *Martial Arts and the Christian*. Kindle eBook, 2012. Soft-Bound Expanded Edition 2015. Amazon.com. Much history, myth, science, literature, philosophy, linguistics, sports, *etc*.

—— "The Many Faces of Kata: The Heart of Combat." *Black Belt Magazine*. Rainbow Publications, Inc. Santa Clarita, CA. Aug. 1986, Vol. 24, no. eight. pp. 60-64, 118. This is a study of martial anthropology and masking principles found in the arts applicable to all. *See* www.laurentbooks.com/ or you can look up the article in Black Belt Magazine on the Internet.

- Lee, Bruce. *Tao of Jeet Kune Do*. Ohara Publications, Inc. Burbank, CA. 1976.

- Lewis, C.S. *The Screwtape Letters* and *The Problem of Pain*. Any edition.

- Maugham, Somerset, W. *The Appointment in Samarra*. 1933.

- Morris, Henry M. *The Genesis Record*. Baker Book House. Grand Rapids, MI. 1987. www.icr.org.

—— *The Defender's Study Bible*. World Publishing. Iowa Falls, IA. 1995. *See* 2006 version. King James Bible.

- Murray, Andrew. *With Christ in the School of Prayer*. A Spire Book. Jove Publications, Inc., Old Tappan, NJ. 1984. Many editions, phenomenal work. One may need this after touring the *Valley*.

- Musashi, Miyamoto. *A Book of Five Rings*. The Overlook Press. Woodstock, New York. 1974. Victor Harris translator. Any translation.

- Nelson, E., Broadberry, R. *Genesis and the Mystery Confucius Couldn't Solve*. Concordia Publishing House. St. Louis, MO. 1995.

- Orwell, George. *Animal Farm* (1945). Any edition.

— *1984*. Harcourt Brace Jovanovich, Inc. New York, NY. 1977.

- Patton, George S. Jr. *Through A Glass Darkly*. (1918) Poem, many editions.

- Pilkey, John. Origin of the Nations. Master Book Publishers. San Diego, CA. 1984. This work is deep, has a lot of myth info.

- Ratti, O., Westbrook, A. *Secrets of the Samurai*. Charles E. Tuttle Publishing Co. Rutland Vermont, Tokyo. 1980.

- Ryrie, Charles C. *Basic Theology*. Victor Books. Wheaton, IL. 1986.

- Sayers, Dorothy L. *The Divine Comedy, Part I: Hell*. (Penguin Classics), Penguin Publishing Group, worldwide with various other publishing dates. 1950.

- Schaeffer, Francis A. *Escape From Reason*. InterVarsity Press, London. 1968. This is volume two of a trilogy, *The God Who is There*, and *He is There and He is not Silent*. The *Escape* is Great!

- Shakespeare, Wm. *Hamlet, Julius Caesar* and *Macbeth*. Any edition.

- Shaw, G. B. *Saint Joan*. Play. 1923.

- Slawson, David A. *Secret Teachings In The Art Of Japanese Gardens*. Kodansha International. Tokyo, New York. 1991.

- Suzuki, D. T. *Zen and Japanese Culture*. MJF Books. NY. 1959. *See Amazon. com.*

- Thurber, James. *The Secret Life of Walter Mitty*, short story (1939).

- Tytler, A. *The Decline and Fall of the Athenian Republic*. No actual record of this book has been found. Apparently, most of Tytler's works have been lost. However, *see Wikiquote* on the Internet for this author.

- Tzu, Lao. *Tao Te Ching*. Random House. New York. 1972. Translated by Gia-Fu Feng and Jane English. Any translation.

- Tzu, Sun. *The Art of War*. Shambhala Dragon Editions, Boston, MA. London, 1988. Thomas Cleary translation. Any translation is good, but Cleary's is very simple and precise.

- Wall Chart, The. *The Wall Chart of World History*. Barnes and Noble. Third Millennium Press Ltd. Lowden Hill, Wiltshire, UK. 1997. Dates may fluctuate. *This is an outrageous work of art and knowledge!*

- Walvoord, John F. *The Nations in Prophecy*. Academie Books. Zondervan Publishing House. Grand Rapids, MI. 1967.

- Watkins, Calvert. *The American Heritage Dictionary of Indo-European Roots*. Houghton Mifflin Publishing. Boston, MA. 1985.

- Whitcomb, John C. *The World that Perished*. Baker Book House. Grand Rapids, MI. 1988. Great stuff about Flood, frozen Mammoths, oil, *etc.*

- Whitman, Walt. *Leaves of Grass*. Many editions.

- Williams, Gareth. *Master Pieces: The Architecture of Chess*. Viking Studio. Penguin Putnam Inc. New York, NY. 2000.

➤ *When St. Kari of the Blade Met Luke Skywalker, Star Wars Jedi Knight* ⚔

"What's that?" Kari asked pointing to the silvery object attached to Luke's waist.

"It's my lightsaber," Luke said cautiously, not knowing where this was going. "It's like your sword, only many years advanced."

"I see me thinks," grinned Kari, "although I cannot see how such a short object labors as a sword. Can you show me how? Here, block my blade." Kari pulled her sharp, simple straight edge and held it so that its steel shaft was stationed off Lukes left shoulder.

"I don't want to ruin your sword," Luke said with a slight grinning shrug. "It will cut your blade in half."

"No it shan't. *C'mon* and try" quipped Kari, her steel blue violet eyes dancing with mirth.

Luke felt compelled to teach the seemingly uncomplicated girl a lesson in advance blade-play. He struck at her sword, but to his amazement, the laser did not cut through Kari's antiquated, plain cross-hilt weapon, as it easily should have.

"I've never seen anything like this," Luke said eyes widening in surprise. "The only thing that resists a lightsaber cut is Cortosis."

"Let me try cutting at you," Kari said, her smile full of delight. As she struck Luke's sword, the neat cylindrical beam of laser light that was Luke's blade fell as one solid piece to the ground and began to eat itself inward and disappear, both ends vaporizing and fizzling, meeting in the middle and ending with a loud "*pop!*"

"How did you do that?" Skywalker asked in amazement. "What's your sword made of?"

Kari smiled. "My sword is made of adamantine eternal belief. It both cut and resisted your blade because I willed it to. All swordplay in the *'Halla* exists on the edge of belief, something you will have to learn if you are to survive here. Learn about the 'Halla, Luke."

Luke awkwardly grimaced. His lightsaber was an amazing piece of advanced technology and here this wispy backwater of a fencing lass had just "out-believed" him, making his well-ahead art of laser swordplay more primitive than the girl's unadorned straightedge. He remembered Yoda's words on failure and belief and felt stupid. The word *Jedi* was not in Kari's vocabulary, Luke thought, but notwithstanding, she seemed more than a Jedi than he.

End *Valley of the Damned*, Volume I, End of Days.

www.ingramcontent.com/pod-product-compliance
Lightning Source LLC
Chambersburg PA
CBHW052027090426
42739CB00010B/1812